A CITY'S LIFE AND TIMES

CAMBRIDGE
in the Twentieth Century

©2007 by the Cambridge Historical Society

Third Printing

All rights reserved under International and Pan-American Copyright Conventions. Published in the United States by the Cambridge Historical Society.

A portion of a chapter from *Snatched from Oblivion* by Marian Cannon Schlesinger published by Little, Brown & Co., copyright 1979, has been reprinted here with the author's permission.

The Cambridge Historical Society
159 Brattle Street
Cambridge, MA 02138
617 547-4252

Interior and jacket design by Linda Manly Wade

Jacket photograph: In 1946, Cambridge turned out to celebrate the centennial of the city's incorporation. Navy marchers strut the parade route up Massachusetts Avenue in front of Cambridge City Hall. (*Cambridge Public Library Collection, Cambridge Historical Commission*)

Manufactured in the United States of America

Library of Congress Catalogue-in-Publication Data

A city's life and times: Cambridge in the 20th century / edited by Daphne Abeel.

p. cm.

20 essays on the history, culture, politics, architecture, literary scene of Cambridge, Massachusetts.

1. Cambridge (Mass.)—History—20th century. 2. Cambridge, (Mass.)—Intellectual life—20th century. 3. Cambridge (Mass.)—Politics and government—20th century. 4. City and town life—Massachusetts—Cambridge—History—20th century. 5. Cambridge (Mass.)—Social conditions—20th century. 6. Architecture—Massachusetts—Cambridge—History—20th century. 7. American literature—Massachusetts—Cambridge—History and criticism. I. Abeel, Daphne.

F74CIC555 2006

974.4'4043—dc22

2006049214

ISBN: 978-1-878284-00-6

A CITY'S LIFE AND TIMES

CAMBRIDGE
in the Twentieth Century

Edited by DAPHNE ABEEL

CAMBRIDGE HISTORICAL SOCIETY
CAMBRIDGE, MASSACHUSETTS

Acknowledgment

The Cambridge Historical Society is deeply grateful to Cambridge Savings Bank for underwriting the publication of *A City's Life and Times: Cambridge in the Twentieth Century*. Beginning with the bank's clerk and treasurer Oscar F. Allen serving as the Society's founding treasurer in 1905, Cambridge Savings Bank has been an ongoing supporter of our efforts to preserve and document the history of Cambridge.

The Cambridge Savings Bank, originally called the Institution for Savings, opened its doors in Cambridge on October 27, 1834 as a mutual savings bank. As opposed to commercial banks, which handled the funds of large investors, mutual banks enabled the average person to deposit small sums of money, such as a nickel or a dime. In 1868, the bank changed its name to Cambridge Savings Bank, and is now one of the largest community banks in Massachusetts. Throughout its history, Cambridge Savings Bank has supported local organizations and programs in an effort to contribute to the social good of the community.

PREFACE

When the idea first surfaced to publish a book that would celebrate the Cambridge Historical Society's Centennial in 2005, it was an undeveloped notion, akin to a fuzzy photographic print still soaking in the developing tray. The image was there, but it lacked clarity and focus. However, as volunteer contributors came forward to write in their areas of experience and expertise, there emerged crisp prints of various aspects of life in Cambridge in the 20th century, the period of time that nearly matches the historical society's existence.

A fascinating and varied volume has resulted, that touches on many facets of the culture and history of Cambridge during this period, now past, but still so immediately present. Readers will find essays on politics, activism, the relationship between the universities and the city, the literary scene, the role of folk music, the city's architecture, its immigrants and its many religions.

Two very different essays describe growing up in Cambridge—one by a leading member of the African American community details life on Worcester Street. The other recalls a childhood as a Harvard professor's "brat." The Coolidge Hill neighborhood, a closely knit community, comes alive in one chapter as does immigrant Jewish Cambridge in another. Two essays bring to the fore the accomplishments of Cambridge women, one singling out the work of Lois Lilley Howe, a prominent architect. And two remarkable local institutions, the Cambridge Plant and Garden Club and the literary publications by students at Cambridge Rindge and Latin School, are testament to the city's traditions and creativity. The collection concludes with a history of the Cambridge Historical Society itself.

Each writer has brought particular enthusiasm and knowledge to his or her subject—thus, each essay has its own peculiar flavor and value. The essays vary widely in length and approach. Some are long and meticulously researched, while others, shorter and more casual, boast a journalistic flavor. While not a consecutive chronicle of the past century, these pieces bring to life much of the great diversity and character of this ever-changing city. And as the pace of change increases, the accounts of what once was preserve for readers the people, the places, the events and institutions that make up the fabric of Cambridge's community life.

For all the contributors' efforts, the Cambridge Historical Society is most grateful.

Those who deserve special thanks and mention for practical assistance and moral support include: Lewis Bushnell, Karen Davis, Luise Erdmann, Ted Hansen, Janet Hawkins, Sally Hild, Michael Kenney, Andrew Leighton, Kit Rawlins, Charles Sullivan, and the councilors of the Cambridge Historical Society.

This collection is certain to entertain and instruct readers of the 21st century and serve as tribute to a city richly endowed with a local history that will always be a subject worthy of interest and study.

Daphne Abeel
Cambridge, Massachusetts
June 2007

A CITY'S LIFE AND TIMES

CAMBRIDGE

in the Twentieth Century

An Overview: Cambridge in the 20th Century

CHARLES M. SULLIVAN

CAMBRIDGE at the beginning of the twentieth century was a burgeoning industrial and academic community that all agreed had a shining future. The city welcomed the Massachusetts Institute of Technology (MIT) when it arrived from Boston in 1916, and a few years later, one historian compared Cambridge's economic potential to that of Detroit. By the middle of the century, however, the industrial sector was in full flight, jobs and property assessments were melting away, and the city's predominantly working-class people found themselves trapped in America's postwar urban crisis, straddled by two prestigious universities that found their undervalued property irresistible and seemed likely to expand until they met in Central Square.

At the end of the century, by contrast, Cambridge had become one of the most prosperous and desirable urban areas in the country. The city had finally brought university expansion into a rough equilibrium with its own needs; Harvard was expanding into Allston and Watertown, and MIT had become an economic engine for the eastern third of the city. Science-based enterprises were flocking to occupy the former industrial precincts, and developers rushed to accommodate them. By 2000, Cambridge had a larger proportion of homes valued at more than one million dollars than any large city in America, and it was struggling to retain its remaining affordable housing.

Newtowne was founded in 1630 as the compromise choice for the capital of Massachusetts, but after the General Court moved to Boston in 1634 the village had few other advantages. Perhaps to make up for abandoning it, the legislature placed the colonies' first institution of higher learning in Cambridge, as it was soon renamed, and designated it as a shire town for Middlesex County. From the beginning, therefore, Cambridge was a highly specialized town, supported by Harvard College and Middlesex County; in its second century, it also became a seasonal residence for wealthy families from Boston and the West Indies.

The opening of the West Boston Bridge in 1793 ended Cambridge's isolation from Boston and triggered the town's first real estate boom. Instead of an eight-mile drive through Brookline and Roxbury or an occasionally hazardous passage on the Charlestown ferry, the village center at Harvard Square was now only three and a half miles from Boston via Massachusetts Avenue and Main Street. The entire territory east of Harvard Yard, with only a few farms and country estates, now lay open for development. Less than a decade into the nineteenth century, Cambridge boasted two bridges and four new highways to Boston, and a land rush was on. The original village was soon known as Old Cambridge, to distinguish it from the new settlements of Cambridgeport and East Cambridge, and Cambridge began a new game, the politics of keep-away.

Old Cambridge lost the Middlesex County courthouse and the registries of deeds and probate to East Cambridge in 1809 and the town hall to Cambridgeport in 1831. Resentful of the growing demands of the new villages for schools and roads, Old Cambridge petitioned the legislature to be set off as a separate town. The new villages blocked this move, and in 1846 the town meeting voted instead to incorporate Cambridge as a city. However, Old Cambridge had already established its reputation as an aloof, insular, and somewhat unwelcoming community—at least for immigrants, tradesmen, and even the emerging suburban middle class. Meanwhile, Cambridgeport and East Cambridge boomed, attracting settlers from across New England, immigrants from Europe, and, after the toll bridges became free in 1854, middle-class Bostonians seeking suburban homes.

Immigration brought Cambridge the challenge of adjusting to a diverse population. African slaves and freedmen had been present in small numbers since the beginning of settlement. A few Germans and Scots had been brought over to work in the glass factories around 1815, but beginning in 1840 large numbers of Irish arrived in America; Massachusetts, a Protestant society for two hundred years, viewed these newcomers as a plague. While Henry Wadsworth Longfellow, James Russell Lowell, and Louis Agassiz brought Cambridge fame as a cradle of the American Revolution and a capital of literature and science, Irish families settled on the fringes of the villages and set to work as laborers, craftsmen, and servants, fueling the industrial growth that transformed the city in the course of the century.

The character of the city at the beginning of the twentieth century is reflected in its census returns. In 1810, Cambridge had a population of 2,323, nearly all of whom were of English descent. By 1900 the population was just over 90,000,* and many nationalities were represented. The predominant ethnicity was Irish, but significant numbers of French Canadians, Italians, Swedes, Poles, and Eastern European Jews were already established, and their communities grew rapidly until the exclusion acts of the 1920s choked off the flow of immigration for more than fifty years.

The generation that came of age in 1900 found Cambridge a modern city. Streetcar service had begun in 1856. Running water and gas for lighting had become almost universal by the end of the 1860s, and twenty years later the construction of sewers had almost eliminated the backhouse and the night-soil carrier, at least in Old Cambridge. Electricity had been introduced in 1887, although gas was preferred for household illumination for at least another decade. Telephone service had begun about 1878, and by 1900 the Old Cambridge exchange had twelve hundred subscribers. The extension of the electric street railways and the availability of inexpensive bicycles in the 1890s greatly facilitated travel. At the end of the nineteenth century, the innovative ideas of the landscape architect Charles Eliot were put into effect by the Cambridge Park Commission, which carried out one of the greatest municipal park projects in America: the acquisition and development of the entire Cambridge frontage of the Charles River.

The Charles River Park project, combined with a marginal sewer, had far-ranging effects. Charles Davenport, a retired railroad car manufacturer, had already formed the Charles River Embankment Company to develop the marshes and mudflats opposite Boston's Back Bay. The Cambridge Park Commission completed Davenport's seawall and constructed a parkway from the Longfellow Bridge to the foot of Ash Street. Near Harvard Square, the old working waterfront was razed and landscaped into its present form. Suddenly, Harvard had an attractive new venue for growth, and in the next thirty years half the population of Saint Paul's Parish was displaced, setting the stage for a century of neighborhood opposition to Harvard. Downstream, Davenport's failed project became the new site of MIT.

In politics, the end of the nineteenth century was a high-water mark for a type of liberal progressivism described as "the Cambridge Idea," while the beginning of the twentieth introduced the class and ethnic struggles that would characterize political debate for decades to come. In the realignment of national political parties after the Civil War, the No-License (or temperance) movement, the Civil Service Reform League, women suffragists, and emerging Irish politicians briefly found common cause in the Democratic Party. The progressives favored nonpartisan elections, professional administration, and public works projects in anticipation of further growth. In 1891 the progressives in Cambridge succeeded in amending the city charter to concentrate power in the mayor at the expense of the aldermen, but this reform backfired less than ten years later when their opponents captured city government.

The election of William E. Russell as mayor in 1884 initiated a period of nonpartisan administration that lasted until 1902. Russell, whose father had represented Old Cambridge in the State House in the 1870s, was the prototype of the twentieth-century Cambridge reformer. He began his career in the common council a year after his graduation from law school in 1880. He stressed efficiency and professionalism in city government and was instrumental in securing the gifts of Cambridge's public library, manual training school, and city hall from the philanthropist Frederick Hastings Rindge.

Massachusetts was a Republican stronghold, but Russell, a Democrat, was elected governor by increasing majorities in 1890 and 1891. His connections through the Irish Democrats of East Cambridge to Martin Lomasney in Boston's West End enabled the progressive element of the party to tap the votes of immigrants and the labor movement. Russell's untimely death in 1896, however, deprived the party of a figure who could unite the reformers and the machine politicians. Without Russell, the Irish wing would no longer support the progressives, and in the election of 1901 party toughs broke up nonpartisan rallies in East Cambridge.

The era of nonpartisanship ended in 1902 with the inauguration of the city's first Irish Catholic mayor. John H. H. McNamee, a bookbinder, came from the elite corps of Irishmen who had dominated the skilled workers at the Riverside Press since the 1870s. He owned a bindery in Harvard Square as well as a number of desirable properties nearby. The progressives, who were well aware of Boston's experience with machine politics, fiercely contested McNamee's candidacy. Although McNamee held office for only one term, his election marked a reordering of municipal priorities to emphasize spending on education, social services, and welfare at the expense of parks and infrastructure. From 1916 until 1942 the Democrats controlled city government, and reform interests remained in the minority.

Good government advocates—sometimes called "goo-goos" by the *Cambridge Chronicle*—labored for thirty years to bring back nonpartisanship. In 1907 George Wright, Richard Henry Dana 3rd, and Stoughton Bell of Old Cambridge successfully campaigned to diminish the influence of party politics by holding city elections in March, and they got the school committee reduced from thirty-three members to five. In 1911 reformers led by Professor Lewis Jerome Johnson and encouraged by former Harvard president Charles W. Eliot nearly secured the approval of a charter that would have replaced all elected officials with a five-member commission elected by

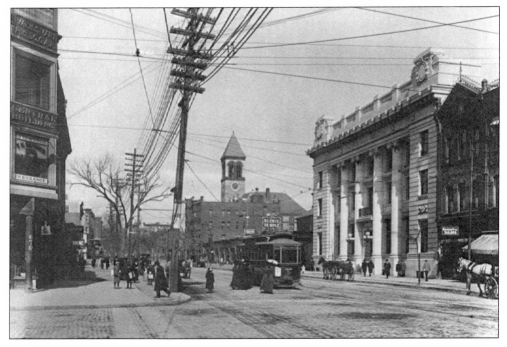

Central Square about 1910. Central Square evolved into downtown Cambridge in the late nineteenth century and soon became the city's administrative and banking center. *(Detroit Publishing Co., Library of Congress collection)*

preferential voting. In 1916, however, the Democratic machine was able to adopt a Plan B government, which strengthened the mayor, abolished the common council, and restructured the board of aldermen as a city council elected by wards.

Professor Johnson continued to advocate preferential voting, and in 1938 he secured the legislature's approval of a new form of municipal government: Plan E, in which a city is governed by a council elected at large by proportional representation. Under Plan E, the councilors elect a mayor from among themselves and appoint a city manager as chief executive. The goals were to place municipal affairs under professional administration and to empower minority interest groups by minimizing the effects of party affiliation.

Cambridge's mayor and council vigorously opposed this reform. When the Cambridge Committee for Plan E presented a petition of eleven hundred voters requesting that the charter change be placed on the ballot, the Supreme Judicial Court had to force the council to accept it. The committee, chaired by the dean of the Harvard Law School, James E. Landis, included industrialist Charles Almy Jr., *Cambridge Chronicle* editor Eliot Spalding, and attorney Henry Wise. The mayor and the council charged that Plan E was a Harvard plot, and that the new School of Public Administration was trying to use Cambridge as a "guinea pig." On October 19, 1938, the council won national attention by voting to set off Harvard as a separate municipality. In a mocking response, brown-shirted members of *The Harvard Lampoon* goose-stepped down Massachusetts Avenue in a "Sudeten burlesque," and MIT students sought *Anschluss* (union) with Radcliffe, Simmons, Wellesley, and the Katherine Gibbs School.

Plan E was defeated by a small margin in 1938, but subsequent developments ensured its later passage. A grand jury investigated Mayor John W. Lyons's administration of a $2.5 million federal grant to build schools, municipal buildings, and bridges, and after a 17 percent tax increase in the spring of 1940, Plan E was adopted by a large majority that fall. Mayor Lyons was soon sentenced to six years in prison for soliciting bribes from architects and engineers.

Plan E brought back nonpartisanship and produced a council on which small blocs of voters found it relatively easy to gain representation. The worst excesses of the old charter were avoided, and the professional management of the city satisfied the reform interests. After their victory, the Cambridge Committee for Plan E transformed itself into the Cambridge Civic Association (CCA), which for decades was the strongest organization in Cambridge politics. Although the CCA rarely won a majority on the city council, it was an effective foil to the loosely organized "independents," or conservative Democrats, until the end of rent control in 1995 robbed it of its most effective issue.

By 1930 the permanent population of Cambridge had risen to its all-time peak of 113,643. The city gave the impression of being completely developed, although a few lots remained in new residential districts like Gray Gardens and Larchwood. Massachusetts Avenue between Cambridge Common and Porter Square was completely transformed between 1914 and 1930 from a street of large, single-family homes to a mixed-use district of apartment buildings and stores. Four-, five-, and six-story apartment houses played havoc with the domestic scale of the main thoroughfares and side streets alike, where building sites were obtained by demolishing unfashionable Victorian mansions. Undistinguished one-story shops and filling stations replaced many private houses that did not succumb to apartment builders. Zoning, introduced in 1924, protected most neighborhoods from three-deckers and apartment buildings, but the dreary appearance of Cambridge after World War II owed as much to opportunistic development as to the enforced neglect of the Depression.

Headline citing the adoption of the Plan E form of municipal government.
Councilors elected by proportional representation and a city manager with
executive power transformed the political landscape of Cambridge. (Cambridge
Chronicle-Sun, *November 7, 1941*)

The crash of 1929, the Depression, World War II, and the postwar flight
to the suburbs halted almost all construction in Cambridge for more than
thirty years; when growth resumed in the 1960s, it was on a larger scale than
before and under new rules. After the war, many of the remaining manufacturers closed or moved, and as the tax base evaporated, the city became desperate for new development. The 1930s had seen the expansion of municipal
health services, public housing, and schools, but little had been accomplished
for the city's infrastructure since the 1890s. Swelled by returning veterans,
Cambridge's population was still 107,676 in 1950 but soon began a steep
decline as the suburbs satisfied the demand for housing. While Harvard
Square prospered and nearby working-class neighborhoods began to gentrify,
Central Square and much of Cambridgeport deteriorated rapidly.

The 1950s and 1960s were stressful for the city. Harvard proposed an
agenda that facilitated its own explosive growth, while MIT acquired scores
of distressed industrial properties in Cambridgeport and around Kendall
Square. Harvard's chief planner, Dean Josep Lluis Sert of the Graduate School
of Design, was also chairman of the Cambridge Planning Board, which drafted a pro-development zoning ordinance that in 1962 abolished the protective
zoning adopted in 1924 and 1943. New residential zones with no height limits supported the universities' plans for high-rise buildings and generated
decades of neighborhood agitation aimed at reducing the allowable density.
Ballooning enrollments at Harvard and MIT put great pressure on Cambridge
during the postwar housing shortage, continuing even when the city's population began to decline after 1950. An affordable housing crisis, caused in
part by the universities' inability to house their growing student bodies, was
addressed by a rent control ordinance that remained in effect until 1995.

Kendall Square was the hub of the city's manufacturing district until about 1950. Manufacturers of office machines, candy, pianos, furniture, soap, rubber goods, metal fasteners, and iron castings are all represented in this photograph. *(Cambridge Planning Board collection, Cambridge Historical Commission)*

The seeds of Cambridge's current prosperity were sown during World War II, when technology and government converged on Cambridge as never before. MIT first attracted federally funded research during the war, and much of Harvard's postwar construction under President James Conant, a chemist, supported science. The renewed vitality of the academic community dampened the postwar flight to the suburbs; many faculty and staff preferred to stay within walking distance, and the ambiance of Cambridge helped retain old graduates and attract new residents.

Considerable discussion in postwar Cambridge revolved around quality-of-life issues. While city hall focused on the redevelopment of Kendall Square and the benefits of the proposed Inner Belt highway through Cambridgeport, activists confronted the threat of overdevelopment. Harvard's expansion generated the greatest concern, as the university grew at the rate of one million square feet per decade. From 1946 through the 1980s, Harvard and Radcliffe undertook at least one major construction project each year, demolishing older buildings, relocating residents, and threatening cherished open space. Leverett and Quincy houses (1958), Peabody Terrace (1963), and Mather House (1967) caused significant displacement in Riverside and further diminished the Kerry Corner neighborhood.

The opposition to Harvard reached a crescendo in 1970, when the residents of Riverside demonstrated at Commencement. In 1972 Harvard agreed to abstain from purchasing property beyond a "red line" and in 1974 published its first long-range plan. In 1981 the city obtained legislation that allowed it to limit Harvard's expansion in residential neighborhoods. The neighborhoods all responded differently, which they were able to do under Cambridge's decentralized political system. Most eventually filed downzoning petitions, which were intended to roll back the 1962 code and limit Harvard's ability to develop the sites it had been landbanking since the 1950s. The Agassiz neighborhood scored an early success in 1974, winning a reduction of allowable density and imposing a height limit of thirty-five feet where none had existed since 1962. In 1977 Mayor Alfred Vellucci (speaking for himself) declared a state of emergency: "*Finito*. No more buildings" (*The Harvard Crimson*, Sept. 30, 1977). Riverside and Kerry Corner residents finally succeeded in downzoning their neighborhoods in 2003, ending a century of conflict with the university.

Other projects also threatened the character of Cambridge. When the Metropolitan District Commission (MDC) extended Memorial Drive from Ash Street to the new Eliot Bridge in 1947, it met little opposition, but the writer Bernard DeVoto editorialized against its further extension through "Hell's Half Acre" to Arsenal Street in Watertown. In 1962 the MDC was authorized to rebuild Memorial Drive as a limited-access highway like Storrow Drive, with underpasses at major intersections. This plan would have destroyed most of the sycamores that the Cambridge Park Commission had planted at the beginning of the century. At about the same time, Harvard Square businessmen proposed the idea of a parking garage under Cambridge Common. The mobilization of Cambridge activists to overturn these projects foreshadowed the intense opposition to the Inner-Belt highway, which continued until 1970, when Governor Francis W. Sargent imposed a moratorium on all limited-access highway construction within Route 128, thus canceling a 1948 plan for the construction of Route 2 through North Cambridge and the Inner Belt through Cambridgeport.

For a decade after President John F. Kennedy's assassination in 1963, the city was torn by a proposal to build his presidential library on the site of the subway yards near Harvard Square. This intense controversy was not resolved until 1975, when the Kennedy family agreed to build the facility in Dorchester. During much of the same period, local opinion was polarized by student demonstrations against the Vietnam War, which caused major property damage in Harvard Square and along the marching routes to Boston.

One of the most important developments of the twentieth century was the extension of mass transit through Cambridge to Alewife. The Cambridge subway, completed in 1912, solidified Harvard Square's position as a transfer station for commuters to many outlying towns. Calls to extend the subway came as early as the 1920s. In 1938 Governor Charles F. Hurley (who lived on Fresh Pond Lane) recommended a $5 million appropriation for an extension to North Cambridge, but it was contingent on a grant from the federal Public Works Administration that did not materialize. In 1945 the state proposed a surface extension from Harvard Square along the river to East Watertown and then north to Arlington Heights, but opposition in Old Cambridge was intense. Conflicts between the transit agency and the city over construction methods and stations stymied proposals in 1956 and 1966. Finally, the availability of federal funding for mass transit improvements (promoted in part by Cambridge's own Thomas P. "Tip" O'Neill Jr., Speaker of the U.S. House of Representatives) provided the catalyst for extending the subway to Alewife.

The actual route remained controversial. One alternative ran under Garden Street, with no intermediate stations. The plan for a tunnel under Massachusetts Avenue and a station at Porter Square was more popular, but North Cambridge residents did not want subway trains running on the surface along the Fitchburg Division tracks. The route finally chosen added a station at Davis Square, Somerville, and required two abrupt turns to orient the line for an eventual extension to Lexington. The work began in November 1977. The Harvard station reopened in September 1983, and the line opened to Alewife in 1986. The 1.2 million tons of excavated rock were used to cap the former city dump, which in 1990 became the fifty-five-acre Danehy Park.

The extension of the subway and the continuing expansion of the universities and university-related businesses brought such prosperity in the 1980s that Cambridge seemed threatened by its own success. In response the city devised a strategy that encouraged redevelopment on its outskirts, away from Harvard Square. The construction of the Cambridgeside Galleria near Lechmere Square in the late 1980s was the catalyst for the ongoing redevelopment of the Lechmere triangle, while the subway's extension to Alewife attracted numerous office and apartment buildings to that area.

The vitality that Harvard Square began to exhibit in the 1970s finally spread in the 1990s to Central Square, which had suffered a pattern of disin-

Research and office buildings on Lansdowne Street in 2005. During the twentieth century, Cambridge evolved from a center of manufacturing to an economy dominated by knowledge industries; instant photography was replaced by electronics, then software, and finally biotechnology in the twenty-first century. *(Cambridge Historical Commission)*

tegration typical of downtowns in older American cities. The gentrification of some of Cambridge's residential districts had actually been under way since 1941. Until then, west Cambridge slowly lost ground as well-to-do householders moved farther from Boston. Restrictions on automobile travel during World War II checked the migration, and rapid increases in building costs and growing congestion after the war persuaded many people to remain in the city; in addition, some who had moved to the suburbs missed city life. First, mansions were updated, and some that were too large for single-family occupancy were divided; rooming houses were reclaimed or converted into apartments; and small houses that once served low-income families were eagerly bought up and improved. Whole districts were renovated, and former working-class areas, like lower Sparks and Foster streets, became fashionable addresses. Between 1980 and 1990, the proportion of Cambridgeport residents with a college degree increased from 30 to nearly 50 percent, a surprising development that reflected the radical improvement in the neighborhood's prospects since the cancellation of the Inner Belt.

In the 1970s and 1980s, skyrocketing property values and the intense demand for townhouses and condominiums led to the demolition of many significant houses in mid-Cambridge and near Harvard Square. These losses and the oppressive density of the apartment buildings and townhouses that replaced them contributed to greater restrictions on demolition and inappropriate overdevelopment. After the recession of the early 1990s, a gold rush mentality prevailed in the Cambridge real estate market, especially in Old Cambridge. The abolition of rent control in 1995 rapidly emptied the community of its moderate-income renters; previously protected apartments were converted to condominiums, and many Victorian houses that had been subdivided were restored to single-family occupancy. Assessed values skyrocketed to levels twenty or more times the prevailing values of the mid-1970s, as wealthy young entrepreneurs poured money into modernizing old houses, sometimes to inappropriate levels of excess.

At the end of the twentieth century, many American cities were desperately trying to attract the kind of well-educated, entrepreneurial young people that have formed a critical mass around the universities in Cambridge. These families and the cutting-edge enterprises springing up near MIT have given Cambridge the financial base to develop affordable housing and create public services and amenities on a scale barely attempted elsewhere. As Cambridge has gentrified, conflicts based on class and racial disparities have diminished, but friction over the adverse effects of development has intensified because the prize—a diverse, humane, and attractive urban community—is valued more now than ever before. The price, however, has been the loss of diversity and economic opportunity, as the prohibitive cost of living in Cambridge has excluded many who might otherwise enjoy it.

CHAPTER NOTES

* Population figures exclude students living in dormitories, who were counted at their permanent residence until 1950. The 2000 census counted 101,355 residents, but 14,663 were living in group quarters (presumably students). Thus the permanent population of Cambridge in 2000 was only 86,692.

The Immigrants of Cambridge, Massachusetts [1]

GEORGE H. HANFORD

LIKE ALL AMERICAN cities, Cambridge is a city of immigrants. The two earliest waves of newcomers to the area were people of the land. First were the American Indians ("Native Americans" in the parlance of the twenty-first century), who moved across North America from Asia. Then, in 1630, came the English settlers, who arrived by sea from the east. The latest wave is now coming, like the first, from the west, from Asia and the Pacific Rim. In between, succeeding waves have caused profound changes in the character of the city as it has been transformed from a seventeenth-century agricultural community into a twenty-first-century high-tech metropolis.

The American Indians in residence when the English arrived were members of the Massachusetts tribe of the Algonquian nation or family of tribes. They were farmers and fishermen as well as hunters, harvesting fish from the Charles and Menotomy (now Alewife Brook) rivers both to eat and to fertilize their crops of corn. They did not have permanent settlements, instead moving their living quarters so they could adapt to the changing seasons and the variable fertility of the land.

Unlike warrior tribes elsewhere, the Massachusetts were hospitable and shared their agricultural knowledge with the Puritan newcomers. As a consequence, the English were able to obtain land in trade, not by force. The Middlesex County records of 1644 note extensive land holdings in Charlestown by the Indians, an ironic admission by the English settlers that the property deeded to them by the Crown really belonged to the Native Americans, who were there first.

The Indians in the area did not last long after the arrival of the English; they succumbed initially to the ravages of smallpox introduced by the settlers as early as 1634, and then virtually disappeared by the end of the seventeenth century. In the 1650s, for instance, the Cambridge Society for the Propagation of the Gospel built a schoolhouse for the education of Indian youth. Called "the Indian College," its popularity with its intended student body—as well as the diminished numbers from which they were to come—can be measured by the fact that only one ever graduated from the institution. With that observation, the eminent Cambridge historian Lucius Paige chose to end his discussion of the local Native American population in 1676.

After the discovery of the North American coast in 1497 by John Cabot, the famed English navigator of Italian lineage, the British Crown claimed all the land of the "new" continent lying between the French possessions to the north (Canada) and the Spanish possessions to the south (Florida). The early history of Cambridge deals primarily with a group of English immigrants who settled in between.

When Charles I put his name to the charter of the Colony of Massachusetts Bay in 1629, he thought he was merely signing the charter of another commercial trading company. The Puritans, however, had other ideas. Disenchanted with the Church of England, they planned to establish the Massachusetts Bay Colony as a community not only to provide a more congenial religious climate but also to serve as a model for a new, more democratic form of government.

With this goal in mind, their leader, John Winthrop, set sail for the North American continent with a small fleet of ships in April 1630. In June and July, the ships arrived with some seven hundred passengers who immediately set out to colonize the land deeded to them by the Crown. The religious congeniality of the group that founded Newtowne (now Cambridge) turned out not to be as great as had originally been hoped, and a sizable contingent set off for Connecticut in 1636.

The Massachusetts Bay Colony chose Newtowne as its capital. It was far enough upstream on the Charles River to be safe from attack by sea, and high enough to be easily fortified against attack by land. After a few years, however, Boston, with its larger and more accessible harbor, became the seat of the colonial government.

Newtowne was selected in 1636 as the site of the first college in the new English territory. Created by the Bay Colony to serve the established church by educating its clergy, the college that became Harvard—today with MIT—attracts scholars from all over the world who are responsible for an important part of the diversity that currently characterizes the city's population.

Most of the inhabitants of Cambridge in the seventeenth century, however, were farmers, not scholars, and some were more privileged than others. Investors in the Bay Colony received two hundred acres of land for each share held, and colonists who could pay their own passage to America were eligible for fifty acres. Indentured servants were not permitted to own land until their period of service, usually about seven years, was completed. These economic inequities grew worse in the middle of the century as land prices fell and wealthy landowners enlarged their holdings.

The clergy being educated at Harvard were originally intended to serve the Puritans' conservative Congregational Church. As time passed, a liberal strain of Christianity grew in the colony. At first it took the form of a faction within the established church, but later it broke away to become affiliated with the Unitarian Church, thereby perpetuating the religious dissension in the community. And there was a further complication in religious affairs.

In the middle of the eighteenth century, a few wealthy men of English extraction, mostly Boston merchants, began to establish estates in Cambridge. Their wealth derived mainly from plantations in Jamaica and Antigua. Politically, these new immigrants were conservatives, members of the Tory party. And they were Anglicans, loyal to the Church of England. Cambridge was, in their eyes, a pleasant country retreat with easy access by boat or bridge to Boston. They built elegant mansions along the road to Watertown, now known as "Tory Row" or Brattle Street. This influx of affluent, aristocratic families marked the end of Cambridge as a rural college town.

The Tories' loyalty to the Crown made them so unwelcome among the democratic Unitarian and Congregational descendants of the first English settlers that, when the Revolutionary War began in April 1775, they were compelled to leave their mansions. In time, however, the wounds opened by the war healed, and slowly the Anglicans returned to live in Cambridge and worship at Christ Church, which they had built in 1760.

Their gradual return and absorption into the life of the community heralded the first stirrings of religious and ethnic tolerance that has slowly evolved in Cambridge over the last two centuries. That growth, however, has had its fits and starts. For a while the Tories' return only added to the tensions between the Unitarians and Congregationalists. Yet the three groups had two characteristics in common: they were of English extraction, and they lived near Harvard Square in Old Cambridge.

These bonds brought Cantabrigians together in common political cause as the settlement on the Charles was transformed during the industrial revolution from a rural, agricultural college town into an urban, manufacturing center. The influx of other European immigrants to run the industries established primarily by the Old Cambridge Anglo-Saxons in East Cambridge, North Cambridge, and Cambridgeport created new communities quite unlike the one around Harvard Square. In fact, they were so different that the citizens of Old Cambridge sought to secede from the city, an idea that died when Cambridge was formally incorporated by the General Court in 1846. Nevertheless, despite the changes in society and the economy that have since diversified West Cambridge, its perception as an Anglo-Saxon Protestant stronghold endures.

The year in which Newtowne became Cambridge—1638—also marked the introduction of black slavery to New England. The first evidence of African Americans in the town dates from the following year, but there seems to have been only a very limited black presence in the seventeenth century. Nevertheless, these few African Americans were, chronologically, the first members of Cambridge's third group of immigrants.

Their numbers were augmented by the slaves, usually known only by their first names, brought to Cambridge by the Tories in the middle years of the eighteenth century. By 1754, the black population of Cambridge was fifty-six—thirty-three men and twenty-three women—and some of them were no longer slaves. By 1771, the Town Valuation identified Anthony Vassal, Neptune Frost, and Prince Cutler as freedmen without property. By 1777, the number of African Americans subject to direct taxation was fourteen. Six years later, slavery was abolished in Massachusetts.

By that time, African American Cantabrigians had already demonstrated their commitment to the new nation. Although the Continental Congress prohibited the enlistment of blacks, General Washington ignored that policy and recruited, along with twenty-one other freedmen and slaves, the same Neptune Frost and one Cato Stedman, both of whom are interred in the Burying Ground next to Christ Church.

These few immigrants of color were the forerunners of the growing African American presence in Cambridge that developed during the nineteenth century. Often more hospitable toward blacks than the surrounding communities, the city attracted a population of around three hundred African Americans by the time the Civil War broke out in 1860, many of whom had come from Boston, where a bitter fight in the 1840s over the integration of schools had ended in a victory for segregation. But it was after the war that the figures began to rise exponentially. By 1880 there were 1,478 blacks in Cambridge, and at the end of the century the city had the second highest number of African Americans in the state.

While Brattle Street serves as the symbol of the Tory presence in the eighteenth century, the African American Trail celebrates the nineteenth-century contributions of black citizens to both the city and the country. During the Civil War, African American Cantabrigians had fought with the Union forces to put an end to slavery. Black businesses were beginning to flourish, and black citizens were becoming involved in all aspects of city life. The trail is a pathway to the homes of some of Cambridge's leading African American citizens.

As the *Cambridge Current* reported in the summer of 1994, "Educational opportunity had made the city a mecca. Many [African Americans] stayed on to devote their lives to serving the city as councilmen, civil servants, clergymen, storekeepers, authors, editors, educators, journalists, lawyers, physicians, realtors, and tradesmen. Others, like W.E.B. Du Bois, went on to become world-renowned social historians and political activists. Together the men and women honored on the trail created new avenues to independence and civil rights." Perhaps one of the least publicly recognized facts is the city's role in providing a haven and then a home to African American men and women who were at the forefront of what became known a century later as the civil rights movement.

It should also be noted that the African American presence in Cambridge did not exclusively comprise descendants of slaves from the southern states. A significant number emigrated from the West Indies. And while most of the southern blacks have maintained their affiliation with the Baptist and related churches, the West Indian blacks from the former British colonies have tended to associate with the Anglican Episcopal Church. A champion of these latter immigrants toward the end of the twentieth century was Father Kenneth Hughes, of Saint Bartholomew's Church on Harvard Street.

Just as religious diversity has flourished in Cambridge's African American community, so that community has not been confined to a single neighborhood. Its largest concentration has been on "The Coast" south of Central Square to the Charles River, while other clusters appear in Cambridgeport and North Cambridge.

By 1830 the population of Cambridge had increased to around six thousand. Most of the new immigrants were Yankees from the other side of the Charles River in Boston. But times were changing. Migration from across the Atlantic had begun in the early years of the nineteenth century and then, for many reasons, accelerated. A decrease in child mortality rates produced a tremendous surge in the European population. The industrial revolution, during which large-scale, factory-dominated enterprises replaced handicraft industries, caused acute social and economic dislocation. And natural disasters, such as food shortages, earthquakes, and volcanic eruptions, spurred the flood of humanity that brought the city's population to nearly one hundred thousand at the beginning of the twentieth century.

Portuguese and Italian workers in a YMCA literacy class, National Casket Company, ca. 1910. *(Cambridge Historical Commission)*

Life for these first-generation immigrants was usually tough. Overwhelming numbers of them lived in abject poverty in crowded neighborhoods with dilapidated housing. Relations among nationalities varied, but British Americans in particular—many of whom had themselves arrived as poor immigrants—tried to distance themselves from the newcomers with whom they competed for work. Religion and language were the main differences.

Numerically, the city's major immigrant groups during the nineteenth and early twentieth centuries were the Irish, the Italians, the French Canadians, and the Portuguese, all predominantly Roman Catholic. Like the Puritans and the Tories before them, they tended to settle in discrete neighborhoods, their social and religious lives centering on parishes where their native language was invariably employed. While the four groups had much in common, they had many differences as well—in their reasons for leaving home, in the timing of their arrival, in their neighborhoods, and in the industries to which they were attracted.

Most came from rural, agricultural backgrounds and provided the unskilled factory labor needed to fuel the new industries. Each group also included a few individuals with special skills and training around whom another self-contained community could be formed. Gradually, as the demands of industry changed, as artisans and tradespeople began to offer goods and services to other than "their own," and as public education helped establish English as the language of daily life, the barriers between the various groups began to disappear, and the homogenizing of the city's population began.

The first influx of Irish occurred early in the nineteenth century. They began to arrive penniless on the East Coast after 1815, when plummeting grain prices in the homeland made payment of the rents demanded by English landlords impracticable. Unable to migrate farther west, as many nationalities were later able to do, many settled in and around Boston.

The victims of Ireland's horrendous potato famine of the late 1840s soon followed, and the number of Irish who came to Boston between 1840 and 1850 grew from 465 to 65,000. In addition to its staggering size, no other migration of the nineteenth century was characterized by such abject poverty. The poorest of peasants, these farm folk came primarily from the southern counties of Ireland—most with no industrial or mercantile skills—and worked as unskilled laborers with minimal pay and often under appalling conditions. Early on they provided the manual labor required in the glass-making and meat-packing factories of East Cambridge, for instance, and later in the brick-making enterprises in North Cambridge.

For the earliest arrivals, the appalling conditions in the factories extended to other areas of their lives as well. Despite the hospitality for which Cambridge later came to be known, the reception given the newcomers by the predominantly British Cantabrigians found its echo in the church-related tensions of twentieth century Northern Ireland. Anti-Catholic feelings were running high, reflected in the sacking of the Ursuline Convent in Somerville by a drunken mob of some one hundred men in 1834. But the numbers of immigrants grew steadily, and the first Roman Catholic church in Cambridge, established in 1843, embraced the victims of the Irish famine.

The Irish were the first of the immigrant groups to establish themselves politically in the affairs of the city, and the first Irish mayor was elected in 1908. The best known of Cambridge's Irish politicians in the closing years of the twentieth century was North Cambridge's Thomas P. "Tip" O'Neill, long a U.S. congressman and Speaker of the House of Representatives. Although predominantly Irish neighborhoods and Irish Catholic parishes continued to exist in East and North Cambridge, by then the immigrants from the Emerald Isle were living throughout the city and had become regular participants in its social, political, and economic life. Meanwhile, other Europeans were on their way to America.

Originally, many Italians left their homeland prompted by the economic depression that afflicted all of Europe in the later years of the nineteenth cen-

John A. Moran Sr., a former glassblower, with his grandchildren on East Fourth Street, ca. 1905 *(Cambridge Historical Commission)*

tury. What fueled a greater exodus, however, were the economic aftereffects of a catastrophic earthquake that hit southern Italy in 1908.

The Italians were attracted to Cambridge by jobs at such enterprises as J. P. Squires Meat Packing and Boston Woven Hose in East Cambridge. Census figures and church records indicate that some of them settled in that part of the city as early as the 1880s, providing the core around which a later, larger influx of Italians established their own community. Most had their roots in southern Italy—from Gaeta on the coast north of Naples, from Potenza inland from Naples, and from Calabria in the foot of the peninsula. They brought variations of heritage and culture, but these differences disappeared as together they created a unique Italian American lifestyle.

Whatever social life existed after long and exhausting working hours was centered on the Catholic Church, initially at Saint Leonard's in Boston's North End. By 1917, however, growing numbers of Catholics had made a local parish necessary, and they rededicated and blessed a "retired" Baptist church in East Cambridge as the Roman Catholic Saint Francis of Assisi. Thereafter, the Italian community established other institutions. In 1925 a parochial school was opened for the children of the parish, and in 1926 the

Society of Saints Cosmos and Damien, the patron saints of Gaeta, began its annual celebration of the saints' feast day.

In an unsigned, undated manuscript in the files of the Cambridge Historical Society entitled "Cambridge's Italian Community," a member of that community observed that the homeland of his fellow immigrants had been one rich with linguistic and cultural diversity. Coastal Italy differed significantly from the interior, and areas long under one particular sovereignty differed in many ways from regions subject to another authority. In America, however, the impenetrable boundaries of the old country disappeared. In microcosm, the blending of local Italian heritages presaged the integration of Cambridge's many immigrant groups, which continues today. The selection of the city's first Italian mayor in 1952 and, later, of four-time mayor, Al Vellucci—one of the most respected local public figures—signaled the political assimilation of the Italian community. Today, florist Sal DiDomenico, whose family has for years helped to put on the annual Italian festival, stands as one of the leading lights of that community.

The majority of the Portuguese immigrants who settled in Cambridge came via the Azores, originally uninhabited volcanic islands colonized by the Portuguese in the fourteen hundreds. About a third of the way across the Atlantic from the Iberian Peninsula, the Azores became a regular port of call for the whaling ships out of Massachusetts. The Azoreans would occasionally sign on and settle in the Bay State when the ship returned to its home port. Finding the area hospitable, they sent word back across the Atlantic and generated a trickle of immigrants that established Portuguese enclaves along the New England coast. One of those nineteenth-century communities was in Cambridge, waiting to welcome the waves that would follow.

The first wave arrived in the 1890s, when the combined effects of the economic depression in Europe and overpopulation on the islands caused many Azoreans to seek a new life in the New World. The second migration occurred in the 1960s, after a devastating earthquake hit the islands. In the first instance, Cambridge proved particularly welcoming, for these immigrants brought with them experience building and repairing ships for the whaling and fishing industries, skills needed by the woodworking companies in East Cambridge. By the time the second wave arrived, a close Portuguese community had been established, ready to help newcomers settle in and find work. One of the leaders in that unifying process was the Reverend Antonio Pimental, founding pastor of Saint Anthony Church (1902), which still serves as the social and cultural center of the community. Today, the entrepreneur Manuel Rogers serves as a recognized lay leader in maintaining that unity.

Currently, the Portuguese American presence can best be observed from Kendall Square, down Cambridge Street and Broadway to the Charles, highlighted each year by the Feast of Corpus Christi. The neighborhood also turns out in force whenever the Brazilian soccer team is involved in World Cup competition. And at the turn of the millennium, Cambridge's Portuguese community was taking pride in the success of its own Cape Verdean singer Cesaria Evora.

The same economic crisis that afflicted Europe in the late nineteenth century spilled over into Canada, where the industrial dynamism of New England led to talk of la fievre aux États-Unis and generated an exodus to the south. The migration came from the Maritime provinces, primarily Nova Scotia, and from the province of Quebec, mostly from the Montreal area. Like the immigrants from Ireland and Italy, the Nova Scotians tended to be farmers who helped meet the needs of industry for unskilled labor. The Quebecoise were more likely to be skilled artisans or experienced tradespeople. But as with the coastal and inland Italian immigrants, the bonds of language and religion were stronger than any differences, and French Canadian enclaves began to appear in New England.

While the Irish, Italians, and Portuguese came directly across the Atlantic, once they boarded ship the French Canadians (Nova Scotians in particular) filtered down through Maine and New Hampshire into Massachusetts and beyond. Many stopped along the way to work in the mills powered by the region's many rivers—in communities like Manchester, New Hampshire, and Lowell, Massachusetts—or to service the fishing industry along the northern New England coast. But many others went on to find work in North Cambridge, slowly replacing the Irish in making bricks from the clay pits and in harvesting ice from Fresh Pond.

It was near Fresh Pond that one of those tightly knit enclaves emerged. The French Canadians built their own church in 1891, almost literally with their bare hands. When they outgrew it and were ready to have a new church built by a contractor, they waited to begin until they had the money in hand to pay for it. Even then, they were parsimonious. Jules Chisholm, a longtime North Cambridge resident for whom the information booth in Harvard Square is named, recalled being assigned by his mother one summer the task of removing the horsehair from the plaster walls of the original church, to be used in the construction of the new Notre Dame de Pitie, which was finished in 1921.

The French Canadians were the first of the four major nineteenth-century immigrant groups to find themselves absorbed into the general population. The exhaustion of the clay pits was at the heart of their migration from North Cambridge toward the end of the twentieth century. By then, the number of parishioners had dwindled to the point that the Diocese of Boston decided to close the church on Rindge Avenue. Today, the church is being used by a French-speaking Haitian congregation.

Homemaking class at the East End Union, 1924 *(Cambridge Historical Commission)*

Joining the Irish, Italians, Portuguese, and French Canadians, the city's largest immigrant groups, were skilled German and English artisans who came over to work in the glass factories in East Cambridge throughout the first half of the nineteenth century. With them came unskilled countrymen to help not only in making glass but in staffing the other industries established near Lechmere Point. There they were joined by Poles, Lithuanians, and Russians, in addition to immigrants from Greece and other Eastern European countries, and by Jews from everywhere, who arrived to help provide the manpower required by the new factories. Indeed, the Poles and Lithuanians arrived in such numbers that they needed their own Roman Catholic churches: Saint Hedwig, dedicated in 1907, for the former, and Immaculate Conception, in 1910, for the latter. Ten years later, Saint Francis of Assisi was erected by the Italians. But, like the French Canadian parishioners of Our Lady of Pity, the pockets of Polish and Lithuanian immigrants and their descendants grew too small to support churches of their own.

In the meantime, the forebears of today's African Caribbean Americans were beginning to populate the West Indies. While Massachusetts was being settled by the Puritans from England, the islands of the Caribbean were being colonized by speculators from Britain, France, Spain, and the Netherlands.

The combination of climate and soil was favorable to the cultivation of sugar, and much of the money used to build the mansions on Tory Row came from the sugar and rum trade between the Continent and the islands.

Growing, harvesting, and processing sugar required much physical labor. With the native Caribe Indians decimated by conquest and disease, plantation owners imported slaves from Africa. Today, the descendants of those involuntary laborers comprise the major portion of the islands' population. For them, the United States has represented a nearby land of opportunity.

In the early years of the civil rights movement, all people of color tended to be identified as "Black." As the country became conscious of its legacy of discrimination, however, it came to realize that not all "Blacks" were descendants of African slaves. Some, it turned out, had come via the West Indies, most of them from the former British colonies after the abolition of slavery. As a result, they brought a culture that was different from that of the stateside African Americans.

Over the last half of the twentieth century, these two black populations tended to coalesce in common cause so that it is now hard to distinguish between them. The point here, of course, is that while Cambridge's original African American immigrants were slaves or former slaves from the South, the African American community that has developed in their wake is a mixture of African Americans and African Caribbean Americans. Perceived as African American, Cambridge's best-known national sports figure, former basketball great Patrick Ewing, is of English-speaking African Caribbean American heritage.

Today, Puerto Ricans comprise the largest Caribbean American presence in Cambridge, part of a larger Spanish-speaking population that includes immigrants from the Caribbean islands as well as from South and Central America. Their presence is responsible for the introduction of bilingual education programs in the schools and the need for Spanish signage in public transportation facilities and elsewhere. They have come not in waves, like the earlier European immigrants, but gradually since World War II. Census figures for 1980 and 1990 show them to be the city's fastest-growing population, and they have tended to find employment in the service area rather than in industry.

The same census figures reveal that, while much smaller in number, immigrants from Asia and the Pacific Rim constitute two of the city's other fast-growing groups of newcomers. And though the mix of African American residents may be hard to determine, dividing immigrants from East Asia into definable communities is more complicated still, except by national inheritance. Attracted to the city in large measure by its education and employment opportunities, for instance, have been Chinese, Taiwanese, Thai, Japanese, Korean, Indonesian, Vietnamese, Cambodian, Filipino, Fijian, Tahitian, and Micronesian populations.

Like the first Native Americans to settle on the banks of the Charles, these latest immigrants have arrived from the west and have, in a sense, completed the latter-day encirclement of the globe by the nationalities represented in the city's population—an encirclement made visible by the twenty-six languages used in Cambridge public schools, by the myriad religions served by its many churches, temples, and mosques, and by the infinite variety of cuisines served in its many restaurants. Cambridge has become, at the turn of the twenty-first century, a truly cosmopolitan city, a far cry from the semi-nomadic home of its first immigrants and from the rural village of the Puritan settlers.

CHAPTER NOTES

1. The author gratefully acknowledges the cooperation of Simon R. Doubleday, associate professor of history at Hofstra University, Hempstead, Long Island, New York, and resident fellow at the Society from 1990 to 1993, in offering advice on early drafts of the manuscript.

The Evolution of Religion in Twentieth-Century Cambridge[1]

ALAN SEABURG

THE EVOLUTION of religious thought, expression, and practice in Cambridge during the twentieth century was dynamic and dazzling, corresponding largely to the ways religion was then developing in much of the rest of the country. As a result, a study of religion in Cambridge in that century also becomes a survey of religion in America over the same period.

PREDOMINANTLY A CHRISTIAN COMMUNITY

As the century began, Christianity continued to be the religious choice of a large percentage of the Cambridge population. Within that faith, the majority of believers belonged to the Catholic Church. Catholicism had grown rapidly in the nineteenth century due to the influx of immigrants from Europe with religious roots in that tradition, and Catholic churches and related institutions were established throughout the city. In the first decades of the new century, the Catholic Church, while consolidating its presence in the community, continued to attract believers and started several new parishes. These were St. Anthony's (1902) in East Cambridge; Blessed Sacrament (1907), St. Patrick's (1908), and Immaculate Conception (1909) in Cambridgeport; and Immaculate Conception (1926) on Alewife Brook Parkway.

St. Anthony's Catholic Church in East Cambridge serves the Portuguese community. *(Photograph by Thomas Dahill)*

It is helpful to have a clear and objective understanding of just what the religious population of the city looked like at this time. Fortunately, the U.S. Bureau of the Census published two studies concerned with the statistics of "religious bodies" in America, one for the year 1906, the other for 1926.

The total population of Cambridge in 1900 was 91,886; in 1906 the federal government estimated that it was 98,544. Of this number, 45,896 declared themselves members of a religious organization. The census then indicated their individual choices. The population of Cambridge at the start of 1926 was 119,700. Of this number, 75,849 claimed a religious affiliation. Again, the census broke down the denominational figures. The table on the next page compares these two sets of statistics.[2]

These figures indicate several significant points about religion in early-twentieth-century Cambridge. The most obvious is the continuing dramatic development of the Roman Catholic Church. That faith increased by about twenty thousand members and came to represent more than half the Christian presence in the city. The second relates to the only other world faith reported in the 1926 census: Judaism. Its share of believers also increased substantially. The Protestant groups on the whole basically held their own in this first quarter of the century, with the exception of Episcopalians, who doubled their 1906 membership figure. Finally, it is of some importance to note that a large percentage of people listed in each survey declared no official connection with

RELIGIOUS BODIES	1906	1926
Adventist bodies	N/A	N/A
African Orthodox Church	N/A	240
Armenian Church	437	N/A
Bahais	N/A	N/A
Northern Baptist Convention	2,918	2,539
Southern Baptist Convention	N/A	N/A
National Baptist Convention	125	561
Seventh-day Baptists	N/A	N/A
Free Baptists	214	N/A
Brethren	65	50
Buddhists	N/A	N/A
Church of Christ, Scientists	186	359
Churches of New Jerusalem	86	116
Congregationalists	2,972	2,516
Evangelical	50	130
Friends	181	N/A
Jewish	65	5,200
Lutheran (Evangelical)	400	711
Methodist Episcopal	1,113	1,277
African Methodist Episcopal	236	355
African M. E. Zion	193	125
Pentecostal Nazarene	166	97
United Presbyterian, NA	240	164
Reformed Presbyterian, NA	50	68
Protestant Episcopal	1,950	4,622
Roman Catholic	33,043	54,436
Salvation Army	130	311
Scandinavian Evangelical	N/A	247
Spiritualists	N/A	680
Unitarians	747	492
Universalists	481	494
Volunteers of America	N/A	59

either a church or a synagogue, although many folks who regularly attended a place of worship did not elect membership in the organization for private reasons. Yet it is suggestive that for a portion of the city, institutional religion offered them no rewarding organizational "home."

A decade later, the story was much the same. While the population of the city declined slightly during the 1930s, it was still well over one hundred thousand in 1936, when the census reported that it had sixty-five churches in fifty-four buildings with a total membership of 72,931. And as it had been at the start of the century, the church of choice for most Cambridge Christians continued to be Roman Catholic.

What was it like, then, to be a Roman Catholic during these decades? "Rather simple," according to the centennial committee of St. John the Evangelist Church, "[for] these were the years of a traditional unchanging Catholic church. It was a triumphalistic church, which held itself distinct from and superior to other Christian religions. The clergy were looked upon as the educated class, whose calling was to communicate church teaching . . . Parishioners were expected to attend Mass . . . were silent spectators . . . and did not receive communion on a regular basis."[3] All this could be summed up thus: "The average parishioner was expected to 'pray, pay, and obey.' "[4] That was the essence of "pre–Vatican II" Catholicism. It may sound negative, but it provided comfort and meaning for its followers. "I sure loved the old parish," said Tip O'Neill of St. John the Evangelist, his religious home—"the Dominican Nuns, the spiritual and social life."[5]

And what was it like to have been a Protestant during the first half of the century? This is harder to answer owing to the many denominations that constitute the movement. Mainline Protestant churches—"the older and larger Protestant bodies, the most socially oriented, the most accepting of contemporary scholarship (both secular and sacred), the most visible religious bodies in America"[6]—certainly had the most members and influence. In Cambridge, that included Baptists, Congregationalists, Methodists, Lutherans, Episcopalians, Unitarians, and Universalists. While there was some membership movement within this group—Episcopalians increased their strength while Unitarians were in decline—it was largely a period when Protestantism was just holding its own. Nevertheless, along with their Catholic counterparts, parishioners of all the various individual churches deeply loved their religious "homes."

A New Multireligious Cambridge

After the Second World War, significant—even dramatic—changes took place in the religious life of the city, changes that proved to be as profound as the influence of Puritanism in the seventeenth century and Roman

Catholicism after the 1840s. Cambridge now became more than a predominantly Christian city. Slowly, the community was being enriched by the infusion of followers from and converts to a number of the world's other major religious faiths—a change not unique to Cambridge but reflected in the history of many other American cities and towns as well. Before discussing this development, it would be wise to examine how the once-dominant Christian community evolved during the remaining decades of the century.

ROMAN CATHOLICISM

The brief papacy (1958–1963) of Pope John XXIII forever reoriented the everyday pastoral life of his Church. Catholics in the United States generally responded favorably, as did the laity around the world, to the innovations in thought and practice that resulted from the ecumenical council—Vatican II—that he called into existence. "The extent of the changes that Vatican II brought about in the Catholic Church," wrote Thomas H. O'Connor, "was truly extraordinary....Almost no aspect of Catholic life, customs, devotion, piety, or ritual remained untouched."[7] Father William J. Leonard, a Jesuit at Boston College, described the effect this way: "Young people now have simply no idea of what it was like to be a Catholic in 1940—or even in 1960."[8]

Cambridge Catholics now worship with mass and the sacraments largely in English rather than in Latin. During prayer, their priests face them rather than the altar. Modern liturgies have replaced those that were familiar to their grandparents, and many religious acts, once required, have become voluntary. It is no longer the rule that fish, rather than meat, be eaten on Friday. Indeed, the very appearance of the religious leaders has changed as traditional habits, cassocks, and dress have been replaced by conventional styles already worn by the congregation.

One of the most far-reaching changes wrought by Vatican II, however, concerned the expansion of the various roles the laity played in the everyday life of the parish and diocese. But Vatican II did more than open to the laity the possibilities of helping to run churches and teaching in parochial schools. It empowered them with "a right and sometimes a duty to express their opinion on matters in the Church that relate to their fields of expertise."[9] As will be seen several decades later during the pedophilia scandal of the late twentieth century, the laity took their duty with the utmost seriousness.

Along with these changes came others. One came by means of a tremendous fire at St. John the Evangelist Church in North Cambridge on the night of December 7, 1956. By morning, the structure was in ruins. "It was like losing a member of your family," said one parishioner, Edward Goulart. The stunned congregation and its cardinal, Richard J. Cushing, vowed to rebuild the historic church, and within less than six years the mortgage necessary to finance the rebuilding was paid in full.[10]

In a change of more lasting significance, the city's Catholic population started to decline as people moved to nearby communities thought to offer better social environments. During earlier decades, when so many Catholic immigrants swelled the population, a dominant feature of Cambridge Catholicism was the need to build churches and religious schools. Now, however, while new Catholic immigrants continued to be attracted to the city, many of the sons and daughters of earlier ones were busy moving out.

There were several reasons for this migration. One was that the earlier immigrants had achieved the American "dream" and been absorbed into its middle class. With better incomes came a desire for more spacious living conditions, which were to be found in the suburbs after World War II. As a result, the need for so many parishes in the inner cities declined, which led the Boston archdiocese early in 2004 to consolidate a number of local churches, including three in Cambridge.

The impact of this population and income shift was perhaps most dramatically seen in Cambridge's parochial schools. Throughout the early decades of the century, enrollment in Catholic educational centers reflected a healthy growth pattern. In 1930, for example, St. John the Evangelist's grammar school in North Cambridge had a thousand students taught by the Dominican sisters, and at its high point, Cambridge supported eleven Catholic grammar schools and four high schools. But during the last half of the century, due to a decreasing student population, several schools—St. Hedwig's, St. Patrick's, St. Paul's, the Sacred Heart, and St. John the Evangelist's—were forced to close or were replaced with regional schools. Indeed, Matignon High School, established in 1947, was the first such central Catholic high school in this archdiocese. Further, lay teachers now served basically all of these schools. As a result, by 2003 the city's fifteen parochial schools had been reduced to four.[11]

Another matter that merits discussion is the effect of the pedophilia crisis on the Roman Catholic Church in this period.[12] During the last quarter of the century, the church's laity gradually learned that a shocking number of priests were sexually abusing the children in their care. Even more troubling for devout Catholics was the clear fact that the leaders of the church had long been aware of the situation and had protected the priests involved while ignoring the pain and suffering of their victims. Cambridge Catholics were not immune to this crisis, for at least two of the accused had served for short periods in the city.

The laity's response was forthright: compassion for the victims and anger at those who had allowed the priests to continue in their jobs. Their anger was expressed in various ways. One was church attendance; the

Reverend George Salzmann of the Harvard Catholic Student Center estimated that attendance at mass dropped about 15 percent at local churches.[13] Another was withholding or limiting financial contributions to church appeals and programs. Perhaps the most significant development to come out of the crisis was the expansion of the laity's role in shaping some church policy. The reforms of Vatican II had already empowered this process, and the sexual abuse crisis furthered the change.

Although a small minority of Catholics decided to leave the church, a majority remained devout followers. As a banner at one meeting of lay Catholics proclaimed, "Keep the Faith, Change the Church." Roman Catholicism is thus still the largest and most influential of the various representatives of Christianity in the city.

PROTESTANTISM

During the 1940s, Cambridge Protestantism underwent roughly two major transitions. The first involved previously stable churches, which now closed, merged, or started to share their space with congregations just getting established. The second consisted of the dramatic increase of "evangelical conservative" congregations in the city. That term refers to a movement composed of Fundamentalist, Holiness, and Pentecostal or charismatic churches.

In 1927 the First Evangelical Congregational Church (called after its move to Prospect Street in 1951 the Prospect Congregational Church) had over four hundred children in its Sunday school program. By 1985, however, its congregation numbered seventy-five at best, so after 158 years as a separate organization, it merged with the North Congregational Church in Porter Square. As one of its deacons explained, "People moved away or died, the neighborhood changed, and the church was left with only a handful of people."[14]

For many Protestant denominations after World War II, this was not an isolated experience. Rather, it became the norm, although the process of a denomination swallowing up its sister churches had begun earlier. At one time, for example, there were three Universalist and three Unitarian societies; today, these traditions find their sole representation in the Unitarian Universalist First Parish in Cambridge, next to the Old Burying Ground in Harvard Square. The Harvard-Epworth Church is another example of this trend, for it is the result of a merger in the 1940s of two Methodist churches, the Harvard Church in Central Square and its offspring in Harvard Square, the Epworth Church.

Some congregations, such as the Emmanuel Baptist Church in Cambridgeport, simply closed their doors and sold their buildings to other religious organizations, while others decided to move to another location, like the Holy Cross Armenian Church in Harvard Square, which in 1996 moved to Belmont. Many other mainline Protestant churches, however, simply decided to become "multicongregational churches." As those involved in the Pluralism Project at Harvard University noted, "It is this that would perhaps astound Puritan visitors most—the growing number of diverse ministries and congregations sharing a common church space."[15]

Among the churches that opted to share their space were the First United Presbyterian Church, St. Peter's Episcopal Church, Faith Lutheran, and the Cambridgeport Baptist Church, all in Cambridgeport; North Prospect United Church of Christ in Porter Square; and the First Church in Cambridge on Garden Street. What is most interesting, according to the Pluralism Project, is the variety of the "ministries and congregations sharing a common church space."[16] Among the religious groups with which the churches above elected to share their space were the Luso American Pentecostal Church, the Brazilian Presbyterian Fellowship, a Spanish Pentecostal prayer group, an Ethiopian Orthodox church, the First Brazilian Church of Greater Boston, the Harvard Korean United Church of Christ, and the Iglesia Bautista Central. Such diversity represents the growing edge of Protestantism.

Yet it is important to note that even within the mainline churches there have been exceptions to the mergers and closings. The University Lutheran Church, for example—founded in Harvard Square in 1928—constructed its attractive modern building in 1950, thereby permitting it to more effectively serve both its congregational and community programs. The Holy Trinity Armenian Apostolic Church arrived in the city in 1945 and by 1961 had built its handsome structure on Brattle Street. And in 1991 the Cambridge Society of Friends welcomed a second gathering of Quakers in North Cambridge, the Fresh Pond Meeting, which is connected to the Friends school it runs there.

Protestantism's significant growth during this century, however, occurred within "evangelical" circles. According to the *Boston Church Directory*, "Most of the increase in number of churches...can be attributed to the increase in Pentecostal, Holiness-Pentecostal, and Baptist churches,"[17] something that holds true not only for Cambridge but also for Greater Boston.

The success of the evangelical Protestant churches can be directly tied to the movement of newer immigrants into urban areas like Cambridge. Previously from Canada, England, Ireland, and various other European lands, immigrants in the last decades of the twentieth century were coming from Africa, the Middle East, South America, the Caribbean, and Asia. Just as their predecessors did, these newer arrivals brought their faith with them, a faith often rooted in the Pentecostal and Holiness traditions of Protestantism. In time they formed their own special congregations in all sections of the city. Some of these were Antioch Temple Church (1962), Trinity Church of God

St. Paul's African Methodist Episcopal Church, Central Square. *(Photograph by Thomas Dahill)*

Zion Pentecostal Tabernacle Church, Central Square. *(Photograph by Thomas Dahill)*

(1980), Iglesia de Dias, M.B., Cambridge (1980), Bethel Assembly of God (1988), Bethel Haitian Congregation (1990), Indonesian Full Gospel Fellowship (1993), Grace Church of God (1998), and Vineyard Christian Fellowship of Cambridge (1998).

These were not the first religious societies in the city to represent the evangelical and conservative side of Protestantism here. Others had come much earlier in the century. The Abundant Life Church, for example, was started in 1917; the Christian Mission Holiness Church was also established in that year. Even earlier, the First Church of the Nazarene (1899) had opened its doors to the community. Furthermore, the First Holiness Church of the Apostolic Faith (1916) and the Pentecostal Tabernacle Church (1927) have long had a connection to the city. What is noteworthy is the new numbers of such organizations and their explosive growth and development.

Assembleia de Deus, 2285 Massachusetts Avenue in North Cambridge. *(Photograph by Thomas Dahill)*

Cambridge Christianity, then, is as lively as it has always been. Indeed, as Diana L. Eck—head of the Pluralism Project and professor of comparative religion and Indian studies at Harvard—has pointed out, "Religions are not fixed and packaged, passed along like boxes of treasures from generations to generations. They are more like rivers, dynamic and changing, bearing the heritage of the past to water the fields of the present."[18]

THE NEW MULTIRELIGIOUS CAMBRIDGE

Cambridge's first synagogue was built in 1901; the first Buddhists came in the 1950s; the first Muslims, in 1958; the first Sufi gathering occurred in 1971; the first Zen Center was established in 1973; and the first Hindu group took shape in 1976. In this manner, and throughout the twentieth century, Cambridge became not just a Christian community but a true multireligious city. The change was not unique to Cambridge. As Professor Eck has pointed out, "America's religious diversity is here to stay...[as is] the opportunity to create a positive multireligious society."[19]

The story of how the neighborhoods of Cambridge have welcomed immigrants who hold beliefs rooted in all the world's living faiths is an excit- ing one. Although this review cannot tell how each group has fared, an account of the beginnings of a few will illustrate what has been taking place during the last decades in our community.

The Cambridge Buddhist Association, which has its temple on Sparks Street, owes its existence to Elsie and John Mitchell, who in 1957 established the nonsectarian Buddhist center. Its current Zen master was trained in Dharma Transmission in the Korean Chogye Order of Buddhism and in the Kwan Um School of Zen. The Cambridge Zen Center, which came into being in 1974, is also of the Kwan Um Zen tradition. It has over thirty residents in its house in Central Square and about one hundred members (the Buddhist

Association has no formal members). Both attract mostly "Euro-American lay practitioners," and their programs include meditation and Zen practice and teaching.

Tibetan Buddhism is represented in the city by the Dzogchen Foundation, which began here in 1991. Its teaching is accomplished through lamas it invites to Cambridge as well as through various meditation retreats. At present, its membership is around 150 and, as with the other two groups, they are mostly Euro-Americans. Buddhist groups are also found in Arlington, Brighton, Brookline, Lexington, Lowell, Lynn, Quincy, Upton, and Wakefield, as well as Boston.

During this same period, Islam also became an increasingly important part of the Greater Boston religious scene. Indeed, by the beginning of the twenty-first century, there were more than ten thousand practicing Muslims in eastern Massachusetts. In 1993 the Islamic Society of Boston opened its own mosque on Prospect Street in Central Square. Here its members —almost four hundred students from nearby colleges and universities —assemble for prayers, festivals, and regular Friday evening services. Islamic groups also exist in Boston, Quincy, Sharon (which has over a thousand members), Wayland, and Worcester. As noted by the Pluralism Project, "Five times a day—in private living rooms, in business offices, in dormitories, and in Islamic centers fashioned from remodeled churches and transformed U-Haul dealerships—the Muslims of New England bow in prayer. They face Makkah, but the path of *shariah*, the 'straight path' of Islam, leads them day by day through the streets of Boston."[20]

If many of these groups are presently small, they are nevertheless growing and exhibit good vital signs. Clearly, they will continue to be a living part of religion in Cambridge during the twenty-first century—part of a movement that can be traced back to Puritan times and to the tribal societies that were practicing religious pluralism before the Europeans arrived. "Looking back," writes Charles H. Lippy, University of Tennessee's distinguished professor of religious studies, "it becomes increasingly clear that the pluralism that came of age in the 20th century was a natural development emerging from forces that had long shaped American religious life.... The Europeans who embarked on colonial settlement brought diverse understandings of Protestant Christianity with them...[and] the history of openness to immigration from diverse sources...paved the way for other forms of pluralism to come to life." Finally, but most importantly for a democratic society, "the legal arrangements of the First Amendment to the Constitution also helped sustain an environment where pluralism would prevail in granting individuals and religious communities considerable latitude in matters of belief and practice."[21]

The Islamic Society of Boston mosque and center on Prospect Street. *(Photograph by Thomas Dahill)*

"I would argue this, first of all," adds the late William R. Hutchison of Harvard Divinity School, "there can be no turning back. Beyond that, I would argue that the logical arguments in favor of a pluralism that goes beyond inclusivity, that is mutually respectful and nonpatronizing, are compelling if one wishes to contemplate any civil religion at all."[22]

What all this means is that Cambridge is now truly a community where all of its citizens may worship freely and with joy in the practice and religion of their choice. It also means that this historical society starts its second hundred years auspiciously, in a city dedicated to seeing that democracy works to serve the needs of its people.

ENDNOTES

1. For an earlier version of this essay, see Alan Seaburg, *Cambridge on the Charles* (Cambridge, Mass.: Anne Miniver Press, 2001), chapter 8.

2. See U.S. Bureau of the Census, *Religious Bodies: 1906, Part 1* (Washington, D.C.: Government Printing Office, 1910), 380–407; and U.S. Bureau of the Census, *Religious Bodies: 1926*, vol. 1 (Washington, D.C.: Government Printing Office, 1930), 383.

3. St. John the Evangelist Centennial Committee, *St. John the Evangelist Church Centennial: 1893-1993* (Dallas: Taylor, 1992), 23.

4. Ibid., 33.

5. Ibid., 58.

6. J. Gordon Melton, *The Encyclopedia of American Religions*, 3rd ed. (Detroit: Gale Research, 1989), xlv.

7. Thomas H. O'Connor, *Boston Catholics: A History of the Church and Its People* (Boston: Northeastern University Press, 1999), 265. For a scholarly examination of how Vatican II affected the life and activities of one Cambridge Catholic church, see Frances O'Donnell, "Vatican II and St. Paul's Parish: An Analysis of the Role of Historical Context in the Creation of Records," Master's thesis, University of Massachusetts, Boston, 1995.

8. Thomas H. O'Connor, *Boston Catholics*, 266.

9. William J. Collinge, *Historical Dictionary of Catholicism* (Lanham, Md.: Scarecrow, 1997), 235.

10. Sarah Boyer, *In Our Own Words: Stories of North Cambridge, Massachusetts, 1900–1960* (Cambridge, Mass.: City of Cambridge and the North Cambridge Stabilization Committee, 1997), 127.

11. It is important to note that the number of students in Cambridge's public schools also declined during this period.

12. For an objective presentation of the matter, see The Investigative Staff of *The Boston Globe*, *Betrayal: The Crisis in the Catholic Church* (Boston: Little, Brown, 2002).

13. The Reverend George Salzmann in conversation with the author, May 2, 2003.

14. Jeremiah V. Murphy, "Church Shuts Its Door after 158 Years," *Boston Globe*, May 27, 1985, 21.

15. The Pluralism Project, Harvard University, *World Religions in Boston: A Guide to Communities and Resources*, ed. Diana L. Eck and Elinor J. Pierce (Cambridge: Pluralism Project, 1998), 40.

16. Ibid.

17. *The Boston Church Directory Millennium Edition*, ed. Rudy Mitchell and Jeffrey Bass (Boston: Emmanuel Gospel Center, 2001), 323.

18. Pluralism Project, *World Religions in Boston*, 5.

19. Diana L. Eck, *A New Religious America: How a "Christian Country" Has Become the World's Most Religiously Diverse Nation* (San Francisco: HarperSanFrancisco, 2001), 383.

20. Pluralism Project, *World Religions in Boston*, 75.

21. Charles H. Lippy, *Pluralism Comes of Age: American Religious Culture in the Twentieth Century* (Armonk, N.Y.: M. E. Sharpe, 2000), 162.

22. William R. Hutchison, *Religious Pluralism in America: The Contentious History of a Founding Ideal* (New Haven: Yale University Press, 2003), 234–35.

Immigrant Jewish Cambridge

ARNOLD SCHUTZBERG

ALTHOUGH the first Jewish immigrants came to Cambridge in 1856—from England via New York—they associated themselves with the newly formed Boston Jewish community and did not establish any Jewish institutions in Cambridge. The Cambridge institutions would appear in time, requiring for their founding the critical mass of Yiddish-speaking "Russians" who came to the city between 1890 and 1924, after which immigration was curtailed by Congress. Sponsored by Massachusetts Senator Henry Cabot Lodge, the legislation grew out of an anti-immigration movement that had its beginnings at Harvard University at the turn of the century.

These immigrants built four synagogues (one was actually in Somerville) and one Hebrew school and established two cemeteries. Their 1901 synagogue on Columbia Street was the first "Russian" structure designed by an architect in Greater Boston. Their 1913 school on Elm Street was the first modern regional structure for after-school Hebrew education. The community was exceptionally active and formed many social, cultural, and philanthropic organizations. They were also active in the initiation and development of various small businesses.

The immigrants worked in the shoe industry and needle trade factories. They managed tailor and fur shops, ma-and-pa spas, fish, meat, tobacco, dry goods, hardware, furniture, stove, junk, recycled bottle, and auto parts businesses. They were painters, building contractors, real estate speculators, ice and kerosene vendors, and fruit and vegetable peddlers.

Cambridge also supported four kosher butcher shops and a Jewish bakery. Live fowl were inspected and prepared for the Friday Sabbath meal at the kosher slaughterhouse, across the tracks on Cambridge Street. Fresh-from-the-oven breads were delivered early in the morning in paper bags by Levy's Bakery, at 815 Cambridge Street, to rear third-floor walk-ups. The heel of the warm rye bread soaked in unsalted creamery butter was a child's reward when he ate breakfast with his early-rising father. There were Heller's National D and Weiner's kosher Jewish food product stores. There were several places to get a corned beef on rye or a brisket dinner.

The immigrants to Cambridge came in families and as young single men and women, leaving parents and brothers and sisters in Europe. They married and had children. Some came directly to join relatives, others only after sojourns in the crowded North or West ends of Boston or the less crowded, peddler-friendly rural Maine.

A small fraction of immigrants returned to the old country because of the absence of piety, or Sabbath observance, in America. Most of the immigrant generation spent their lives in their adopted city and died after long, productive lives. The lives of their European cousins, sisters, and brothers, on the other hand, were short-circuited by genocide.

They learned just enough American English to make a living and to get their naturalization papers. Their children became professionals or successful entrepreneurs and left the city for the leafy suburbs. Only a few first-generation immigrant enterprises survived. They include Temple Beth Shalom (the Tremont Street *shul*)—the last of the four Cambridge synagogues whose cornerstone was laid in 1924—the S&S Restaurant, Legal Sea Foods, Pill Hardware, and Hyde Shoe (Saucony).

Jewish immigrant Cambridge spanned about one hundred years, from 1856 to 1956. The story of this community is told here in terms of some of its institutions.

THE CIGAR MAKERS

The earliest Jewish immigrants in Cambridge came from England in the 1850s. They resided mainly in the Central Square area and made cigars. Other occupations included antiques dealer, barber, bookkeeper, chiropodist, clothing dealer, crayon artist, cracker factory worker, fruit and vegetable dealer, gold leaf artisan, hairdresser, house painter, optician, peddler, and veterinarian.

The *Cambridge Chronicle* said that "Cambridge single-term councilman Harry W. Joel was brought at age 4 by his 28-year-old London-born peddler father, Samuel W. Joel, from his Salt Lake City birthplace to

Cambridge in 1870...here was a small colony of Jewish families...concentrated around...Pearl Street. Religious services were held in private homes."

Most English Jews of this period were not very observant, but they associated themselves with the small Jewish community at Ohabei Shalom, the first synagogue in Boston. The Cambridge Londoners withdrew from that synagogue in 1859 and joined the short-lived (fifteen years) Beit El Congregation of Boston, also known as the Hollanders. Burial in consecrated ground was a traditional as well as a religious practice for most Jews of the period, and this congregation purchased land for a Jewish cemetery in Melrose.

The Hollander Synagogue dissolved about 1874, abandoning its chapel on Gloucester Place and the weekly Sabbath service. They met only on the High Holidays, when they rented Red Men's or Paine Memorial Hall. The congregation retained its corporate status to maintain the Melrose cemetery.

The Boston United Hand-In-Hand Society was incorporated on April 11, 1877, to supply sick benefits to Jews of good moral character who had been married according to Jewish law and custom. In case of death, funerals, burial lots, headstones, and endowments to heirs or next-of-kin were provided. Three Cambridge residents—Michael Busnach, Joseph C. Joel, and Samuel W. Joel, all active members of the cigar makers' union—were signatories of the corporation. Dues were set at twenty-five cents a week. A cemetery was acquired in West Roxbury, and the first interment was a child of the cigar maker Alexander Barnett of East Cambridge.

With the exception of Michael Busnach and his wife, Maria, who settled in Cambridge in 1856, all of the early immigrant community and many of the next generation were buried in the Hand-in-Hand Cemetery in West Roxbury. Maria and Michael were buried in 1892 and 1893 in the Hollander Cemetery in Melrose.

In 1922 Solomon, Michael's eldest son, received an elaborate Grand Army of the Republic funeral and interment in the Hand-in-Hand Cemetery. He was one of the six surviving members of the first company in the country to answer President Lincoln's call for volunteer troops. Their names are inscribed in brass on a tablet inside the entry to Cambridge City Hall.

Marriage and burial are both traditional activities associated with publicly acknowledged religious ritual. In general, the community relied on the Hollander *chazan* (lay religious practitioner rather than ordained rabbi) to officiate at their weddings and funerals. With a lack of qualified religious officials, the community turned to available but compatible local clergy. The choices were quite broad.

The radical Reform Rabbi Fleischer of Adas Israel Synagogue officiated at the 1905 Solomon-Lemon wedding in St. Georges Hall, Central Square.

The wedding was catered by Strachan (that is, it was not kosher), suggesting that a significant portion of the English colony had an Americanized level of Jewish observance not common to their East European brethren. Rabbi Aaron Gorovitz (the Orthodox Cambridge and Somerville city rabbi from 1910 to 1924, who was traditionally observant) officiated at the second wedding of Harry Joel's younger brother Arthur in 1911. Rabbi Samuel Abrams of the conservative South End Ohabei Shalom Synagogue led the 1924 funeral of Elizabeth (Busnach) Lemon, the first Jewess born in Cambridge, in 1856.

In 1913 the building on the corner of Pearl Street and Massachusetts Avenue—which had housed Michael and Solomon Busnach's cigar store, Henry and Samuel Busnach's barbershops, and Lewis Lemon's antique furniture business, "Old Curiosity Shop"—was torn down to make way for Harris Ginsberg's three-story Harvard Bazar, which extended the entire block to Green Street. This event marked the end of the English and the ascendance of the Russian immigrant Jewish business community. In 1914 Samuel Busnach died of "tobacco heart" and was buried in the Cambridge city cemetery. It seems that in addition to smoking too many cigars, he married out of the faith and thus was not permitted burial in consecrated ground.

Other names associated with the English community were Aaron, Berlyn, Barnett, Cohen, Fonseca, Keezer, Levy, and Poliak. Only Poliak was associated with the 1901 groundbreaking of the Beth Israel Synagogue.

CONGREGATION BETH ISRAEL, THE FIRST SYNAGOGUE

In 1880 the civic, economic, and social conditions of traditional Jews in Czarist Russia were such that emigration became an active option. According to a U.S. government report, between 1880 and 1914 more than ninety thousand Jews informed immigration officials in ports across the United States that their final destination was Massachusetts; some headed to Cambridge.

It is clear that the Eastern European Jewish immigrants followed the pattern of all nineteenth-century immigrants who came into the port of Boston. They settled with their predecessors in the neighborhood next to the port—the North End. Former church structures were available to be converted into synagogues and to meet the religious and communal needs of the new population.

As they became familiar with the country and sought better housing and business opportunities, these immigrants moved to the suburbs. Some preferred to keep their families in familiar surroundings and developed only business ventures outside the city. Others inverted this process. Cambridge and Somerville had distinct advantages over the North End with respect to housing (it was significantly less concentrated), demand for services, and business potential—not to mention space for keeping a horse and storing goods. The

Congregation
Beth Israel at 238
Columbia Street.

suburbs, however, lacked the Jewish institutional structure of the common meetinghouse and synagogue, and no churches were available for conversion as in the North End.

The first public acknowledgment of a synagogue in Cambridge appeared in the *Cambridge Chronicle* on October 6, 1900. (The two other Cambridge newspapers had no coverage.) Under the heading "Synagogue to Be Built," the article told of the holiday services held on September 30, 1900, in Prospect Hall, where the number of attendees was sufficient to warrant the communal fundraising meeting. Thirteen hundred dollars was pledged to erect a building to serve as a synagogue and religious school. Except for its proximity to Central Square, the location of the building was unspecified. The cost was estimated to be between ten thousand and twenty thousand dollars. The building was to be designed and built by architect Nathan Douglas.

The corporation was formally organized eight months later, on June 6, 1901. The officers were Israel Nesson, president; Charles Snow, treasurer; and five directors, with the building to be known as Congregation Beth Israel of Cambridge. Its purpose was to be a "Synagogue for the Public Worship of God." The directors held their first meeting on June 13, 1901.

On June 24, 1901, the article "Cambridge Hebrews New Synagogue" in the *Cambridge Chronicle* reported on the "imposing cornerstone laying ceremony which took place on Monday, June 19, 1901, between 11 a.m. and 6 p.m. at the building site on Columbia St." The lot, measuring 80 by 109 feet, accommodated a building footprint of 50 by 75 feet. Erected on the site were a grandstand and booths elaborately decorated with American flags and tricolor bunting, and the occasion produced pledges totaling over one thousand dollars. In addition, bricks to be used in construction were sold as a fundraising scheme for between one and one hundred dollars apiece. Building fund assets as of that day were estimated at four thousand dollars.

The cornerstone laying ceremony included addresses by the four English-speaking rabbis from the South End and by local politicians. Notably absent was the Orthodox rabbi from the North End, who was probably not proficient in English. (The spoken language of the new immigrant Jews was Yiddish.) According to the newspaper, the congregation consisted of "the best class of Hebrew citizens of the city."

The article estimated the "Hebrew" families in the city to number about four hundred, with an additional hundred in Somerville. The seating capacity in the main sanctuary was designed for five hundred men, with a separate balcony for three hundred women. It is clear that the design was meant to meet the needs of the existing population and did not allow for significant growth. Congregation Beth Israel was issued a certificate of incorporation, No. 9161, by the Commonwealth on July 3, 1901. On September 20, 1901, the *Cambridge Chronicle* reported the building to be "nearly completed at a cost of about $30,000," in time for celebration of the "Hebrew New Year."

The communal roots of the immigrant Cambridge community were tied to orthodoxy, traditional Judaism associated with the 1888 Baldwin Place Synagogue in Boston's North End—the "mother synagogue." Its official name was Beth Israel, and its "chief rabbi" was Rabbi Moshe Zevulun Margolies. Cambridge's synagogue was its offspring.

The first Boston-area use of the name "Beth Israel" had occurred in 1849 and was associated with Cambridge, but it was short-lived. The congregation, formed when a "Polish" secession of about a hundred members from Ohabei Shalom took place, appears to have lasted only one season. A High Holiday service was held, and a burial society and cemetery were established on Kidder's Lane (next to the Catholic cemetery on Rindge Avenue). The Polish ascendance over the German minority in Ohabei Shalom quashed the nascent revolt, though, and the Beth Israel congregation and its burial society were dissolved.

The new immigrants rejected the radical Reform Judaism of the preceding German Jewish immigrant community, Adas Israel. They rejected the negation of Jewish ethnicity, the mixed or family seating, the introduction of organ music, the designation of Sunday rather than Saturday for Sabbath observance, prayer service "decorum" and other innovations that were considered radical, un-Jewish, or too foreign.

The one thing the newcomers did accept from the veteran American Jewish community was its taste in architecture. They found the 1885 synagogue erected by Adas Israel to be truly American and the apex of modernity. There was nothing like it in Eastern Europe. Thus the new citizens of Cambridge essentially copied this architecture to demonstrate solidarity with the earlier Jewish community, patriotic allegiance to the new homeland, and the desire to be perceived as a modern pioneer congregation in a new settlement.

As well as being the first Jewish house of worship in Cambridge and the first suburban Boston synagogue, this synagogue was also the first designed by an architect and built by late-nineteenth-century Russian immigrants. Since the common name of a synagogue was ascribed to the street where it was located, this one became the Columbia Street Synagogue or *shul*. It took an additional two decades for Jewish enclaves to establish themselves in the streetcar suburbs of Roxbury and Dorchester and build other grand synagogues.

ANSHEY SFARD, THE SECOND SYNAGOGUE

Charter 7699 was issued on May 6, 1898, and congregation Anshey Sfard became the first group in Cambridge incorporated by the Commonwealth for "establishing and maintaining a permanent place for religious worship according to the Hebrew faith." A. J. and Jacob Andelman—the brothers of Frank Andelman, who is acknowledged to have emigrated from Russia to Cambridge in 1890—were two of the seven organizers of the corporation. Before 1895, there were not enough Jews to sustain the minyan (quorum) of ten men required to conduct a communal religious service. According to the December 30, 1954, oral testimony of Lena Andelman, the Jewish residents of Cambridge had to go to Boston to participate in religious services. By 1895 there were enough Jewish families in Cambridge to form a minyan, and services were held in private homes. In 1897 there were about twenty-five Jewish families, and a small hall was rented for the High Holidays.

At the 1901 laying of the Beth Israel cornerstone, a committee representing the Anshey Sfard Bnay Yaacob Society of East Cambridge and Somerville contributed the largest single gift toward the construction of the new synagogue. The *Cambridge Chronicle* confirmed the merger of Congregation Aghal Jacob,[1] the first Somerville Jewish congregation, with Anshey Sfard (Men of Spain). Kahal Jacob received Commonwealth charter number 7416 on October 8, 1897.

The Hebrew name *Anshey Sfard* confirmed that the incorporators were East Europeans associated with the "Polish" (Hasidic) mode of Jewish worship. The Hasidic religious movement of the mid-nineteenth century in

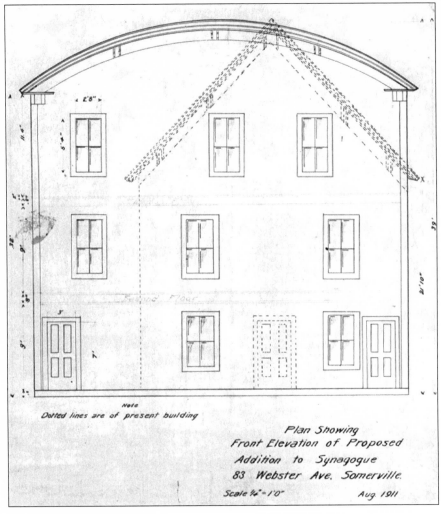

Architectural drawing made in 1911 of proposed revision to the Anshe
Sfard Synagogue, built in 1903.

Eastern Europe had dropped the prevalent Ashkenazi rite of the region and
adopted the Spanish version, developed before the 1492 expulsion of the Jews
from Spain. The difference is of only minor significance.

On December 30, 1902, Boruch Rosenbaum, one of the incorporators
of Kahal Jacob, purchased a two-and-a-half-story wooden building at 85
Webster Avenue, Somerville. On August 28 of the following year, Barnet
Rosenbaum, a builder and architect, submitted the required plans to the state
building inspection department to assure that the modified building would
meet the safety standards required. The 1911 modification drawings show the
original sanctuary to have seating for no more than thirty men, and the only
provision for women appeared to be associated with monthly access to the

mikvah (ritual bath). It is assumed that the congregation met and observed their rituals in a minimally modified structure. The property was officially transferred from Rosenbaum to Anshey Sfard on February 28, 1906. Additional seating for men and separate seating for women were added in 1911.

The American Jewish Year Book of 1907–08 identifies the officers of Anshey Sfard Congregation at 85 Webster Avenue, Somerville, organized by December 1, 1902. It claimed to have twenty-five members and an income of $350—compared with Beth Israel's sixty-five members and $3,000 yearly income. The Anshey Sfard group was observing its tradition in private homes and rented facilities before apparently achieving, in part, its goal with the pending dedication of Beth Israel in September 1903. Why, then, did the Anshey Sfard group purchase and modify a separate property to perform the same function?

In addition to meeting the geographic needs of the constituents for daily prayer (the two synagogues were separated by three short city blocks), there was both a cultural and an economic division between the two communities. The Anshey Sfard people essentially preferred a smaller place of worship, in keeping with the small towns of their homeland. They regarded the Beth Israel Synagogue as too grand for their modest purposes. Most of the Anshey Sfard people occupied a lower economic class and were probably more traditionally observant than the more upwardly mobile, assimilating leadership of the Beth Israel congregation. Junk collectors and dealers were uncomfortable with manufacturers, real estate developers, and high fashion tailors. The Beth Israel group also included persons whose origins were in Lithuania and who retained the Ashkenazi rather than the Hasidic, Polish rite. They broke away in 1906 and formed Agudas Ashkenazim.

Agudas Ashkenazim, the Third Congregation

After Beth Israel's completion and dedication in 1903, a controversy over the mode of liturgy is reported to have arisen. This led to a civil court suit, with a judge ruling that the two modes of worship should be used for alternating six-month periods. The reliability of this report is questionable since the observant immigrant parties would likely have preferred to take the controversy to the Jewish religious court in Boston, Bet Din, before initiating civil court proceedings.

The first public indication of the existence of a "Benevolent Ashkenaz Society" in Cambridge was a notice in the September 27, 1907, *Jewish Advocate* with the title "A Synagogue for Cambridge." It read: "The increase of Jewish population in Cambridge demands that another synagogue should be erected in the city to take [the] place of existing residential and meeting room places of worship. The Benevolent Ashkenaz Society has therefore convened a mass meeting which will be held in Malta Temple hall, 40 Prospect St., Cambridge, on Sunday evening, October 7 at 7 p.m. Chief Rabbi Wolf Gabrial Margolis, Leo J. Lyons and Max Mitchell will address the meeting." A state charter was reported to have been issued to Congregation Agudas Ashkenazim of Cambridge in 1908.

The *Jewish Advocate* next referred to the group in the October 6, 1911, front-page headline "Cambridge to Have Another Synagogue." It reported that Agudas Ashkenazim of Cambridge had held annual services at Prospect Hall for the past six years, suggesting that Rosh Hashanah services began in a rented hall in 1905, two years after the dedication of the Beth Israel synagogue. After the 1911 Yom Kippur Kol Nidre service in Prospect Hall, a Harvard professor reprimanded the assemblage by suggesting that they "build a synagogue [because it is] shameful to hold services in a dance hall." The following Monday, committees were organized and officers selected.

The house at 8 and 10 Tremont Street was purchased on December 15, 1911. Both sides of the house were rented to immigrant Jewish families, although daily and Sabbath services were held at number 8. When the number of congregants was high, as during the High Holidays, various halls were rented.

Congregation Beth Israel and Agudas Ashkenazim are first listed in the Cambridge City Directory of 1914 under "Hebrew Churches." Ashkenazim is misspelled and is accompanied by the wrong address of Tremont Court. These errors were finally corrected in the 1920 directory.

THE HEBREW SCHOOL

In the summer of 1895, before the first synagogue was built, nine women organized the Cambridge Hebrew Ladies Educational Society, hoping to teach Jewish children the Hebrew language and undertake other charitable endeavors. Articles in the *Cambridge Chronicle* and the *Jewish Advocate* describe an active Hebrew free school that took place in the basement vestry of the synagogue. The instructional emphasis was on Yiddish, rote learning, and religious themes in the manner of the traditional Polish or Russian *cheder* (school).

The Hebrew Literary Association movement, Shochrei Sfat Ever, was initiated in the West End of Boston in 1904 by recent young Russian immigrants who brought with them the new revolutionary nationalistic approach of learning Hebrew by using the same language in conversation as well as instruction, Ivrit B'ivrit (*Hebrew* in Hebrew). The West End school met in an unheated, cheerless third-floor flat with no local communal support and last-

The Elm Street
Hebrew School.

ed only three years. In 1906 about 150 Cambridge and Somerville residents
formed their own Hebrew literary association and school. Meetings and classes were held at 280 and 508 Windsor Street (now the location of Roosevelt
Towers).

From 1906 to 1912, a competition existed between the traditional and
modern schools. According to a 1911 census of Hebrew Schools in the *Jewish
Advocate* of July 14, 1911, the Jehudia School had twenty-five pupils;
Shochrei Sfat Ever, sixty-five. The Beth Israel minutes indicate that it took a
committee four months to arrange the amalgamation of the two schools.

In 1911 the Cambridge and Somerville Hebrew Literary Association
purchased a forty-by-one-hundred-foot property on Elm Street. The property
included a wooden structure that was probably used as a school before it was
torn down to make way for a new building two years later. The Cambridge
Hebrew Ladies Educational Institute bought a three-decker at the corner of
Windsor and Palermo streets to use during the construction period.

On Sunday, February 8, 1914, a two-story brick building housing both
the Hebrew School and the YMHA (Young Men's Hebrew Association) was
dedicated with a ceremonial march from Congregation Beth Israel. The Amer-

The 1923 Hebrew School graduation class.

ican and Zionist flags were raised. That building, at 178 Elm Street—with *Zion* worked in Hebrew script into the Star of David motif over the front door—was designed by Nathan Douglas. The cornerstone, engraved "C & S HL, AUX, 1913," confirms the year of emplacement. In addition to being the first such structure in Cambridge, it was also the first school in Massachusetts built by late-nineteenth-century East European immigrants. Earlier schools used modified structures or family housing.

THE YW-YMHA BUILDING

The Young Men's Hebrew Association was organized in 1910 and by 1911 was actively looking for a property to buy for its own use. The mutually beneficial decision to combine efforts with the Hebrew Literary Association resulted in their new headquarters being the first Jewish Center in New England.

The building on Elm Street was left entirely to the Hebrew School when the YW and YMHA moved from the site in March 1929. The YMHA purchased a former Baptist church known as Beacon Hall at 249 Hampshire Street—adjacent to Inman Square on the Somerville border. It appears that the stock market crash and the onset of the Depression set off an ambitious program of growth and membership expansion, including a major renovation

The 1923 Spot Pond immigrant outing of the Young Men's and Young Women's Hebrew Association.

of the two-story structure, projected to include a complete gymnasium, an assembly hall, a cafeteria, and living quarters for Jewish students attending nearby colleges. Beacon Hall was razed in June 1932. A gas station on the site lasted for some forty years, until it was torn down in 1974 to make way for the Cambridge Portuguese Credit Union bank, the current occupant.

CONGREGATION YAVNAH: THE FOURTH CONGREGATION, THIRD SYNAGOGUE

The first meeting of the new Congregation Yavnah was held in a three-decker at 242-244 Western Avenue on October 16, 1917. It received its official charter on January 4, 1918. On September 28, 1919, its name was changed to include a religious school, Talmud Torah.

A review of the 1920 census and the Cambridge City Directory reveals that the twenty or so Yavnah directors, or incorporators, were a combination of older Ward 3 Cambridge residents and families from the North End and West End of Boston who moved into Cambridge's Ward 7. Some of the membership was active in Congregation Beth Israel. At its largest, the Jewish population of Ward 7 never exceeded 20 percent. The economic base of the group was small business, which included junk collecting, insurance, real estate, plumbing, tailoring, printing, upholstering, and auto parts.

Author's father, Harry Schutzberg, carrying the Temple Beth Israel's Thirteenth Torah Scroll in a 1957 ceremony.

The small enclave of Jews who found work and housing in the Riverside section of Cambridge had been displaced from the synagogues and Hebrew school. Thus the community was motivated to purchase a lot, hire an architect—S. S. Eisenberg—and build a synagogue at 10-12 Howard Street. Although the original drawings show the building to be of clapboard, sufficient funding must have been found to finish the building in brick.

The interior arrangement of the two separate platforms required for housing, storing, and reading the Torah scrolls used at Beth Israel was modernized (some would say Protestantized) by combining them. A simple balcony cantilevered over the rear third of the sanctuary's main chamber provided seating for women. The basement accommodated the school and other social and business activities. The two-story, flat-roofed exterior reflected a Byzantine, or Oriental, character, rather than the Germanic Rundbogenstil of Beth Israel.

BETH ISRAEL CEMETERY

In 1919, the May 23 and June 1 minutes of Congregation Beth Israel document the conclusion of a committee that the "Cemetery grounds at Everett were found suitable," but the asking price of eighteen thousand dollars for two acres was too high, and one acre was not considered worthwhile. The problem of cost seems to have been overcome, however, since the cemetery was incorporated four and a half years later, on December 1, 1923. This cemetery was the last resting place for most of the East European Jewish community who made Cambridge home.

Temple Ashkenaz

In 1924 Congress further constrained Jewish and Italian immigration, from eastern and southern Europe, respectively. That was also the year that the Jewish immigrants from Lithuania who settled in Cambridge were sufficiently motivated to build the last immigrant synagogue. They decided to tear down the existing two-family structure that had been used since 1911 for daily and Sabbath observance. The new building was essentially an upgraded copy of the Yavnah Synagogue on Howard Street and was designed by the same architect. Essential to this accomplishment was the civic and religious philanthropy of the Sugarman family, whose contributions came from their successful paper bag business.

The traditional immigrant Jewish community had previously rejected the Reform movement's use of the term *temple* instead of *synagogue*. They believed there was only one temple, in Jerusalem, which was destroyed for the second time by the Romans in a.d. 70. The Reform movement adopted the term to indicate their rejection of Jewish nationalism and the association of their religion with patriotism toward their native country. By the 1920s, the ideological arguments were abandoned and *temple* was deemed acceptable in traditional Jewish circles. The first Conservative synagogue in the Dorchester-Roxbury community was Temple Mishkan Tefila, built in 1925.

The milestone of the erection of Temple Ashkenaz in 1926 reflected the end of the communal leadership of European, Yiddish-speaking rabbis. Rabbi Gorovitz moved into 11 Boardman Street in Cambridge as Mayor James Curley of Boston appointed a Jewish chaplain to the Prison Point Jail in 1916. It appears that Rabbi Gorovitz was accepted as the communal rabbi of the three extant Cambridge congregations and of Anshey Sfard of Somerville in 1917. The Temple Ashkenaz Golden Book records him as its rabbi from 1917 through 1924.

From about 1912 to 1916, the only function of professional religious personnel was to perform weddings. Cantors were engaged separately for the High Holidays. Religious services were essentially provided by knowledgeable lay personnel, with nominal congregational compensation.

After the era of the European rabbis, Beth Israel and Temple Ashkenaz engaged rabbis born and educated in the United States who were graduates of

American Conservative and Orthodox seminaries. Sermons previously given only in Yiddish were henceforth given in English.

TOWN AND GOWN

I would be derelict not to mention Judah Monish,[2] an Italian born of Converso parents who came to Cambridge in 1720. In 1722 he was appointed the first instructor in the Hebrew language at Harvard College, after his public conversion to Christianity in Harvard Hall. He married and lived in Cambridge for some thirty-eight years, selling hardware in the marketplace to supplement his income. Church records suggest he continued to celebrate the Sabbath on Saturday. He died in 1764. His house, now replaced by a brick apartment building, was on JFK (formerly Boylston) and Winthrop streets and is described in the *Proceedings* of the Cambridge Historical Society. *The Jews of Boston*, pages 30 to 34, discusses this personality in depth.

Another immigrant, Harry Austryn Wolfson, came to this country from Russia in 1903 and settled in Scranton, Pennsylvania. There he learned English by completing grammar and high school and taught Hebrew in a program similar to the one started by the Hebrew Literary Association in Cambridge in 1906. At the age of twenty-one he entered Harvard and, during that first year, lodged with his uncle in Roxbury; thereafter, until his death in 1974, he lived in Cambridge, except for short absences for a research fellowship in Europe and World War I army service. (His name is not listed on the bronze plaque in front of Temple Beth Shalom that commemorates the Jewish men from Cambridge who served in that war.)

Despite his many years in Cambridge, Wolfson had no known relationship with the city's Jewish community. This is surprising; he was observant, and the Jewish institutions in Cambridge were closest to him. Apparently, however, he worked constantly, and his social and intellectual ties were to the centers of Boston Jewish life—the North End, the West End, and Roxbury. He is credited with introducing Judaica (Jewish studies) into American universities, beginning with Harvard.

CONCLUSIONS

The Yavnah Synagogue disbanded in 1934 and its Torah scrolls were given to Congregation Beth Israel. The building became a harpsichord workshop and is now owned and occupied by the Gurdjieff Society of Massachusetts, an organization associated with a twentieth-century philosopher and spiritualist.

In "Old Rite Unites Temples," *Life* magazine reported in its June 24, 1957, issue that the laymen of Anshey Sfard formed a procession outside their synagogue and marched to Cambridge. Those carrying their Torahs assembled under the protection of a wedding canopy to form the core of the procession. They met a second procession of the laymen of Beth Israel carrying their Torahs at the entrance of the Beth Israel Synagogue; the cantors, accompanied by musicians, sang psalms. The two delegations then marched into the synagogue, where the Anshey Sfard Torahs, the spiritual embodiment of the congregation, were placed in the Ark. The Anshey Sfard structure was subsequently torn down and the land used as a parking lot. It is now a site for affordable housing called Union Place.

The Hebrew School on Elm Street closed in 1951. It was sold and is now a Portuguese social club.

The Cambridge Jewish Community Center, on the corner of Harvard and Lee streets, was purchased in 1952. It served as a Hebrew school and a community center until its sale in 1977.

In 1962 Temple Beth Shalom was formed by the merger of Congregation Beth Israel and Temple Ashkenaz. The Tremont Street location of the latter was selected because of its lower maintenance costs and its proximity to Mid-Cambridge, the new center of gravity of Cambridge's Jewish population. Temple Beth Shalom is the museum and repository of all the artifacts of the immigrant Jewish community in Cambridge. Some of the notable artifacts are the Torah scrolls; the brass memorial (*yahrzeit*) nameplates from Anshey Sfard, Beth Israel, and Temple Ashkenaz; the bronze plaque listing participants in World War I; and the Golden Books of Congregation Beth Israel and Temple Ashkenaz.

The Beth Israel building on Columbia Street is listed on the National Register of Historic Places. The interior was converted to ten artist studio-condominiums in 1976. The Cambridge Historical Commission has committed to the installation of its blue oval marker to commemorate the property's historic significance.

Beginning with the establishment of the Jewish Community Center and Temple Beth Shalom, the leadership of the Jewish community was passed from the founding immigrants to their children, thereby ending the Jewish immigrant era. Other than the S&S Restaurant and the bronze likeness of Benjamin Roseman (the "mayor" of Inman Square) mounted on the Inman Square fire station, little remains of the pioneering immigrants' legacy beyond the religious edifices they built.

The reasons few of their institutions survived are complex but basically boil down to the law of supply and demand. A synagogue requires that a community demand its services, and that sufficient buyers of seats exist to participate in the High Holiday services. These tickets, together with the minimal core membership dues, provide the funds to maintain the property, the artifacts, and possibly a rabbi and his family. The immigrants were nostalgic for their European traditions, but the American experience affected their religious observance. By mid-century, the Conservative religious movement, which permitted Jews to drive to Sabbath observances rather than walk, dominated. Judaism had overcome its Orthodox origins.

American Judaism today is diverse, including even the nonreligious or ethnic. The Reform movement, in which the fulfillment of all Talmudic and traditional laws is optional, has superseded the Conservative movement. The first generation born in America did not observe Jewish traditions as their immigrant parents had, so there was less demand for the services provided by the synagogue. Only a small fraction of the new generation remained in the city in which they were born. Most eventually left for the suburbs.

Because of Cambridge's educational attractions, the influx of Jewish citizens has proven larger than the exodus of native Cantabrigians. Currently, the city's Jewish population is estimated to be a larger percentage than it was during the immigrant period, and it continues to increase, although it is significantly more transient and not as family-oriented. In the past, Jewish immigrant Cambridge centered on the Columbia Street area and gradually moved to Mid-Cambridge, but it was never a concentrated enclave, and very few Jews lived in North or West Cambridge. Today, the Jewish population is dispersed throughout the city. Owing to their diversity and the degree of civic integration, the Jews of Cambridge lack the many organizational and social structures of the previous immigrant community.

Traditional Jewish European immigration to Cambridge dwindled even before World War II. The postwar Hillel Foundation collegiate movement satisfied the religious needs of both professorial families and students and made no demands on families or individuals. Hillel essentially concentrated on the educational institutions it served but abandoned Jewish communal institutions.

The Eitz Chaim congregation in Cambridgeport and the Cambridge Chavurah in North Cambridge are outgrowths of the educational community and provide nontraditional alternatives. The Beth Shalom congregation preserved the traditional approach for the observant by retaining Holocaust survivor Reb Moshe Holcer Z"L (of Blessed Memory), the last *shamus* (sextant) of the Beth Israel synagogue.

Rabbi Ben Zion Gold, a former director of Hillel at Harvard, conducted the funeral of Reb Holcer on August 10, 2004. Gold eulogized the ninety-one-year-old Holcer, observing that his congregation was essentially made up of seventy-year-old men when Beth Shalom began. In the 1970s, Reb Holcer had encouraged young people to attend the Simhat Torah celebration, the holiday that commemorates the end of the weekly readings of the five books of

Moses), inaugurating the now-famous annual Tremont Street event and revitalizing the community. The congregation tries to preserve the traditional practice—only men are counted in the *minyan*—but it also offers egalitarian services, which count women. The Kesher Community Hebrew School After School is a nonaffiliated learning community established in 1992.

ENDNOTES

1. *Aghal* is a misspelling of the Hebrew word *Kahal*, or congregation.

2. Judah Monish is covered in depth in *The Jews of Boston*, ed. Jonathan D. Sarna, Ellen Smith, and Scott-Martin Kosofsky (New Haven: Yale University Press, 2005), 30-34.

Cambridge Modern, 1930-1970: One Architect's View

DAVID N. FIXLER

CAMBRIDGE in the twentieth century assumed a significant global role in extending the frontiers of human knowledge while remaining firmly grounded in the mythic American past. Despite its long association with tradition, there was never any doubt that modernity—as a function of philosophy, reason, science, and economy—was an established and largely welcome presence, which was therefore deliberately engaged in terms set out to suit the local culture. Over the course of the century, this engagement had a profound physical as well as intellectual impact on Cambridge, not the least of which was the city's emergence as an internationally recognized center for both architectural design and architectural education.

The impetus for this paper started with two incidents in my childhood that together—for reasons unknown to me at the time—were largely responsible for both my affection for and my lasting association with the modern movement in Cambridge after the Second World War. First, walking around Cambridge as a child, I was mesmerized by the process of the construction of two of the icons of modernity in Harvard Square, Josep Lluis Sert's Holyoke Center and the Carpenter Center by Le Corbusier. Second, in 1966, I visited a friend whose family had recently moved to one of the original houses at Six Moon Hill, in Lexington, designed by the founding partners of The Architects Collaborative (TAC), this one by Norman Fletcher.

Here was both a house and a community that spoke to me even then of the freedom and exhilaration of modern residential space and of the possibility for a more sophisticated alternative to the idea of low-density community from that of the prevalent, numbing forms of suburban development. I also understood, in absorbing the intellectual and aesthetic lessons of these sojourns, that this work was very much the product of a culture nurtured by the academic and research communities in Cambridge, and that what I came to understand as a "Cambridge Modern" sensibility was in fact a highly sophisticated regional adaptation of international modern architecture to the unique brand of civilization that Cambridge had for so long represented.

Cambridge Modern can be defined as a significant component of the regional impulse that was becoming more overtly prominent in modern architecture—a trend that was reified by the modern movement's first historian of record, Sigfried Giedion, in the 1954 edition of *Space, Time and Architecture.* Fueled in the late 1930s and 1940s by the presence of global influences such as Marcel Breuer from Central Europe and the Bay Area aesthetic of Northern California in the person of William Wurster at Harvard and MIT, respectively, Cambridge Modern, especially as it evolved after the arrival of Walter Gropius, is also a variant of the quiet reaction against International-style modernism that became associated with the postwar welfare state in Scandinavia and northern Europe (and to some degree with Italian neo-realism). This aesthetic exploited the possibilities of using a traditional material palette—in this case the wood, brick, and granite (now transformed to the exposed concrete frame) of New England—in a contemporary way.

However, it is misleading to assume that these architects were seeking merely to develop a contemporary interpretation of traditional New England architecture. In fact, a new paradigm was emerging that represented a profound cultural shift in the attitude of this region toward nature. Whereas, for centuries, nature had been regarded as an adversary, to be resisted and overcome in a harsh northern climate, modern building technology now permitted the interaction of interior space with the outdoor environment to a degree unprecedented in history. The relaxation of physical boundaries that this shift produced, particularly as it was explained in the early designs and theoretical writings of Le Corbusier and Mies van der Rohe and contemporaneously developed in the modern residential architecture of both the Bay Area and the Los Angeles Basin in California, was highly influential in the development of a new modernist sensibility in New England.

The seeds of modernism were present in Cambridge long before there was any structure that could be identified as representing the work of the modern movement. As a place embodying both a tradition of progressivism that sought to accommodate traditional cultural values and the embrace of social justice in an appropriate contemporary fashion, Cambridge nurtured an intellectual community that catalyzed a distinctly modern sensibility toward architecture, planning, and the intellectual world through most of the nineteenth century.

It should be remembered that both H. H. Richardson and Louis Sullivan—two of the most adventurous and progressive American architects of the nineteenth century—spent their undergraduate years at Harvard and MIT respectively (MIT was still in the Back Bay in Sullivan's time), and that three of Richardson's finest works, the Stoughton House on Brattle Street and Austin and Sever halls for his alma mater, were executed in Cambridge. Theirs was not, however, a culture of the artistic avant-garde; rather, it sought to understand and temper the visual signs of modernity in order to allow their assimilation within the broader context of the modernism that was beginning to permeate local culture.

As "modern architecture" began to be defined after World War I, there emerged on the one hand the strong coupling of abstract art, social action, and a celebration of industrial process that characterized the European avant-garde movements—presented to the American public in 1932 as the "International style" in a book and exhibition by Henry-Russell Hitchcock and Philip Johnson at the Museum of Modern Art in New York. On the other side stood Frank Lloyd Wright, whose architecture had strong roots in craft-based movements such as Art Nouveau and who remained throughout his career a singular spokesperson for the continuing values of agrarian Jeffersonian democracy.

One form of mediation between these positions came in the personages of Rudolph M. Schindler and Richard Neutra, two Viennese architects who were drawn to the United States by the work of Wright and ended up introducing the architecture of the European modern movement to Southern California (and America) in the early 1920s. Another was Cambridge, which fell, both geographically and as a state of mind, somewhere in the middle while creating a niche very much its own. Here was nurtured a modernist sensibility that was filtered, refined, and subsequently redefined through the particular lens of Cambridge culture; one that, in its effort to accommodate the moral conservatism of its roots, tempered potentially disquieting aspects of the avant-garde while providing those same roots that exist in Wright's early work as an interpreter of Richardson and Sullivan. This enabled a softening of the social rhetoric and the hard edges of European modernism, added a northeast American and perhaps more cosmopolitan perspective to Wright's agrarian rhetoric, and engendered a unique style of its own.

The house was the original crucible out of which modern architecture evolved in Cambridge, both physically—in works built in west Cambridge in the 1930s and 1940s—and conceptually, in the studio designs and early office commissions of many young Cambridge architects. These houses were commissioned, designed, and built by a group of people who understood and

Koch House, Buckingham Street, 1937, Carl Koch and Edward Durrell Stone, architects. View of original house prior to addition of the third floor mansard roof. *(Eric Stoller/ESTO)*

believed in progress and in the potential of modernity as manifested in research and technology to elevate the human condition. Many of the clients for these houses were the academic and professional individuals largely responsible for the birth and flowering of the post-industrial information revolution, and there is growing evidence, as further research is done on the history of this era, that the convenience, openness, freedom, and spirit of community represented by the modern house formed a significant component of the philosophy and the lifestyle aspirations of many of these individuals.

Although Sigfried Giedion would have us believe that Walter Gropius arrived at Harvard in 1937 to a world untouched by the impact of European modernism, there was in fact before this time much interest and discussion on the subject among the local academic and professional community, and a modest though important corpus of projects and built work reflected this new sensibility in Cambridge and its cultural hinterland. Given its long association with progressive causes, it is perhaps fitting that the earliest work to be realized in the new mode was by a woman—Eleanor Raymond's house (1932) in Belmont.

Philip Johnson house, 9 Ash Street, 1941, Philip Johnson, architect. View from the interior living space looking out to enclosed courtyard. *(Eric Stoller/ESTO)*

Raymond was trained at the Cambridge School of Architecture for Women before Harvard admitted women to its school of design, and she produced a number of houses between 1932 and the early 1950s that embodied the technical and aesthetic principles of the modern movement as well as a nascent sensitivity to environmentally sustainable design while being thoroughly grounded in the tradition of New England domestic architecture. Her major work in Cambridge is the 1935 Frost House, at Longfellow Park, a transitional work with a loosely Colonial Revival plan and massing but with a strong horizontal emphasis in the fenestration and cladding and in the suppression of the roof line (with a low-pitched hipped roof) that tied it unmistakably to European modernism.

Early examples of more fully realized modern houses in Cambridge include Howard Fisher's design for a modular steel-paneled home (1935) on Coolidge Hill and the International-style home (1937) built by Carl Koch and Edward Durrell Stone for Koch's parents on Buckingham Street. The Koch house, a building that creates an intimate and private garden space as an extension of its glazed living area, was a particularly significant work, for it was the first work in Cambridge that embodied the full aesthetic vocabulary and dynamic, open planning of European modernism, most notably, in this case, Mies van der Rohe's Lange House in Krefeld, Germany, of 1927–30 (plan), his Tugendhat House in Brno, Czech Republic, of 1931 (elevation), and his ongoing explorations into the court-house type.

The typology of the Miesian court-house is most purely demonstrated in the house that Philip Johnson designed and had constructed for himself as a student at the Harvard Graduate School of Design (GSD) in 1940–41. A single-story, flat-roofed pavilion on a corner lot, completely opaque to the street, with a wall entirely of glass that opens onto an enclosed courtyard, the house on Ash Street is perhaps the purest example of one of the most significant architectural explorations of the 1930s. Here Johnson takes full advantage of the notion of Cambridge as a laboratory for ideas—in this case giving full physical realization to an intellectual and artistic experiment that Mies had studied in countless iterations on paper from 1931 to 1940, none of which, given the dire economic circumstances and later political conditions of the time in Germany, had ever been executed.

A third significant pre–World War II modern house in Cambridge is a brick villa at 45 Fayerweather Street designed by Walter Bogner, a professor of architecture at Harvard, in 1940, the same year that he built his own residence next to the new houses of Gropius and Marcel Breuer in Lincoln. Built on the site of an older Queen Anne structure, the Fayerweather Street house presents an L-shaped design that encloses a garden defined by the rubble stone walls of the foundation of the previous house. Despite the severity of the street facades (very much like the Lange house, cited above, and other works in brick by Mies of the late 1920s and early 1930s), the garden elevations of this house are elegantly proportioned, with generous areas of glass that bespeak a luxurious accommodation to and interplay with its site.

This strategy recalls, both in form and in spirit, the sophistication of Alvar Aalto's Villa Mairea in Noormarku, Finland, of 1937–39—a work that eloquently communicates the possibilities of successfully accommodating the highest aesthetic aspirations of international modernism with an acute regional sensibility. Widely published at the time of its construction, the Villa Mairea was featured in a 1938 exhibition of Aalto's work at the Museum of Modern Art in New York and is a work with which Bogner was doubtless familiar.

In 1935 Joseph Hudnut became the dean of the Graduate School of Design with a mandate to move from the Beaux-Arts toward a curriculum that reflected the contemporary direction of the architectural avant-garde. Hudnut believed that modern architecture was still very much "in the process of formation" and that, with proper leadership, Harvard could guide the course of the new architecture—in education and practice—into a maturity that would reflect the "pattern of contemporary ideas" and be more than just "specific to our day...conformable to our technique, adaptable to our uses and observances."[1] He understood and advocated to Harvard that the quickest and most effective way to bring this change about would be to lure one of the titans of European modernism to the GSD to become chair of the department of architecture.

In 1937, after courting both Mies van der Rohe and J. J. P. Oud of the Netherlands—two central figures in the International-style exhibition—Hudnut realized that Walter Gropius, one of the founders of the Bauhaus in Dessau and an accomplished architectural educator, would be the best choice, both pedagogically and personally. It is important to understand, however, that Hudnut did not seek, nor did Gropius initially advocate, the recreation of the Bauhaus at the GSD. Hudnut rather imagined—and hoped—that Cambridge could become the crucible for the evolution of an enlightened, humanist modernism, different but not uncoupled from the significant architecture and urbanism of the past.

This would be artistically adventurous yet sensitive to local form and regional character, and would be the result of the synergy of the social and artistic values of European modernism with the progressive intellectual tradition in Cambridge that had helped to define modern thought in America beginning in the early nineteenth century. It was also an evolutionary approach that built on the urban theory of Camilo Sitte and Hudnut's mentor Werner Hegemann, which emphasized the importance of space and context in the creation of urban form.

The formidable personality and international reputation of Gropius made it difficult over time for Hudnut to counter what he saw as the growing entrenchment of an orthodox modernism based on the principles espoused both by Gropius through the Bauhaus and by CIAM (the Congrés International d'Architecture Moderne), the group responsible for formulating and codifying much of theoretical basis of European modernism. Neither of these bodies supported the broad, historical base and plurality of views that Hudnut felt were necessary for a richer approach to a new architecture and urbanism. Though Gropius clearly gained the upper hand pedagogically in the 1940s and established the general direction that the GSD was to assume through the 1950s and much of the 1960s, the modernist edifice that he constructed—one that taught largely without history or any real emphasis on the palpable spatial aspects of creating architecture—eventually proved overly doctrinaire and limiting in its ability to provide students with the full complement of tools necessary to create a truly humanist modernism.

This modernism was envisioned by Hudnut, and by many architectural theorists since the late 1960s, as one that could accommodate the complexity and contradictions of modern life in an appropriate contemporary fashion without resorting to pastiche. Following what can in hindsight be seen as the necessary historicist reaction to the constraints of orthodox modernism, there has been a reassessment of the more diverse views held by Hudnut. In addition, with the recognition that the modern movement is now itself a part of history, there remains a sense that Hudnut perhaps better anticipated what would be required for modernism as an idea and an architectural ethic to successfully flourish both in the culture of this region and as part of a more sophisticated, if less ideologically pure, modernist project.

While the impact of Gropius and his Bauhaus and GSD colleague Marcel Breuer on the architecture of Cambridge and the Northeast were really to be felt only after World War II, this move had a more immediate effect at MIT. John Burchard, the head of the Bemis Foundation (which was affiliated with the MIT School of Architecture), having met Alvar Aalto and experienced the architectural tour de force of his Finnish Pavilion at the New York world's fair of 1939, invited Aalto first to lecture on the problems of housing and construction in Finland and then to teach at MIT in the fall of 1940.

MIT was also in the process of defining a new educational model to supersede its Beaux Arts architectural curriculum, and Burchard saw in Aalto someone whose credentials as an accomplished modernist could match those of Gropius while helping MIT to define and pursue its own evolving modernist pedagogy. Aalto was already establishing himself, in questioning some of the more restrictive aspects of the "functionalist" doctrine advocated by CIAM, as a modernist more concerned with understanding how architecture could improve the human condition rather than focusing on processes of industrial rationalization and standardized minimalist housing. Although the Russo-Finnish winter war of 1940–41 cut short Aalto's initial sojourn at MIT, his strong ties to the institute and his friendship with William Wurster, dean of the MIT School of Architecture, brought him back to Cambridge in 1946—both to teach and to build.

As testimony to the overlapping currents of thought in Cambridge and in the architectural world at this time, in 1939 MIT built the first fully modern structure on an American college campus—the alumni pool, by resident faculty member Lawrence Anderson, with Herbert Beckwith—at the same time the last and most prominent piece of its Beaux Arts main group (the lobby and dome of Building 7, which gives the school its grand entrance on Massachusetts Avenue) was being completed. The alumni pool is a simple functionalist box of buff brick with one wall entirely of glass, placed in what was then MIT's "backyard," to the northeast of the main group. Given the emphasis on physical culture in the rhetoric of modernist discourse, it is perhaps not surprising that the alumni pool, as one of the earliest institutional modern works in America, should be a communal exercise facility.

A similar focus on communal housing and buildings dedicated to fostering social interaction was instrumental in prompting both Harvard and MIT to reconsider their models for student housing after World War II and to commission works that would give Cambridge its first internationally significant modern buildings—the Harvard Graduate Center by Walter Gropius and his office and MIT's Baker House by Alvar Aalto. Baker House and the graduate center were both commissioned in 1946 and opened in 1949. It was these two buildings—each in its own very different way—that truly announced the arrival of modern architecture in Cambridge. Both are structures designed by world-renowned modernists (and memorialized by Sigfried Giedion), both embody many of the essential attributes of Le Corbusier's canonic five points of modern architecture of 1926, and both claim to have drawn unique inspiration from their locus in Cambridge. There the similarities end.

The Harvard Graduate Center comes as close as any complex of buildings in the United States to realizing the *Gestalt* of the modernist housing estates of Central Europe of the 1920s and 1930s and in that sense remains pure to the principles that Gropius developed as both an architect and an educator in his years at the Bauhaus. It also marks the architectural debut of The Architects Collaborative (TAC), the office formed by Gropius with a group of his former students and other second-generation modernists to carry out in practice a working model of the collaborative ethic he had always encouraged in the studio. TAC, its later offshoots, and several other practices, such as those founded by former Gropius teaching assistant Hugh Stubbins and Josep Lluis Sert, created a center of architectural energy in Harvard Square, fueled and peopled in large part by Harvard and MIT, that attained international significance after World War II.

The graduate center is often cited as a more dynamic, modernist interpretation of the traditional Harvard pattern of buildings placed in loose quadrangular arrangements around a common green space, and it was sanctioned at the time by President James Conant of Harvard as an appropriate model for extending the school's campus north into Cambridge. Iconic as it has become in the history of modern architecture, the graduate center remains a radical exercise for Cambridge that has never been a completely comfortable fit. Like Mies van der Rohe's contemporaneous buildings for the Illinois Institute of Technology in Chicago (where Mies had been appointed head of the school of architecture in 1940), the residential buildings were constructed of an industrial buff brick with steel sash hung over a steel frame, an aesthetic more appropriate to the industrial areas of East Cambridge than to the residential Agassiz district. Perhaps more than any subsequent work by TAC and its contemporaries, the graduate center came to be identified with the "Harvard box," which critics saw as the result of an overly dogmatic application of a Bauhaus-based system—designed initially as an *Exzistenzminimum* ideal to house the European working classes—that tried to stretch the boundaries to which it might best be suited while paying only superficial heed to its particular physical and cultural environment.

Harkness Commons, the centerpiece of the graduate center, is, however, an underappreciated work that best exemplifies Gropius's ideal of the building as an extension of the Bauhaus *Gesamkunstwerk*. It presents two primary elevations to the law school: a gently curved façade of limestone and steel-framed glass, with bold but restrained accents in blue glazed brick focused on a sculpture by Richard Lippold (recently moved) that anchored the green space of the quadrangle, and a short but powerful entry façade announcing its presence to the length of Holmes Field. Its interior, originally embellished with artwork in different media by Herbert Bayer, Jean Arp, Josef Albers, and Joan Miró, comprises an ensemble of interpenetrating spaces on three levels that weave around a central ramp.

This space was a quintessential example of the materially modest but artistically energetic mid-century modern aesthetic. Recent renovations to the building have introduced a contemporary style that has compromised the delicate, often minimalist palette of light, material, and color that are essential to the successful realization of this aesthetic. These changes, though well intentioned and welcomed by the users, nonetheless offer stark testimony to the necessity of better understanding the particular qualities of mid-century modern design in order to sustain this architecture with care and sensitivity.

Baker House exhibits a more idiosyncratic and conceptually more complex interpretation of an appropriate modern response to the environment created by MIT, the riverfront, and the old industrial fabric of East Cambridge. The commission was championed by William Wurster, who had come from Berkeley in 1944 to serve as dean of the MIT School of Architecture, thereby initiating the long, fruitful, and iconoclastic (from an orthodox modernist point of view) intellectual synergy between these institutions that continued through the second half of the twentieth century. Conceived to optimize the number of rooms that would receive river views, Baker House is a six-story serpentine slab of dormitory rooms clad in the "lousiest brick in the world,"[2] bisected by a series of pavilions in glass, steel, wood, and stone that define an axis of communal spaces leading back to the heart of the MIT campus. The wave form, though a fundamental design trope of Aalto's work (and *aalto* means "wave" in Finnish), can also be read here as a metaphori-

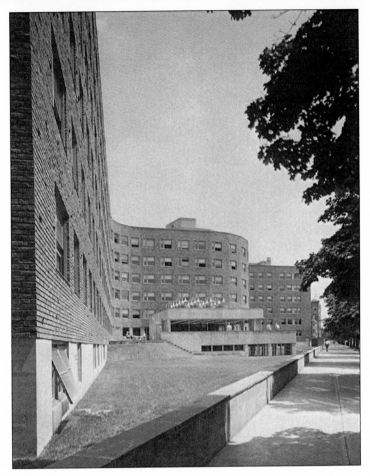

Baker House Residence Hall, MIT, Alvar Aalto, architect. View from the west of undulating south facade, and glass and stone dining pavilion. *(Eric Stoller/ESTO)*

cal response to the bow-front townhouses of Beacon Hill and the Back Bay, on a scale meant to be read from across the Charles. This is Aalto's first use of exposed brick on a major work, and it is clear from his writings and other buildings of the 1950s that his exposure to the brick Georgian vernacular of Boston and Cambridge had a considerable impact on his architecture, especially his subsequent work in Finland. Baker House in turn gave direction to later architects in this region seeking to reintegrate the use of brick in an appropriately modern direction; it is best illustrated by Hugh Stubbins's 1959 Loeb Drama Center for Harvard on Brattle Street, which would add a deeper regional flavor to the next generation of modernism in New England.

The limestone-clad, ribbon-windowed dining commons in Baker House, the ultimate destination of the long axis back to Building 7, is a pure, but also quintessentially Aaltoesque, expression of international modernism that, however modest, is one of the finest spaces of its kind in the world. As is true of the graduate center, architectural drama is carried out in Baker House with minimal means; the building is austere and straightforward, befitting the lean economic conditions still present in the aftermath of the war, but Aalto manages, in this relatively humble structure, to make a profound connection between the need for individuality and the desire for community—one that still resonates with MIT's students today. The connection of the communal and the private is revealed through a monumental constructivist stair, hung off the north side of the building, which also simultaneously recognizes and acknowledges the rough industrial context of MIT.

While completing the work on Baker House, Aalto was also commissioned by Harvard to design a poetry reading room for the 1949 undergraduate Lamont Library. Lamont is an early work in the modern idiom of Shepley, Bulfinch, Richardson and Abbott, the successor firm to H. H. Richardson's practice, which also designed the B&B Chemical Lab (later Polaroid) of 1938 on Memorial Drive, the first fully developed modern industrial building in Cambridge. At the corner of Harvard Yard at Quincy Street and Massachusetts Avenue, Lamont is the first modern structure in Harvard Yard and Harvard Square, and it represents a definitive break with precedent both for Harvard and for Shepley, Bulfinch, the architects of the neo-Georgian river houses of the 1920s and 1930s. Its design is an understated though demonstrably contemporary response to its brick Georgian context that also takes considerable cues in massing and detail from Aalto's own 1932 library for Viipuri, Finland (now Vyborg, Russia), the first great library of the modern movement.

After World War II, the second generation of modernists, trained by Gropius, Breuer, Anderson, Wurster, and their colleagues, began, with their peers across the United States, to finally practice modernism as the new norm for American building. While corporate America responded enthusiastically to the economy and ubiquitous modern image of the glass and steel office building, in Cambridge and its cultural hinterland the development of modernism was championed by the educational, research, and residential market—driven by a core of academics and research professionals who fully embraced the promise and possibilities that modern architecture, and a modern way of life, could lead to a more efficient and comfortable future.

An immediate local result of the impact of Aalto's influence and Wurster's tutelage was the design by a group of young architects—Carl Koch, Ralph Rapson, Robert Woods Kennedy, and Vernon de Mars (several of whom were recent MIT graduates)—of 100 Memorial Drive, the first large exercise in modern housing in the region. The complex features an E-shaped plan that, like Baker House, maximizes the views of the river from the living units; it employs skip-stop elevators (that stop at every other floor) for economy in construction and is clad with a frank and elegantly detailed skin of brick and steel sash stretched over a steel frame. One hundred Memorial Drive won the Boston Society of Architects' prestigious Harleston Parker Award for the most beautiful building in the metropolitan Boston area in the early 1950s, and it remains one of the most successful and popular complexes of its type in the region.

In the mid-1950s, Aalto's Finnish compatriot Eero Saarinen was commissioned by MIT to design an auditorium and a nondenominational chapel in the field between Baker House and the main group. A radical exercise in the exploration of pure geometric form, Kresge Auditorium is conceived as one great, wood-lined space under a dome in the shape of a triangular segment of a large sphere, with each of the three vertical "slices" creating a lobby space around the theater, glazed in great arcs of steel and glass curtain wall. The chapel is a cylinder, faced with the same rough, water-struck brick specified by Aalto on Baker House, set in a moat that is accessed through a low pavilion of steel, glass, and wood. These clearly space-age structures helped to set the tone for MIT as an institution symbolizing innovation, bringing unprecedented design along with unprecedented science and technology to the marshy lowlands of East Cambridge. It is this tradition of innovation in building—of Baker House and the work of Saarinen—that MIT cited in the 1990s as it embarked on a building campaign designed to reinforce and expand its leadership role in extending the boundaries of institutional architecture, more of which will follow at the end of this essay.

Scandinavian design, particularly that of Finland, had a great impact on the postwar design culture of Cambridge. It began with Aalto's experience at MIT, when he also tried to open a local outlet for his Artek furniture line. While it was never a successful venture, the aesthetic promulgated by Artek and reflected in spaces ranging in scale from a residential living room to the three council chambers of the UN headquarters (designed and donated by Sweden, Denmark, and Norway) resonated with a local culture seeking contemporary alternatives to the harder, more industrial designs associated with the International style. The broader culture that evolved around this sensibility also produced a healthy local craft revival in contemporary furniture and innovative, world-renowned design in fields such as lighting, architectural acoustics, and audiovisual equipment. These were a direct outgrowth of the burgeoning high-tech community in this area.

In 1953 Benjamin Thompson founded Design Research (DR) in a storefront converted from a house on Brattle Street, a commercial venture that featured a variety of home and personal furnishings hand-picked by Thompson from Europe and Japan. It was an enterprise that began a revolution in taste and had a significant impact on American fashion and lifestyle accessories through the 1970s (and is undergoing a revival today). Most famously, Thompson's exposure at the Brussels exposition of 1959 to the clothes and fabrics of Marimekko of Finland, and a subsequent exhibition at DR of contemporary design from Scandinavia, concentrated the impact of a design culture that meshed perfectly with the northern European architectural aesthetic that was already, through the influence of architects such as Aalto, Breuer, and Serge Chermayeff, transforming the domestic design vocabulary of the northeastern United States.

DR flourished in its small storefront for sixteen years before moving into a new, signature building at the corner of Brattle and Story streets. This concrete and glass structure, designed by Benjamin Thompson, set a standard for commercial architecture and retail design that resonates to the present day (the building is now occupied by Crate and Barrel, a successful enterprise that based its original retail philosophy largely on the model of DR). It also completed the group of mid-1960s structures at 44 and 46 Brattle Street, by Sert, Jackson Associates and TAC, respectively (1966–69), that filled in the block between the Brattle Theater and Story Street.

These buildings—housing each of these architects' offices, the original Charrette and Stone Reprographics stores, and the Harvest Restaurant (owned and designed by Ben Thompson), as well as other retail and commercial tenants—created a richly diverse though broadly unified ensemble that came to define a particular brand of refined, post-Brutalist modern architecture. Employing a vocabulary of concrete, glass, and wood paneling, the ensemble speaks well to the scale and ambience of Cambridge without having to use traditional motifs, particularly brick (except as pavers). The buildings are in their own way contextual, with an ethic of accommodation that posits a quiet mediation of the assertiveness of Le Corbusier's Carpenter Center (built just before these structures and discussed later) and that sought to create a workable paradigm for a new style of commercial modernism that could flourish in Cambridge.

No one better defined the leading intellectual edge of this direction than Josep Lluis Sert, a Catalan architect, urbanist, and CIAM colleague of Gropius's and Le Corbusier's who had a gift for cultivating personal relationships and took over as dean of the GSD in 1952. Sert brought a more muscular Corbusian, Mediterranean aesthetic to Harvard and to Cambridge, and as the author of *Can our Cities Survive?* (1942)—the first major work to promote the CIAM urban agenda in America—expressed a more profound concern for the issues of urban design and city planning than had been evident at Harvard during the Gropius years.

Through the scale and volume of his buildings and urban design schemes, Sert left an important legacy in Cambridge and Boston. His earliest work is also his most regional: a house for his family and, around the corner, a modest conference-residence center for the Harvard Divinity School that introduced Sert's own distinctive interpretation of the wood-clad, white-windowed local vernacular, a language that would evolve in scale and material in his subsequent work. The Sert residence extends and elaborates the courtyard house typology first built by Johnson on Ash Street into a still modest but highly complex procession of indoor spaces grouped around three courtyards. This unique synthesis of Sert's own interpretation of the Mediterranean courtyard house vernacular is filtered through the 1930s Miesian experiments and executed in an appropriate, contemporary New England material palette.

By the early 1960s, Sert had gained sufficient local clout to enable his practice to garner major urban-campus design and building commissions from both Harvard and Boston universities, which had a significant impact on the growth and image of these institutions and on the urban future of Cambridge and Boston. Sert executed three major commissions for Boston University, including its law school tower, an interpretation of Le Corbusier's proposed 1930s high-rise for Algiers and perhaps the most Corbusian skyscraper realized since the master's 1938 ministry of education in Rio de Janeiro (with Oscar Niemeyer). Harvard also commissioned three major projects, one of which, the Peabody Terrace housing complex for married students, remains to this day a source of controversy between Harvard and its Riverside neighbors.

The first of the Harvard commissions was Holyoke Center, a mid-rise (ten-story) structure built to house many of Harvard's central administrative functions as well as shops, the university's health services, and a bank. The complex is set back from Massachusetts Avenue on a Seagram Building–style plaza that provides a well-scaled, lively pedestrian relief valve to the congestion of Harvard Square. One of the first structures in this area to be built using architectural-quality exposed reinforced concrete, with a metal curtain wall system featuring spandrels in primary colors and white *brise-soleils* (sun breaks), Holyoke Center creates a locus, like a transplanted Corbusian *Unité d'Habitation*, that identifies Harvard Square from a distance. Despite the bulk and vocabulary of Holyoke Center, it can be argued that Sert took a measured and ultimately successful risk in seeking to alter the urban character of this part of Cambridge with an uncompromising, provocatively modern structure.

One of the shortcomings often cited in the design of mid-century modern architecture is a tendency toward a lack of warmth and human scale at the pedestrian level. In the evolution of its plaza and through-block galleria

Peabody Terrace, Harvard University, 1963, by Sert, Jackson and Associates, Josep Lluis Sert, architect. *(Bruner Cott and Associates)*

over the last fifteen years, the interventions in Holyoke Center have subsequently provided a positive illustration of how a modern building of this kind can provide an infrastructure upon which fine-grain embellishments can be layered on an often raw and even harsh structure in order to engender a subtle transformation that enlivens the streetscape and refines and improves the experience of the user. It is precisely this kind of challenge that is facing architects charged with extending the lives of the buildings of the modern movement, and the Holyoke Center results display the quality of space that a thoughtful intervention can produce.

Peabody Terrace is a housing complex for married graduate students that includes three high-rise residential towers punctuating a complementary group of low-rise apartments and community amenities. Like the Gropius–TAC Graduate Center, Peabody Terrace is perhaps the best example in this region of another CIAM urban paradigm, in this case the typology of an ensemble of low-rise structures anchoring a series of towers in a park-like setting. This is a European idea, beginning with Le Corbusier's utopian urban projects of the 1920s and 1930s, that has been executed with only limited success on either side of the Atlantic.

Universally admired in the design community, largely reviled by the lay public, and with both advocates and opponents among its residents, Peabody Terrace has been cited over the years (along with its contemporary, Boston City Hall) as the quintessential example of the disconnect that emerged between high design and popular cultural taste in the course of the twentieth century. It can be argued, however, that as both architecture and urban design, Peabody Terrace is far more successful than Harvard's other, less publicly controversial attempts at modern high-rise architecture—notably, Leverett and Mather houses, along the river, and especially Minoru Yamasaki's bizarre and somewhat alien William James Hall, across from the former Busch-Reisinger Museum on Kirkland Street.

However, the bitterness that has lingered in the Riverside community as the result of Harvard's construction of Peabody Terrace in the mid-1960s was instrumental forty years later in Harvard's decision to abandon its attempts to put up a building that had the potential to point the way toward a mature, twenty-first century Cambridge Modern sensibility. This was Renzo Piano's design for Harvard's Fogg Museum at the corner of Western Avenue and Memorial Drive, a potentially ravishing exercise in the contemporary interpretation of the use of wood cladding on a post-and-beam frame that would have created a vibrant cultural destination on what was a garden stand with a large parking lot. The lesson here is the constant reminder of the degree to which modernism, as it continues to be associated with foreign influence and the consequent perception of its insensitivity to context and local concern, has never become fully assimilated into the broader culture of this region.

Sert's last major commission for Harvard was the undergraduate Science Center of 1973, a polyglot structure that occupies the bend in Oxford Street opposite Memorial Hall and the Lowell Lecture Hall. Like Holyoke Center, it is organized around an interior street that unites the diverse masses that proceed up from a lecture hall hung from spider-like trusses to the stepped central eight-story volume. An ambitious exercise in campus design, it has become more successful with the changes that have occurred since its completion, particularly the creation of the pedestrian mall that now covers Cambridge Street and its renovation and expansion (2003) by Leers Weinzapfel Associates.

No discussion of the architecture of Cambridge in the twentieth century can be complete without a mention of Harvard's Carpenter Center for the Visual Arts, the only work of Le Corbusier—arguably the most influential architect of the century—in North America. Le Corbusier was over seventy years old at the time he designed it and famously never visited the site after being awarded the commission (which was in large part won for him by Sert, who pledged the support of his Cambridge office to execute the design). The

Carpenter Center has long been criticized for the rather deliberate manner in which it ignores its Beaux Arts Georgian (and quintessentially Cambridge) context. One may argue, however, that conceptually, and on many levels, it is in fact an appropriate response to its program and client. As a pavilion in the context of Quincy Street, rotated to deny any pretense of frontality and bisected by a circulation ramp connecting it to Prescott Street beyond, the Carpenter Center makes a very strong statement about the fundamentally anti-urban nature of much of Cambridge and about the pervasive American unease with the traditional European forms of urbanism that Le Corbusier spent much of his career trying to reform.

The Carpenter Center, an exposed, reinforced concrete and glass structure in a brick and clapboard Georgian neighborhood, is true and consistent to the relentlessly critical nature of its creator. Harvard wanted to make a statement with this building about its commitment to the visual arts and to the necessity of having this commitment reflected in an appropriately modern, if not avant-garde, fashion. At the same time, Le Corbusier realized that given his age, and his inability to secure work in the United States before this occasion (beyond his ultimately compromised and personally unsatisfying role in the design of the UN headquarters in New York), the Carpenter Center would very likely remain his sole commission in North America and should therefore be invested at every opportunity with expressions of the full range of his critical thought as it had evolved over the previous forty years. To this end, he added design tropes of his early work, such as the glass block wall, to his contemporaneous *béton brut* (raw concrete) aesthetic of sculptural concrete forms accented with a dynamic circulation spine and concrete *brise-soleils* shielding walls of glass. Whether Le Corbusier really understood that the spaces beneath the ramps facing Prescott Street would be as awkward as they appear to many was beside the point; the Carpenter Center is a lexicon that exists as a reminder, for the denizens of Cambridge and the American people, of the ideas that forever changed architecture in the twentieth century.

In addition to the work of Sert, the impact on Cambridge of Le Corbusier's Carpenter Center can be seen in James Freeman's delicate, reinforced-concrete-frame homage to the "Unité," in the Riverview Apartments of 1960 on Mount Auburn Street, and in the projects executed by I. M. Pei's office for MIT in the mid and late 1960s, particularly the Dreyfus Chemistry Building. MIT also built several of the purest examples of the corporate, International-style metal-and-glass curtain wall buildings to be found in Cambridge: Buildings 16 and 56 by Anderson, Beckwith and Haible of 1956, and the elegant Compton Laboratories (Building 26) by Gordon Bunshaft of Skidmore, Owings and Merrill, 1955.

The end of the modernist ascendancy was heralded by the mid-1960s in the realization of several simplistic, reductive interpretations of the early work of Le Corbusier (particularly the Villa Savoye of 1929), blown up in scale and transformed in material in a definitive turn to a more superficial and ultimately less confident approach to architecture. The first of these is the MIT Student Center, by Eduardo Catalano. In this building—and subsequently in the 1970 Optics and Guidance Laboratories by TAC, built for the government complex at Kendall Square that was originally to have housed NASA (before the 1968 election)—we see modernism simultaneously turning in on itself and the next generation of architects developing an amnesia about what these forms and spaces meant to those who were responsible for their creation.

The most prominent and certainly most poignant of these apparitions is the current home of Harvard's GSD, John Andrews's Gund Hall of 1969–72. As a highly publicized commission by a graduate of Harvard's architecture program, Gund Hall was initially intended to be an appropriately modern structure in which to house the most influential modernist school of architecture in the country. In fact, it is an uneasy and impractical work, with a Quincy Street façade that pays linguistic homage to the Villa Savoye with its *pilotis* (columns), cantilevered, ribbon-windowed upper levels (offices and classrooms) and partially glazed first floor (library), but without any of the proportional élan, scale, delicacy, or real architectural raison d'être of the original. This, in turn, is grafted onto an interesting but incongruous cascading glass shed that houses the design studios. The open-tier "tray" configuration of the studios is meant to foment dialogue and community, but when fully populated the effect is more often the cacophony one associates with the prototype for this type of structure, the train sheds of the great nineteenth-century railway stations.

It is thus ironic that at almost precisely the moment when the completion of the Carpenter Center signaled the apogee of the acceptance of European modernism into the culture and fabric of Cambridge, its end was foretold by the appearance of these architectural simulacra—packages with the wrappings and gestures of the icons of the 1920s, now cut adrift in both space and time. The uncertainties produced by the cultural unrest of the late 1960s, the 1973 energy crisis, and the growing public dissatisfaction with the shortcomings of much that was associated with the modern movement eventually caused even the most stalwart of the postwar practices—particularly those of Gropius (TAC) and Sert—to abandon the principles on which they were created and to succumb to the new historicism that ended modernism's hegemony. Of particular note here is Sert Jackson's large retail and office project in the heart of Harvard Square (housing part of the Harvard Coop, the GAP, and other concerns), ca. 1979. From a planning and massing perspective this is a clever if not a masterful work, a large program carefully woven at modest scale into a dense, irregular, and delicate urban fabric. However, the attempts at contextualism in the design of the facades, with abstracted references to the vertical punched openings and colors of a traditional brick building executed without evident understanding or conviction, display a fall from the robust aesthetic manifest in Sert's earlier work at Holyoke Center and 44 Brattle Street—confident works that only fifteen years before had been able to engage this same context in a meaningful, stimulating dialogue on their own terms.

Where or what is modernism today? In contemplating the future of architecture from the vantage of the GSD in the late 1970s—when the attack on modernism was at its highest pitch—Peter Smithson, an eminent mid-century British architect, made a prescient remark. He noted that at a comparable juncture in the history of Renaissance architecture (some sixty years after its inception), we were just getting to Bramante and the High Renaissance, with Mannerism and the Baroque yet to come, implying that modern architecture had perhaps reached a hiatus if not an actual state of crisis in the trajectory of its development, but that its impact on history was far from over. While the nineteenth-century taxonomy of the progression of styles is no longer universally accepted as the best tool for the analysis of change in the arts, it is nonetheless worth considering this remark. The "post modern" moment (as seen by Smithson and as opposed to the postmodern future) was thus to be viewed as a time of pause and reflection in which to assess both the mistakes and the triumphs of the previous half-century and to allow history to catch up and give perspective to what architecture might become in the decades ahead.

Smithson has proven prophetic, but not without some critical loss. The last two decades have in fact seen a resurgence in modernism and the production of some extraordinary buildings that certainly can be said to carry the torch of modernism—as an aesthetic exploration, not a social movement (a notable exception is the growth of an environmental conscience that has fueled the push toward sustainability in both planning and construction). Some examples of these works include the aforementioned design for a riverfront museum by Renzo Piano, and MIT's newest ventures into the world of high design with the completion of Frank Gehry's Stata Center and Steven Holl's undergraduate residence, Simmons Hall. MIT is also planning an extension to its Media Lab by Fumihiko Maki, a Japanese architect educated under Gropius and Sert at Harvard. Based on a meticulously developed language of abstract form and spatial manipulation, Maki's work has succeeded in creating an architecture of meaningful synthesis to an extent found in few of his contemporaries today. Furthermore, the emergence of East Cambridge as a world center for biotechnology has produced at least one building show-casing the state of the art in sustainable design, the very modernist Genzyme headquarters by the German architects Benisch, Bensich & Partner, with engineering by Buro Happold of Great Britain. These are all buildings designed by architects who hail from outside this region, and they reflect the tendency that peaked at the end of the twentieth century by corporations and institutions throughout the developed world to tap the best of the world's architectural resources in creating "signature" buildings. In Cambridge, however, they can be seen as merely the continuation of a tradition dating back to the 1940s that already includes luminaries such as Aalto, Gropius, Le Corbusier, and James Stirling (the Sackler Museum at Harvard).

This is still architecture by committed modernist architects, but we must acknowledge that, bereft of its utopian promise and much of its social mission, it is no longer the architecture of the modern movement as it came to be understood between the end of World War I and about 1970. This loss continues to be mourned by many who continue to seek new meaning and purpose in architecture (and who admit to harboring "nostalgia for the avant-garde"), and it has resulted in the formation of advocacy groups for the understanding and preservation of modern architecture around the world, most notably Docomomo International.

This loss of innocence and the recognition that architecture can no longer be viewed as a Manichaean struggle for the ascendancy of an enlightened modernity over the dark forces of oppression and decay—linked in the mid-twentieth century with classicism and traditional urban form—has been made possible both through the rediscovery of history and through the critical analysis of modernism as a part of history, rather than its end. The next generation of architects have thus come into practice armed with the knowledge, insight, and (let it be said) ideological freedom—if not complete confidence—to pursue a diverse design agenda that includes, without being limited to, further explorations into the technical and artistic possibilities of contemporary architecture.

These explorations are taking many forms, such as the buildings for MIT, Harvard, and Genzyme already cited, many of which lend credibility to Smithson's notion that modern architecture may be well into its Baroque phase. There is a theory of the cultural impact of natural rhythms, developed by Michael Young in a series of lectures at Harvard in 1988 and later published as *The Metronomic Society*, that posits the principle that society— and convention—are grounded by "cyclical oscillations embodied in individual and collective habits." These oscillations periodically shift from the predominance of cyclical time, producing stasis, and linear time, which introduces novelty and change. In the visual arts, stasis is reflected as calm, refinement, and repose, while novelty and change introduce dynamism of form and space.

Although these tendencies have always coexisted to some degree in modern architecture, there is both a self-consciousness and heightened sensuality evident in even the most geometrically rigorous buildings today, through the unusual, ambiguous, and often disturbing use of materials and light, that clearly place today's architecture in the realm of novelty and change. Thus our era has moved beyond the cultural stasis of mid-century modernism—a moment in time as fleeting as that of the High Renaissance of Bramante and Raphael—and the changes that were first manifest in the mannered work of architects such as Eero Saarinen and Paul Rudolph in the 1950s have progressed to the point where the "High Modern" moment itself is a source of nostalgic reflection and Baroque interpretation.

Cambridge and its institutions will continue to monitor, explain, and at times drive these trends. It will likely avoid the most extravagant manifestations of the "New Baroque" in modernism, but neither will it likely become a center for architecture of severe, Apollonian purity. Though never flamboyant or excessive, the buildings, like the people, will be thoughtful and most probably will have something to say.

ENDNOTES

1. Jill Pearlman, "Joseph Hudnut's Other Modernism at the 'Harvard Bauhaus,'" *Journal of the Society of Architectural Historians* 56, no. 4 (1997): 465-66.

2. Aalto quoted in Goran Schildt, *Alvar Aalto, The Mature Years*. (New York: Rizzoli, 1991), 159.

Lois Lilley Howe: America's First Woman Architect

LARRY NATHANSON

"I think about how much we owe to the women who went before us—legions of women, some known but many more unknown. I applaud the bravery and resilience of those who helped all of us…to be here today."—Ruth Bader Ginsburg

GROWING UP in the house at 3 Gray Gardens East, I was totally unaware of its architectural or historical significance. Many years later, I came to reoccupy the same house and asked my neighbors Beryl and Ralph Beatley about the history of both the house and the neighborhood. Suddenly, in their knowledgeable and articulate answers, a new world of Cambridge history opened up for me. In addition to a learned discussion of the origins of Gray Gardens East (the former estate of Edwin Dresser, an early Cambridge millionaire and manufacturer of the first address-appointment books) and the importance of Asa Gray (the first full-time academic botanist in America, after whom the street was named), they casually noted that my house had been designed by a woman named Lois Lilley Howe.

A few brief trips to the Cambridge Historical Commission, the Cambridge Historical Society, and the MIT archives revealed that Lois Lilley

Lois Lilley Howe in 1949 (center).

Howe was the founder, in 1893, of the first successful all-women architectural firm in the United States and the first elected woman member, and later fellow, of the American Institute of Architects. In short, she was a pioneer in the fight for career opportunities for women in America. Almost immediately, my curiosity was aroused about the background of this woman who ignored the advice of her parents, friends, vicar, and teachers to achieve a goal that had been denied American women up to that time.

It should be noted that this short paper focuses on Howe's cultural and historical background. The architectural commentary is largely confined to her houses in Cambridge, although they represent only eighty-two of the approximately 426 projects completed by Howe and her firm—which eventually included Eleanor Manning, who joined the firm in 1913, and Mary Almy, who joined in 1926. Thus this paper makes no claim to being a comprehensive review of all of Howe's architectural achievements.

FAMILY BACKGROUND

Lois Lilley Howe was born in Cambridge in 1864, never married, and dedicated her life to the pursuit of her career. Her family came from central Massachusetts. Her paternal great-grandfather, Estes Howe, was a physician in Belchertown. As a boy he was a drummer in the pre-Revolutionary British

Army in the French and Indian Wars. In the Revolutionary War he served as a military surgeon under General Horatio Gates and was cited for "distinguished service and courage." He was offered the Order of the Cincinnati in 1795 but declined. George Washington suggested that such distinctions might lead to elitism—even restoration of the aristocracy—in the fledgling and egalitarian America.

Samuel Howe, Howe's paternal grandfather, was educated at Williams College and Litchfield Law School (in Litchfield, Connecticut; the first law school in the United States). He practiced law and was appointed a judge in the Court of Common Pleas in 1821. Because of his concern about the paucity of law schools, Howe established his own. As was often the case in nineteenth-century America, his wife died in childbirth, at the age of twenty-four. He was married again, in 1813, to Sarah Robbins, who was Howe's grandmother.

Lois Lilley Howe's father was named Estes, after his grandfather, and like him was a physician and later an entrepreneur. He was a bright and precocious child who was educated at Phillips Andover, Harvard College (from which he graduated in 1832 at the age of eighteen), and Harvard Medical School (1835). He started a medical practice "out West" in Ohio.

Estes Howe's first wife, Harriet Spelman, bore him two daughters but died of "fever" at the age of twenty-three. This tragedy, coupled with his disillusionment with medicine as a career, caused him to return to Cambridge in 1844. There he met and married Lois Lilly White, Howe's mother, in 1848. She was the sister-in-law of James Russell Lowell, a professor of modern languages at Harvard and one of the prominent poets and liberal intellectuals of the day. (He lived at 33 Elmwood Avenue, one of the most architecturally significant Georgian mansions in Cambridge.)

Lois White Howe had four children, the oldest of whom was Lois Lilley Howe. Estes's political orientation was liberal: first he belonged to the Free Soil Party and then the Whigs, which became the Republican Party in about 1856. Thus, by 1860 the family was squarely behind the candidacy of Abraham Lincoln.

Estes Howe was described by his contemporaries as a man possessed of an "eager, inquiring mind" who "loved nature." He prospered as the treasurer of the Cambridge Gas Light Company and was active in the Cambridge Water Works. He was so well known for his intellectual prowess that in 1861 he was invited to join the Saturday Club, whose members included the likes of William J. Stillman, Jeffries Wyman, John Holmes and Oliver Wendell Holmes, Amos Binney, Ralph Waldo Emerson, and Louis Agassiz. Emerson described Estes in a poem (dedicated to him) as of "generous heart and solid sense."[1]

Howe was thus born into a family in which intellectual accomplishment was taken for granted. Her family and their circle of friends included many, if not most, of the city's intelligentsia. The Cambridge of that time was described by Ruth Huntington Sessions as "a country-like suburb, connected to the city of Boston by a long bridge, and its inhabitants a rare company: a concentration of the best minds of the time....Their fine houses and their gracious and ready hospitality and informal courtesy made for a rare neighborhood."[2]

Howe's family championed not only iconoclastic but courageous and principled causes. Its members were closely associated with the abolitionist movement, a sympathy not shared by most Boston Brahmins. Senator Charles Sumner (a close family friend), James Russell Lowell and his first wife, Maria Howe Lowell (Howe's aunt), William White (her maternal uncle), Clara Howe (a half-sister), and Sarah Tracy (her maternal grandmother) were all active abolitionists. Sarah Tracy was a participant in the Underground Railroad, a clandestine network of people who aided and assisted enslaved people in their escape to freedom. When the family voted for Lincoln in 1860, they were occasionally harassed, and at school Clara was subjected to derisive and racist ridicule.[3]

CHILDHOOD AND ADOLESCENCE

Lois Lilley Howe's childhood in Cambridge was, by current standards, bucolic. The family lived at 1 Oxford Street, the current site of the Harvard Science Center. They owned one acre of land on which they kept a cow (milked daily) and other domestic animals. She attended Miss Olmsted's and then Miss Page's elementary schools from 1868 to 1877. Then she switched to the public Cambridge High School (then located on the corner of Fayette Street and Broadway), from which she graduated in 1882. Whether she chose not to attend a girls' "finishing school" on principle or due to her father's financial reverses is not clear.

At about the age of twelve Howe remembered "noticing a story and a half house and deciding gravely that it should have dormer windows." Between 1875 and 1880, Ware and Van Brunt's Memorial Hall was being constructed on Kirkland Street, across from her house. She became fascinated with the project and spent so much time there on the way to and from school that the workers hailed her as "the little superintendent." In high school, moreover, she had a schoolmate, Mattie Sever, whose house in Kingston she visited on several occasions. "[It] is one of the finest old New England Houses in existence," Howe commented, "and its beauty sank into my heart at once—never to be forgotten."[4]

During this time the family was struck with tragedy. In 1879 Samuel, Howe's eldest brother (Harvard 1871, HMS 1875), and James M. and Susan H. Howe, her aunt and uncle, died. The depression of 1879, together with Edison's invention of the incandescent bulb, resulted in a marked reduction in the family's financial status. Then, in 1883, James R. Howe (Harvard 1881)—her "most brilliant," youngest brother—also died.

EDUCATION

Although these events, which occurred when Howe was in her teens, must have had a severe emotional impact on her, she continued her education. She was admitted to "the Annex," the term for the embryonic version of Radcliffe (which was not incorporated until 1894), but she "had no desire to go to college." Instead, because of her early interest in architecture and design, she decided to attend the School of the Boston Museum of Fine Arts. There her interest in architecture persisted, although her "masters and pastors" (in her words) all attempted to direct her toward illustration, which was regarded as a suitable career for a woman. C. Howard Walker, who was foremost among her teachers in this regard, stated that she "should have to learn to swear, and most of the time should think the occupation tedious."[5]

Estes Howe died after a long illness in 1887. Because of the family's reduced circumstances, the Oxford Street house was sold and another built at 2 Appleton Street, the site of "old Mr. Choate's asparagus patch." This apparent downturn in fortune, however, had an indirect but salutary effect. First, Howe met and made an excellent impression on Robert Peabody, an architect and the brother of the man who bought the Oxford Street house, the Reverend Francis Peabody.

Because of the suggestions Howe made about architectural improvements to her former house, Robert Peabody became a close friend and lifelong patron. In addition, the architect of the new house, the construction of which both excited her interest and furthered her experience in architecture, was none other than Francis H. Chandler, of Cabot and Chandler, who became the director of the MIT School of Architecture in 1888.

When she applied to MIT in 1887, therefore, Howe was accepted. It should be remembered that MIT, a Morrill Act (1862) Land Grant school, admitted women long before other Massachusetts institutions did. Howe inadvertently applied for the "partial course," a two-year program scheduled to graduate in 1890, rather than the regular three- to four-year program. The curriculum consisted of Freehand Drawing, Architectural History, Pen and Ink, Watercolor, Business Law, Contracts, Working Drawings, Strength of Materials, Five Orders, Iron Construction, and Heating and Ventilation. The school was known for its "overwhelming Beaux Arts tradition, utterly unworkable buildings, and emphasis on form, not function." Her graduating class included one other woman, Sophia Hayden—who was in the full program (class of 1890) and became a friend—and sixty-five men. One of her classmates wrote a short but sympathetic poem:

I thought I saw an architect,
Climb up the Tech's high stairs,
I looked again and found it was,
A Lamb midst crowds of bears.
Poor thing! I said, poor lonely thing,
I wonder how she dares.[6]

Early Career, 1893–1900

After graduation, Howe worked as a librarian and draftsman until 1892 in the firm of Allen and Kenney. In 1891 the "bold and novel" idea had emerged of having a competition, limited to women, for the design of the Women's Pavilion at the World's Columbian Exposition of 1893. Howe submitted a design but won only Honorable Mention behind Sophia Hayden's winning proposal.

Sadly, Hayden experienced so many frustrations while dealing with the final plan and its construction that she developed "brain fever" (presumably a nervous breakdown) and never pursued what had seemed a most promising career. Ironically, this was attributed in part to the domineering role of another woman, Mrs. Potter Palmer of Chicago, who was chairman of the women's board of governors for this project.

Howe used the five hundred dollars in award money from this competition to pay for part of her "grand tour" of Europe in 1892–93. The designs seen in some of her buildings doubtless stem from her observations on this trip. On her return in 1893, she opened an architectural practice by herself, first at 73 Tremont Street, then at number 101 (the Paddock Building) in 1901. To my knowledge, this became the first successful, continuous women's architectural practice in the United States. Many of Howe's early houses were for clients who were also part of her extensive network of acquaintances, friends who lived in the western part of Cambridge. In fact, of the twenty-two houses Howe designed or renovated in Cambridge that are singled out below, all were within three quarters of a mile from her own house.

There is little commentary in the writing either about or by Howe concerning her relationships with her clients. Word of mouth must have accounted for most of her new referrals. Clearly, she related well to her clients, probably in part because they had backgrounds, tastes, and values similar to her own. She also appears to have had the interpersonal skills necessary to overcome the male chauvinism of her times.

ARCHITECTURAL STYLE

Howe's first complete domestic dwelling, in 1893, was the Potter house at One Kennedy Road, next to the Cambridge Historical Society's Hooper-Lee-Nichols House. It illustrates many of the architectural elements that she would use in later, more sophisticated structures, including a gambrel roof, portico, center hall and center stair plan, and classical detail.

The general objectives of Howe's architecture, as best described by Doris Cole and Karen Taylor in *The Lady Architects* (1990), were ease of living, good circulation, and a concern for everyday needs. A single woman, Howe had many women friends with similar lifestyles. As a result, she designed houses with the needs of single or independent women in mind. Most of her houses were of modest size and designed for middle-class people. Her use of the Colonial Revival style stemmed both from her love of early New England architecture and from a reaction to what she felt was the heaviness and excessive ornamentation of Victorian architecture. In general, Howe favored simplicity of design over unnecessary elaboration.

Her use of classical detail, however, was very much her own. She meticulously drafted the particulars of moldings for portico or fireplace for each of her houses (those whose blueprints I have been able to review), adding her own stamp to these adaptations. In many of these houses, a room was designed for domestic help in which, interestingly, the molding detail was simpler than that in rooms to be used by the owner, reflecting class distinctions of the day.

Her adaptive use of new materials as advanced technologies became available demonstrated her "modernist" attitude. In her approach to architecture, she was largely a creature of the twentieth century: eight of the twelve new houses and all of the seventeen major renovations she designed in Cambridge used contemporary concepts and technologies. Many of the houses, for example—especially in the 1920s—had steel I-beam support at the ground level. She was one of the first to use stucco as an exterior finish when that durable, cement-like material was introduced. Even more daring was her use of colors for stucco; she often favored warm earth tones (sometimes whimsically referred to as "a maiden's blush").

The domestic dwellings, especially after 1900, were thoughtfully planned for optimal use of space in both city and country locations. Her classically inspired rather than Victorian plans emphasized comfort over orna-

The house at 4 Gray Gardens West, designed by Lois Lilley Howe, 1922. *(Photograph by Lewis Bushnell)*

ment, with fewer but bigger rooms and large windows that brought natural light into living spaces.

Howe's city houses, as might be expected, were somewhat more formal, with classical design details, central halls and stairs, and rooms arranged for urban activities (music, study, sewing, formal entertaining). The summer houses were "breezier" and often shingled, with wide piazzas, roof overhangs, and informal decorative detail. Although Howe did build a few institutional structures, the great majority of her projects were domestic, including houses, and such outbuildings as carriage houses and barns.

Howe's firm completed approximately 426 documented projects during its forty-four years, about 85 percent of which were renovations rather than original designs. She invented the term *renovising* to describe the integration of the goals of renovation and revision in a single coordinated process. This term certainly is applicable to the twentieth century, where "adaptive reuse" is part of the jargon of modern architecture. It signifies a combination of respect for the historic with an understanding of current needs.

Most of the firm's work was in New England, with more projects in Cambridge than in any other single place. An important exception was an

The house at 15 Traill Street, designed by Lois Lilley Howe, 1898. *(Photograph by Lewis Bushnell)*

eight-house project in a planned development for working-class people in Mariemont, Ohio, carried out in 1913. These houses, simple in decoration and plan, used the local limestone as a primary building material. Nevertheless, with a total of eighty-two projects—buildings and renovations—in Cambridge between 1894 and 1929, the Howe-Manning-Almy firm had, and continues to have, a major impact on the architectural appearance and history of the city.

CAMBRIDGE ARCHITECTURE

The following table lists all twelve original buildings and ten (of seventy) selected major renovations, grouped chronologically, that were developed by Howe's firm in Cambridge. An asterisk (*) indicates a building originally designed by the Howe-Manning-Almy firm; all others are renovations. The "date" column refers to the time of design or the date of renovation by Howe. The owner is the individual contracting with the firm. (TLA refers to Cole and Taylor, *The Lady Architects*, 1990.) Renovation houses include mention of the original architect where possible.

|	|	|	|	|

Lois Lilley Howe, 1893-1912

NO.	DATE	OWNER	ADDRESS	COMMENTS
1.	1893*	Potter	1 Kennedy Road	First house by Howe. Gambrel roof. Portico. Colonial Revival, twin chimney, center hall. Adjacent to CHS. (Renovated by Howe in 1913 with third-floor addition; tile fireplace, wood paneling, homey window seat, work area.)
2.	1894*	Merrill	11 Vincent Street	Boxy, clapboard, gambrel roof and dormers. Corner turret.
3.	1895*	Oliver-Lowell	33 Elmwood Avenue	Carriage House. Simple design. Gabled roof. Raised center section. Eyebrow arches over doors, "awkward vitality." (TLA)
4.	1898*	Henshaw	15 Traill Street	Shingle. Broad gable in front.
5.	1900	Scudder	17 Buckingham Street	Gabled with peak overhang. Stick style 1880. (Extensive renovation, 1999)
6.	1900*	Maynadier	49 Hawthorn Street	Straightforward, center entrance. Twin chimney. Classic, open, front portico. Three-story. Palladian second-story detail over portico.
7.	1901	Griswold	23 Craigie Street	Original architect unknown, 1857. Second renovation by Howe, 1904. "Good renovation results in good proportions and circulation in a three-story Classic Revival house with butt-joint boards. House has a gutsy Thomas Jefferson quality. The awkwardness comes off as quite pleasant and charming and straightforward . . . someone working out ways of doing things . . . This house by Howe has a similar quality. House has a grandness of texture, a sense of free-flowing spaces." (G. Gund)
8.	1902	Hooper-Eliot	25 Reservoir Street	Gambrel roof, gables. Center front entrance. Two-story bay flanked with Corinthian columns. Dormers and Georgian detail; broken-scroll pediment. 1873 Sturgis-Brigham, original architects.
9.	1903	White	19 Reservoir Street	Mansard roof; second-story overhang. Front porch and portico.
10.	1904*	Munroe	17 Traill Street	Center gable with projecting bay over entrance. Two chimneys. Second-story overhang. Long roof. (Not in TLA)
11.	1906	Stetson	128 Brattle Street	Half-timbered Tudor Revival. Originally by Ralph Adams Cram, 1892. Renovation by Howe in *House Beautiful*, 1916. (Further renovation, 2000)
12.	1908	Runkle	8 Willard Street	Clapboard saltbox, center-entrance Colonial.
13.	1909	Davis	57 Lake View Avenue	Center entrance, clapboard, Mansard roof. 1871 house stripped of ornament.

*Buildings originally designed by Howe's firm.

Howe and Manning, 1913–1925

NO.	DATE	OWNER	ADDRESS	COMMENTS
14.	1916	Wentworth	35 Bigelow Street	1873 house. Renovated for Cambridge VNA.
15.	1916*	Cornish	15 Fayerweather Street	Sited with narrow end to the street. First seventeenth-century-type Colonial Revival house in Cambridge Gabled roof, dormers, second-story overhang. (Renovation, 1998)
16.	1918	Stevens	229 Huron Avenue	1897 house. Additions plus "sleeping porch."
17.	1922*	Frothingham	4 Gray Gardens West	House for the independent woman. Georgian Revival, sited on triangular lot. Brick, hipped roof, pedimented porch, 8/12 windowpanes. Published in *House Beautiful*, 1935. Steel beams in basement. Spaces for privacy, entertainment, maid-companion, guests. Gray Gardens West Trust. Garden design, Fletcher Steele.
19.	1923*	Chapman	3 Gray Gardens East	Stucco (color 'maiden's blush'). Asymmetrical Colonial Revival with "studied picaresque quality" (TLA). Large living-parlor-dining space. Simplified version Colonial balustrade. Cyprus molding and other details custom designed. Steel I-beams in basement. Efficiency of space plan and traffic flow. Designed for a single woman. (Renovated by Howe in 1932 and by R. Kennedy in 1996)
20.	1923*	Hart	14 Gray Gardens West	Brown shingle exterior. Steep gable roof, prominent chimney. (Extensive renovation, 1970). Small but efficient use of space and "never lonely." (W. von Moltke)

Howe, Manning, and Almy, 1926–1929

NO.	DATE	OWNER	ADDRESS	COMMENTS
21.	1926*	Almy	111 Coolidge Hill Street	Rectangular red brick Georgian Revival. Hipped roof. Designed primarily by Almy, but similarities to the Frothingham house (1922). Part of the Coolidge Hill development, ca. 1924.
22.	1928	Simmons	11 Gray Gardens West	Large clapboard with hipped roof. Original designed by Putnam-Cox, 1923. (Renovated by LLH, 1929, and by T. Bolton, 1995)

*Buildings originally designed by Howe's firm.

LATER CAREER, 1901–1937

Having completed five original houses by 1901 in Cambridge alone, Howe was proposed for membership in the American Institute of Architects (AIA) by her friend Robert Peabody. Although there had been a prior honorary female member of the AIA, Howe was the first elected female member. This distinction doubtless bolstered her prestige and acceptability, and by 1913 her firm had enough business to add Eleanor Manning as a partner.

Eleanor Manning, who had graduated from MIT in 1906, came from a working-class background and was especially interested in architecture that working-class people could afford. She was active in a variety of social causes and worked on local, state, and national housing committees. Her addition to the firm made it the fourth-oldest multiple-partner female architectural firm on record in the country (the others were Julia Morgan's practice in San Francisco, 1904; Florence Luscomb in Waltham, Massachusetts, 1909; and Anna Schenck in New York, 1912). Howe's firm, however, was the first established, and it achieved by far the longest tenure.

In 1913 Howe published a modest book of drawings, *Details of Old New England Houses*, that she had made over the years. The Mariemont, Ohio, project mentioned above was completed the same year. She took a leadership role in the community of Boston professional women and in 1914 became an officer in the Women's Club of Boston (for which she remodeled a clubhouse). In 1916 she achieved the added distinction of becoming the first female member of the Boston Society of Architects. In 1918 she became chair of the Naples Table, a group at MIT devoted to issues of concern to career women; in 1919, she chaired the MIT Women's Association.

Howe's practice continued to do well, and in 1926 a third principal, Mary Almy, was added. Almy had attended Radcliffe and—after a period of teaching in secondary schools—the MIT architectural program. Despite the handicap wrought by childhood polio, she mastered draftsmanship, mathematics, and business administration skills, which were a great asset to the firm.

Howe was elected the first female Fellow of the AIA in 1931. She served as vice president of the Cambridge Historical Society around 1935 and as president of the Cambridge Plant and Garden Club in 1952. She was also a prominent member of the Cambridge Shakespeare Club and a participant in Unitarian church groups.

With the onset of the Depression in 1929, building construction suffered severely. By 1937 it was clear to Howe and her partners that their firm was no longer fiscally viable. Accordingly, they decided to dissolve the business. Howe was seventy-three. She continued to be available for "consultation,"

The house at 3 Gray Gardens East, designed by Lois Lilley Howe, 1923. *(Photograph by Lewis Bushnell)*

and both Manning and Almy maintained solo practices for some years thereafter. The firm had survived for forty-four years and had completed some 426 projects. It had proved to the American public, to the American architectural establishment, and most of all to American women with career aspirations that women could succeed as architects.

In 1958 there were about three hundred licensed women architects in the United States, of whom about seventy-five were in active practice. In 2002 women comprised 19.9 percent of all licensed architects (up from 13.7 percent in 1999) and 20.7 percent of principals or partners of architectural firms. Success in the struggle for equality in career opportunities for women in architecture is still a way off.

THE SIGNIFICANCE OF HOWE'S ACHIEVEMENTS

Lois Lilley Howe came from a principled and independent-minded family whose circle included some of the finest minds of the day; the Cambridge of her time was an extraordinary intellectual and social environment in which to grow up. It is interesting to note that her classmate Sophia Hayden, although possibly more talented, failed to achieve Howe's success, possibly because she did not enjoy the same degree of family and social support or lacked the wherewithal to overcome the obstacles of her time.

Howe's achievements were remarkable. She did not think in terms of advancing the rights or opportunities of women but simply strove to fulfill her own personal goals. In so doing, she served as a role model for other women who hoped to succeed in what was then a man's world of architecture. Howe wished to design buildings that were simple and efficient, buildings that served the needs of, among others, single and independent women like herself. She believed that architecture could help solve social problems. In acting on this conviction, she served as an example for women who wished be architects and as a beacon for all women with professional aspirations.

ENDNOTES

1. Ralph Waldo Emerson, "Poetical Notes about an Adirondacks Camping Trip of the Saturday Club in 1861," in E. W. Rhinehart, "Lois Lilley Howe, FAIA, 1864–1964," *Proceedings of the CHS* 43 (1975): 153–72.

2. Lois Lilley Howe, "Dr. Estes Howe: A Citizen of Cambridge," *Proceedings of the CHS* 25 (1939): 122–41.

3. Ibid. 137.

4. Lois Lilley Howe, "Memories of 19th Century Cambridge," *Proceedings of the CHS* 34 (1952): 59–76.

5. Ibid.

6. Ibid.

BIBLIOGRAPHY

Cole, Doris, and Karen C. Taylor. *The Lady Architects*. New York: Midmarch Arts Press, 1990.

Hail, Christopher, *Cambridge Buildings and Architects*. Harvard/Radcliffe Online Historical Reference Shelf.

Howe, Lois Lilley. "MIT '90, 1864–1964." Cambridge: MIT Fiftieth Reunion Program, 1940.

———. "Dr. Estes Howe: A Citizen of Cambridge." *Proceedings of the Cambridge Historical Society* 25 (1939): 122–41.

———. "Memories of 19th Century Cambridge." *Proceedings of the CHS* 34 (1952): 59–76.

———. "The Cambridge Plant Club." *Proceedings of the CHS* 35 (1953): 17–33.

McCavitt, M. J. "Howe, Manning and Almy Papers," 1883–1973. Manuscript Collection MC-9. The libraries of MIT. Institute Archives and Special Collections. Processed April 1980.

Reinhardt, E. W. "Lois Lilley Howe, FAIA, 1864–1964." *Proceedings of the CHS* 43 (1975): 153–72.

Sibley, F. P. "Miss Lois Lilley Howe, Noted as an Architect." *Boston Globe*, July 12, 1934.

"The Absolute Majority of the Population"[1]: Women in 20th Century Cambridge

EVA S. MOSELEY

"WE LOOK AT all of history, but we look at women first." So said Patricia King, then director of the Schlesinger Library on the History of Women in America, in a 1988 video.[2] This is a useful perspective in Cambridge as elsewhere—adding people, events, and ideas without taking anything away—which may even alter one's view of familiar times and places.

Women and girls make up more than half the population, and in the twentieth century they did more and more of what men did: they got more education in larger numbers, became more active politically, and took up any and all occupations and professions. (Even in the nineteenth century, women were factory workers, teachers, nurses, and, in smaller but significant numbers, doctors, lawyers, Protestant ministers, writers, photographers, and social workers—a profession women invented.)

What women also did that men didn't have to do was assert their equality, both as human beings and as citizens. Feminist movements were among the major trends of the twentieth century. The "first wave" women's movement (which was not called that until the "second wave" began in the 1960s) was launched at the Woman's Rights Convention in Seneca Falls, New York, in July 1848. Thanks to Elizabeth Cady Stanton, suffrage—seen by many at the convention as too radical a demand—became the focus of the movement, especially after the Civil War, when African American men were enfranchised but women were not.

Cantabrigians stood on both sides of the suffrage question. In 1892 Hannah Luscomb took her daughter Florence—who would live in Cambridge at various periods of her long life (1887–1985)—to a suffrage convention, where Susan B. Anthony spoke. "I guess you might say that was my introduction to the women's movement," Florence Luscomb said in 1974.[3] Later she worked for suffrage herself and was one of the first women to vote.

In the late 1890s, a Harvard professor had his class of nearly seventy Radcliffe students write about suffrage for women. Only two wrote in favor: Maud Wood and Inez Haynes. Together they went on to found the College Equal Suffrage League, the first of many such leagues throughout the United States.[4] And on Class Day at the private Berkeley Street School, one lone girl marched as "class suffragette," her classmates regarding her "with black disapproval" before she was taken away by "two...males with brass buttons and helmet-shaped hats."[5]

Abbie Brooks Hunt, a middle-class woman who lived on Lancaster Street and for many years kept a diary rich in quotidian detail, attended some suffrage events. On January 28, 1914, the Economic Club met at Symphony Hall, and Hunt recorded that "both Suffrage and Anti-Suffrage was talked of...; it was very ——," but alas, the adjective is illegible.[6] On April 28, 1914, she "went to a great Anti-Suffrage meeting in Faneuil Hall," which was "most interesting," probably not how an avowed suffragist would have described an "anti" meeting.[7] When there was a referendum on women's suffrage in 1915, she did not write at all, and on August 26, 1920, when women were enfranchised with the ratification of the Nineteenth Amendment, Hunt was unaware of it or had no comment. She did vote that November, however: "I cast my first vote for President of U.S. & I voted for Harding—the straight Republican ticket, except for Lt. Governor."

One of the arguments women used during their seventy-two-year suffrage campaign was that the vote would make them better able to apply their domestic skills in the public sphere. Women had long used voluntary associations to overcome some of the limits on their participation in public life, influencing and changing society without claiming political power. In a section of her book on women's voluntary associations, the historian Anne Firor Scott compiled a list of issues, reforms, and innovations tackled by women's groups, in corrections, education, housing, public health, recreation, "the social evil" (prostitution and venereal disease), and other categories, all concerns throughout the country.[8]

The Mothers' Club of Cambridge (MCC), for example, started a vacation school for boys on Hilliard Street in 1896, adding girls in 1897. The boys' carpentry class was oversubscribed; one boy waited for someone to cut a finger "so I'd get his chance."[9]

The MCC then promoted playgrounds in Cambridge's more congested neighborhoods. Rindge Park Playground, open in 1902 for eight weeks in July and August, accommodated seventy-five or more children a day. The same year, the MCC's "municipal housekeeping" included a playground at Pine and Eaton streets, where a small lot was cleared of trees, leaving the largest stumps. "[If] not objects of beauty, they were objects on which the children could climb and play," says the Playgrounds Committee report—a use to which Cambridge tree stumps are still being put. There were also swings, a sandbox, and an open area for "basket-ball, bean-bags, ring-toss, blocks." A paid staff of three women oversaw a daily average of two hundred children, "who would play on the street if there were no playground." When it was hot, the children made scrapbooks; the girls played with dolls, sewed, or read.

In 1902 the playground was open from June to September, except when it was closed for a week due to smallpox. In 1903 attendance increased. Although the playground was too small, assistant teacher Gladys Abbot proclaimed its good effects: "Children that were timid have become confident, and many of them that were inclined to be little bullies have learned to settle disputes with tongues instead of fists, at least in the Playground."[10]

By 1907, Cambridge had nine playgrounds. "Some big boys came" to one of them one day, the committee reported, "and when told they were too big for the playground they went away, but in an hour a third of them returned with babies, pleading to be allowed to 'mind babies in the sand.'"

The Playgrounds Committee's 1910 report begins with the notice that "hereafter the city of Cambridge will have full charge of the playgrounds," and on March 19, Mayor William F. Brooks invited Mrs. Charles (Helen) Almy, who had chaired the committee, to join the new Special Commission on Playgrounds.[11] This pattern of a public need noted by women and met through their voluntary efforts, then taken over by a local government or institution almost invariably headed by men (with women still doing much of the work), was repeated thousands of times in cities and towns across the country. The former Cambridge city councilor and mayor Barbara Ackermann calls city government "a householder's job."[12]

The MCC was only one mothers' club among at least five founded in Cambridge between 1878 and 1919. Generally, they aimed to educate members to be better mothers by hosting talks on relevant topics by members or "expert" speakers. At the fifth meeting of its first season (1899–1900), the Mothers' Discussion Club considered children's obedience, the speaker advocating "unquestionable obedience" and members disagreeing "as to this form of obedience and the methods of enforcing it. Some advocating telling the reason why, others holding that obedience should be enforced without question, others again that the reason should be told after the obeying."

Other topics also concerned children: how to teach them "the deference and respect that we showed to our parents," whether to pay children for "their little services" or give an allowance. At the sixth meeting, the physical education expert Dr. Dudley Allen Sargent "took up the different parts of the body in order, said that a large head indicated brains and a small neck out of proportion to the head indicated lack of physical force to support the brain." He advised every mother to have "a table of average weight and measurements to compare her child's growth." The flavor of those gatherings may also be gleaned from the report of the fourth meeting: a paper entitled "What we shall give our children to read" was followed by a discussion of "Miss Alcott's books, some upholding them, others condemning them as tiring, too sentimental and emotional. It was decided to serve tea after the meetings."[13]

The Cambridge Home Information Center (CHIC), in existence from 1927 to 1975, originally provided instruction in cooking and household management. A home economist was present one day a week at its office on Brattle Street, and it had a "scheme to train household assistants"—which sounds like an attempt to deal with that old bugaboo of middle- and upper-class families, "the servant question." Earlier, Charles R. Lanman, professor of Sanskrit at Harvard, had kept a "Household Record of Servants" (1889–1915), a recital of comings and goings at 9 Farrar Street and a record of wages.[14] The professor kept the accounts, though Mrs. Lanman presumably hired and managed the help.

The record was peppered with comments. One nurse, employed at the house for five weeks, "knew too much and did too little"; another "became exceedingly impertinent and excitable" and was let go after three months. Yet another nurse was "faithful, and very kind to our little daughter" but "not physically strong, and after Thomas was a few weeks old, she felt unable to keep on." Mary Chambers, however (employed for nineteen months), was "simply invaluable to us—a faithful, kind, and most acceptable nurse. I shall always be thankful that she stayed so long." Her replacement lasted thirty-eight days.

Then there were the cooks. One was "wasteful and slovenly," another "excessively disobliging" though "very neat" (barely eight months). Another, "too old to do much," lasted three days, as did the next, a "blear-eyed Cyclops." A period with no cook or nurse or "second girl" was an "Interregnum." Though some comments sound uncharitable ("forgetful, unintelligent, can't read"), the penultimate entry hints at the ambiguous relations between mistresses and servants: "Mary Hayes (Irish) young & inexperienced. Had tonsillitis. Mrs. L. cared for her for some days. She went to her brother's & then left." The women were largely Irish, and many came from Nova Scotia or Prince Edward Island. One longs to have the servants' side of the story.

Abbie Hunt, who also had an Irish servant, wrote on January 28, 1910: "Hannah Mahoney has been with me ... twenty years today, a good faithful servant & one of the best friends in the whole world to us all. I gave her $5.00, I wish I could have given her $500.00."[15]

After World War II, the CHIC gave up its office and its initial goals. For a time it conducted educational trips to museums, historical sites, and craft studios, and then just held luncheons with speakers at members' houses.[16] This evolution was typical of many clubs. Meeting topics were no longer confined to household management and child rearing, but there was less activism. The CHIC also seems to have succumbed to the dilemma facing women's groups in the 1970s: older members did not want (or were afraid) to go out to evening meetings, while younger members could not go to daytime meetings because they had jobs.

Unlike the CHIC, the Cambridge Plant and Garden Club—formed in 1966 when the Plant Club (1889) merged with the Garden Club (1938)—persists and has changed with the times. It has expanded its interests to include the preservation of "wetlands near Cambridge Cemetery" (that is, Hell's Half Acre, now a project of the new Charles River Conservancy, another organization founded by a woman) and the redesign of Winthrop Square Park, as well as household and other hazardous waste, water pollution, and additional environmental issues.[17]

Mary Isabella de Gozzaldi, president of the Plant Club from 1903 to 1906, worked on another of her multiple interests during this time. From 1904 to 1905 she chaired a "Committee of Ladies" in the Hannah Winthrop chapter of the Daughters of the American Revolution, its task to index Lucius Paige's *History of Cambridge*. In the course of this work, she realized that the city needed a way to collect and preserve historical materials, and so she became one of the founders, and a vice president, of the Cambridge Historical Society.[18] She was also concerned with the education of her daughter and other girls.

In 1900, the Mothers' Discussion Club heard a paper, "The Public Schools," in which a Mrs. Richardson praised their "modern buildings." She declared

that the ventilation and plumbing were well considered and frequently inspected, that the teachers were carefully selected, the discipline excellent, and in the case of her child the methods were far superior to a private school in inducing attention and interest in work.... The drawbacks...were the lack of appliances for nature work and the lack of beauty in the rooms.... [and that] the medical examinations might be improved by being more thorough.[19]

Mary Gozzaldi might not have agreed with the comparison to private schools, for she was a devoted alumna of Berkeley Street School (as was her daughter) and served as first president of the alumnae association. Founded in 1861-62 by Lyman Richards Williston as Irving Street School, it later moved to 17 Berkeley Street. The curriculum, designed to "fit students for the entrance examinations to Radcliffe and Bryn Mawr," included French, German, Latin, and Greek; ancient, European, and American history; arithmetic, geometry, and algebra; and sciences, geography, current events, history of art, and drawing.[20]

Addressing the first meeting of alumnae at the Berkeley Street School on June 4, 1912, Mary Gozzaldi claimed that "few private schools for girls round out the half century."[21] This no doubt referred to the fact that many schools for girls were run by an individual woman, meeting in her house and expiring when she did—or when she was too old or unwell to carry on. Such schools and small female academies in fact had a long history, with curricula emphasizing the traditional graces expected of a marriageable young lady: piano, embroidery, French, and so on.

Three years before Gozzaldi's remarks, Edith Lesley had launched Miss Lesley's School in her house at 29 Everett Street. Miss Lesley's differs in at least two ways from other private girls' schools of the time: its mission, to train kindergarten teachers, was more specific; and it still exists today, having evolved as Lesley Kindergarten School, Lesley Normal School, Lesley College, and (in 2000) Lesley University.

Begun by Friedrich Fröbel in Germany, the kindergarten movement was brought to the United States by Elizabeth Palmer Peabody in the mid nineteenth century. "Kindergarten education will soon become established as a permanent unit in our national educational philosophy," Lesley explained on the first day of her school. "Teachers trained as specialists in this field are alarmingly few.... I plan not merely to set up just another training school; I plan for us to be different: to consider the individual of basic importance; to inculcate the ideal of gracious living; and to foster the tradition of American democracy."[22] Whether gracious living and democracy are compatible is an open question, but soon Lesley added the training of elementary school teachers, then a home economics course and a Program in Management of the Tea Room.[23]

In 1939 Edith Lesley gave her school to a board of trustees to turn into a college, and by 1943 it was accredited to grant four-year degrees rather than the previous two-year certificates. As Lesley College offered evening courses for teachers, graduate education developed, and in 1953 the state approved the granting of master's degrees. In 2005 men were admitted to undergraduate, in addition to graduate, programs. While Lesley now offers programs in education, human services, and the arts, not only in Cambridge but also at its Boston campus and at more than two hundred sites in twenty states, it has also grown in place to more than fifty buildings, including historic 29 Everett Street.

Another school, begun in 1914 by Agnes and William Ernest Hocking (a Harvard professor) on the back porch of their house at the foot of Shady Hill, carried its name with it when it moved to Coolidge Hill in 1926. An early prospectus tells us that "the coöperative open-air school" admits both boys and girls from the age of four or five; children learn in nine classes, and the aims are "those which inspired its founders: to keep childhood alive to an open-mindedness and a love of learning; to provide life with all possible richness and fullness; to secure freedom *with* self-control." A later letter recalls the open buildings and old-fashioned stoves: "In the extreme weather their effectiveness depended upon how freely logs were fed into them."[24]

Shady Hill School was headed first by Agnes Hocking and then, from 1921 to 1949, by Katharine Taylor, by all accounts a remarkable educator. She added a teacher apprentice program, increased the school's size and gave it a national reputation, and maintained its balance of freedom and discipline. Although trained in "progressive" education, she called Shady Hill a good school rather than a progressive one. Fellow educator Ella Lyman Cabot wrote to Taylor from 101 Brattle Street after a visit to the school: "No bored children, almost no self-conscious children, or showing off bragging children, and an extraordinary minimum of punching little boys considering how many little boys of punching age are there.... [Some schools] accent appreciation, or discipline, or correlation, or passing your exams, or being 'socially minded.' I think you do all of these."[25]

Like many people who made their mark in Cambridge, Taylor had migrated to the city, in her case from Chicago. Another midwestern educator, Ada Louise Comstock, came to Radcliffe College from Moorhead, Minnesota, by way of the University of Minnesota and Smith College. Comstock had been Smith's first dean and had been denied the title of "acting president" when she served that function—between two male presidents.

Comstock served as Radcliffe's first full-time president between 1923 and 1943. Begun in 1879 as the Society for the Collegiate Instruction of Women (Harvard Annex for short), Radcliffe had been incorporated as a college in 1894. It had no faculty, for its raison d'être was to give women a Harvard education, which it did, but in separate classes.[26] While turning a "provincial school into a national institution," Comstock had to struggle to preserve Radcliffe's charter—in which Harvard had agreed to certify that Radcliffe's degrees were equivalent to Harvard's—in the face of President A. Lawrence Lowell's hostility. After James Bryant Conant succeeded Lowell in

1933, Comstock and Provost Paul Buck of Harvard engineered an agreement by which, starting on July 1, 1943, the Faculty of Arts and Sciences assumed "complete responsibility for the undergraduate and graduate education of Radcliffe students." Most classes were to remain separate, but the exigencies of World War II soon made them coed, though everything else was still separate—and not equal.[27]

Two years after Comstock came to Radcliffe, Cecilia Payne came to the Harvard Observatory from Cambridge University and was soon the first person to earn a Ph.D. in astronomy at Harvard. Her major contribution was "the demonstration that normal stars all have essentially the same chemical composition," and she proved that it is possible to combine hard, sustained scientific work and family life. Her long career was, however, a succession not only of professional achievements but also of instances of exploitation and at times exclusion. Being a woman made no difference intellectually, she believed, but "on the material side, being a woman has been a great disadvantage. It is a tale of low salary, lack of status, slow advancement."[28] Only after many years of doing the work of a faculty member without the pay, title, or status was she made a professor and chair of the Department of Astronomy.

It was this kind of treatment, as well as their tiny numbers, that with the impetus of the women's liberation movement led women faculty members to meet on December 2, 1969, to discuss the proposed merger of Radcliffe and Harvard, "both in itself and in relation to the larger question of the place of women in the University." At the second meeting of the group on January 13, 1970, "Bobbie Cohn reported on her interviews with women lecturers....[E]ach lecturer felt that she was an exception and that rules had been bypassed as a favor to her, for which she felt grateful....[S]ome...thought that hiring women was against the rules in the 'real' system."[29] That year women held one of 483 tenured positions (the one being the Radcliffe chair meant only for a woman); they were 4.6 percent of assistant professors and 15.5 percent of lecturers, including language instructors, research associates, and the like.

The women convinced the Faculty Council to appoint a Committee on the Status of Women at Harvard, which investigated the problems of female faculty and graduate students. Its recommendations included tying the percentage of women in faculty positions to the percentage of women Ph.D. students, a permanent committee on women, various maternity benefits, part-time graduate study, and better provisions for day care.[30]

The School of Science at MIT undertook a similar study in the 1990s. At the start, junior women faculty felt "well supported" by their departments and did not expect their careers to suffer due to gender bias. They did worry that "family-work conflicts" would affect their careers more than those of men. In contrast, according to the report, "many tenured women faculty feel...excluded from a significant role in their departments. Marginalization increases as women progress through their careers at MIT [and is] often accompanied by differences in salary, space, awards, resources, and response to outside offers...with women receiving less despite professional accomplishments equal to those of their male colleagues." The investigating committee, using both data and interviews, found that "the difference in the perception of junior and senior women faculty about the impact of gender on their careers...repeats itself over generations." Young women believe that gender discrimination has ended, but as they age they realize "that the playing field is not level at all."

In response to the committee's interim report, Dean Robert Birgeneau addressed issues of space, resources, etc.; increased female participation in department activities; and made efforts to recruit more women at all ranks. One senior woman had thought that being "unhappy at MIT for more than a decade...was the price you paid...to be a scientist at an elite academic institution." After the committee's work, she said, "my research blossomed, my funding tripled.... It is hard to understand how I survived those years—or why."[31]

Founded in Boston in 1865, MIT accepted its first female student, Ellen Swallow, in 1870. She was allowed to study chemistry *gratis* so that, as she learned later, the president could deny she was a student in case trustees or other students objected. A young MIT instructor, Robert Hallowell Richards, proposed to her in the chemistry lab. She started a Woman's Laboratory at MIT in 1875 and ran it until 1882. From 1884 until her death in 1911, she was an instructor in sanitary chemistry, and she invented the field of home economics.[32] All this happened before MIT moved to Cambridge in 1916 (as did Florence Luscomb's years as an architecture student).

Between Ellen Swallow Richards and the women scientists of the 1990s, quite a few alumnae and women faculty succeeded in their fields, though in minuscule numbers compared with men. Katharine Dexter McCormick (1875–1967) earned a B.S. in biology in 1904 and used her knowledge of endocrines—and her private fortune—to work with various experts to try to find a cure for her husband's mental illness and with Gregory Pincus to develop "the pill." A suffrage leader, she later supported Planned Parenthood and built women's dormitories at MIT, "ending the long-standing excuse" that MIT could not admit more women "because no housing was available."[33] Vera Kistiakowsy (b. 1928) came to MIT in 1963 after teaching and doing research in nuclear and particle physics elsewhere and became professor *emerita* in 1994. She had been a director of the Council for a Livable World, which works for the abolition of nuclear weapons. Sheila Evans Widnall (b.

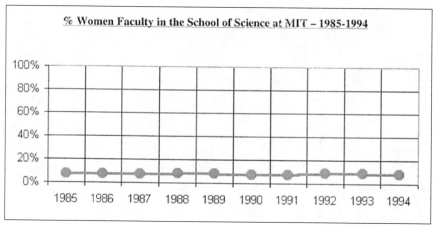

Graph showing percentage of women faculty in the School of Science at MIT, 1985-1994. *(From a special edition of* The MIT Faculty Newsletter, *March 1999)*

1938) has three degrees from MIT. She taught aeronautics there from 1964 to 1993, has edited journals in her field, and holds several patents. From 1993 to 1997, she served as secretary of the U.S Air Force.[34]

Faculty and students are, of course, not the only women at a university. Since 1636, Harvard has relied on women to cook, clean, wash, and later to type, file, do research, and so on (as the Harvard Union of Clerical and Technical Workers [HUCTW] put it in a slogan used during its organizing drive in the 1980s, "Harvard Works Because We Do"). This necessary but invisible cohort became famously visible in 1929. On December 21 Harvard chose to fire the Widener Library "scrubwomen" rather than pay them the state-mandated minimum wage of thirty-seven cents an hour. (Harvard paid thirty-five cents; MIT was paying forty-seven cents for comparable work, the State House sixty cents.)

The scrubwomen's story brought Harvard and President Lowell adverse publicity nationwide. Investigations and student pamphlets followed, and soon a group of alumni—led by wealthy socialist Corliss Lamont—raised enough money to pay the women the difference between what they had earned and what they should have earned since the minimum wage was enacted in 1920. On December 25, 1931, Lamont divided $3,880 among them, but "Harvard...remained recalcitrant," and the women did not get their jobs back. As it would do again decades later, "Harvard...claimed that its 'prestige' compensated for lower wages." (Again, the HUCTW had a succinct comment: "We Can't Eat Prestige.")

To replace the scrubwomen, Harvard hired men to clean Widener; because the minimum wage did not apply to them, they were paid only thirty-two cents an hour. In this case, protective legislation that applied only to women backfired. It had been a bone of contention among feminists, some advocating protective legislation for everyone, others arguing that it was politically impossible to secure protection for men.[35] The former were allied with the National Woman's Party, which in 1923 began to advocate an equal rights amendment, the latter with the League of Women Voters (LWV).

The LWV worked (and continues to work) on many issues of concern to voters. One item of business left unfinished by the suffrage amendment was jury duty for women. Pearl Katz Wise of Cambridge led a statewide legislative campaign in 1948 that secured this right, and Agnes Goldman Sanborn, an officer of the LWV of Cambridge (LWVC), served on a jury from October 1 to November 2, 1951, about which she wrote:

> This was the second or third session to which women jurors were called and it was therefore a novel experience for the women, the men jurors, and the court officers.... Usually [during the long waits] the women sat on one side in the so-called pool room, the men on the other.... Though there were a few foolish people and big talkers, on the whole both men and women seemed a conscientious group.... I was favorably impressed by the women. All of them were serious about their responsibilities.... The ones who came from an ordinary middle class housewife's background had a lot of common sense gleaned from the daily experience of life, and I felt that they put it all over me.

Although Sanborn learned that "accurate recall and honest intention" are always in question, "I shall never believe that the juries did not make a real effort to arrive at the truth."[36]

A bacteriologist originally from New York, Sanborn had moved to Boston when her husband became secretary of the Museum of Fine Arts, and to Cambridge (7 Meadow Lane) in 1933 so their daughter could go to Shady Hill School. She was vice president of the LWVC and editor of its newsletter, co-founder and president of the Cambridge Community Center, and, later, a major supporter of the Committee of Responsibility, a Vietnam War-era organization that helped wounded Vietnamese children.[37] Earlier, as chair of the LWVC's committee on international affairs, she had helped get the Lend-Lease Act passed. Enacted in 1941, it enabled the president to sell, grant, lend, or lease war supplies to countries whose defense was considered vital to the defense of the United States. Before and during World War II, the Sanborn

Pearl Wise with children and a feathered pun on her name, during one of her runs for Cambridge School Committee, 1948, 1950, or 1952. *(Photograph by Robert O'Neil, from Pearl Wise papers, Schlesinger Library, Radcliffe Institute, Harvard University)*

house (which from 1940 to 1974 was at 147 Brattle Street) was filled with students and refugees.

World War II refugees were the focus of another undertaking by Cambridge women, initially a group of Harvard faculty wives "deeply disturbed by [their] plight." Seeing that social agencies helped with immediate needs but left unmet "a need for a long range plan to fit the refugee into the community economically and socially," the women opened a shop with a large window at 36 Church Street, above the present Border Cafe, on May 2, 1939. There "the refugees could sell the products of their skills and provide small services then unobtainable in Cambridge," such as mending, dressmaking, cake baking, and photography. Mary Mohrer, herself a refugee from Vienna, was in charge. Like the other women, "she knew nothing of merchandising" but she knew languages, had good taste, and learned "to adapt the best of European taste to that of a new country." So sweaters would be made with less heavy yarns and pastries with less costly ingredients. Patronage fell off during a very

Olga Schiffer, wearing a dirndl and rolling dough at the Window Shop, 1940. The shop, with its tearoom, was then at 102 Mt. Auburn Street. *(Photograph from the records of the Window Shop, Schlesinger Library, Radcliffe Institute, Harvard University)*

hot summer, but when Mohrer wore an Austrian dirndl to work one day, orders began to pour in from near and far.[38]

In November 1939 the shop moved to 102 Mount Auburn Street and began to serve tea, then lunch, despite the inconvenience of a basement kitchen. In 1941 the Window Shop was able to buy 56 Brattle Street, adding 5 Story Street in 1950. By 1959 it had employed 451 people from twenty countries. Some were wives of men retraining to practice their professions in the United States, others were like "the former judge over 70 years old who otherwise would not be employable"; he typed and mimeographed the daily menu for what became a first-class Viennese restaurant. Labor policies were progressive, including part-time work, job sharing, morning hours for mothers, health insurance, and—for those who reached fifty-five—a cut in hours without a cut in pay.[39]

After a visit to the shop, Eleanor Roosevelt wrote about it in "My Day," her newspaper column. Would-be emulators wrote for advice from the Midwest and the West, and Alice Cope, the shop's president, spoke on the radio, at social welfare conferences, and before the President's Commission on

Immigration. The shop continued to serve new waves of refugees, especially Hungarians in 1956, but changing tastes meant a drop in revenue. The shop and restaurant closed in 1972, and 56 Brattle Street was sold to the Cambridge Center for Adult Education. For some years the Blacksmith House, a café and bakery still featuring Viennese pastries, continued to use part of the building and the courtyard; now the Hi-Rise Bread Company runs the café. Meanwhile, the Window Shop scholarship fund for foreign students continued until 1987.[40]

In its heyday, the Window Shop advertised in the LWVC's *League Items*. It offered to mend runs in nylon stockings, which were hard to come by during World War II.[41] Agnes Sanborn, the league's wartime service chair, led a "Do Not Hoard" campaign and promoted Defense Bonds and Red Cross blood drives.

The LWVC tried not to neglect "other essential matters."[42] Among these was a self-supporting high school lunchroom—an issue that Elizabeth Bancroft Schlesinger, chair of the league's education committee, had addressed since 1934, when she surveyed other cities and learned that lunchrooms in Boston, Lynn, Medford, and Somerville were self-supporting and served healthful food. Cambridge, on the other hand, had no hot food or salads, sold candy throughout the lunch period instead of at the end, and cost the city $5,000 to $10,000 a year.[43]

Schlesinger's suggestion to cut staff salaries was guaranteed to annoy some, as was her campaign in 1932 to stop school committee members from "dining extremely well in the midst of the depression" at public expense. The committee's chairman, Raymond FitzGerald, accused Schlesinger of "picayune prying into public peccadillos."[44] That didn't stop her from also taking on the issues of nepotism and corruption in the appointment of teachers, as in the 1942 case of domestic science teacher Gertrude Trant, who did not meet the city's requirements, already lower than the state's. "Having elected the teacher...the School Committee at the same meeting piously moved to raise the requirements for the position to those proposed by the State Department [of Education]," Schlesinger wrote.

Schlesinger's further efforts to make the school committee honest entailed a discussion with Mayor John H. Corcoran and an angry letter from him. "It is quite apparent to me," Corcoran wrote, "that you have no real desire to cooperate with me in regard to school matters.... I consider your statement regarding my position as a deliberate insult.... I feel that...it would be an absolute waste of time for me to hold any further discussions with you."

Ten years later, she was still at it. A 1952 letter to the editor of the *Boston Herald* pointed out that an "examination procedure for all appointments and promotions" had been set up to replace "political horse-trading." But, Schlesinger continued, "now this program is ignored and in its place four school committee members sneak their appointees, including three relatives, through the back door of politics into the school system, avoiding the front door of open competition."[45] She campaigned, too, for the accreditation of Massachusetts teachers' colleges and against teachers being solicited for funds for political candidates.

When Schlesinger died in 1977 at nearly ninety-one, one condolence letter paraphrased Camus: she "sought respite...in the very thick of the battle."[46] Originally from Columbus, Ohio, she and her husband, Arthur M. Schlesinger Sr., had come to Cambridge in 1924, when Harvard appointed him professor of history. They lived—and she composed her critical letters and reports—in the house she designed, at 19 Gray Gardens East. She also researched and wrote articles about women before women's history was a discipline, and she encouraged her husband to "remember the ladies."

Schlesinger evidently relished her role as a citizen gadfly, but there were other women who chose to go into politics.[47] Pearl Katz Wise, an LWVC activist, was the first female city councilor elected under Plan E. Wise was another immigrant to Cambridge, born in Russia in about 1901 and raised in Connecticut. Barbara Ackermann—the first woman mayor (1972–73) and one of a growing number of women to follow Wise on the school committee and city council—could have spoken for Wise, a mother of four, when she wrote: "What pushed me into politics was my parental interest in our public schools. Once I was in I was hooked."[48] Privately, Wise was chair of the education committee of the Cambridge chapter of Hadassah, president of the LWVC (1942–45), and founder and first president of the Parents-Teachers Association at Cambridge High & Latin. Once in politics, she served three terms on the school committee (1949–55), one as vice chair, and was largely responsible for the construction of three new schools, the inauguration of a federally funded hot lunch program, and the establishment of a library in each public school. She then served four terms on the council. Politics seemed to come naturally to her; as one of her daughters wrote, at ninety-five Wise was "working the floor" of her nursing home "like an old pro pol..., getting favors, extra help, etc."[49]

In 1957, the city's boards and commissions had a total of five women members and forty-two men. Noting this discrepancy, Wise filed a council resolution for equitable representation. In 1959, when she urged Mayor John J. Curry to appoint women to the Housing Authority, he responded, "I have never consciously discriminated against women at any time in my life."[50] Concerned with racism as well, Wise got the city to observe Negro History Week and ban race discrimination in public housing. She initiated a conservation commission and secured group health insurance for city employees and pensions for widows of former employees.

Another major concern was affordable housing. In 1958 Wise voted against the Riverview project (corner of Mt. Auburn and Sparks streets). As she wrote to a constituent "there was no guarantee that those displaced would be able to return to live in apartments within their financial reach," and "I am against the bull-dozer approach in seeking answers to housing problems."[51] She voted against other urban renewal projects as well, and as she left the council, she earned effusive thanks from Julia Hamilton Smith, writing on behalf of the Riverside Neighborhood Association:

> We owe you our gratitude for your courage when you...challenged the right of the government to take away people's homes under Urban Renewal while others sat in silence. The minority groups such as ourselves need leaders who understand our problems.... [W]e have been deceived by many who received our support and votes,... but [who] after the election turned a deaf ear to our pleas.[52]

Smith, an African American woman who had taught in Washington, D.C., for forty-three years, moved to Cambridge in 1947 to live with her brother at 12 Lee Street. Active in the YWCA and the Cambridge Community Relations Committee, she saw to it that blacks were hired in stores under the Fair Employment Act. Like Wise, she opposed urban renewal and especially the "Inner Belt" highway, convincing her neighbors that it would destroy a swath of Cambridge, including their "lovely residential area." Although she had escaped the "bitterness, indignity, humiliation of racial bias that thousands of Negroes have...been forced to endure,...conscious of the horrible injustices of hate...bigotry, and vengeance,...whenever I could, I raised my voice in protest."[53]

Racism and other forms of prejudice have always been issues in Cambridge. In 1910 the Mothers' Club Playgrounds Committee had asked its workers, "On your teams composed of various nationalities, has there been any race feeling?" (At that time, "race" could refer to nothing more exotic than having Irish, Jewish, or Eastern European roots.) The answers, according to the committee, "proved that whatever small amount there was at first disappeared as the work went on." Abbie Brooks Hunt reported on several events involving what are now called "minorities." On April 13, 1917, "Jennie & I went to a Patriotic Man meeting for colored people at our church [probably the First Unitarian Church in Harvard Square]. It was very interesting and the music was beautiful—A colored glee club of about 20 men sang."[54] On March 20, 1929, she remarked, "I sold my house this P.M. to a Mr. & Mrs. McCullough.... He is a policeman & they seem to be nice respectable Irish people, I hope the neighbors will not mind."

In a 1949–50 report, the executive director of the YWCA wrote that Cambridge "is about 75% Roman Catholic with many different racial and nationality groups...[that] do not mix.... The Y.W.C.A. is one organization that definitely brings people together."[55] Indeed, the group has pioneered good race relations both nationally and internationally, though some might find its being "a movement rooted in the Christian faith as known in Jesus" problematic, even if it "draws together...women and girls of diverse experiences and faiths."[56] When the YWCA of Cambridge grew out of the Woman's Christian Temperance Union in 1891, active members had to be church members, though "any other young woman of good moral character" could be an associate member.[57]

The Cambridge YWCA was founded for the "temporal, moral, and religious welfare of young women who are dependent upon their own exertions for support," but some church leaders opposed it for doing "Christian work not part of church work."[58] The organization struggled and thrived nevertheless. It has changed with the times, adding coed activities, groups for older women, summer camps, and classes in auto mechanics and self-defense. It has extended its work to the suburbs. And, with the school department, it has held prenatal classes for pregnant teens. When it built a new residence in 1964, it had to turn away more than one hundred applicants. That spring, it collected books for Mississippi, "since many public libraries in the south are not open to colored people." Clearly, the Cambridge "YW" was part of the struggle to overcome racial and other prejudices.[59]

At the Shady Hill School, Katharine Taylor had encouraged black parents to apply and had worked to make their children's experience at the school positive—rare among private schools in her day. At the Window Shop, as business improved and fewer refugees came, "Negroes were employed who proved most satisfactory and who said that the Window Shop was the best place in Cambridge for Negroes to work."[60] And at Agnes Sanborn's memorial service, her daughter recalled that

> some time in the mid forties, a Cambridge restaurant refused admittance to a black person. Out marched Agnes, taking me with her, and we joined a small group of sign-bearing pickets.... I was scared, but proud, and figured that if she could do it, so could I—I've avoided crossing picket lines ever since. Agnes took it for granted that...such unfairness must be challenged.[61]

Elizabeth Schlesinger criticized Lucy Wilson Benson, then head of the Massachusetts LWV, for not taking the lead on civil rights even when the

Cambridge and Northampton leagues had expressed some concern over the matter.... It is also quite depressing to read that you believe that in our own state "the League will never be able to be far ahead of the community as a whole." This was not always so.... You certainly were ahead of the current thinking on the council reform.... Our difference lies in the choice of issues to work for.[62]

In 1944, at the request of the American Defense–Harvard Group (which was organized during World War II to carry out various projects to aid the war effort), Schlesinger wrote "Instruction, Research, and Community Work at Harvard, Bearing Upon Problems of Group Prejudice and Conflict." She found little relevant activity, except for "community activity...carried on by one small group of Harvard instructors who are called upon again and again." In a characteristic dig, she added that "the writer is inclined to the view that the Harvard staff is not particularly distinguished from the community at large in respect to its prejudices, or its attitude toward prejudice."[63] Schlesinger's observations are not far from those expressed in the 1949 YWCA report, which continues as follows: "There is definite cleavage between Central and Harvard Squares, i.e., the so-called town does not approve of Harvard, and Harvard Professors and Laboratory Assistants, as its own report states, do not know Central Square exists."

In writing about her response to racism, Julia Smith declared, "God reigns, & is a just God.... Righteousness must prevail," a sustaining faith evident also in the story of the Pearson sisters, Satyra P. Bennett and Ozeline P. Wise. The Pearson family hailed from Jamaica, where one grandfather had been a slave. Both sisters lived at 26 Mead Street and were devoted to St. Paul A.M.E. Church at 85 Bishop Allen Drive, holding numerous offices as "a sisterly team" —as trustee, Sunday School superintendent, and on various committees. Wise was the first African American employee of the Massachusetts Banking Department and a passionate advocate of education for black youth. "Parents and guardians," she wrote, "I advise you to make the sacrifice to keep your children in school as long as possible, encourage them to press forward, and assist them all you can.... Children, go to school, learn your lessons, go as far as you can."[64] Bennett was for a long time treasurer of the Cambridge Community Center (while Agnes Sanborn was president).

Together the sisters founded the Colored Charitable Health Association (CCHA) in 1948, with Bennett as president and Wise as treasurer. By 1955, the first C stood for Citizens'. "Our goals are aiding and sustaining research for Arthritis, Heart Disease, Cancer and Birth Defects," a 1970 statement explains. "We were founded...for the purpose of making the public more

Ozeline Wise, an active member of St. Paul A.M.E. Church and co-founder of the Citizens' Charitable Health Association, ca. 1982. (Portrait by Judith Sedgwick for the Black Women Oral History Project, Schlesinger Library, Radcliffe Institute, Harvard University)

health conscious and to make an annual monetary contribution to national health drives."[65]

While the Pearson sisters and the CCHA focused on major illnesses, others were concerned with reproductive issues. A 1940 poll by Massachusetts birth control activists on repealing restrictive laws showed citizens favoring repeal by a comfortable margin, but referenda in 1942 and 1948 were defeated, largely through the efforts of the Catholic Church; priests' homilies instructed parishioners to vote no. In 1966 the legislature finally permitted birth control information and devices, for married people only.[66] In 1974, a year after Roe v. Wade made abortion legal, the Women's Community Health Center (WCHC) began its short life, first at 137 Hampshire Street, as "the only women worker owned and controlled licensed free-standing clinic in Massachusetts." It offered educational and medical programs, "work[ed] politically on local and national levels..., and struggle[d] to create a viable workspace" for those who worked at the center. It opposed unnecessary Caesarean sections and episiotomies, drugs to slow or hasten labor, and the separation of mother and newborn.

In 1978 the WCHC moved to 639 Massachusetts Avenue. Self-help groups chose their own topics, and the center offered pregnancy screening, first-trimester abortions, child care during medical hours, and Spanish- and Portuguese-speaking staff. But while the center met the needs of many women, it faced "harassment," and financial difficulties were a major factor in its dissolution in 1981.[67]

The WCHC was one of several Cambridge institutions that attempted to carry on their work as collectives, eschewing leadership and hierarchy. New Words Bookstore also began in 1974, a four-woman collective in a one-room storefront on the Cambridge-Somerville line. In 1976 it moved to 186 Hampshire Street, where it carried books by and about women and nonsexist, multicultural literature for children and teens; hosted readings; and became an "informal community center." In 2002, suffering the fate of the many independent booksellers who have been done in by chain stores and the Internet, it ceased to be a bookstore and became the Center for New Words. According to the center's web site, "The Center for New Words is dedicated to a simple mission: To use the power and creativity of words and ideas to strengthen the voice of progressive and marginalized women in society."

The saga of the New Words experiment as a collective is for now buried in its unprocessed records at the Schlesinger Library, but one can get some insight into the difficulties from the documents of Bread & Roses, a conglomeration of small feminist collectives that flourished in Cambridge from 1969 into the early '70s. A "Draft Internal Statement" of October 10, 1969, declares that "Bread and Roses is an organization of socialist women" and that it should "fight against male supremacy as it exists in all institutions and in its structural base, the bourgeois family." Along with questions about membership and decision-making, the document asks:

> How do we deal with our bureaucratic problems?—getting and renting an office, fundraising, setting up agendas and chairmen for meetings.... Many organizations have an executive, or steering committee to deal with certain functions. If we want no such thing, we have to find some other way to handle it.
>
> [One suggestion was] a secretary to do the minutes. This is a shit job and should be paid.... It may be possible to rotate it but that's a big bureaucratic hassle.[68]

Another Bread & Roses document also asks numerous questions, including the following, under the heading "Women's Culture":

> 1) What is women's culture? What is its relation to drop-out culture? To freak culture?

2) Have we developed a sense of community? What communal forms, institutions, services, have we created? Is developing communal forms a priority? Do communities cut us off from other people?

And under "Organization, Structure, Leadership and Non-leadership":

Is it possible to develop a structure which meets our needs, the needs of new women, and is able to divide leadership and shitwork functions in some equitable way?.... What are the possible forms of leadership? Can leadership be different from elitism?[69]

As, by their own admission, these were educated, mainly white (and in Bread & Roses, though not other groups, disproportionately Jewish) women, and as they were breaking new intellectual and social ground, the soul-searching was earnest and nearly endless. Eight women "started a friendship group," asking "why the [women's] movement [was] so competitive." Another Bread & Roses document echoes that concern as it addresses a question posed earlier, "Do communities cut us off from other people?" Some members chronicled the evolution of this group:

As we became personally vulnerable and supportive, we began to feel a real sense of responsibility to the people in the group—and a sense of commitment to the group itself.... As we began to participate and trust each other, we became almost giddy and condescending when we thought about how much better our group seemed to be than other groups we knew.... Naturally, this attitude caused a lot of hostility among women and men outside our group.[70]

But it wasn't all *Sturm und Drang*; the Bread and Roses women learned to use a potent weapon: humor.

WBCN wrote and ran a...spot announcement for the Riverside Drug Dependency Unit, which asked for volunteer doctors and therapists. "And," it glibly continued, "if you're a chick, they need typists." The male supremacist assumption was that "chicks" by their very nature type; we do fifteen words a minute at birth and work our way up. Many phone calls later, they modified it to, "If you're a chick and can type, they need typists." No men need apply. It's beneath male dignity, and besides, men will be too busy being those doctors and therapists, which, presumably, no "chick" can ever be.

Could a radio station get away with an ad that ran, "And if you're black, we need janitors?"

Then, on Friday, February 13, 1970, thirty Bread & Roses women "stormed the offices of...WBCN," got the station manager to grant them an hour of air time on March 8 (International Women's Day), and presented him with eight live baby chicks as a Valentine's Day present, "pointing out that *women* are *not* chicks."[71]

Amaranth, a feminist restaurant at 134 Hampshire Street, mirrored this incident in its "woMenu," which included Casseopeizza and a chickpea-spread sandwich called "Don't Call Me Chick" Delight. Run by a collective, Amaranth held shows of women's artwork, performances by musicians and poets, and discussions about housing and other current issues. But customers and money were in short supply, and a "severe financial and emotional crisis" soon led the women to close Amaranth's doors.[72]

The women's liberation movement continued, of course, and continued to wrestle with important issues. A flyer that used capital letters only when needed for emphasis asked, "is women's liberation a 'lesbian plot'?" The flyer argued that

> women in bread and roses must begin to understand lesbianism, and deal with their fears and misconceptions about it. if gay liberation is given a verbal approval in a manifesto...women who are not gay must be prepared to defend this position to people outside the movement.... we will all be ACCUSED of lesbianism at some time.... if someone, female or male, asserts that women's liberation is a bunch of dykes, how would you respond?

Further probing about the attitudes of "straight" feminists points to a divide that for some years vexed the women's movement, and not only in Cambridge.[73]

International Women's Day was an annual focal point for the movement. On March 8, 1971, feminists marched from Park Street in Boston to Harvard Square. Either some or all participants (memories vary) went on to 888 Memorial Drive, still identified by a sign over the door as the Hingham Knitting Factory but by then a Harvard building in minimal use by the Architectural Technology Workshop. There were twenty women in five teams, one of which had gone ahead that morning, loosened the boards on a basement window, and detained the one man at work there until the others came. Relays of women—about two hundred in all—occupied the building for nine days, demanding that Harvard provide a women's center. Supporters brought blankets, flashlights, and groceries, including a lot of peanut butter, and the occupiers learned to deal with overloaded plumbing and with electricity: Harvard turned it off; they turned it back on. They organized day care for their children and held lengthy political discussions. The teams took turns keeping watch, and when the police came and read an injunction demanding that they leave, the women made so much noise that they could not hear it, making the injunction invalid. Later, when they learned that the police had a court order to evict them, they declared victory, painted their faces, left a note on the door, "Sorry, MDC police, we could not wait,"[74] marched noisily to Harvard Square and then to Old Cambridge Baptist Church, and issued a statement:

> Today, those of us who have lived in and built a women's center in a Harvard building...have won a victory.... Our commitment to a women's center is well on the way to completion. We decided to leave the building so that the love and energy generated in the last eight days can be used towards the further creation of a center for women, rather than in the courtroom with legal hassles.

The second sentence turned out not to be an idle boast. Susan Storey Lyman, then director of the Radcliffe Fund and later chair of the Radcliffe board of trustees, gave the women $5,000 for a down payment on a building; the gift was ostensibly from Harvard but was actually Lyman's own money.[75] As a result, there has been a Women's Center at 46 Pleasant Street since January 1972, "a place where we can learn to meet our needs and change society through collective alternatives in service, education, and action. The struggle to gain control of all aspects of our lives—our bodies, our jobs, our social roles, and our creativity—is the struggle of every woman."[76]

The center launched, or became affiliated with, many programs and groups. The Boston Area Rape Crisis Center was an instance of "women helping women," but it also worked with police departments, mainly in Cambridge. "As part of the in-service training program of the police force," reads one document, "we have met weekly...with veteran officers...to "demythify" rape and to create an awareness as to the feelings of rape victims...[so] that the police officers will better understand all aspects of rape and be more sensitive in the investigation of rape cases."[77] Other projects included Self-Defense for Women, the Feminist Therapy Research Project ("writing a manual on women's experiences with traditional therapy"), a Women's

The building at 888 Memorial Drive, then owned by Harvard University, during the feminist takeover. The women occupied the building for nine days in March 1971, declaring it a women's center. *(Photograph by Marie T. Gamache, Women's Center, Cambridge)*

School, Transition House (a battered women's shelter), and the Tooth and Nail Collective, "working to improve the physical structure of the Center." Anyone who reads the weekly *Cambridge Chronicle* can see how busy the center continues to be.

The critique of the "bourgeois family"—together with beliefs about living communally, or at least cooperatively—brought about a wave of housing arrangements different from the single-family "American dream." In 1957 at the age of seventy, Florence Luscomb began living in cooperative houses, "a classic example of an elderly person living on a fixed income" as real estate prices were climbing. Her housemates were in their twenties and thirties, students or working people "interested, as she was, in cheap rent and left politics." For them it was an "experiment in communal living," for her a permanent arrangement.[78] One group that included Luscomb moved together from 10 Kirkland Road to 11 Russell Street; Luscomb also lived with ever-shifting groups at 29 Bowdoin, 37 Pleasant, and 64 Wendell streets.

"If you expect me to cook I must have a sink free of other people's dirty dishes. FL."[79] This note, found among her papers, evokes the benefits and frustrations of communal living: the ease of coming home to a hot meal (and congenial company) when it's someone else's turn to cook, the unevenness of the cooperative impulse. Steven Seidel, who lived with Luscomb on Pleasant Street when she was in her early eighties, remembers her as reliable and

Cambridge anti-apartheid activist Caroline Hunter, center, with Nelson and Winnie Mandela in the early 1990s. *(Photograph by Caroline Hunter)*

independent, up to date on current events, a source of wonder to her house-mates, and in demand as an anti–Vietnam War speaker.[80] In the 1970s she was the essential speaker about women's history, a living link between the first and second wave women's movements. Whatever one's views about women's liberation, it is clear that Luscomb, Bread & Roses, and the Women's Center have been part of a movement that has profoundly changed American society.

One woman, not a member of Bread & Roses, who joined in the occupation of 888 was just beginning to work toward profoundly changing another society: South Africa. Caroline Hunter, with a brand-new degree in chemistry (1968) from Xavier University in her native New Orleans, had been hired as a bench chemist by Polaroid, a company reputed to be concerned with social justice and good to minority employees. There she met her future husband, Ken Williams, who had started as a janitor but was soon, thanks to his skill, working as a photographer. One day in October 1970, she and Williams happened on a badge tacked to a bulletin board; it bore a Polaroid picture and had been issued by the South African Bureau of Mines—one of the infamous passes that all black South Africans had to carry. Polaroid's instant film made it feasible to "shoot" people quickly, and its cameras were easy to carry to remote areas.

The next weekend, Hunter and Williams distributed a flyer: "Polaroid Imprisons Black People in 60 Seconds." They launched the Polaroid Revolutionary Workers Movement (PRWM), were fired (Williams in January 1971, Hunter in March after her suspension in February), and testified to the UN Special Committee on Apartheid on February 3 and before the U.S. House Subcommittee on Africa on May 5. Meantime, Polaroid responded by asking the pair how they found out and by insisting that the passes were a small part of its business and that Polaroid was not in South Africa. The PRWM continued its active boycott until Polaroid left South Africa in 1977, and the divestment movement broadened to other companies and spread geographically, continuing until Nelson Mandela was released from prison in February 1990. Hunter and Williams found jobs at the Cambridge Public Library; after apartheid ended, she visited South Africa, finding enormous inequality between whites and blacks and, in the black townships, poverty, squalor, energy, and hope.[81]

Hunter is one among many Cambridge women whose activities have had an international impact. When Katharine Taylor retired from Shady Hill, she chaired the Unitarian Service Committee's child care project in Germany (1949–53) to promote services for children during that period of reconstruction, and she continued to work with international education agencies, such as the Fellowship in Israel for Arab-Jewish Youth.[82] Radcliffe's Ada Comstock helped found the International Federation of University Women and was vice chair of the Institute of Pacific Relations, an independent research agency with affiliates in Asia and Europe.[83] Gisela Warburg Wyzanski, of 39 Fayerweather Street, who herself was forced to leave her native Hamburg because of Nazi persecution, worked with Youth Aliyah during the 1930s to enable Jewish children to escape from Europe to Palestine. Olivia Abelson—of 5 Ashton Place, then 218 Hamilton Street—a math teacher originally from Philadelphia, was a mainstay of the antinuclear movement in Cambridge.

Another kind of international reach comes with immigration, which has contributed to Cambridge's vaunted diversity. The program for the Tercentenary banquet honoring Mayor Richard M. Russell on November 13, 1930, lists International Festival Committees by ethnicity: American, Afro-American, Franco-American, Greek, Irish, Italian, Jewish, Lithuanian, Polish, Scottish.[84]

One Lithuanian family is made faintly visible by a small group of documents that neighbors rescued from the trash when the second and last daughter died in 2000. Jenny and Andry Sawicz were themselves immigrants, married in 1930, had two daughters, Genevieve and Adele, and owned rental property at 92-94 Pine Street. In the 1940s and '50s, Genevieve worked variously for S. S. Kresge, the city's recreation department, Wolf & Smith Druggists, Gorin's department store, and the Edwin R. Sage Company.[85]

Of course most Cambridge women lived "ordinary" lives. Many worked in stores, as did Genevieve Sawicz, others at Draper Laboratories or NECCO or the Boston Woven Hose Company, in offices at Harvard, Lesley, or MIT, as dental assistants, nurses at Cambridge City or Mount Auburn hospital, in city offices or libraries, as waitresses at the Wursthaus or Honey Bee or Turtle Café, at home as dressmakers, at night cleaning offices, and so on. And many put in thousands of hours of volunteer time with organizations already mentioned, or at East End Settlement House or Margaret Fuller House, or at their churches. At Christ Church, for instance, in addition to managing the flowers, linens, silver, and brass for services, for many years the women held a Thursday Study and Work Day for lectures and discussion, sewing, knitting, church office work, and the like. In 1956–57 the Tuesday Sewing Group sent layettes, operating gowns, and other items the members had made to agencies from Alaska to Puerto Rico. Women still raise money for the church and for related causes, partly through the Thrift Shop, which began in 1968 when the Shady Hill Thrift Shop on Huron Avenue closed and its experienced workers were willing to help start the shop on Farwell Place. We know more about these women than those at some other churches because two volunteer women archivists, Erika Chadbourn and Louise Todd Ambler, have consolidated and organized the church's records.[86]

Nearly all, even the accomplished professional women, had absorbing domestic duties. Though Ada Comstock married only at the age of sixty-six, a week after leaving the Radcliffe presidency, the last three presidents were all mothers as well as academics. The three scientists mentioned above—Payne-Gaposchkin, Kistiakowsky, and Widnall—each raised two children. Pearl Wise, the politician, had motherly advice for her son David:

> Keep a daily record of outlays. Keep a monthly record of your heating bills.
>
> Have all estimates for work you and Enid may be contemplating put in writing.
>
> Do not do business with relatives of relatives.
>
> Because your house is small, [electric] fixtures should not "hang down."
>
> Paint bookcase and chests gray like the floor, but you can use bright red or bright blue on inside shelves.[87]

There is also a less pleasant side of domestic life. Transition House is one of several efforts to respond to domestic violence. Less dramatic but probably

Women workers at Boston Woven Hose Co. in Cambridge, 1912. Women and men apparently worked in separate departments and probably at separate tasks. *(From the records of Boston Woven Hose. Co., Cambridge Historical Society)*

more common are Cambridge's many current divorcées. Abbie Hunt was also divorced—in 1906. There is no diary for 1901–06, but there are hints of trouble in the summer of 1900, when Freeman Hunt goes to Petersham—or does he? Then, on March 29, 1907: "I got my paper from the court...'the decree absolute' today & so my married life is ended." We get a glimpse of her feelings only obliquely:

3 March 1907: Mrs. Tobey called this P.M. She has lost her youngest sister & she told us that this sister had undergone the same terrible experience which I have.

7 March: Beth came in the evening & read us some of <u>Frank Elwell's letters to Mina</u>. (She is suing for a <u>separation</u> & he wants a <u>divorce</u>), he is a horrid man.

Someone, perhaps a relative, has noted at the end of the 1914–18 diary that a "girlhood friend...informed Abbie of some of Freeman's obvious 'adultery.' But Abby [sic] in getting divorce charged drunkenness, not adultery." Whether this was to protect his reputation or her own we don't know. We do know that when, in 1929, Freeman's mental state deteriorated after he was "knocked down by an auto," Abbie was solicitous and even contributed ten dollars a month for his keep in a mental hospital. And from the others she mentions, we gather that divorce was not quite as rare at the time as some like to think.

Perhaps what has changed most in matters pertaining to sex is not reality but perception and candor. On July 17, 1918, Hunt writes that her daughter Edith, married and living in Albany, "has been having a dreadful time, her maid was taken ill & the Dr. found she had Gonorrhea (the horrid creature) and poor E. has had the house to clean & disinfect and do the work until she can get another maid." The word *gonorrhea* is underlined twice. Hunt clearly finds a poor woman infected by a lover (or perhaps a rapist) as blameworthy—"horrid"—as a man who wants to dump his wife. Perhaps it isn't a fair comparison, but in 1975 Katharine Taylor, a "spinster" then almost 87, wrote to a younger woman:

I can well understand your plight, for several young women friends...are going through something very similar. The men they would like to live with are not free, so they are together intimately when feasible, and one such couple have been waiting several years until the man's children are older and until he can work things out with his wife without too much damage.... Somehow our society seems to be becoming more flexible and freer about such relationships, outside of marriage "till death do us part." I think it is all to the good.[88]

Change is always a mixed bag, and one can both agree and disagree with Katharine Livermore, who in 1957 wrote a rueful poem for the forty-fifth reunion of the Berkeley Street School Association. She compares—then and now—clothing, household duties, education, and technology and concludes:

Schools and the world, since our young day
Are changed indeed, and I must say
I liked the times much better then.
I wish we had them back again.[89]

But if we had them back again, we would not have Susan Hockfield as president of MIT, Margaret Marshall as Massachusetts chief justice and former university counsel at Harvard, Alice Wolf as former mayor and current state representative, and many other women in prominent positions; nor a Women's Commission to look out for women's interests; nor women on the police force, fighting fires, and on construction sites; nor young women assuming that that is how things are, unaware of what it took to get here.

Cambridge has changed, too. In 1955 the city was losing population, and Pearl Wise worried over it: "City tactically well run," she wrote. "What is lacking is civic pride, joy of living in Cambridge.... People need to be excited and want to stay here."[90] Now nearly everyone wants to stay here. Surely we owe that in large part to the many women mentioned here and the many more who helped make Cambridge an exciting place to live.[91]

ENDNOTES

1. Dean Robert J. Birgeneau in his introductory comments to "A Study on the Status of Women Faculty in Science at MIT," *MIT Faculty Newsletter* 11, no. 4 (March 1999).

2. The 1988 video in which King was speaking was about the Arthur and Elizabeth Schlesinger Library on the History of Women in America at what was then Radcliffe College and is now the Radcliffe Institute. King was director from 1973 until her untimely death in 1994.

3. Interview on WHN, March 19, 1974. Florence Luscomb papers, Schlesinger Library, MC 394, no. 1.

4. Barbara Miller Solomon, *In the Company of Educated Women: A History of Women and Higher Education in America* (New Haven, Conn.: Yale University Press, 1985), 111.

5. Class Day, Berkeley Street School, May Thirty-First 1912, 13–14. Records of Berkeley Street School Association, Schlesinger Library, MC 238, no. 5. The British women used the term *suffragette*, which was generally pejorative here, where *suffragist* was the preferred term.

6. The elusive adjective looks most like *spicy*, which is unlikely, and may have been meant to be *inspiring*, with the first two letters omitted. All Abbie Brooks Hunt references are to Parmenter-Hunt Diaries, Cambridge Historical Society.

7. Of four referenda held in various states that year, the percentage of *ayes* was lowest in Massachusetts (35.5 percent), which one author ascribes to its being the "origin and home of the anti-suffrage movement" and to the influence of some "leading [Catholic] clerics." Eleanor Flexner, *Century of Struggle: The Woman's Rights Movement in the United States* (Cambridge, Mass.: Harvard University Press, 1959), 270–71

8. Anne Firor Scott, *Natural Allies: Women's Associations in American History* (University of Illinois Press, 1991), 185–89. Scott derived the headings and the specific topics under them from Mary Ritter Beard's *Women's Work in the Municipalities* (1915).

9. Papers of Helen Jackson (Cabot) Almy, Schlesinger Library, A-84, no. 1.

10. Ibid., no. 2.

11. Ibid., no. 6. The full title was Special Commission to Investigate and Report on the Subject of Playgrounds for the City of Cambridge; Almy was to be "the member appointed by the mayor."

12. Barbara Ackermann, *You the Mayor? The Education of a City Politician* (copyright Auburn House Publishing Co., 1989), xii. Quotation reproduced with permission of Greenwood Publishing Group, Westport, Conn.

13. Records of the Mothers' Discussion Club, Schlesinger Library, B-13, no. 3. Miss Alcott would probably have agreed that much of her work was too sentimental.

14. Household Record of Domestic Servants, 1889–1915, in Charles Rockwell Lanman papers,

Harvard University Archives, HUG4510.36. Passages quoted courtesy of Harvard University Archives and Sally Cushman Lewis, granddaughter of Charles R. Lanman. Ms. Lewis told the author in a phone conversation on November 11, 2004, that Professor Lanman was kind but short-tempered and was known to yell at the servants, thus perhaps accounting for some of the early departures. Similar but briefer and more cryptic notes appear in a notebook of Sarah W. Dana for 1871: Dana family papers, Schlesinger Library, A-85, v. 38.

15. Parmenter-Hunt Diaries, Cambridge Historical Society.

16. Records of the Cambridge Home Information Center, Schlesinger Library, MC 276.

17. Records of the Cambridge Plant and Garden Club are at the Schlesinger Library. Information included here is from the finding aid.

18. Mary I. de Gozzaldi papers, Cambridge Historical Society, folder 19.

19. All quotes from proceedings of the Mothers' Discussion Club are from the club's records in the Schlesinger Library, B-13, no. 3.

20. Records of the Berkeley Street School Association, Schlesinger Library, MC 238, no. 1.

21. Ibid., no. 3.

22. Edith Lesley in Carole Brandon, "An Investigation of the History of Lesley College: A Work in Progress," unpublished paper for course HED 630, Fall 2000, p. 4. Thanks to Ms. Brandon for the use of her unpublished compilation of Lesley history.

23. Ibid., 5-6.

24. Papers of Katharine Taylor (unprocessed), Schlesinger Library, no. 34. The letter, November 17, 1964, is a typed carbon copy to Taylor from A.M., probably Alva Morrison.

25. Ibid., no. 39.

26. For a more detailed account of Radcliffe's complicated birth and difficult history, see Sally Schwager, "Taking Up the Challenge: The Origins of Radcliffe," in Yards and Gates: Gender in the History of Harvard and Radcliffe (New York: Palgrave Macmillan, 2004), 87–108.

27. For a good brief biography of Comstock and a list of additional sources, see the entry by Barbara Miller Solomon in Notable American Women: The Modern Period, eds. Barbara Sicherman and Carol Hurd Green (Cambridge, Mass.: Harvard University Press, 1980), 157–59. The Harvard-Radcliffe Agreement is summarized in Radcliffe Quarterly 27:3, Aug. 1943, 26. See also the following in Yards and Gates: "The Changing 'Harvard Student': Ethnicity, Race, and Gender," by Marcia Synott, 195–207, especially 198–99, and Ruth Hubbard, "Memories of Life at Radcliffe," 229–32.

28. Cecilia Payne-Gaposchkin, An Autobiography and Other Recollections, 2nd ed. (Cambridge, Eng.: Cambridge University Press, 1996), viii (in Introduction by Virginia Trimble), 226–27.

29. Records of the Committee on the Status of Women at Harvard, Schlesinger Library, MC 172, no. 1.

30. Ibid., no. 48.

31. For source ("A Study on the Status of Women..."), see note 1.

32. For a brief biography, see the essay by Janet Wilson James in Notable American Women: A Biographical Dictionary, ed. Edward T. James, et al. (Cambridge, Mass.: Harvard University Press, 1971), vol. III, 143-46.

33. See the entry by James Reed in Notable American Women: The Modern Period, 440–42.

34. Information from Who's Who in America, 2003-04.

35. For quotes and a much more detailed account, see the excellent essay "Fair Harvard? Labor, Law, and Gender in the Harvard Scrubwomen Case," by Linzy Brekke, in Yards and Gates, 159–72.

36. "Five Weeks of Jury Duty" (typescript), January 30, 1952, in Agnes Goldman Sanborn papers (unprocessed), Schlesinger Library, no. 46. She wrote at the behest of Elizabeth Borden

of the Women's Archives (forerunner of the Schlesinger Library), whose letter of November 19, 1951, is also present.

37. Agnes Goldman Sanborn papers, Schlesinger Library, especially nos. 42–46.

38. The dirndl consists of a sleeveless bodice, usually black or navy, fastened with buttons or a drawstring and attached to a gathered skirt, often of a print fabric. An apron may be added. A white peasant blouse with short, puffy sleeves completes the outfit.

39. See various histories in Records of the Window Shop, Schlesinger Library, MC 427, nos. 1, 5, and 6, and in no. 18 the history by Ilse Fang in *Germans in Boston* (Goethe Society of New England, 1981).

40. Upon dissolution it donated its assets to the Boston Foundation, Northeastern University, and Radcliffe College.

41. League Items 15:9, June 1942, in Pearl K. Wise papers (unprocessed), Schlesinger Library, no. 39.

42. Minutes of 1943 annual meeting in Records of the League of Women Voters of Cambridge, Schlesinger Library, MC 264, no. 19v.

43. Elizabeth Bancroft Schlesinger papers (unprocessed), Schlesinger Library, no. 8.

44. Ibid., no. 2.

45. Letter to the Editor of *The Boston Herald*, March 18, 1942, and other items in ibid., no. 9.

46. Letter from a U.S. senator (signature illegible) to Arthur Schlesinger Jr., in ibid., no. 6b.

47. One of them, Florence Lee Whitman, was elected to the city council in 1925 as one of four at-large councilors, along with eleven ward representatives. She had already served two terms on the school committee (1915–16, 1924–25), school suffrage having been extended to women in the 1870s in recognition of their presumed (and often actual) special concern for children. Information about Whitman supplied by Glenn Koocher.

48. Ackermann, *You the Mayor?*, xi.

49. E-mail message from Abigail Simons to Eva Moseley, 1996. Wise was a candidate of the Cambridge Civic Association but did not always follow the CCA line.

50. Papers of Pearl Katz Wise (unprocessed), Schlesinger Library, nos. 86, 88.

51. Letter from PKW to Enricus Everetze (no date), in ibid., no. 85. These apartments, now condominiums, are among the most expensive in Cambridge.

52. Typescript letter "Written for this occasion by Miss Julia H. Smith," (no date, 1963?), in ibid., no. 90.

53. Unpublished memoir, 1971, Schlesinger Library, A/S651. See especially 38, 61–64, 69.

54. Here, as elsewhere, Hunt's thoughts and feelings tend to be so conventional that one can't be sure what she really believed, and many entries are quite opaque concerning her response to events.

55. Records of the Young Women's Christian Association of Cambridge (unprocessed), Schlesinger Library, no. 139.

56. 1972 annual report, in ibid., no. 134.

57. 1891 leaflet, in ibid., no. 35.

58. See "The YWCA in Cambridge" by Frances Cooper-Marshal Donovan, in *Proceedings of the Cambridge Historical Society* 36: 41–51 (1957).

59. *Your Y News*, May 1964, in YWCA of Cambridge records, Schlesinger Library, 36.

60. Muller history, p. 7, in Records of the Window Shop, Schlesinger Library, MC 427, no. 6.

61. "A Memorial Service for Agnes Goldman Sanborn, 1887–1984, February 12, 1984, Library, Museum of Fine Arts, Boston, Mass.," in Sanborn papers, Schlesinger Library, no. 43.

62. Typescript cc. of letter from EBS to Mrs. Benson, July 15, 1964, in papers of Elizabeth B. Schlesinger, Schlesinger Library, no. 14.

63. Ibid., no. 15.

64. "Education—Its Advantages to Our Group," (no date, 1950s?), 4, in papers of Ozeline Wise and Satyra Bennett (unprocessed), Schlesinger Library, no. 17.

65. Ibid., no. 28. Biographical information from Wise obituary in no. 33 and for Bennett, no. 18, 26, 27.

66. See, for instance, David J. Garrow, *Liberty and Sexuality: The Right to Privacy and the Making of Roe v. Wade* (New York: Macmillan, 1994), 91, 101, 118, 269.

67. Information from WCHC publications in manuscript department control file, Schlesinger Library.

68. Papers of Annie Popkin (unprocessed), Schlesinger Library, no. 30.

69. Ibid., no. 39.

70. "A Boston Women's Group," by Marya Levenson, Judy Ullman, Marcia Butman, Nancy Hawley (no date), in ibid., no. 5.

71. Statement presented to WBCN and press release, in ibid., no. 30. The recollections of one participant, Rochelle Ruthchild, differ somewhat from what these records tell us: "I remember driving in my 1969 Saab and hearing Charles Laquidara on WBCN announcing that Project Place needed volunteers and 'if you're a chick and can type,' they needed us. I was outraged, and I remember mentioning it at a Bread and Roses meeting. A group of us from Bread and Roses planned the action against WBCN, including getting the baby chicks. When we came in to their office, they were stupefied and agreed to give us one hour of airtime.... Somewhere in the course of this, I interviewed Laquidara.... He said that women's voices were too high for radio, among other stupid things...." E-mail message to Eva Moseley, June 18, 2004.

72. Papers of Rochelle Ruthchild (unprocessed), Schlesinger Library, no. 11.

73. Flyer in ibid., no. 12.

74. The MDC was the Metropolitan District Commission, which administered parks and roads, including Memorial Drive in Cambridge. Its successor agency is the Department of Conservation and Recreation.

75. Thanks to participants Nancy Falk, Tess Ewing, and Rochelle Ruthchild for details of the occupation. Ewing has documents about it and Bread & Roses that are eventually to go to the Schlesinger Library. Ruthchild (letter to Eva Moseley, December 27, 2004) is the source of the information about the funds, for which Sue Lyman never took credit publicly.

76. Ruthchild papers, Schlesinger Library, no. 14.

77. Boston Area Rape Crisis Center, vol. 1, April [1975], in ibid., no. 22.

78. Sharon Hartman Strom, *Political Woman: Florence Luscomb and the Legacy of Radical Reform* (Philadelphia: Temple University Press, 2001), 12–13, 260.

79. Florence Luscomb papers, Schlesinger Library, MC 394. Some addresses listed in no. 53; note re: dishes in no. 59. Wendell Street address in Strom, *Political Woman*, 7.

80. Interview by Eva Moseley, May 21, 2004.

81. Williams died in 1998; Hunter is an assistant principal at Cambridge Rindge and Latin School. Information from interview by Eva Moseley, May 19, 2004, and from papers in Hunter's possession, eventually to go to the Schlesinger Library.

82. Katharine Taylor papers, Schlesinger Library, no. 1.

83. Entry in *Notable American Women: The Modern Period*.

84. Program in papers of O. Wise and S. Bennett, Schlesinger Library, no. 10.

85. See Sawicz family papers, Cambridge Historical Commission. The neighbors who rescued

the papers believed that many more had been lost.

86. Information from records of women's groups in Christ Church Archives.

87. Typescript, September 12, 1972, in Pearl Wise papers, Schlesinger Library, no. 14.

88. From a letter (typescript, cc.) of April 7, 1975, in Katharine Taylor papers, Schlesinger Library, no. 19.

89. Berkeley Street School Association records, Schlesinger Library, MC 238, no. 27.

90. Notes in Pearl Wise papers, Schlesinger Library, no. 112.

91. I have included no doctors, lawyers, social workers, artists, or tenant activists; omitted Italians, Portuguese, Hispanics, Chinese, other Asians, and other important ethnic groups, important families with notable women such as the Cannons, and individual famous women such as Julia Child, Joyce Chen, and May Sarton (who appears in several manuscipt collections cited here: Luscomb, Sanborn, Taylor). There is much more to say about women in the history of Cambridge!

The Never-Boring Political History of Cambridge in the 20ᵗʰ Century[1]

GLENN KOOCHER

SEVERAL CONSISTENT themes flow through the complex but never boring political history of Cambridge during the twentieth century. As the face of the city evolved dynamically and defied predictability, and as commerce diversified to match the changing economy, the city's politics exhibited both familiar and novel qualities.

In the 1900s Cambridge was both a melting pot and a stew. Old Yankees clashed with waves of immigrants from Eastern Europe, Canada, the Pacific Basin, and Central and South America, and with migrating southern African Americans, for whatever benefits the political system had to offer. In the 1990s the city's census tracts listed the wealthiest and most economically disadvantaged populations within walking distance of each other. By 2006 Cambridge public schools included students from more than seventy nations. The voting lists were almost as diverse.

As immigrants earned the rights of citizenship, fought for political strength, and influenced the course of municipal affairs, others who chose the city as a place to study, work, and live also wove their way into positions of power and influence. In fact, a dominant political theme of the 1900s was the struggle to win and keep a share of political power and all it provided: patronage, social services, education, regulation of the economy, control of

A last hurrah: former Mayor Al Vellucci, left, shares a laugh with incoming Harvard President Neil Rudenstein at the 1991 Harvard Yard picnic. It was Rudenstein's second day on the job and Vellucci was waging his final city council campaign. *(The Cambridge Chronicle)*

the housing stock and the determination of policy. Invoked at almost every turn were ethnic, religious, and class politics. Invariably, political campaigns arose around two factions: self-styled "good government" reformers from "Avon Hill and Brattle Street" versus populist challengers under various banners who claimed a closer connection to the people.

The "us against them" concept played out well through most of the 1900s; central issues included the licensing of alcoholic beverages ("No-License" had been the law since 1886), political patronage, urban renewal and development, administration of the schools, and—the dominant theme of twenty-five of the last thirty-five years—rent control.

No less important was the presence of two of the world's great universities. Founded in Cambridge in 1636, Harvard was the bastion of Yankee power and elitism and a constantly expanding institution in the geographic center of the city. The Massachusetts Institute of Technology, which moved to the city from Boston starting in 1915, became an international center of science, technology, and urban planning. Over the years, they coexisted in a state ranging from selectively harmonious to adversarial to a more common détente. They also served as frequent and convenient political targets in the community at the same time as they attracted people and ideas that would affect the city's political life and distinguish Cambridge from its neighbors. If the Parliamentarian Edmund Burke was correct in noting that the individual may be foolish but the species wise, his heirs might point to Cambridge's civic history to prove his point.

The Charter of 1911

The government that had developed after the city's incorporation evolved by the turn of the twentieth century into a bicameral system with a mayor, a twenty-one-member common council, and a board of alderman. It was a partisan, party-driven system in which political patronage vied with the emerging concept of "good government." A school committee of fifteen, no less divided, supervised the superintendent of schools and oversaw an educational system that assumed as one of its tasks the transformation of new immigrant and first-generation American children into citizens. Charges of political favoritism, patronage, and corruption, all exacerbated by the rhetoric of the times, might seem tame by today's standards, but the amount of government mismanagement was sufficient to keep a strong and active organized "reform" movement in place.

As chair of the Cambridge Charter Association, Lewis Jerome Johnson, a Harvard professor, proposed a major change in the framework of the local government that had been in place since 1891. Distressed by budgetary mismanagement, construction overruns, patronage, and a structurally unsound framework, he led the campaign to put before the voters a "commission" form of government to focus on the right work and to "get the right men in office." While the initiative was defeated on November 7, 1911, the proposal introduced four significant changes whose time had not yet come:

- nonpartisanship, by removing party labels from local races
- the consolidation and compacting of legislative and administrative authority
- the right of initiative, referendum, and recall
- "preferential voting," the forerunner of the proportional representation (PR) form of government that has made Cambridge unique among twenty-first-century American cities, a system so new that it put fear into the hearts of political power brokers

Johnson's proposal replaced the common council and board of alderman with a five-member city council acting as an administrative commission. The plan included a mayor, who would chair the city council and supervise the administration. Rounding out the quintet of commissioner-councilors were supervisors of finance, public works, public property, and health. The school committee was reduced to five members. The whole concept was modeled on successful practices in Houston, Dallas, Des Moines, and Haverhill, Massachusetts.

Local initiatives by citizens, referenda on legislative matters, and the right to recall elected officials by a petition of 25 percent of the voters were instruments of genuine reform. But the proposal also represented a second major goal: to weaken the political bosses, who had long been a target of reformers.

Supporters of the 1911 reforms cited the endorsements of the former Republican president Theodore Roosevelt, the Democratic New Jersey governor Woodrow Wilson, and Wisconsin's Progressive "Fighting Bob" La Follette to show how the plan posed no threat to anyone. Still, the local Democratic power structure and entrenched political interests waged a bitter campaign to defeat the plan, 6,073 to 5,272—although the principles behind the failed proposal remained very much alive to surface another day.

Left for future reform efforts was the concept of preferential voting, an early version of which was used at the time in Boulder, Colorado. Voters there ranked candidates in numerical order to allow for the transfer of votes from second choice to first choice, to eliminate primary elections and empower the true majority. Unlike the PR plan of 1941—the plan in use today—the 1911 proposal was restricted to first, second, and "other" choices, but it incorporated, for the first time, the concept of a single, transferable ballot.

The Campaign of 1915

Mindful of the strong base of support to eliminate patronage and establish good government, Democratic forces grasped another of the four charter options (Plans A, B, C, and D) offered to cities by the legislature in 1915. If the failed commission model of 1911 represented one alternative, a strong mayor and city council of fifteen was available as Plan B—and was put before Cambridge voters that November.

To ensure adequate representation of both the majority and minority, the city council included eleven members elected biennially from each ward and four more members at large. A mayor, elected separately, chaired the school committee, now a seven-member body elected at large in staggered three-year terms. Critics of the earlier format had argued that reducing a government of thirty-six to one of five would reduce opportunities for up-and-coming public-spirited candidates, forcing them to select the school committee as their only other option. However, advocates of a fifteen-member single legislative body, the city council, saw it as a compromise over a cumbersome bicameral system.

Not nearly as radical as Johnson's 1911 plan, Plan B called for nonpartisan races and was enough of a reform to rally the Citizens Municipal League (CML) to action against the rival "Democratic Citizen Ticket." Joining the league in support of the 1915 proposal was the Republican-dominated Public School Association (PSA), the "good government" advocate for education. The PSA called for an end to a "dictatorial" majority on the school committee and opposed its political patronage. It called for innovations like open bidding for purchasing and creating an administrative structure to promote professional leadership by the new superintendent of schools, M. E. Fitzgerald, who had recently succeeded the deposed Frank Parlin.

The Nineteenth Amendment had not yet brought universal suffrage, but women had both voted in school committee elections and served for many years. In fact, women had been represented on the board as early as 1880. Just before the 1915 election, the Equal Suffrage Club sued to extend voting rights for women to the mayoral race under the 1915 charter, arguing unsuccessfully that the chief executive was to be the chair of the school committee—a body for whom women could vote. Among the strongest opponents of women suffrage were the liquor dealers, whose products were available only from druggists for "medicinal purposes," for women were viewed as predisposed to Prohibition. Cambridge would remain, on the surface, "dry" until the end of Prohibition.

On November 2, 1915, the Charter of 1891 yielded to the new Plan B government. The CML candidate for mayor, Wendell D. Rockwood, assumed office, and a full slate of PSA-endorsed candidates took over the school committee. Another milestone occurred in 1925 when Florence Lee Whitman, a veteran of the school committee, was elected as an at-large member to become the first woman to sit on the city council.

For the next two decades, Cambridge politics focused again on political patronage as the dominant issue. The popular, colorful mayor, Edward J. Quinn, provided stability from 1918 through 1929. He was succeeded by Richard M. Russell, the scion of a distinguished family of progressive political leadership. Russell's grandfather had held public office, and his father, William E. Russell, had served as a youthful mayor in the 1880s before becoming the state's youngest and first Democratic governor. He managed local affairs efficiently, but the Depression hit the city hard, and people turned to their political leaders for jobs.

It was during this period that two men, who would become prominent figures in American public life, emerged from different neighborhoods with perspectives that typified the two ends of the Cambridge political spectrum. A Pulitzer Prize–winning historian and chronicler of the Kennedy administration, Arthur Schlesinger Jr. spent his youth in Cambridge and attended the

Peabody elementary school and, for a time, Cambridge High and Latin. The son of a Harvard professor, he counted many Irish classmates among his chums but described their political patrons as people who "regard[ed] the schools as repositories for ill-qualified friends and relatives" (among them was his social studies teacher, who explained that residents of Albania were known as Albinos, complete with white hair and complexions). Schlesinger's mother regularly observed "exasperating" school committee meetings and served on the library board. When she was unceremoniously replaced in 1939, she called the board "a nice, quiet little pond where any politician can cast his line and pull out a job for someone."

Across town, Schlesinger's contemporary Thomas P. O'Neill Jr., the son of a turn-of-the-century common councilor and patronage-dispensing super-intendent of sewers, was beginning a political career in the state legislature. In 1945, three years before he became the first Democratic Speaker of the Massachusetts House of Representatives, O'Neill was pressured by his parish priest to run for and serve a two-year term on the school committee—and, more specifically, to deliver jobs for his neighbors. That both Schlesinger and O'Neill earned venerable status among the nation's liberal establishment—the former as a presidential adviser and historian, the latter as Speaker of the U.S. House of Representatives—demonstrates the dichotomy and uniqueness of the Cambridge political experience: one person's patronage is another's impropriety.

In 1936 the popular North Cambridge druggist John D. Lynch, a former member of the school committee and city council, assumed the mayor's chair. He had built his base on customer and constituent service, and it did not hurt that he was an officer of the neighborhood bank in these difficult economic times. He was, however, unseated by John W. Lyons in a bitter 1937 race. In the meantime, property taxes had risen substantially and charges of corruption in government characterized the tone of local elections.

THE CAMPAIGN FOR PLAN E

Out of this period emerged a reinvigorated campaign for reform. The Cambridge Industrial Association had organized a special committee on tax-ation as early as 1934, citing as an example of mismanagement the fact that the city had five blacksmiths but no horses. In April 1936, under the leader-ship of the prominent businessman Stoughton Bell—and with his close asso-ciates Eliot Spalding (future editor of the *Cambridge Chronicle*), Professor Johnson, and Johnson's son, Chandler—the Cambridge Taxpayers Associa-tion was organized. Its goal was the reduction of property taxes, efficient gov-ernment, and ultimately the structural reform of local government. Joining them was the League of Women Voters, an active and influential political group. The Lyons administration gave them plenty to use as ammunition in the battle for change.

Lawmakers had offered municipalities the option of a city manager form of government in Plan D, but with the support of the legislature, reformers introduced an option known as Plan E in 1937. Unlike the commission format and the strong mayor-council structure, Plan E featured a city manager like Plan D, but most importantly it added proportional representation, a major improvement to the preferential voting plan that Johnson had proposed in 1911. This revision—a system of voting based on the Hare System developed in England in the 1830s—used a single transferable vote. It had been introduced in America thirty years earlier and was very popular in many Ohio cities.

The strengths of the Plan E charter over Plan B were fourfold. First, a professional city manager, hired at the pleasure of a nine-member city council, would hold strong administrative authority, including autonomy over most personnel appointments and wage and benefits administration, to reduce patronage and improve the efficiency of government. In theory, politics would be taken out of city affairs (as another Cantabrigian of an earlier period, William James, might have said, "a fine theory, brutalized by a vicious set of facts"). In fact, the charter rendered illegal any attempt by a city councilor to influence personnel or to interfere with the city administration—an ominous provision, but one that no judge would enforce in the next sixty-five years. However, some compromises found their way into the charter to ameliorate potentially fatal opposition; to secure legislative support for the creation of the Plan E Charter, lobbyists for police and fire department personnel retained for the city council the right to set their compensation. Similar restrictions did not apply to the school committee, which kept the power to approve or reject personnel recommendations, policy, and administrative action until the 1993 Education Reform Act gave to the superintendent of schools the administrative and personnel powers similar to those of the city manager.

Second, the city council and six school committee members would be elected at large. The city council would then choose from among themselves a mayor, to act as ceremonial head of the city with limited other powers. The mayor would chair both the council and school committee.

Third, voters would elect the council and school committee using PR. Complex enough to require three weeks to count the votes cast in 1941, the system, still in use, requires voters to list candidates numerically in order of preference. By eliminating weaker candidates and transferring their votes to the next highest choice on the ballot, eventually all nine council and six school committee candidates are elected. The essence of the system was determining a "quota" of votes to serve as the threshold of election and which only nine councilors and six committee members could reach mathematically. Once candidates reached that quota, they were declared elected and received no more transferred ballots. Thus, a discrete political faction that made up a large enough bloc of voters could channel its votes from its weakest to its strongest candidate and assure election. This new system eliminated the need for a primary election.

Finally, by creating a way for residents to vote for all other candidates without compromising their special interests, Plan E created within the city a "single-member district." Candidates would be encouraged to campaign city-wide and urge voters to select them with a first choice or number-one vote; the 1 on bumper stickers and literature became the signature of a Cambridge candidate. However, candidates would not want to alienate other candidates, lest they miss the opportunity to capture the transfer votes later in the balloting process—thus making elections less bitter. In fact, an examination of campaign literature from the 1950s through the present shows far greater diplomacy and focus on issues than what voters received through the end of the Depression.

There were two campaigns for Plan E. The first, fought in 1938, was unsuccessful, but the narrow, 1,300-vote margin was encouraging enough for the Cambridge Taxpayers Association to revive the Committee for Plan E in 1940. James M. Landis, dean of the Harvard Law School and a member of the Roosevelt "Brain Trust," led the committee in name while a devoted core of hard-working reformers, many recruited from the League of Women Voters, directed the effort.

The campaigns were bitter, with inflammatory charges and counter-charges at one level. Voters could, however, find the debate stimulating, with political literature and editorials sufficiently detailed to resemble a local version of *The Federalist Papers*. Supporters pointed to the mismanagement by Mayor Lyons, the trading of scores of jobs, politics in the schools, and poor municipal services. They appealed to underrepresented factions that had been shut out of influence because their citywide base had been overwhelmed by majorities in neighborhoods under the ward system. Critics, on the other hand, were quick to point out that the likes of Adolf Hitler had used PR to advantage in his rise to power and that fascists and communists supported the system.

The November 5, 1940, elections were especially important for Cambridge voters. Franklin D. Roosevelt was on the ballot, seeking a third term. Congressman Robert Luce, a Waltham Republican, fought for his political life against Cambridge's Thomas Eliot, the son of a Harvard president, author of key parts of the Social Security Act, and another member of FDR's brain trust. If Luce's vaguely camouflaged prejudice wasn't enough to exacerbate the undercurrent of ethnic warfare (such as advertisements that included Eliot among the New Deal's "intellectual punks" and citing Thomas Corcoran and Benjamin Cohen as his associates in campaign literature),[2] the opponents of Plan E also played to class distinctions in their own campaigns.

Elected officials who might otherwise have attacked Plan E and proportional representation more aggressively were cautious after initial canvassing revealed a growing base of support for reform. Moreover, as war enveloped Europe, voters worried increasingly about civil defense.

Voters may have had other things on their minds as well, such as the state races for governor and attorney general as well as the seven referenda on the ballot. Plan E was skillfully sandwiched in between three measures to keep liquor licensing, which had been restored with the Twenty-First Amendment, and three questions on lotteries and funding for Old Age Assistance. If booze was offensive to old guard Republicans, licensing, lotteries, and old-age benefits were attractive enough to Democrats to keep some voters in a "yes" frame of mind.

At the same time, Mayor John Lyons was rumored to be the target of investigations for bribery in connection with several major construction projects. A grand jury indictment was anticipated but not ready at the time of the election, though it was a significant factor nevertheless. His conviction, resignation as mayor, and subsequent imprisonment would come after the election.

With a solid base of support in Republican precincts and enough strength in neighborhoods where high property taxes, political corruption, and a sense of having been left out trumped political patronage, voters turned the defeat of 1938 into a significant 59–41 percent margin of victory. They also turned Luce out of Congress. But so complex was the new PR system that 14 percent of all voters left their ballots blank on the question. In the next twenty years, opponents of PR would appeal to voters—unsuccessfully—four times (1953, 1957, 1961, and 1965) to repeal the system.

THE ERA OF PLAN E GOVERNMENT

Plan E changed the politics of Cambridge significantly, starting with campaigning. Under PR, slate balloting was critical. Voters needed to be reminded of how best to direct their votes to candidates who shared, for example, their political views, racial or ethnic heritage, or neighborhood. They also needed to be educated on how to vote.

None of the potential candidates knew how to judge their own strength or how transfers might play a role. In 1941 eighty-three candidates ran for city council and twenty-eight for school committee.

The Committee for Plan E quickly transformed itself into two parts after the 1943 elections. The Cambridge Research Association became a tax-exempt institution, to provide the studies necessary to analyze the implementation of a strong and efficient municipality. The Cambridge Civic Association (CCA), on the other hand, became the political arm in 1945. Dominated by the new, nonpartisan coalition forces of progressive Democrats and old guard Republicans, the CCA waged regular, highly organized campaigns for the city council and school committee, mastering the art of slate voting. Over the years, the CCA's endorsement became a brand of sorts, a label that many voters trusted to guide them.

Unlike the CCA factions, other political interests remained more focused on the candidate. It was city councilor Michael Neville who appears to have been the first to use the word *independents* to define those not associated with the CCA. The label stuck. In election after election, the CCA battled Independents for majorities. For decades, neither side captured more than a single-member majority at any election.

The CCA focus remained on efficient, good government without political patronage, well-planned economic development, good schools, and unity in the election of a mayor in order to tip the balance of power on the school committee. Independents interpreted these same goals differently and found unity harder to achieve. Because they were rarely organized coherently at election time, no faction dominated the other, but many ad hoc coalitions were formed over the years to support mayors, city managers, or public policies.

Electing the mayor was particularly critical because, under an opinion of the city solicitor in effect early in the 1940s, only emergency business could be conducted without a duly elected mayor in the chair of the city council and school committee. In 1946, John D. Lynch became the only person to serve as a strong mayor under one charter and a ceremonial mayor under the other with his victory on the 309th ballot. Two years later, Cambridge received national attention when it took four months, thirty-five sessions, and 1,321 ballots to elect Michael Neville as mayor. It was less traumatic in 1970, when Alfred E. Vellucci had to wait until March 30 to win the first of his four mayoral terms. Moreover, by the early 1970s, a new city solicitor had opined that, in the absence of a mayor, the city council could act with the senior member presiding. In 1985 another city solicitor gave the vice chair of the city council—sometimes referred to as "the vice mayor"—the same power, and Francis Duehay took a step unprecedented in any Plan E city before or since when he claimed the right to chair the school committee after the death of Mayor Leonard J. Russell.

The first Plan E city council elected John H. Corcoran as its mayor and quickly appointed John B. Atkinson as city manager. Atkinson was an industrialist whose base was the shoe industry, but he put his administration together and proceeded to control taxes and improve services. He was, however, fiscally conservative—too conservative, for example, to address Cambridge's desperate need for new schools (the average age of its twenty elementary schools was fifty years) and a more solid infrastructure. Moreover, he battled with the city council and school committee over the salaries of municipal workers. A court suit that upheld teachers' raises despite Atkinson's objections cost thousands of dollars to resolve.

In 1952 Atkinson was unceremoniously replaced without notice by John Curry, principal of the Roberts School (now Fletcher-Maynard Academy). Curry, whose appointment had been planned by an ad hoc coalition, oversaw both a major school construction program and the first phases of urban development.

The Politics of Us vs. Them and the Events of 1965–1972

CCA and Independent relationships hovered between states of collaboration and détente, with elections and the occasional highly partisan crisis emerging to remind voters that political differences were at play. A few of these crises explain why each side always kept a close eye on the other.

One such disruption took place in December 1952 when the school committee celebrated the holiday season by convening in executive session and forcing from the compliant superintendent, John Tobin, a series of personnel appointments that were blatantly patronage-ridden. So burdened with family members and friends was the roster of beneficiaries that the *Cambridge Chronicle's* Eliot Spalding labeled it "Family Night."

Tobin was no stranger to patronage, nor would he be the first superintendent of schools to command the attention of political activists. His father, Daniel J. Tobin, had headed the International Brotherhood of Teamsters and served as an advisor to President Roosevelt. His son's promotion to the superintendency in January 1945 was, in part, achieved by calls to school committee members directly from the White House. But a 1947 study by a twenty-three-member blue-ribbon team of experts, headed by Alfred D. Simpson of the Harvard Graduate School of Education, produced a scathing assessment of the Cambridge Public Schools, and Tobin became a target of educational reformers.

The patronage scene of 1952 was repeated in December 1956 and January 1957—again with Tobin as superintendent—with a series of "Family Night II" meetings. The appointments made during those meetings were ultimately rescinded, however, following overwhelming pressure from the public, a spirited campaign, and a referendum.

In the early 1950s, urban renewal was an important priority. The city took slum properties along Main Street and Broadway and worked with developers to produce Technology Square, the first of a thirty-year series of developments in the area. In the early 1960s, the Johnson Administration located a major center for the National Aeronautics and Space Administration (NASA) at the contiguous Kendall Square area, and by the end of the century, it had blossomed into the Kendall Square economic boom. This was foresight and planning at its best. Edward A. Crane, who had served on both Plan B and E city councils and who served four terms as mayor over sixteen years, was the principal political negotiator who, along with MIT officials, helped put together the plan for Technology Square. A huge man, at six-foot-five, with a larger-than-life reputation, he held considerable influence with City Manager Curry.

Economic development also ran the risk of displacing people, and taking land meant the loss of homesteads. Technology Square replaced unsalvageable slums and displaced very few tenants. But a project that emerged in the late 1950s, known as the Donnelly Field Project, threatened the loss of more than two hundred homes in a 114-acre site along the Cambridge, Windsor, and Willow street borders. The CCA strongly supported the plan to revitalize this area, while Independents fought to protect the homesteads of their long-time constituents. The plan might have steamrolled through had it not been for the courageous actions of city councilor Pearl K. Wise. Wise had been part of the Committee for Plan E and had served on the school committee under the new system. No stranger to community organizing, she had mobilized the citywide PTA and the League of Women Voters. She was a committed liberal and social activist who objected to the federal requirements that urban renewal take over properties officially deemed "decadent." What may have been decadent to urban planners was home to hundreds of Cambridge families, Wise argued. Old as they might have been, they were also well-kept, well-loved residences. She refused to support the plan, and it failed as a result.

As part of the resolution, the city created the Wellington Harrington Citizens Committee, the first true "citizens' participation" planning process. It was a step that helped create a social activism movement and furthered the belief that "citizens' participation" was a right. This new way of thinking heavily influenced Cambridge politics later in the century.

At the same time, an Inner Belt highway was proposed along Brookline and Elm streets, through the heart of the city. Originating with a major 1948 regional transportation plan, the roadway was viewed as inevitable by many officials. At first, civic leaders focused on steering the roadway to a less destructive path. As they did with the Donnelly Field Project, Independents took the lead in opposition in order to save the heart of their constituency.

They would not stand by as a three-hundred-foot roadway carved a swath through their neighborhood, taking eleven hundred jobs, displacing fifteen hundred families, and costing the city an estimated $375,000 in tax revenue.

A number of CCA leaders were resigned to the Inner Belt's being constructed. They pointed to the benefit of reducing truck movement, easing traffic congestion in general, and making the area more attractive to technological business interests. The Independent leadership objected strenuously, led by city councilors Charles Watson and Edward and Walter Sullivan and state representative John Toomey, who as chair of the House Ways and Means Committee swore that no bonds would be approved to fund the state's share of the project.

The city rallied around the theme adapted by city councilor and MIT history professor Thomas H. D. Mahoney, a Cambridge native who transcended political labels. During World War I, the king of Belgium had refused to give in to a German demand for clear passage through his nation. Identifying Cambridge with Belgium, Mahoney made "Cambridge Is a City, Not a Highway" the battle cry against the Inner Belt.

With Tip O'Neill working the political angle in Congress and Crane calling for an alternative route over the existing railroad bed along an extension of Route 2, skillful political activists were able to create enough delays for the "inevitable" to become undone. Governor Francis Sargent finally killed the project in the early 1970s.

During the campaign of 1965, change was in the wind. Shortly after the election, the former city councilor and mayor Joseph E. DeGuglielmo put together a bipartisan coalition to fire city manager John Curry. Critical to his plan was the support of a highly respected Independent councilor, Daniel J. Hayes, who would become mayor. More important was the recruitment of Cornelia B. Wheeler, a city councilor of unquestioned political integrity and a resident of Coolidge Hill with Boston roots reaching back to Revolutionary times. Wheeler was determined to wrest power from Crane and get more involved in municipal policy. The pressure on her was almost unbearable because of Curry's record of success, but she held to her position to remain in the coalition and to replace him with DeGuglielmo, who had retired from the city council two years earlier (the waiting period required by the Plan E Charter). The CCA held forums in which Wheeler's judgment—not her integrity— was questioned as she was confronted by friends and supporters. Still she remained adamant, bolstering a small cadre of good government advocates who had tired of Curry.

DeGuglielmo was installed as city manager in 1966, but his term did not last long. At the next election, a new working coalition that included Edward Crane took office and replaced him. Mahoney chaired the search committee that involved public participation for the first time. In 1968 the city council elected James Leo Sullivan, the dynamic town manager of Milton and a Somerville native, as its new city manager.

In 1970 a series of events brought unprecedented disruption to the city's social and political life. It took three months for the City Council to elect Mayor Alfred E. Vellucci. In February racial turmoil broke out in the hallways and on the grounds of Cambridge High and Latin. Students of the Black Student Union and their parents began to demand that attention be paid to their issues, first in school and then in the community at large.

Next, on April 15, riots erupted in Harvard Square, a result of growing tensions over the war in Vietnam. A year earlier, the Harvard campus had been mobilized after a student takeover of University Hall. Now, state police in riot gear marched along Massachusetts Avenue, dispensing tear gas as broken windows and shattered glass littered the sidewalks. Angered further by the footsteps of police in formation, a growing number of students became aroused and aware of their political potential. A year later they would turn their energies to voter registration and turnout in the municipal election.

Then, City Manager Sullivan was fired. The coalition that had unseated DeGuglielmo was not the same group that had elected Sullivan. Crane was left out of that equation.

As city manager, Sullivan had wasted no time in moving forward and upsetting the Independents and Crane. By June Crane had assembled another coalition to oust Sullivan. He recruited Thomas Coates of the CCA slate to join him, further enraging the progressive element. The hearings over Sullivan's firing, held in the crowded auditorium of Rindge Technical School (Cambridge High and Latin School and Rindge did not merge until 1977), took on a circus atmosphere and attracted a lot of attention. Civic activists, already mobilized over Vietnam and eager to exploit their energy by using a local issue, put together an alliance of old guard CCA support and social progressives and formed a Save Our City Manager coalition, also called SOC'M. But Sullivan was fired and replaced by John M. Corcoran, who had been the assistant city manager.

Meanwhile, five days after Sullivan's firing, more turmoil visited the school department. When the superintendent of schools, Edward Conley, and his deputy, David Hockman, surprised the school committee with their early retirement notices on June 16, a battle ensued over whether to conduct a wide search for a replacement or to appoint, as tradition held, the most senior administrator at hand, assistant superintendent Frank Frisoli. Frisoli was the son of one of the most respected East Cambridge families and DeGuglielmo's brother-in-law. He considered the promotion a virtual birthright and fought for it, going so far as to insist that he would not accept an "acting" appointment. The school committee, under a nominal CCA majority but with Vellucci's support, called for a nationwide recruitment effort, and Frisoli relented. Most observers had little doubt that Frisoli would prevail in the long run, even though Vellucci and DeGuglielmo had been rivals for a similar constituency over the years.

In October Frisoli called the police to another riot at Cambridge High and Latin and exacerbated relations with the city's African-American community. Six months later, in the middle of the formal search process, two CCA-endorsed school committee members, Donald Fantini and Lorraine Butler, effectively changed their political affiliation. Becoming Independents, they joined with three others to appoint Frisoli, stopping the superintendent search in its tracks and leaving an outraged minority of two: Francis H. Duehay, a Harvard education school dean, and David A. Wylie, an emerging reform-minded activist who would help define the next generation of liberal, local politics as one with a global vision.

Frisoli, like Corcoran, believed that Cambridge residents deserved priority for Cambridge jobs. This rang true with generations of citizens who resented what they perceived as the condescending attitude of the CCA and the elitist views of Harvard.

Thus the election of 1971 became one of the most important and defining moments of the era after Plan E. With their constituencies energized at levels not seen since 1940, the CCA had a political agenda that was twofold: return the city managership to a professional urban administrator, and replace Frisoli with the best superintendent America had to offer. There was no middle ground and no ambiguity tolerated at candidate endorsement forums. The sides were carefully defined. Several additional slates were drawn up to incorporate the more radical political alliances, with a goal of channeling those votes to a strong social progressive. Party discipline was enforced at unprecedented levels among the progressive slates.

Voters elected five CCA city councilors, who then chose Barbara Ackermann as mayor. Among her colleagues were, for the first time, two African Americans: Henry Owens, the son of a prominent and successful businessman, and Saundra Graham, the first self-styled radical to join the council. Graham was a social activist and a consummate pragmatist and quickly became one of the architects of a major social agenda.

Ackermann had tangled with Tobin during her years on the school committee and articulated the progressive political agenda, and she was among the most passionate critics of the Inner Belt. She also strongly opposed Sullivan's firing. She joined three carefully screened CCA-endorsed school-committee colleagues to fire Frisoli, but not before some of the most intense, bitter hearings in the city's history took place. The public hearings, prefaced not only by Frisoli's promise to fight his dismissal but also by shouts, allegations, and even fights in the audience, were broadcast live on local public television for all of Greater Boston to view.

While the new city council could not agree on a new city manager and Corcoran survived for two more years, the school committee appointed Chicago's district superintendent, Alflorence Cheatham, an African American, as its new superintendent.

Cheatham's appointment pleased the newly empowered African-American community, which disliked Frisoli. The relationship between African Americans and the CCA had been successful but fragile. African Americans had served on the common council and school committee early in the century. However, under Plan E, virtually every credible black candidate had carried a CCA endorsement, and no black had been elected without a heavy supplement of transfer votes from the CCA slate.

In 1945 the Reverend Kenneth deP. Hughes might have been elected to the school committee had the CCA not been so timid about his left-wing politics and instituted a "no minister" policy in making endorsements. In 1959 school committee member Gustave M. Solomons became the first person of color under Plan E to win public office in Cambridge. In 1963 Thomas Coates was elected to the city council. Henry Owens, who bucked his colleagues over the effort to find a new city manager, lost his bid for endorsement in 1973 and subsequently relinquished his seat.

Still, the aftermath of the period was that the lines that separated CCA and progressive voters from independent constituencies were thick. Sensing the need to bring people together again after the election of 1973, a bipartisan coalition was formed to elect Walter J. Sullivan as mayor in return for the "retirement" of John Corcoran, support for Superintendent Cheatham, and the return of James Leo Sullivan as city manager. No one but Walter Sullivan and his Independent colleague Leonard J. Russell could have made the new coalition's agenda work. Russell, an Independent who had run on a platform of professional city management and who did not sacrifice his conscience to political advantage, had finally won election to the office that he had sought unsuccessfully three times. Walter Sullivan made an art form out of constituent service, a skill carefully cultivated by his brother, the former Mayor Edward Sullivan, and his father, Michael A. "Mickey the Dude" Sullivan. (His son Michael succeeded Walter on the city council in 1993 and as mayor from 2002-2005.) His family had been prominent in politics even before his father's election to the city council in 1935, and he was the city's most popular elected local official. More important, his reputation and his personal integrity, like Russell's, were untarnished. The public supported the arrangement, which ushered in a new era of administrative stability to local government.

When James Leo Sullivan retired as city manager in 1981, the city council handed the reins of authority to his deputy, Robert Healy. So confident was the public in this change of power that Healy's appointment was made without a public process, a formal search, or public outcry. When Superintendent Cheatham resigned in April 1975, and when the position became vacant again in 1984, broad public participation helped identify new superintendents, demonstrating convincingly that an era of local patronage politics was ending.

The enduring legacy of the period was to shift the CCA's political agenda from simply good, economical, and corruption-free government to a socially active, liberal platform. Many among the old guard remained loyal to the CCA, as they had few alternatives. A few CCA stalwarts, alienated by the movement toward enforced "political correctness" and the unwavering support of rent control, defected to palatable Independents. To understand what drove the CCA and good government factions to the left, one must understand the politics of rent control.

The Other Big Political Issue: Rent Control

The dominant theme of Cambridge politics over the last part of the century was rent control. Thus no discussion of Cambridge is complete without a clear understanding of how rent control affected the fabric of local life.

Cambridge has long been among the nation's most crowded cities. Add the growing number of students at the universities in and around the city, transient workers commuting to Boston, and older residents in apartments, and it's clear that demand for housing far outpaces supply. Rent controls after World War II were extended by state law until 1955, after which—during the 1960s—rents skyrocketed. When local rent control was first introduced in the city council, there was strong but not overpowering objection. Pressure to protect longtime residents in apartments and a plan that excluded owner-occupied single-, double-, and triple-unit houses from any rent regulation were enough to overcome the forces against rent control.

The CCA and tenant activists had worked for several years to develop the political strength to support a rent control program, and they knew how to count votes at election time. Proportional representation is designed to be a good vehicle to transfer votes among like-minded voters, and tenant activists knew how to develop a slate card. They became among the most influential members of the CCA board that handed out endorsements every two years. At one point, as many as thirteen thousand tenants—a voting bloc

The legendary count, 1991: at one of the last week-long vote counts, in the days before PR voting was computerized, election official Monique Thorne waves off an onslaught of incoming ballots at Longfellow School. *(The Cambridge Chronicle)*

large enough by itself to elect nearly a majority on the city council—walked to the polls, knowing that keeping their low rents required supporting the CCA slate card. Later, the Cambridge Tenants Union also produced an effective slate card. Add to this support a number of liberal small property owners whose houses were exempt from rent control and the support of one or two traditional Independents, including the unflappable Vellucci, at every election, and a majority capable of overwhelming any opponent was formed.

The impact was unmistakable at election time. While candidates articulated the time-tested issues for sound development, good civic management, and good schools, the real issues were, as pundits pronounced regularly, "rent control, rent control, and rent control." Supporters considered rent control rational social policy. They called for rent protection of the diverse population and advocated reasonable rents and zealous enforcement of the program's regulations. Opponents called it tyranny of the temporary majority and labeled it a punitive system enforced by an anti-landlord, pro-tenant Rent Control Board and its frequently criticized, obnoxious staff. Leaders among the small property owners identified many prominent citizens, including several with considerable wealth, who occupied rent-controlled apartments.

In fact, for most of its twenty-five-year history, there were few changes to the rent control ordinance. To support modification or changes that might weaken the ordinance was to risk the loss of the valuable political endorsements and placement on the election-day slate card, effectively writing one's political obituary. When strategists began converting apartments to condominiums to avoid regulation, tenant advocates secured the city council's approval of an anticonversion ordinance. It was not unusual for the city to have "ordinanced condominiums," converted from apartments after 1979, that could not be legally occupied by their owners.

In 1993 a creative attorney who owned an "ordinanced condominium" crafted a ballot question for the next statewide election, pleading his case to the voters of Massachusetts rather than to the tenants of Cambridge. On November 8, 1994, voters narrowly voted to support the ballot question, and rent control was effectively rescinded.

Tenant advocates demanded that the city council approve a home rule petition for the legislature to restore rent control as they knew it, a strategy that would have effectively overturned the ballot question. Unfortunately for them, Governor William Weld, a Cambridge resident and libertarian, while indicating his willingness to approve ameliorating legislation, joined House Speaker Charles Flaherty, himself a Cantabrigian, in defining what might pass muster. They told the city council that any legislation concerning rent control would face legislative defeat or a certain gubernatorial veto unless it contained protection only for senior citizens, disabled people, and low-income families; a reasonably administered short-term administrative structure; and a short period during which rent control could be completely phased out.

Under the terms of the bill Weld signed, only 9.4 percent of rent-controlled units remained under the program during the two-year phase-out. More than 14,600 rental units were deregulated.

A New Era Begins — 1995 and Beyond

The demise of rent control changed the face of Cambridge politics as no other change had done. Many tenants left the city, including families who relied on affordable housing. Rents rose quickly until the recession of 2000–2004 leveled them off. More important, the issues changed.

Proposition 2½, adopted in November 1980, had put a cap on local property taxes and took from the school committee its autonomous budgeting power. Soon afterward, the rolls of municipal employment began to shorten. No longer dependent on blue-collar municipal jobs that had previously driven the political agenda, patronage, to a large extent, dried up as a political issue.

After 1995 the issues of managing development, providing transportation services, improving the quality of municipal services, protecting the environment, building an expanded public library system, establishing a multipurpose senior center, expanding elderly programming, and ensuring high-quality public education to serve the most diverse population in the city's history dominated the agenda. Social progressives also raised international issues, a legacy of the peace movement and the large cohort of social activists who remained in the city after the Vietnam era.

Moreover, disenchanted "old guard" advocates of good government drifted elsewhere. They found the social activism of the remnants of the CCA, not to mention the foreign policy of some members, hard to accept. The CCA, tottering without purpose after rent control and known to a dwindling few, remained as the group with the good-government brand, but it went into sharp decline and virtually disappeared by 2005.

Furthermore, the Plan E era was practically free of corruption. No elected official had been indicted for misconduct while in office since Lyons went to jail in 1940. A thirty-year period of stable administration in the hands of two professional city managers, James Sullivan and Robert Healy, improved services, expanded parks, maintained public safety, kept taxes reasonable, and fostered careful growth. Because development had secured a solid and diverse economic base for the city, taxes were low compared to those of other eastern Massachusetts communities. What remained of patronage was more professional than political, one group arguing that they were more competent than the other.

Moreover, proportional representation gave to the city elective bodies that more closely, if not perfectly, reflect the community than do others with majority and plurality winner-take-all systems. The mandate to conduct an election campaign across the city, to reach out to other constituencies and remain accessible, has helped draw out candidates of all stripes and achieve a measure of credibility even among the potentially disenfranchised.

The time to focus on issues had come. Majorities necessary to elect a mayor became hard to predict, as labels no longer applied. Thus, citizens in 2007 might find it difficult even to define one noble faction from another. The computerization of the proportional representation voting count has even taken the drama out of what used to be reliably a week-long but socially healing vote-counting process.

The hundred-year period that began with political turmoil, partisan battling, and crusades to end corruption and patronage ended with those very same issues—except that in 2005 they played out at the state and national, not the local, level. As political historians have noted, periods of tranquility lull us into complacency only to be toppled by new issues, crises, and economic development. Indeed, given time, the species has proven wise.

ENDNOTES

1 The author would like to express special thanks to Susan Flannery and the staff of the Cambridge Public Library for their assistance in the research and preparation of this paper.

2. Luce was clearly playing to the prejudices of the city's Protestant establishment by referencing these prominent members of the Roosevelt Administration, one Irish and the other a Jew.

A Hundred Years of Activism — Or Was It?

BILL CUNNINGHAM

IF WE COULD roll back the clock—and the asphalt—and revisit the cobbled streets of Cambridge a hundred years ago, we would surely encounter active citizens in Central or Harvard Square. Whether any of them could be called "activists" is another matter. The word activism, which becomes common only around 1980, hardly appears in our newspapers before the late 1960s. Standard English dictionaries differ quite a bit in their definitions, except that they all use the word action. Politically, of course, your average activist may be all talk.[1]

So we may be speaking in a new way about something long familiar, or we may be on to some objective shift in our political culture. Here we will use our word tentatively, leaving aside for the moment what, if anything, distinguishes activism from advocacy—or from active citizenship in general.

What happens to the activist who gets elected to office or appointed to a city board? Before 1916, local politics in Cambridge was a far more streamlined affair than it is today. Each year citizens elected mere handfuls of officials: a mayor, a board of assessors, a bicameral city council, and a fifteen-member school board.[2] Except for school committee positions, women could neither vote for nor run for municipal office. Thus, at the turn of the century, they appear as "pure" activists.

A hundred years later, the city manager has a seemingly endless supply of seats to fill on boards and commissions. Whether this has increased or diminished the ranks of the city's activists is an open question.

In some sense, the twenty people who founded the Cambridge Historical Society in 1905 were themselves activists. After all, nobody paid them to do it. We note that Yankee and Scottish names predominated among the founders, that membership was limited, and that new members had to be accepted by a two-thirds vote of the membership.[3] It may be a stretch to describe these people as taking vigorous action on a controversial issue, but in a way, they were. Among "old stock" Americans at the time, anxiety about the future was leading to a new emphasis on the past. The tide of immigration, largely Catholic and Jewish, had been rising for twenty years. The local historical associations springing up around the country were part of a larger effort to preserve a certain heritage and cultural memory in the form of "antiquities."[4]

In Cambridge, of the 1905 census population of 97,434, two-thirds were immigrants or the children of immigrants. By far the leading countries of origin were Ireland (nearly 11,000) and Canada (over 10,000), and these figures do not even include migrants from rural New England, nor Afro-Americans, mainly from North Carolina and Virginia.[5]

The immigrants themselves developed a rich community life, as recorded by practitioners of the new profession of social work, such as those whose essays were first published almost fifty years after they were written in Robert Woods and Albert Kennedy's fascinating *Zones of Emergence*. Social workers found an abundance of voluntary energy among the people. The Irish created countless sodalities, societies, and strong temperance organizations, and led social lives that centered on the Catholic Church. The Jews organized relief societies and social clubs, including a Protective and Political Association that acted to defend against the violent attacks to which they were subjected by street gangs. Vigorous activism was also described among African Americans, but as "a childish delight in multiplicity of organization," a comment indicating how vigorously racism existed in Cambridge as well.[6]

Whatever their opinions on immigration, the attitudes of the social workers who wrote those essays were similar to those of Cambridge academics such as MIT president Francis Amasa Walker and Harvard professor Albert Bushnell Hart, who helped found the Immigration Restriction League in 1894. Their beliefs were in line with the poet and sometime Cambridge resident Thomas Bailey Aldrich, who declared that "human gorillas should be closely questioned at our gates."[7]

The temperance movement, ushered in by the Women's Christian Temperance Union, had a somewhat more modern attitude toward diversity. The movement had its basic constituency among middle-class Protestant churches and the industrialists who attended them, but as we have noted, working-class Catholics were also members.

Among the founders of the Cambridge Historical Society was Henry W. Higginson, whose family boasted many public figures. None was more famous than Thomas Wentworth Higginson, an abolitionist who recruited and led African American troops in the Civil War, fought for women's rights, advocated cultural pluralism, and in 1905 cosponsored the formation of the Intercollegiate Socialist Society. He was, however, concerned with studying socialism—not putting it into practice. Definitely not an egalitarian, he was a staunch believer in "woman's innate domesticity" and in the "childlike Negro."[8]

Florence Luscomb, who graduated from MIT in 1909 with a degree in architecture, was in many ways a twentieth-century Higginson. She took the lead, as an organizer of the struggle for women's suffrage and later as a founder of the Massachusetts League of Women Voters. She also persistently ran for office with minor parties.

Luscomb brought an almost aristocratic sense of personal privilege to her lifetime of dedication to the downtrodden. A leaflet promoting her 1938 congressional candidacy on the People's Labor ticket announced that she "comes from old American stock," flaunting a list of ancestors distinguished in military, political and judicial affairs.[9]

In 1911 two Harvard professors, James S. Ford and C. W. Killam, founded the Cambridge Housing Association. Ford became a national authority on housing reform; Killam served in a host of Cambridge civic clubs and municipal boards over five decades. Believing that overcrowding and fire hazard were the city's biggest housing problems, the two professors became leaders in the drive to outlaw further construction of wooden three-deckers—as Ford wrote, "to remove a source of fire risks and of depreciation of property values." For him, the "filthy habits of the recently arrived immigrants" increased the danger.[10] When a proposal was put forward in the midst of the housing crisis of the early 1920s to again allow construction of three-deckers—provided they be built of nonflammable materials—it was opposed by the Cambridge Welfare Union, the Cambridge Housing Association, and the League of Women Voters, organizations which had come to institutionalize the activist interests of social workers, housing reformers, and the victorious women's suffrage movement.[11]

In the area of housing, middle-class reformers were challenged by other types of activism, including that of the Socialist Party.[12] Tenant complaints about "rent profiteering" had reached such a point by April 1919 that Mayor Edward Quinn set up a "rent and housing committee" as a sort of rent grievance board. Its meetings were sometimes attended by "delegations" of tenants from neighboring addresses. At one such meeting, attorney J. Joseph Foley suggested that a "way to beat the landlords will be for all the tenants to stick together and refuse to pay exorbitant rent. There will not be enough officers to evict them nor enough teams to cart away their property....You may call this revolution or call it what you want but when men are driven to the wall they become desperate."[13]

In January 1921 a Boston landlord foreclosed on the apartment building that still stands at 881 Massachusetts Avenue and tried to raise the rents by eleven dollars a month, turning off the heat to press his demands. The tenants "banded together for mutual protection," hired a lawyer, petitioned the bank, and refused to pay the disputed sums.[14] In the meantime, Governor Calvin Coolidge had already responded to the postwar housing crisis by signing the state's first rent control law.[15]

There was a nationwide wave of labor and social unrest after World War I, by which time Cambridge was the second industrial city in Massachusetts (after Boston). Perhaps the nastiest local strike was at the Squire meat-packing plant in East Cambridge. Mobs in the hundreds attacked strikebreakers, while an anticommunist Cambridge Citizens League formed to support the employers.[16]

The prominence of communist and socialist ideas and activities during the 1930s caused those years to be dubbed The Red Decade. Unless associated with middle-class radicals, working people themselves—organizing and engaging in strikes and direct action—hardly appear in the newspapers at all but crowd the dim edges of the media stage, mostly nameless and without discernible features.[17]

Alfred Baker Lewis had emerged in the course of the 1920s as the head of the Socialist Party in Massachusetts and its perennial candidate for governor. A former attorney, he was a vestryman at St. James Episcopal Church in Porter Square. In the depths of the early Depression, Lewis had a handsome residence built for himself at the corner of Raymond Street and Gray Gardens East. When a reporter baited him about a socialist leader spending so lavishly, he replied that "by building he had helped to relieve unemployment" and that he continued to collect rent and interest on his holdings because "I feel it is better to use the economic freedom that money gives me to work for a better social system."[18]

In 1938 Baker inherited the then-princely sum of two million dollars from the estate of his grandmother, Henrietta R. F. Baker of Philadelphia. Right away, he bought a downtown Worcester office building; next, he purchased fifty-two pieces of residential property from the Worcester Five Cent Savings Bank, said to be the largest single residential transaction in that city's history at the time.[19]

The tradition of elite leftist activism in Cambridge is thus not new. Other prominent Socialist Party figures included Professor S. Ralph Harlow, candidate for U.S. Congress, Rev. George Lyman Paine, and Professor Alfred Sprague Coolidge, sometime candidate for state treasurer.[20]

The Communists and anarchists were a rougher lot, and radicals were frequently arrested for speaking in public without a permit. A crowd of three hundred at a 1929 Communist rally on Main Street was dispersed for this offense. In the summer of 1932, Jane Rosane and Nettie Jackson were arrested at Washington and Portland streets while addressing a gathering of two hundred at a labor demonstration. Four months later, two women were arrested in "a jeering crowd" of four hundred for obstructing Norfolk Street and, again, for speaking without a permit. In 1935 the Communist Party was holding weekly meetings in front of the First Baptist Church in Central Square, right across from the recently constructed police headquarters. These rallies were legal but not always peaceful. One was broken up and about 150 onlookers scattered after "a girl speaker declaimed that the masses were strong enough to overcome the police."[21]

Fervent working-class activism lay behind the many strikes of the 1930s, and Cambridge came out of the decade far more unionized than it had gone in. No labor conflict was more bitter than the 1933 strike at Hyde Athletic Shoe, which involved nine hundred workers, street battles with scabs, and other violence. According to court records, the Hyde picketers were mostly women, mostly with Portuguese family names, and they were convicted despite showing evidence of bruises inflicted by Cambridge police. In one Hyde "riot," police fired live ammunition toward a crowd of workers. Wellesley professor Harriet B. Hawes demanded the transfer of three cops from the Hyde strike detail, accusing them of acting as "a private police force," arresting "all they possibly can."[22]

Picket-line violence was not the only grievance Cantabrigians had against their police in the 1930s. One of the officers on the Hyde detail, Lieutenant Robert L. Douglas Jr., was accused of brutality several times during the decade. And early in July 1936, James Dunn of 16 Magee Street complained that while on desk duty, Lt. Douglas had flatly refused to send an ambulance to the aid of Dunn's sick son. At least five hundred persons attended a subsequent public meeting where other complaints about the ambulance service came up.[23]

Yet while people were roused to activism against what they perceived as abuses, police officers might be considered activists in their own right. The Depression was an era of foot patrols and police athletic leagues. Police officers doubled as welfare investigators, and some took on the role of social workers. Only a month after the meeting about the ambulance issue, Metropolitan District Commission (MDC) officers found a recently evicted East Cambridge family living in the woods in suburban Weston. Our old friend Lt.

Douglas helped the family apply for welfare and gave them money from his own pocket to tide them over.[24]

The adoption of Plan E—city-manager government and proportional representation—was the outcome of decades of activism, mostly of individuals from business and academic life and the Republican Party. The League of Women Voters sponsored lectures on city-manager plans beginning in the 1920s, with league leaders like Mrs. Henry R. Brigham joining men like Stoughton Bell, John H. Corcoran, and professors Killam, Lewis L. Johnson, and Joseph H. Beale in launching a series of reform organizations such as the Cambridge Union (1927), the Cambridge Taxpayers Association (1932), the Cambridge Committee for Plan E (1938), and the Cambridge Civic Association (CCA, 1945).[25]

Typical of such organizations, the Cambridge Union board included five members each from the city's most prestigious clubs—the Cantabrigia, Cambridge, and Economy clubs. In those days, middle-class civic life was organized into a plethora of such associations. Several new ones were organized in the early 1930s, including the Progressive Club of Cambridge, the Neighborhood Civic Union (African American), the Cambridge Civic League (Jewish professionals and businessmen), and the assertively inter-ethnic Cambridge Cosmopolitan Civic Union.[26]

Each club had officers, committees, and events that demanded lots of time from volunteers. Of course, there were individuals who filled many seats at once. Our old housing reformer, Professor C. W. Killam, simultaneously served as head of the Cambridge Taxpayers Association, the Cambridge Club, and the planning board. In 1934 he was named by Mayor Richard M. Russell to the board of the newly established Cambridge Housing Authority.[27]

The long, intermittent struggle for charter reform in city government culminated in two ballot campaigns for Plan E. Defeated in 1938, the reform forces became more aggressive in 1940. They packed city council meetings and brought a lawsuit against the 1940 budget. Both sides had to mobilize for almost three years, an experience of activism that marked the city's politics for years to come.[28]

In the years immediately after World War II, another housing crisis took center stage throughout the nation. Rent control had been imposed during the war, and in Cambridge the initiative to retain wartime regulations came from the Harvard Teachers Union. In short order, the American Veterans Committee joined in and took the lead. Attorney and World War II veteran Channing Beucler, a prominent spokesman, and a leader in the veterans' push for more public housing, exposed "tactics employed by the opposition in bringing race, color, and religion into this fight." African American residents organized through their churches, and a major fight against discrimination in housing ensued. The Cambridge Civic Association supported many of these efforts.[29]

Around 1950 a different kind of activist took over the burden of defending rent control. Benedict Fitzgerald was a music teacher in the Cambridge public schools with a brother who had served on the school committee. As executive secretary, Fitzgerald did most of the talking for the Cambridge Tenants Council, whose rank and file activists were mostly women. At the time, the rent law had to be renewed every year, a fact that kept interest in the issue continuously high.[30]

Rent controls expired in 1956. The twelve years that followed saw the hard-won victories of activists against urban renewal and the Inner Belt highway, the saving of the sycamores along Memorial Drive, and the coming of the federally funded Cambridge Economic Opportunities Committee (CEOC).[31]

At first, active Riverside residents, like others in Cambridge, had welcomed the promise of urban renewal, believing it simply meant that the government would help to fix up their homes and neighborhoods. In 1961 came the disillusionment. Hearing that "entire blocks would be cleared for new residential structures," five hundred residents jammed a public hearing at the Community Center on Griggs (now Callendar) Street. Representatives of the Cambridge Redevelopment Authority (CRA) reassured residents at a second meeting at the Western Avenue Baptist Church that it would be "two, three, four years before some families will have to move."[32]

Dorothy Sullivan of Howard Street—for one—who had been actively pro-renewal, now opposed the Houghton plan, named for the Houghton school (which was replaced by King in 1970). The plan envisaged "relocation" for eight hundred of the neighborhood's two thousand families. Said Enricius Evereteze of the Riverside Neighborhood Association: "It seems that the city no longer wants to tolerate the people of color who are so well integrated in the Houghton area."

In February 1962 the spotlight shifted to Area Three. City officials and the chamber of commerce testified at a city council meeting for the Donnelly Field plan, which would have replaced, with large blocks, many of the existing structures within a 114-acre area. The plan was rejected by 150 residents, even though it meant losing funding for the new Harrington School. The crowd at the next public hearing was larger and angrier still, but the council voted 5-4 to take the land anyway. On May 14 an anti-urban-renewal crowd of three hundred "nearly raised the roof" at city council, according to the *Cambridge Chronicle*. When a renewal proponent referred to "blight" in his neighborhood, Councilor Alfred Vellucci declared, "Homes are not blight!" Then, on May 28, Councilor Pearl Wise turned against the urban renewal

Reunion of activists at the rededication of the Inner Belt mural, October 15, 1995. Left to right: Hannah Malenfant; Acadie Waddell (granddaughter of Anstis Benfield); Anstis Benfield and grandson, Benjamin; unknown; Connie Yee, holding sign, "Cambridge is a city"; Barbara Ackerman; Rebecca Hall, holding sign, "Beat the belt"; Virginia Digdon; Gordon Fellman (left of Digdon); Rev. John Snow (behind Feldman); Steve Kaiser (in plaid shirt); Charlie Watson (in soft hat); former state rep. William P. Homans Jr.; Bill Joyce; and Marie Dottin. *(Photograph by Anstis Benfield)*

plan in a decisive vote that effectively stopped the bulldozers in their tracks. The move cost Wise the support of the CCA. She never ran for re-election and thus returned to the world of unelected activism.

The fight against the Inner Belt highway plan peaked a few years later. This time the activists were readier and the people more organized.[33] For several years, Massachusetts cities and towns retained veto power over new highways on their turf. Governor John Volpe got this repealed in 1965 and quickly set a deadline for Cambridge to decide where to put its section of the Inner Belt. The crisis spawned two new grass-roots organizations: Neighbors United and Save Our Cities. The former was organized by Catholic priests whose parishes were in the path of the planned highway; the latter was started by two activists, Ansti Benfield and Bill Ackerly, who had not known one another previously. In the mass meetings called by the priests, the affected neighbors discussed tactics from letter-writing to "direct action." Volunteer planner-advocates tried to help by working for a "realistic" alternate-route compromise; the rank and file generally opposed compromise.

Gordon Fellman, in association with Barbara Brandt, produced a book about the Inner Belt fight shortly after its successful conclusion. They saw two distinct kinds of activists, whom they labeled the Middle Americans and the Organization Class, and concluded that "while organization-class allies had a key role in helping the Middle American citizens of Brookline and Elm Streets keep away the Inner Belt, they did so by taking over the battle and waging it on their own terms, without actively involving the neighborhood people." The highway planners, members of the same 'class' as the professionals who opposed the highway, "apparently interpret[ed] the fact of little protest to mean that residents living on a proposed route do not mind very much the possibility of moving. Our data indicate, by crucial contrast, that while Brookline-Elm residents were strongly opposed to moving, most were deterred from protesting by a deep sense that people like themselves are too insignificant to influence government decisions."[34]

In truth, Benfield and Ackerly did not fit into this schema very neatly. Nevertheless, the movement against the highways spread to the suburbs, where people did believe they could influence government. The urban-suburban alliance was a vital factor in Governor Francis Sargent's decision to scrap the highway plan.[35]

The activism that emerged out of the cultural and political upsurge of the 1960s bore a new stamp. The disruptions brought about by the Vietnam War, urban renewal, university expansion, television, birth control pills, and a host of other factors help to explain the change. Cambridge may have reflected some of these changes earlier than other places, but it was hardly unique. In the past some of the city's students had gone off campus to support trade unionists and civil rights organizers. In the 1920s they had supported Sacco and Vanzetti. In the 1930s others had aided the Irish scrubwomen's strike at Harvard and attacked the Nazi diplomats the university had invited to its 1934 commencement.[36]

In the 1960s there were more students and fewer working-class families living in the neighborhoods, and the line between campus and community had become blurred. At just this time, journalists began to use the word activism more and more often to describe what was going on. Civil society is arguably the home base of activism. But the steady growth of government, especially the federal government, radically reshaped civil society. The War on Poverty, Model Cities, Volunteers in Service to America (VISTA), and tax-exempt foundations poured money and resources into lower-income neighborhoods, sponsoring new agencies and "organizations" in an effort to channel the new conflicts and energies.[37]

All of these factors can be seen in the renewed struggle over rent control, the quintessential activist issue in Cambridge after 1970, which, as noted above, first arose in Cambridge during and after World War I. In the summer of 1968, CEOC released a survey of some two thousand older residents, which found that over half "face[d] an existence in which they cannot afford the basic necessities of life." CEOC staff organizers tried to persuade people not to bring the rent control issue into the citywide housing meeting they were planning. They felt it would be too divisive. But the largely elderly crowd of nine hundred, who jammed St. Mary's Parish Hall for the September 14 Housing Convention, remembered the 1950s.

Every neighborhood caucus brought rent control resolutions to the floor, and a committee was formed to draw up an ordinance. The neighborhood caucuses formed the basis for the neighborhood planning teams, designed to draw lower-income people, particularly tenants, into neighborhood organizations normally dominated by middle-income homeowners.

Meanwhile, the newly founded local Peace and Freedom Party (PFP), which had already written a rent control ordinance, began a petition campaign to put it on the 1969 ballot. The PFP was led by Progressive Labor, a pro-Maoist organization influential in Students for a Democratic Society (SDS). These groups were activist but had few material resources; they had very few paid staff members, and to accept government or foundation funding was tantamount to "being co-opted by the system."

The strength of neighborhood activism had been apparent a few months earlier when the grief and outrage at the death of two-year-old Willis Moore forced the city to change Western Avenue and River Street to one-way roads.[38] This had been my first experience of the Cambridge neighborhood I lived in—my kids played with the Moore kids—as a mobilized community, one that exhibited a kind of quotidian activism seldom indexed, referenced, or categorized.

Nevertheless, it was the 1968 rent control petition that served as my real introduction to activism. I learned that to get rent control, and then to keep it, required a sustained effort to understand, organize, and communicate with a wide range of people. It required some people to do this almost all of the time, and many people to do it some of the time. Both supporters and opponents of rent control had to be relentless. Politicians had to be nimble. Although some other reforms encouraged activism, none did so more than rent control.

Now let's look again at the question we asked ourselves at the beginning of this essay. Is activism a new thing, or is it just a relatively new word? All of the examples we cited above are largely related to government operations. So are the two biggest issues we didn't discuss: zoning and public schools. And it goes without saying that the role of government in society grew steadily over the hundred years of our survey.

Land-use issues, including transportation and housing, are the focus of a preponderance of the energy that goes into local activism, and the constant struggle over what will be allowed or encouraged to happen on the city's land, especially in one's own backyard, has nurtured a sort of "culture" of activism. The universities and the professionals they train also occupy a far bigger social space than they once did. In Cambridge, this is both literally and metaphorically obvious, but the mass media was the first to identify the "student activist" as a type.

In the past, recognized civic leadership was monopolized by wealthy white males. Working-class and minority leadership may have been much more diverse, but it was submerged. Rich white guys still wield disproportionate power but now must share the stage. For all these reasons, today's activist lives in a world very different from that of the civic leader of 1905.

It is also now clear that we've been trying to describe more than one social role with a single word. Fellman and Brandt's Middle Americans, or Herbert Gans's West Enders, may not seem to qualify as activists at all. But we have other words, so let's use them. People who take an active part in community politics may be called advocates, organizers, or active constituents. By the latter I mean people who will write letters, attend meetings, and sometimes emerge as advocates or organizers in their own right.

Look over the street listing, the city's annual survey of its residents. It is remarkable how many of them—of us—have been active in public life at one time or another. But not everybody can be in the spotlight at once, which is one reason more citizens haven't been counted as activists. Still, the story of activism over the past hundred years is clearly the story of many thousands of men and women of all classes and nationalities whose names were never printed in the newspaper and will never be seen in any book. There are not enough bricks in the sidewalk to commemorate those whose lives and deeds made this city what it is today.

ENDNOTES

1. The word didn't appear at all in the Dictionary of American English (1938). Currently, we have: "A doctrine or policy of advocating energetic action" (Oxford); "direct, often confrontational action" (American Heritage); "direct vigorous action in...a controversial issue" (Merriam-Websters Collegiate). William Safire (Safire's New Political Dictionary, [New York: Random House Reference, 1993]) thinks it replaces the earlier term agitator.

2. Arthur Gilman, ed., The Cambridge of Eighteen Hundred and Ninety-Six, A Picture of the City and Its Industries Fifty Years After Its Incorporation Done by Divers Hands (Cambridge, Mass.: Riverside Press, 1896), 80.

3. Cambridge Historical Society Proceedings, June 19, 1905–April 24, 1906 (Cambridge, Mass.: Cambridge Historical Society, 1906).

4. Michael Holleran, Boston's "Changeful Times": Origins of Preservation and Planning in

America (Creating the North American Landscape), (Baltimore: The Johns Hopkins University Press, 1998), 234. Preservation increasingly became part of a matrix of class and ethnic definition; the audience for patriotic education shifted from us to them.

5. Cambridge Tenants Organizing Committee, *East Side, West Side, 1900-1920* (1975).

6. Robert A, Woods and Albert J. Kennedy, *The Zone of Emergence: Observations of the Lower Middle and Upper Working Class Communities of Boston, 1905–1914* (Cambridge, Mass.: The MIT Press, 1962) 72, 76, 81. Kennedy spoke of "the coming of the filthy races" to Cambridge without feeling the need to specify who they were. Nat Hentoff describes ethnic violence, especially against Jews, in *Boston Boy* (New York: Knopf, 1986).

7. Barbara Miller Solomon, *Ancestors and Immigrants: A Changing New England Tradition* (Cambridge, Mass.: Harvard University Press, 1956), 102; for Aldrich, 88.

8. Tilden G. Edelstein, *Strange Enthusiasm: A Life of Thomas Wentworth Higginson* (New Haven: Yale University Press, 1968) esp. 372, 373. Edelstein comments: "An attitude of noblesse oblige was satisfactory to Higginson only when those beneath him were no less generous in acknowledging their debt." 181.

9. "The Answer to the Present Crisis: Vote for Florence H. Luscomb" (1938).

10. *Cambridge Board of Trade Bulletin*, February 1916; *The Boston Globe*, March 11, 1916.

11. *Cambridge Chronicle*, October 8, 1922. The fact that these organizations continued to oppose this type of housing construction shows that their concerns were broader than fire safety—"not in my backyard," or NIMBY, as we might say today.

12. *Cambridge Chronicle*, October 11, 1919.

13. Ibid., April 4, 1919; June 8, 1920.

14. Ibid., January 22 and January 29, 1921.

15. Mass. Gen. Acts of 1920, 555, 578. Monica R Lett, *Rent Control: Concepts, Realities, and Mechanisms* (Piscataway, NJ: Transaction Publishers, 1976) 20.

16. *Cambridge Chronicle*, January 11 and November 15, 1919.

17. Organized labor—even if it includes in its ranks the majority of all the adult citizens in the community—is generally regarded as a "special interest" that must be represented; businessmen, on the other hand, are often regarded, not as representing business as a special interest, but as serving the community as a whole. Edward C. Banfield and James Q. Wilson *City Politics* (Cambridge, Mass.: Harvard University Press, 1966), 282.

18. *Cambridge Chronicle*, September 30, 1927; July 31, 1931; March 6, 1931; March 20, 1931.

19. Ibid., June 29, 1939.

20. Ibid., July 29, 1932; October 18, 1933; June 23, 1938.

21. Ibid., September 4, 1931; June 10, 1932; October 7, 1932; May 2, 1935.

22. Ibid., April 14, 1933; May 26, 1933; July 21, 1933; August 18, 1933; June 9, 1933.

23. Ibid., July 16, 1936.

24. Ibid., August 13 and August 20, 1936.

25. Ibid., February 25, 1927; March 10, 1928; May 6, 1927; July 15, 1932; August 4, 1938.

26. Ibid., March 9, 1928; May 8, 1931; May 30, 1930; March 18, 1932; January 16, 1931.

27. Killam was appointed to the board despite the fact that he questioned "whether any city is under any obligation whatever to provide homes and municipal services, fire, police, sewer, water, lights, and education to all classes of the population." *Cambridge Chronicle*, March 23, 1934.

28. *Cambridge Chronicle*, October 13, 1938; November 3, 1938; April 27, 1939; May 18, 1939; April 11, 1940. *Cambridge Tribune*, March 28, 1941; *Harvard Crimson*, March 11, 1941.

29. *Cambridge Chronicle*, November 26, 1946; December 12, 1946; August 12, 1948; July 31, 1947.

30. Ibid., March 20, 1931; August 31, 1950; May 21, 1953.

31. What follows is mostly taken from Cunningham, *Which People's Republic?* (1999), esp. 16, 17.

32. *Cambridge Chronicle*, July 20, 1961.

33. Cunningham, esp. 21.

34. Gordon Fellman (in association with Barbara Brandt), *The Deceived Majority: Politics and Protest in Middle America* (Piscataway, NJ: Transaction Press, 1972), 131, 94. Herbert J. Gans, *The Urban Villagers: Group and Class in the Life of Italian-Americans* (Glencoe, NY: The Free Press, 1962) makes a similar point: "The caretakers' [Gans's equivalent of Fellman and Brandt's 'organizing class'] blindness to the nature of West End life stemmed in part from their being middle-class people who did not live in the area, but even more from their missionary outlook," 151. Gans's reference is narrowly relevant to our concern, since many of the West End's refugees ended up in Cambridge. See also Chester Hartman, "The Housing of Relocated Families," in James Q. Wilson, ed., *Urban Renewal: The Record and the Controversy* (Cambridge, Mass.: MIT Press, 1966), 295.

35. Alan Lupo and Frank Colcord, *Rites of Way: The Politics of Transportation in Boston and the U.S. City* (Boston: Little Brown & Company, 1971).

36. *Cambridge Chronicle*, August 12, 1927; August 10, 1929; March 21, 1930; May 16, 1930; June 29, 1934.

37. Bill Cunningham, *Which People's Republic?*, unpublished ms. available online at http://bridgenews.org/background/WhichPeople.pdf/view?searchterm; 22, 23, and for the following paragraphs, 24-28.

38. *Cambridge Chronicle*, July 25, 1968.

Town and Gown in the 20th Century

O. R. SIMHA

CAMBRIDGE'S town-and-gown relations in the twentieth century reflected the worst and the best of the community's capacities and talents. While both sides suffered from the traditional perception that conflict was the natural state between them, most of the stresses between town and gown can be understood in terms of competing agendas.

Each of the city's educational institutions was driven by distinct academic and social missions and shaped by financial and political realities. Cambridge, in turn, had its own aspirations and dreams that it aimed to realize on its own terms rather than as an adjunct to the academic institutions it hosted. Yet during periods of external threat, the sides often came together to achieve great success. When, in dire straits, Cambridge asked for help, the universities came to its aid. When the institutions were threatened, Cambridge was there to provide support.

Cambridge began the century as home to two secular institutions of higher learning: Harvard University and Radcliffe College. Lesley College was established in 1909, and in 1916 MIT moved across the river from Boston. Other, smaller institutions arrived over the course of the century. The larger institutions were often perceived as rich and powerful and able to do as they wished, but in reality their fortunes were profoundly influenced by the changes in the city's demographics and the actions of the city's political leadership and public agencies.

Many of the misunderstandings between town and gown grew out of their fundamentally different governance structures. The "academy" is a self-governing, self-perpetuating autocracy; leaders are chosen by a select few for long terms with the specific purpose of defending and extending the academy's aspirations. The "town," on the other hand, is a raucous, rough and tumble expression of democracy, where to survive leaders who stand for election every two years must reflect at least some of their constituents' loves, hates, fears, and biases. There were, however, demonstrations of leadership and unity of purpose that illustrate how town and gown could act together under certain circumstances to address problems and opportunities of mutual interest.

In 1900 President Charles William Eliot of Harvard was completing thirty-one years in office. Formerly a professor at MIT, he brought to Harvard a passion for changing a hidebound college into a modern university hospitable to a new kind of student body, one chosen on the basis of merit rather than ethnicity, race, or religion. That goal was aided by the funds left to Harvard in 1905 by Daniel Buckley to endow scholarships for Cambridge public school graduates, making merit-based access to Harvard a financial reality for families of modest means.

Such innovation in one of Cambridge's earliest colonial enterprises—education—was not limited to Harvard. In 1909 Edith Lesley, a pioneer in early childhood education, opened a school for women who wanted to prepare for careers teaching young children. These students, who came mainly from immigrant and working-class families, saw the profession as their avenue to improving their mobility and social standing.

In 1909 A. Lawrence Lowell, the complete Boston Brahmin, succeeded to the presidency of Harvard, and with him came the full measure of the prejudices, self-assurance, and arrogance of his caste. He found the institution to be full of messy dichotomies. Eliot had enriched the curriculum and invited students to seek their own specialties through elective courses of study, something Lowell saw as an invitation to anarchy. The "well-rounded" Harvard man was Lowell's goal. He imagined a version of an Oxford or Cambridge college where a gentleman would be formed who would rise to his standard.

But his standard had a dark side, characterized by his caste's religious bias. Lowell pressed for quotas for Jewish students, fearing that Harvard would become dominated by the children of immigrants. He informed the town, however obliquely, that Jews, Italians, Irish, French Canadians, Portuguese, and others of their ilk need not apply—at least not in too large a number.

This shift in policy sent a clear message that, unlike Eliot, who saluted merit from any quarter, Lowell would protect the college from the influence of the "newer races." He began by insisting that freshmen all live in the col-

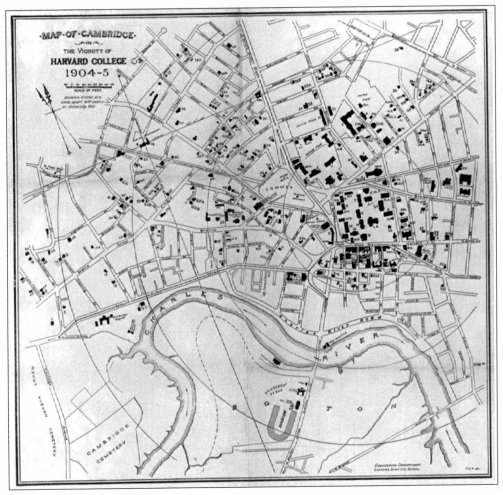

A 1904-05 map of Harvard University; university properties are shaded.
(Cambridge Historical Commission)

lege. One consequence, perhaps unintended, was to draw students away from
neighborhood rooming houses, thereby reducing an informal and economically important interaction between town and gown. Lowell's housing policy
also undercut the more exclusive private residences along Mount Auburn
Street's "Gold Coast" that catered to wealthier students. These had been built
by private developers, who by 1912 had lost many of their customers to Lowell's new policies and were anxious to sell their properties to the university.

Meanwhile, from the Boston end of the Harvard Bridge, MIT's new
president, Richard Maclaurin, was casting his eyes on the undeveloped land
facing the new Charles River basin. In 1909 he proposed that "Tech" move
to Cambridge. The idea developed traction as the Cambridge industrialist

Everett Morss, president of the Simplex Wire and Cable Company, and other MIT alumni recruited supporters for it.

Harvard's Eliot had tried three times to draw MIT into the Harvard fold and had failed. So it came as no surprise that President Lowell voiced his opposition to Maclaurin's idea. He feared that MIT would add to the tax burdens of the city, which would lead to demands for compensation to the town from both institutions.

When other cities began to compete for MIT, Cambridge civic associations and the city council invited the school to settle in Cambridge. Whether the spirit of competition or a sense that MIT could offer Cambridge access to new technologies and employment opportunities was at play, it appeared that the community had chosen a university rather than tax relief.

By October of 1911, the MIT Corporation had acquired forty-six acres of soggy land at the edge of the Charles River and was planning its new campus. The following year the new subway line to Harvard Square opened, guaranteeing easy access to the campus from the Kendall station.

The design for the MIT campus was entrusted to William W. Bosworth, who produced a handsome campus for the school and a new front door for Cambridge. The new buildings, of classical design, serenity, and symmetry, were a sharp departure from the Cambridge brick that had dominated the city's architecture. Built in reinforced concrete and clad in limestone, they presented a new image of the city to the world. In 1916 the new buildings were finished, ceremonies celebrating MIT's move to Cambridge were completed, President Maclaurin became a Cambridge resident, and the faculty and students got down to work.

The following year, the United States entered World War I. MIT was training aviators, engineers, and radio operators, and Harvard was providing new officers for the armed services. Cambridge industries were producing material for the war effort. Mobilization took many people from both town and gown; many never returned.

Lack of funds in the years after the war made it difficult for MIT to exploit its new campus and to pursue all of its educational aspirations. It would lose its president to illness, and it struggled for leadership and resources for the next decade. But it valued its graduates, and it had some dedicated friends who would see it through hard times. On the other hand, a couple of bright spots appeared in the Cambridge economy when the Lever Brothers Soap Company built its new plant in Kendall Square and the Boston Woven Hose & Rubber Company installed itself on Broadway, just north of the MIT campus.

At Harvard, President Lowell was determined to leave a legacy of residence-based education that would bring the undergraduates inside the university's walls, thereby further isolating students and creating conditions that fueled the conflict between town and gown. To give substance to his goals, Lowell expanded the university's land holdings and in 1922 commissioned a new plan for the school's further development.

In 1924 a forward-looking member of the MIT Corporation acquired additional undeveloped land for the school on the west side of Massachusetts Avenue. The original owners had intended this site to replicate a Back Bay neighborhood, but the land had lain fallow and become an informal dump. Only a warehouse and a state armory stood at the corner of Massachusetts Avenue and Vassar Street. The city approached MIT for land to extend Vassar from Mass Ave to Memorial Drive. MIT provided the land, and a number of businessmen developed warehouses on Vassar Street that added to the city's tax base. Billboards advertising their wares were erected, the most famous being the Heinz 57 and Cain's mayonnaise signs.

By 1925 Cambridge's population was reaching a peak of 120,000, and MIT was under pressure to accommodate more of its students on its somewhat isolated campus. It added new dormitory space on Ames Street.

Over the next two years, Harvard began to implement its new housing plan, and the city started to experience economic woes as its expenses outstripped its resources. By 1928 members of the Harvard Corporation were expressing concern about the university's expansion and its impact on real estate revenue in the Cambridge budget.

The universities represented an estimated fifty million dollars in tax-exempt property, and Cambridge, facing the need to demand more taxes from residents, sought the universities' assistance. The result was the first formal Payment in Lieu of Tax (Pilot) agreement, which included Harvard, Radcliffe, and MIT. Signed in 1929, it provided for payments for land taken off the tax rolls for twenty years after this date. The agreement was a watershed in town-gown relations and suggested that there were limits to tax exemption for educational institutions.

But 1928 was a lucky year for Lowell at Harvard. Edward Harkness, a Yale alumnus, provided the funds for the president to fulfill his dream of creating undergraduate houses that would attract and serve his kind of Harvard student: white, Protestant, middle and upper class, and drawn from across the country.

Following the stock market crash in 1929, the universities and the town began to reflect on the economic troubles confronting them. Harvard raised its tuition 33 percent, from three hundred to four hundred dollars. Enrollment nevertheless remained stable, since Harvard was now drawing its students mainly from families who could afford the higher tuition. It was the less well off who felt the doors close. With the exception of Cambridge students eligible for the Buckley scholarships, the demographic profile of the university was changing, and the shift was not lost on the city's residents.

By 1930 more than half of the freshman at Harvard came from private schools. The "preppies" often brought with them social biases that revealed a cruel streak. Some students living in the Harvard houses along Bow and Mount Auburn streets would heat copper pennies on their steam radiators. When a "Cambridge urchin" would pass by, they would toss the hot pennies to the street and watch with amusement as the children singed their fingers trying to pick them up. Many decades later, these stories still color the relationship between the town and gown.

A new generation of leadership was moving into place in the city and at the universities to handle these difficult times. Karl T. Compton came to Cambridge from Princeton to lead MIT. He was expected to reinvigorate the Institute and bring the school's finances under control. At Harvard ordinary employees' wages had been cut while faculty salaries remained intact. In contrast, in 1931 MIT withheld 10 percent of salaries over five hundred dollars as a reserve to tide it over the crisis, later distributing the funds to those who had suffered the deduction. In 1932 the institute felt it necessary to increase tuition from four hundred to five hundred dollars, and enrollment dropped as a result. But with the help of Gerard Swope of the General Electric Company, MIT was able to establish the Technology Loan Fund, an interest-free fund that allowed able students of modest means to attend the university.

Compton also focused on building MIT's scientific capacity, which would soon be critical to the country's ability to defeat Germany and Japan in World War II. It would also serve to establish the basis for a new economic era in Cambridge.

In 1933 James Bryant Conant became president of Harvard, putting scientists at the helm of both large institutions in Cambridge. Conant shared some of Lowell's views on the makeup of the student body, and he worked to establish a national scholarship program that would bring in students from across the United States. He also established the Celtic Chair, to engender a more cordial relationship between Harvard and the Irish Catholic community in Boston, which exercised considerable political clout.

But old injuries die hard. In 1936 Michael Sullivan was elected to his first term on the Cambridge City Council, setting the tone for a contentious relationship with Harvard for many years to come. Two sons and a grandson would follow him, serving as councilors and mayors of the city.

Harvard continued to struggle with the issue of the proportion of scholarship students entering as freshmen. The claim was that too many scholarship students could undermine the fiscal health of the institution. That message was heard clearly by aspiring Cantabrigians of modest means, and it never went down well.

Meanwhile, the municipal government had slipped into habits of nepotism, favoritism, and questionable financial and contract behavior, which led to a movement to change the established political order. Harvard Law School's Dean James M. Landis, the League of Women Voters, and volunteers for good government led a good-government movement, determined to clean up the city. Plan E, which featured a government of professional management and city council elections by proportional representation, was their preferred mechanism. In 1938 their first attempt to effect change failed, but they persevered and ultimately won in 1940. Representatives of the "gown" were now engaging in the political process, and they would continue to struggle for power with the independent "townies."

The city's expenses were climbing, and Mayor John Lyon called on the universities to contribute one hundred thousand dollars to the city. The universities were not inclined to do so, given what appeared to be a bloated city budget rife with political appointments. The tensions between town and gown grew as the new members of the city council joined the fray, with Michael Sullivan attempting to close down two student theatrical productions at Harvard and John Toomey, later the powerful chairman of the House Ways and Means Committee in the state legislature, adding his voice to the chorus.

The year 1940 ended with a change in the city's form of government and the indictment of Cambridge mayor John Lyon for taking bribes. But the following year was of even greater significance. With the U.S. entrance into World War II, town and gown shifted into high gear for the war effort. MIT needed Cambridge's cooperation in suspending a number of building restrictions to allow for the construction of the now famous Radiation Laboratory's research facilities. The laboratory would develop the radar equipment that many claim won the war. This and other wartime research would set the stage for a postwar economy based on the electronics, computer, and biotech industries.

But wartime did not entirely suspend the city's desire to seek new revenues from the gown. In November 1942, with gas rationed, bicycles were becoming the preferred mode of travel around the city. A new ordinance that required all bicycles to be registered for a twenty-five-cent fee was introduced, entitling the owner to a license plate and ID. Unregistered cyclists could be liable for a twenty dollar fine. Well over a thousand university students and staff contributed to this new source of income.

By the end of the war in 1945, the city and its institutions realized that nothing would be the same again. The GI Bill brought thousands of veterans to Cambridge to pursue their education. Older, serious, many with families, they needed housing or, in some cases, places to park their trailers. Cambridge was asked to continue to suspend some building restrictions to accommodate them, and the Cambridge Housing Authority helped to facilitate the housing of some of these new Cambridge residents.

But old habits still lingered. Cambridge tried to put the federally sponsored veterans' housing on the tax rolls, and only after the federal government stepped in was it agreed to come up with a formula that would pay the city a sum in lieu of taxes. At the same time, Harvard showed equal self-interest. Anxious to control costs being mandated by new federal programs, the university tried to get an exclusion from the Social Security Act for its employees. Fortunately, wiser heads prevailed; the Harvard treasurer warned that the university would earn only deep resentment from its employees and forgo much good will from the public.

The good-government movement, led by university graduates, faculty, and staff—having changed the form of governance and put in place a professional management system for the city—now turned its attention to the Cambridge schools. Critical of the conservative school administration controlled by political families and personalities, they initiated a review of the school department in 1945 by the Harvard Graduate School of Education. The subsequent Field Study Report was very critical of the Cambridge school superintendent and his management of the school system, leading resident supporters of the school department to reply to the Harvard critique with anger. Cambridge parents did not wish to have their children "experimented" with by Harvard academics who they felt were influenced by questionable ideologies. At the center of the controversy was probably the ill-founded perception that the university wanted control of the school system and questioned the competence of the resident community to guide the education of its own children. The incident led to a long chill between Harvard and the Cambridge School Department—to the detriment of both.

By 1946 housing was becoming a serious issue, with many new students taking up the available housing inventory. Some student families lived in prefabs, and the universities were trying to develop new housing to meet the pressing needs. In 1947, with students living in wartime research buildings converted to barracks, MIT commissioned the distinguished Finnish architect Alvar Aalto to design a new senior dormitory. In 1948 the school leased land to an insurance company to build 270 apartments at 100 Memorial Drive for both MIT staff and the public. Harvard was beginning to plan for additions to its graduate residences and the expansion or construction of new undergraduate houses.

In 1949 James R. Killian became MIT's president, bringing to the job a desire to work with Cambridge to solve old problems and to create a new sense of cooperation. That same year, the city councilor Michael Sullivan, long a nemesis of Harvard, died in office. (His son Edward succeeded him on the city council the following year.) President Killian spent much of his first year in office gearing up for a major fundraising campaign that would put MIT on track to expand its wartime discoveries, something that would have a major effect on the future of Cambridge's economy.

By 1950, the old industrial base of Cambridge was faltering. The soap manufacturing at Lever Brothers in Kendall Square, the Squire's meatpacking plant in East Cambridge, the woodworking firms such as Kaplan Furniture, Irving and Casson, and the American Casket Company were heading into the sunset. The confectionery industry, long a Cambridge stalwart, was beginning to loosen its ties to the city. The Daggett Chocolate Company would be gone in a few years.

The abandoned space, however, would be essential to the emergence of a knowledge-based economy in Cambridge. A score of electronic companies and research and development firms began their days in the old factory buildings of Cambridge, where MIT and Harvard researchers and graduates were incubating a new financial base.

This slow transition was not an immediate boon to the city, which was still losing tax revenue and jobs at a rapid pace. But the institutions were growing, and job opportunities for able Cantabrigians were multiplying. These jobs, at least for some MIT employees, meant more than food on the table. Employment brought with it the opportunity for tuition support for their children. Maintenance workers, seeing their children graduate from MIT, would experience a bond with the school that could not easily be equated to a holiday bonus or a Christmas turkey. At Harvard, on the other hand, the relationship between Harvard and its employees—despite good intentions—was characterized as "feudal" by the faculty committees examining the situation.

At mid-century the Cold War was in full swing, and town and gown issues gave way to questions of academic freedom, loyalty oaths, and political affiliations. Many Cambridge politicians supported loyalty oaths for what they thought were patriotic or politically advantageous reasons. They were less concerned about the implications for academic freedom than they were motivated by the desire to keep the loyalty of their aroused supporters. The Red Scare and McCarthyism threatened the very core of Cambridge's institutions. At MIT, President Killian fought the forces that were prepared to do great injury to the universities. "The Institute is opposed to communism," he said. "It is equally opposed to the communistic method of dictating to scholars the opinions they may have and the doctrines they teach."

Harvard changed leaders in 1953 with the arrival of Midwesterner Nathan Pusey, who had been president of a small college in Appleton, Wisconsin. There he had had close personal relations with citizens and town officials and had been lionized in the national press for his willingness to stand up to Senator Joseph McCarthy's witch hunt for communists at American institutions. But he was not prepared for the rough-and-tumble political atmosphere in Cambridge.

As the universities embraced the opportunities provided by increasing national support for research, they attracted bright graduate students from all over the world who were not always met with friendship or hospitality from Cambridge landlords. Alice Rossi, a distinguished sociologist, studied the attitudes of rooming house landlords toward MIT graduate students. Her results showed some deep-seated prejudices and a record of painful behavior toward foreign students, particularly Africans, and toward American black and Jewish students. The study led to the requirement for a nondiscrimination pledge from all landlords who wished to place their rooms or apartments with university rental-listing services.

The 1954 Federal Housing Act energized the city to take advantage of federal aid. Mayor Edward Crane established the required Citizens Advisory Committee to assist the city with its renewal planning program, and the presidents of both Harvard and MIT served on the committee, as did a wide variety of citizens from all parts of the city. For many ordinary Cambridge residents, this was the first time they had any contact with the leaders of the celebrated institutions. Meeting to address citywide issues was a novel experience for all involved. Cambridge was ultimately deeply influenced by these events, focusing as they did on local issues of economic development, jobs, taxes, education, and housing, which were of equal importance to the city and to the institutions.

The city's efforts to plan for its future had the benefit of a number of talents from the university community. The head of the City Planning Department at MIT and the dean of the Harvard Graduate School of Design, both Cambridge residents, served on the planning board. Mark Fortune, the city's planning director, and his small and talented staff formulated a vision in 1957 that showed how the renewal of the city could occur in a rational way. Many of the ideas in this plan were ultimately realized through the cooperation of the city, the universities, and the business community.

By 1958 both Harvard and MIT had established planning offices to address their long-term planning and development needs. Both explored ways to meet their institutional needs that would be in concert with the city's goals. Pusey established the new post of assistant to the president for community affairs at Harvard and charged it to "deal with the manifold problems connected with the University's day-to-day existence in a large urban area." The MIT Planning Office was given a broad mandate to plan for MIT's growth but also to seek ways of developing useful and cordial relations with the community.

With its reputation for taking an active role in community affairs, MIT's leadership was called on to help the city in 1958. Lever Brothers was closing its Cambridge soap plant; the employees had been given notice, the property put on the market. Next door, the Rogers Block redevelopment project, undertaken by the city several years earlier, lay moribund. The land had been cleared, but there was little commercial interest in redeveloping property next to an aging soap plant. Mayor Crane asked President Killian if MIT could help. Out of their conversations emerged a proposal to establish a partnership between MIT and the real estate development firm of Cabot, Cabot and Forbes to redevelop both the soap plant site and the Rogers Block into a new research and development center, to be called Technology Square. This unusual venture was the first step in the revitalization of the city's commercial and industrial economic base.

In 1959 Julius Stratton stepped into the MIT presidency, having led one of the institute's most important wartime laboratories. He brought with him an enthusiasm for good relations with the city and better facilities for students.

In another corner of the city, the far-sighted and talented president of Lesley College, Trentwell Mason White, was planning for its future. White's early career in the theater had given him a sense of flair and imagination, and he helped the college become a leader in early childhood education and in education for special needs children. Several Cambridge businessmen and corporations, including Livingston Stebbins, the Carter Ink Corporation, and the Welch Candy Company, supported him.

Lesley had long since developed relationships with the Cambridge school system, and as its reputation and enrollment grew, it wanted to expand its services. The college began to purchase homes in the Wendell and Mellen streets area, next to its existing facilities. One of the college's motivations was its sense that the impending expansion of Harvard University would preempt its own aspirations to develop a more efficient and economical campus. Although Lesley's actions alerted the Agassiz neighborhood to the threat of two expanding institutions, the college wisely established a number of satellites for its laboratory schools to limit its need to intrude into the neighborhood. Lesley Ellis and Lesley Dearborn on Concord Avenue and Lesley Lowell, laboratory schools for elementary and special needs students, were among its initiatives. In another pioneering effort, the college developed a program of foreign language instruction for elementary school children.

The year 1960 was another town and gown watershed in Cambridge. A major revision of the zoning ordinance was being debated, and the proposed changes would introduce new ways of constraining university expansion. Allowances for high densities in the existing university precincts was to encourage concentrated development, and increased height limits would help the universities build up, not out.

That same year, James Killian, now chairman at MIT, announced the Technology Square development at a Chamber of Commerce meeting, raising hopes for a renaissance in the city's economy. MIT and Harvard both embarked on fundraising campaigns to support an increase in student housing, prompting complaints from Cambridge landlords and developers of rental housing, who called the competition unfair. But the rising market for housing quickly made it clear that there was room for everyone in the enterprise.

Meanwhile, in recognition of how rapidly times were changing, Harvard finally permitted women to attend all classes at the university on an equal basis with men. The Inner Belt highway issue, which had first become a concern in 1952 and would not be resolved until 1971, was also heating up. And President Kennedy was announcing that with MIT's help, the United States would put a man on the moon. (Interestingly, many of the laboratories that would get us to the moon lay along one of the routes proposed for the highway.)

Unintended consequences fueled other controversies, such as when Harvard completed additions to its student housing along Memorial Drive without realizing that students would soon dominate the use of the Corporal Burns playground, elbowing out residents of the Riverside neighborhood. It was another item in the list of the university's offenses that would long be remembered.

With passage of the amended zoning ordinance in 1962, expansion of the universities was guided by a new set of rules that encouraged concentrated development and required off-street parking. Student housing and laboratories were being built, but little was being done to meet the community's housing needs. Even the city's housing authority was running into resistance from traditional neighborhoods when it tried to find sites for elderly housing.

The following year brought town and gown into conflict in unexpected ways. Some members of Harvard University were encouraging the Metropolitan District Commission to resolve the traffic problems at the intersection of Memorial Drive and Boylston Street (now John F. Kennedy Street) by building an underpass. Such an action would have required removing several of the stately sycamore trees that had been planted almost a hundred years earlier by the Cambridge Parks Commission. The residents of the adjacent neighborhoods led a campaign designed by the father of American public relations, Edward L. Bernays, called "Save the Sycamores," which defeated the proposal. Another misadventure was Harvard's attempt to develop the land at the Sachs estate, bordering the Somerville line and the Harvard Divinity School, for much-needed junior faculty housing. The neighbors in this case, largely senior Harvard faculty, opposed the plan, complaining at the city's planning board about the insensitive manner in which the university administration was determined to destroy their peace and quiet. These events suggest that it was not always clear where town and gown began and ended.

The assassination of President Kennedy in 1963 was especially painful for the Cambridge community. Both town and gown had shared in his triumphs, and then, so abruptly, he was gone. The subsequent battle over the location of the Kennedy presidential library will go down as one of the great ironies in the city's history. The neighborhoods of Harvard Square opposed the library for fear it would bring unwanted traffic to Cambridge, so it was built on a site overlooking Boston Harbor, next to the University of Massachusetts. In hindsight, the construction of Harvard's Kennedy School of Government and the development of commercial buildings in the area probably produced more traffic in Cambridge than has ever plagued the Kennedy Library in Boston.

In 1964, frustrated by the continued lack of much-needed housing, MIT and Harvard established the nonprofit Cambridge Corporation in the hope that it would take the lead in getting the construction of more community housing under way. In 1965 the Cambridge Planning Board, in an effort to give sensible guidance to the development of the city, published "Suggested Goals for a Cambridge City Plan"; in addition to defining areas for housing and recreation, it outlined the districts where the universities could develop in a rational fashion.

Nineteen sixty-five was also the year that NASA, looking for a home for its electronics research center that would be close to MIT and other universities in Boston, began its search in Cambridge. A proposal to create a redevelopment project in Kendall Square to accommodate NASA and simultaneously create a new commercial center was presented by the Citizens Advisory Committee to the city council. A major difficulty for the city was how it would pay for its share of the project. MIT stepped forward to provide the city with the financial credits it needed to proceed. With this support, the ground was laid for capitalizing on the initiatives that had started with MIT's Technology Square. The renewal of the city's economic base in East Cambridge was now under way.

In 1966 MIT appointed a new president. Howard W. Johnson, a youthful forty-four, was a great supporter of the city's efforts to revitalize its economy and to preserve its historical heritage, and he was determined to make his views known. He presented his ideas for a new era in town-gown relations at the annual meeting of the Cambridge Chamber of Commerce. His optimism led him to encourage students to serve in the community. He sought friendships with city councilors. But President Pusey, now somewhat more cynical about the city's representatives, told Johnson, "Be careful, Howard, they are difficult." Johnson recalls that he later came to know exactly what Pusey meant. He recorded in his memoir, *Holding the Center*, that "town gown relationships are always complex. Fraught with difficulty [they demand] constant attention."

With new leadership in the city—Mayor Daniel Hayes and City Manager Joseph DeGuglielmo—there seemed to be a new opportunity for amity. The city leadership asked the institutional leadership for help in developing a cooperative spirit that could help Cambridge move forward on a number of fronts. Chairman Killian and President Johnson at MIT directed the institute's planning office to identify new financial resources for the city. The planning staff helped the city prepare requests to federal agencies that ultimately won it "Model Cities" funds. They also identified professional resources that allowed Cambridge to take a fresh look at the divisive issue of the Inner Belt highway and design a unified strategy for defending the city from this threat, ultimately demonstrating that it was an unnecessary element of the state's transportation plan.

There were, however, some issues that continued to elude resolution: housing and the city's educational system. In 1967 Harvard labor economist John Dunlop chaired a committee on faculty recruitment and retention; it concluded that the improvement of the Cambridge schools and better housing were essential to the university's ability to hire and keep good faculty. Not long after that, Pusey appointed a faculty committee to look into how the university should deal with the city. Daniel Patrick Moynihan was a member of the committee whose report said, among other things, "The unremitting scandal of Harvard's relationship to its community has been its relationship with the working class."

The Pilot agreements established in 1928 were once again up for renewal in 1968, and both universities renewed them, although somewhat differently. Harvard's officers chose to introduce a percentage of income on real estate as a basis for its payment; MIT continued the longstanding policy of contributions based in part on the average tax levy for land.

It was also in 1968 that the city council agreed to go forward with the Kendall Square Urban Renewal project to accommodate the NASA Electronics Research Center. But the country was at war in Vietnam, and the turmoil between the city's young and old was palpable. The universities were the locus of student pressures to change society: Harvard was perceived to be part of the establishment that had led the country into the morass, and MIT was seen as making the military instruments that sustained the policies of the national administration. Passions ran high, and ultimately a small group of radical students was able to create the conditions for violent confrontation. The "takeover" of the Harvard administration building in 1969, followed by Pusey's call for assistance from state and local authorities, resulted in the famous "bust." But it also presented in vivid terms the cartoon of the gown being attacked by its own progeny and calling on the town to save it from harm. The irony of two hundred officers mostly from working-class backgrounds expelling the privileged students of the middle and upper classes from what the town had always seen as the impregnable tower of the elite was historic.

It was a time of citizen manifestos and demands, and calls for the city and the institutions to solve the social and shelter problems of the community abounded. The opportunity to participate in the revolutionary fervor was too delicious for some. The faculty and students at the Harvard Graduate School of Design soon became the source of protest graphics and housing-need reports—some of questionable integrity—that called people to the barricades. It was another student-worker alliance that burned brightly for a while and then faded into oblivion when self-interest replaced political passion.

In this atmosphere, in January 1970 some MIT students, after crafting a metal ram, broke into the president's office and presided there for some days. The administration decided to let the adventure run its course and avoided a violent confrontation. In time the intruders left, having learned that MIT was more interested in solving problems for the future than in inflicting pain for past injuries.

Throughout this period, the housing issue continued to be the nagging irritant that kept the conflict between town and gown alive. Dissatisfied with the rate of progress, in 1969 MIT announced the acquisition of the Simplex Wire and Cable property and a program for building seven hundred units of turnkey housing for the elderly for the Cambridge Housing Authority. Known as the L. B. Johnson apartments in Cambridgeport, the Millers River apartments in East Cambridge, and the Daniel Burns apartments in North Cambridge, they were the largest single contribution to affordable housing for the elderly in the city's history.

Competition for housing resources in a city that had become one of the principal destinations of the "liberated" young of the country was making things increasingly difficult for both town and gown. The resulting rise in the cost of housing was laying the ground for the introduction, in 1970, of rent control. The author of the rent control ordinance, Assistant City Manager

Residents of the Riverside neighborhood, angered over Harvard projects in their neighborhood, stormed the 1970 Harvard Commencement. *(Harvard University Archives)*

Justin Gray, was sure it would be only a temporary measure, quickly rescinded when the housing crisis passed. As it turned out, it became the polarizing issue in the city's politics for many years to come. It had many unintended consequences, and it shaped the political climate in which town and gown lived in ways that few could have imagined.

Other events in which town and gown were intertwined emerged during the year. The sudden cancellation of the NASA project by the Nixon Administration galvanized the city to ask its institutional and political friends to find a compatible federal use for the site, and the U.S. Department of Transportation's transportation research center became the site's new tenant. But the most dramatic town-gown event of the year was the protest at Harvard's Commencement by Saundra Graham, a Riverside neighborhood activist, against the university's proposed development of university housing on the Treeland site (later Mahoney's Garden Center) on Memorial Drive. Graham won that fight and went on to win election to the city council and state legislature. Thirty years later, she found herself again confronting Harvard on its proposal to build, first a museum, then, after protests, student housing on the

Saundra Graham, neighborhood activist, center, leads a protest at the 1970 Harvard Commencement over the university's projects in the Riverside neighborhood. *(Harvard University Archive)*

same site. Although the faces representing Harvard had changed, the university's relentless application of political and economic power allowed it finally to achieve its objective—at a price.

The following year, 1971, both MIT and Harvard appointed new presidents. Jerome Wiesner, who had been President Kennedy's science adviser and who was deeply committed to ending the war in Vietnam, took over at MIT, while Derek Bok, dean of the Harvard Law School, became Harvard's president. Nevertheless, the major news of the year for both town and gown was Governor Frank Sargent's decision to eliminate the Inner Belt highway from the state's transportation plan.

The 1970s were full of excitement for both the city and its institutions. It was a muscular time: civility had slipped into the background, and "demands" had replaced "requests for consideration." Yet the outside world continued to influence the common agenda. Nixon's announcement that he would begin a war on cancer energized scientists and citizens alike. The scientific resources that would come to Cambridge would require new facilities and attract new researchers. Their intense activity helped to create the structure for the science-based industries that came to form the backbone of the city's economy two decades later.

The dominant atmosphere at the time, however, was of cultural and political revolution. "Hippies" and "flower children" camped in and around the universities. Challenges to traditional authority were rife in both town and gown. Sexual liberation and the "People's Republic of Cambridge" were the standards that flew in the face of the institutions that were trying to protect the principles of rational discussion and respect for individual rights.

Political events that focused on the role of university laboratories in national and international policy occasionally got out of hand. The police responded at times with clouds of tear gas, but in the main, most of the activity was limited to debate and discourse. It was a time when new political leadership, drawn often from university graduates, began to emerge. David Sullivan, an MIT alumnus and no relation to the Cambridge Sullivans, took a leading role in the Cambridge Civic Association. Elected to the city council, he had an agenda that was intended to change the balance of power in the city. Not inconsequential to his objective was the fact that eighteen-year-olds had recently gained the right to vote.

The city now began to make formal, annual requests to all tax-exempt landowners for a Pilot based on their land holdings. MIT and Harvard were already participating, but Lesley College and other smaller institutions, challenged by the difficult financial times, demurred.

By 1973, MIT had sold its interest in Technology Square, having produced some 900,000 square feet of new tax-paying buildings. But next door, the Cambridge Redevelopment Authority was faced with another federal government decision: to abandon a portion of the twenty-odd acres of land that it had reserved for its electronics research center. Eleven acres were now available for other uses, and Mayor Barbara Ackermann appointed a citizens' committee to review the options for development. Despite the cries for more mixed-income housing from MIT and the surrounding neighborhoods, some city councilors opposed new housing, apparently fearing that it would change the political balance in the neighborhood. This shortsighted view was abetted by a combination of forces that saw the eastern end of the city solely as a cash cow.

The end of the Vietnam War in 1975 brought much relief to town and gown, but only a year later a new controversy erupted. This time it involved recombinant DNA research. Ethical and safety discussions had been going on for some years, and in 1975 a national conference in California proposed standards for conducting such research. Mayor Alfred Vellucci, however, aware of the interest of some Harvard faculty in building a laboratory for this research, saw an opportunity to demonstrate his skill at reminding the university—and those "elitist know-it-alls in this city's academic quarters"— that the public might have something to say about the issue. Hearings were conducted, and Vellucci generated much national publicity for Cambridge and himself. Frank Duehay, a city councilor and Harvard alumnus, moved to put the matter out of reach of political maneuvering by sponsoring a resolution that would have the city manager establish an advisory committee to review it. After much controversy, an ordinance was passed that established a biohazards committee to oversee all university and commercial recombinant DNA research in the city. Many other university towns adopted this model legislation.

Notwithstanding moments of cooperation, continued concern about institutional expansion into residential neighborhoods prompted the passage the following year of a home rule petition, which allowed the city to restrict institutional expansion into low-density residential neighborhoods. The principal impact of this new authority was to convey to Harvard that its development opportunities in Cambridge were narrowing. It was time to look to other pastures for its growth. So Harvard looked across the river and began purchasing property in Allston.

As these development and neighborhood pressures mounted, Lesley College contemplated leaving Cambridge for a less contentious place. Ultimately deciding that its mission could best be achieved in Cambridge, it resolved to seek solutions to its need for nearby space. It also began a summer school program for the Cambridge schools and established at the college the Cambridge Partnership for Primary Education. Lesley's close ties to the Cambridge school system were in stark contrast to the cool relations that had prevailed with Harvard.

By 1984 Paul E. Gray had been inaugurated as president of MIT, and fourteen years had passed since the school had acquired the Simplex property. After endless difficulties, the institute had designated a developer, Forest City Enterprises, and the city had then empanelled a blue ribbon committee to recommend criteria for development. In 1988 Cambridge, MIT, and Forest City Enterprises finally came to terms on a plan for the area, to be called University Park. The city council passed the necessary zoning changes and the project proceeded. By the end of the century, University Park was generating five million dollars a year in taxes and supporting 4,500 new jobs.

Another opportunity for cooperation that year came with the renovation of the Kendall subway station. MIT and the Cambridge Historical Commission worked with the MBTA to create a design that continues to educate and delight residents and visitors alike. In addition, on the occasion of the renewal of the Pilot agreement with Cambridge, Harvard agreed to make some of its housing resources available to the community at a deep discount.

The final decade of the century reflected the growing parity of power between town and gown. With new legal authority, the city was able to exercise more control over institutional land use. Furthermore, pressures on the institutions for more direct contributions to the city's welfare, and Cambridge's willingness to use its legal powers to slow or deflect institutional aspirations, were increasing.

The institutions' response was to try to minimize friction with their neighbors and the city council. Early in the nineties, Harvard announced an increase in its PILOT payment and a commitment to the Cambridge Partnership for Public Education. It made new commitments to increase affordable housing and agreed to include a branch library in a faculty housing project on Observatory Hill.

In 1990 Charles Vest came from the University of Michigan with midwestern optimism and a friendly outlook to become MIT's president. One of his chief missions was to repair the negative perception of universities that had developed during the Vietnam War and rebuild the relationship between MIT and the U.S. Congress.

The following year, Neil Rudenstine became president of Harvard. He tried, like others before him, to consolidate the administration of the university. But the effort to move toward one Harvard policy on many issues, including town and gown relations, faltered before the Harvard principle of "every tub on its own bottom." The time-honored tub principle was a financial tradition that gave the Harvard deans great control of their own affairs, including their growth and expansion plans. Rudenstine exhausted himself early in his tenure and, after taking a short leave, returned to spend most of his efforts on fundraising. At the end of his incumbency he sponsored a number of initiatives in housing and education with Cambridge and Boston that were characterized by Duehay, now mayor of Cambridge, as "a magnificent step forward."

At Lesley, Margaret McKenna, the new president, oversaw the school's physical expansion through the acquisition of the nearby Porter Exchange, a building whose owners had fallen on hard times. The university then reached out to form a more extensive relationship with Cambridge public schools and their teachers. Its "Yes to Education" program provided support for seventy Cambridge students from the Harrington School, and it offered tuition discounts to teachers and city employees.

With some important battles won, Cambridge continued to press its universities for more openness about their plans and how they could serve the common interest. In 1991 Mayor Kenneth Reeves appointed a city council committee on university-community relations and got the institutions to agree to submit an annual report to the planning board and city council on their population, housing, and growth expectations. The city also continued its efforts to derive more revenue from the institutions. Frank Duehay, who had returned to the city council, commissioned a study of the issue. Prepared at the Kennedy School of Government, it outlined the pros and cons of the different ways in which the universities could compensate the city, concluding that the current arrangements were, in fact, a better solution than the alternatives.

The city now took every opportunity to extract a quid pro quo when the institutions required public approval or special services. One instance was the conflict over a "wet shelter" for alcoholics. In 1974 Justice Lawrence Felony of the Cambridge District Court had asked MIT for permission to use a site on Albany Street for two trailers that would be used by a Cambridge alcohol and drug rehabilitation program, CASPAR, until permanent quarters were available. MIT agreed to lease the land for a dollar a year with the understanding that the site was reserved for student housing. Then, in 1992, MIT asked permission to connect two of its buildings under a public way. The previous year, it had given CASPAR notice that it wanted to move forward with its student housing on Albany Street and hoped the city would finally provide the program with a permanent home. No neighborhood in the city wanted CASPAR in its precincts, and Cambridge said it preferred to have the rehab program remain at MIT. The institute planner then crafted a proposal that would accommodate the city in exchange for public rights of way and easements through its campus. In 1993 the city and MIT agreed on a formula that would accomplish their mutual objectives.

In 1994 a group of small property owners who felt unfairly burdened by the Cambridge Rent Control Law managed to bring the local issue to a statewide vote. When the referendum won, rent control ended in Cambridge, Boston, and Brookline, with profound effects on town and gown. Pent-up demand and artificially suppressed rents collided, and rents began to climb rapidly. Little rental housing had been built during the rent control years, so rising rents pushed many older and long-term residents out of the city. Cambridge's efforts to increase the number of affordable housing units—by levying a requirement on new housing or by boosting contributions to the housing fund—did not slow the tide. The universities felt the impact of these changes as their students tried to find housing in Cambridge. They built some additions to their housing stock but not enough to keep up with the growth of student enrollment.

The sense of empowerment that a new generation of leadership in Cambridge was developing soon began to be clear to both the universities and the city. A new kind of resident activist, frustrated by the pace of dealing with traffic, the erosion of open space, and inadequate controls over development, spurred residents' call for a better quality of life. They identified new commercial development as the culprit in generating traffic, pollution, and parking problems. They saw university developments, particularly those that bordered residential areas, as excessively dense and overbearing. They began to use all

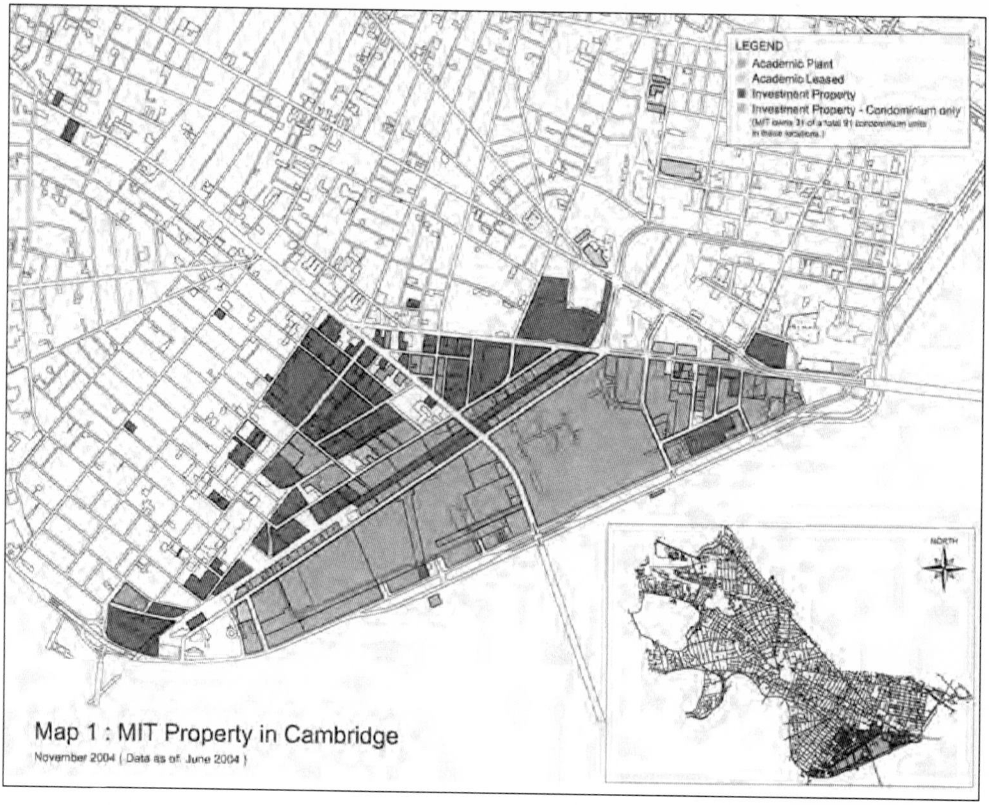
LEGEND
Academic Plant
Academic Leased
Investment Property
Investment Property - Condominium only
NORTH
Map 1 : MIT Property in Cambridge
November 2004 (Data as of June 2004)

Shaded areas indicate property owned by the Massachusetts Institute of Technology in Cambridge, November 2004. *(Cambridge Community Development)*

the legal tools at their disposal to redress the balance that they believed had been lost. Legal suits and zoning petitions were now the favored tools; every development was contested.

At the same time, the city's demography was changing again, with a growing distance between economic classes and races. New immigrants, representing a variety of ethnic, racial, and language groups the city had not contended with before, were making new demands. The city was getting richer as a result of new, technology-stimulated development, but it was becoming more expensive to live in. For the universities, this became a serious issue. For politicians, the easy way out was to blame the ills on the institutions, claiming that they were not paying their fair share. The lack of an acceptable response from public agencies and boards to the issues of traffic and development finally led to a citizen's petition to revise the city's zoning ordinance. The new changes reduced allowable densities, limited building heights, restricted university campus development, and imposed new restrictions in the city's industrial zones, institutional districts, Cambridgeport, and East Cambridge.

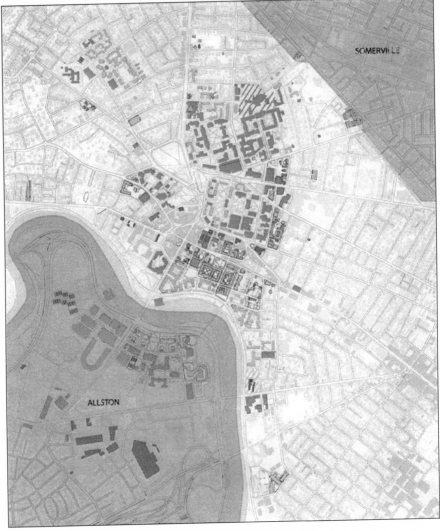

Harvard University Town Gown Report, 2004. Harvard properties are shaded. *(Cambridge Community Development)*

The success of this rezoning and the subsequent proposals from the Citywide Growth Management Advisory Committee curtailed the institutions' development opportunities. Some began to focus on areas outside Cambridge for their future. Lesley developed programs to be delivered across the country; Harvard looked to Boston's Allston neighborhood and Watertown; MIT tried to use the land it had assembled in Cambridge over the years to meet its current and future needs.

Meanwhile, the old themes were still being played out, with new demands for institutional financial contributions and calls for additions to the city's affordable housing inventory and for middle-income housing. Acquiring more land for public facilities was also high on the agenda. Harvard announced a housing loan program that addressed the expansion of affordable housing in an innovative way. MIT proposed ways to improve traffic safety on Memorial Drive and Massachusetts Avenue; it also gave additional parkland to the Cambridgeport community and agreed to redevelop a building site in Central Square for two community theater groups.

The extensive interactions between the universities and the school system continued in spite of the unrelenting difficulty of dealing with an educational system trying to serve a racially and economically divided community. Over time, one set of social divisions and prejudices had been exchanged for others. An educational system that had begun by providing immigrants with their first steps up the ladder of social mobility was now struggling to meet the demands of a new and more diverse population.

Nevertheless, town and gown could look back at the end of the century on a city that had come full circle: a prosperous industrial and university town had fallen into decay and had been revived, thanks in part to the intellectual capital of its universities. From time to time, Cambridge had been able to overcome its penchant for tribalism, take advantage of new opportunities to support its economy, and select leadership that could cross the boundaries between town and gown and help the city fulfill its promise. On occasion, the universities had been blessed with leadership that recognized residency in Cambridge as an opportunity for creative service, though they tended to react to the town's challenges rather than take the initiative. Both town and gown had to acknowledge, however, that to engage their talents and resources in creative and useful ways would always be a work in progress.

Cambridge: A Congressional Battleground

MICHAEL KENNEY

CAMBRIDGE HAS OFTEN BEEN a battleground in congressional races from 1904 to the present, but for almost half that period the city's voice in the U.S. House of Representatives came from Boston, Somerville, or the western suburbs. That "not from here" representation has usually been the result of Cambridge's being divided among several congressional districts. Yet even at the beginning of the twentieth century, when Cambridge was the dominant community in the Eighth District, its congressional voice was that of a Winchester Republican, Samuel W. McCall—with the votes of Republican-leaning suburban towns outweighing those of city voters.

Frederick S. Deitrick, the Democratic Cambridge state representative who had run unsuccessfully three times against McCall, won the seat in 1912 when McCall retired—only to lose it to Frederick Dallinger, a Cambridge Republican, in 1914. Dallinger's win led off a twenty-six-year period during which Cambridge was represented by a Republican: Dallinger for sixteen of those years, defeating a string of Cambridge Democrats; Harry Thayer of Wakefield for one term; and Robert Luce of Waltham for six years.

That pattern was broken only by the New Deal victory in 1934 of Richard Russell, a Cambridge Democrat, a former mayor, and a son of the progressive governor William E. Russell. But Luce recaptured the seat in 1936 and held it until he was defeated in 1940 by the Cantabrigian Thomas H.

Campaigning in 1946. During Memorial Day ceremonies, John F. Kennedy, then running for Congress, places a wreath on the John W. Weeks Memorial Bridge. With him, from left, were officers of the Hoyt Post VFW: Women's Auxiliary President Blanche Simarde; Jr. Vice Commander John W. Hamilton; Post Commander Frank Lynaugh; and Sr. Vice Commander John Roderick. *(John F. Kennedy Library/Cambridge Historical Commission)*

Eliot, a Brahmin New Dealer who had played a major role in fashioning the Social Security Act of 1935.

Meanwhile, during the 1930s, Republican-friendly gerrymandering had moved several Cambridge wards into districts dominated by Boston, Somerville, and the rural and suburban towns represented by the Lowell Republican Edith Nourse Rogers. And in 1942, when another gerrymander put all of Cambridge into the Boston-based Eleventh District, the seat attracted the attention of James Michael Curley, then seeking to recoup his political fortunes after a string of defeats for mayor, senator, and governor. In the primary, Curley defeated Eliot using familiar smear tactics, including a Curley or Communism billboard.

Then, with the 1946 election looming and his son John home from the war, Ambassador Joseph P. Kennedy convinced Curley to give up the seat and run again for mayor—setting up one of the classic "battleground" contests.

The neophyte JFK was the celebrity candidate in a field of seventeen, but he had a formidable opponent in Cambridge's state representative (and future mayor) Michael Neville. With Cambridge and Somerville casting some 40 percent of the vote, "My father thought he owned the district," Neville's son recalled years later.

But Kennedy owned the airwaves, the subway and trolley cars, and the billboards (some ninety of them at nine thousand dollars a month). And he staged an event that became part of Cambridge political lore—a reception at the Commander Hotel on the Saturday evening before the June primary. Cambridge Common had been wired for sound, and the nearby streets were clogged as some fifteen hundred Cambridge women turned out in their spring finery to be greeted by a receiving line that included Rose Fitzgerald Kennedy and her husband, Jack himself, and his sister Eunice.

As the future mayor Walter J. Sullivan recalled, Neville "never knew what hit him." He held Cambridge, but only by 1,134 votes out of 16,068; Kennedy carried the district with 42 percent of the vote, nearly twice that of Neville. Kennedy gave up the seat to run for the Senate in 1952, setting up a second "battleground" contest.

Considering that Thomas P. "Tip" O'Neill Jr. would hold the congressional seat for thirty-six years, it requires turning back forty years of political history to realize that his initial victory was not at all a sure thing. O'Neill's chief rival was Michael LoPresti of East Boston, the state senator whose district included East Cambridge (his son Michael Jr. would follow him in the state senate). The contest became one of ethnic rivalry between the long-dominant Irish and the Italians who had supplanted them in East Cambridge, East Boston, and Boston's North End.

In the closing days of the race, O'Neill was hit by two charges stemming from his position as speaker of the Massachusetts House (he was the first Democrat to hold that position). As John A. Farrell recounts in his biography, *Tip O'Neill and the Democratic Century*, two weeks before the primary it came to light that O'Neill had "shepherded an arcanely worded bill through the State House" that granted Curley a pension roughly equal to what he would have earned as a congressman. The deal had been cut the year before, when Curley had hinted that he might run for the congressional seat, throwing a curve into O'Neill's own plans to run.

Then, just as O'Neill was weathering that flap, it was charged that as speaker he had "pigeonholed" a bill to extend the life of the legislature's Committee to Curb Communism. "The long arm of Moscow has reached into the State House," charged Representative Edmond J. Donlan of West Roxbury.

But O'Neill had one card to play: Archbishop Richard J. Cushing. At a communion breakfast the Sunday before the primary, Cushing called for an end to "the ungrounded judgment of the vileness of others," and, Farrell wrote, "From more than one pulpit that Sunday, a parish priest informed the faithful that [O'Neill] was a patriotic American and no Communist dupe." LoPresti carried East Boston and the North End, but O'Neill "clobbered" him in Cambridge, 13,404 to 4,528, and won the primary by 3,262 votes.

Spool forward to perhaps the greatest "battleground" contest of them all, the 1986 race to succeed O'Neill. With $3.8 million spent, it was among the most expensive congressional primaries in American political history to that date. With fifty-one forums all focused on issues, it was the most debated. And with the presence of Joseph P. Kennedy II, there was not just celebrity but a sense of excitement rarely seen before in a campaign.

Cambridge would account for just over 20 percent of the vote, but the campaign of the local candidate, James Roosevelt Jr., had never taken off. The city's liberal-academic establishment was more congenial to Mel King, a Roxbury community activist with the status of liberal folk hero, and especially to the liberal George Bachrach of Watertown, who represented part of Cambridge in the state senate and also had considerable appeal in the liberal and upscale precincts of Arlington and Belmont. Joe Kennedy was the brash outsider. Acknowledging Kennedy's star quality, Bachrach would often greet and startle voters he encountered on the street by saying, "Hello, I'm not Joe Kennedy."

In tracking polls throughout the spring and summer, Kennedy held a consistent lead that generally hovered around 35 percent. Then, just a week before the September primary, a *Boston Globe* poll showed a race that had narrowed to just five points. Bachrach saw his opportunity to "sharpen the differences" with an issue likely to galvanize liberal voters in Cambridge: the bombing raids against Libya earlier that year, in which there had been civilian casualties—and which Kennedy had supported.

In *The Race for the Eighth*, Gerald Sullivan and I recounted the Bachrach attack as it was played out in television debates and candidate forums. The climax came on the Wednesday before the primary, first at a Cambridge forum on national security.

Bachrach: Would you support doing it again, Joe? Would you support doing it again?

Kennedy: You bet I would support...

Bachrach: Even if it took civilian lives, Joe?

Kennedy: Yes I would...

Coming and going: Joseph P. Kennedy II, left, greets House Speaker
Thomas P. O'Neill Jr. outside a Cambridge polling place on Primary Day,
September 1986. After his victory that fall, Kennedy would succeed O'Neill in
Congress. *(The Boston Globe)*

Then, at a television debate that night, Bachrach dropped what he
thought would be the bombshell: documents suggesting that a consortium of
Arab banks, including three controlled by the Libyan leader Muammar
Khadafy, had a lien on Kennedy's Citizens Energy Corporation.

Bachrach: The question is simple. Yes or no, are you in hock to Colonel
Khadafy?

Kennedy, as Sullivan and Kenney reported it, "looked momentarily startled, but then looked directly at Bachrach. When he spoke it was with a barely concealed anger: 'Excuse me, George. You've accused me of being for a raid
on Libya. Libya offered Sirhan Sirhan asylum after he killed my father. And
for you to think for one second...that [Citizens Energy] would have anything
to do with any oil coming out of Libya is just totally off-base.'"

When Bachrach realized the next morning how his "best shot" had played out, he said that he began "to prepare the people around me for what was going to happen." What happened was a Kennedy walkover, with 52 percent of the vote—remarkable in a twelve-person race. Bachrach even lost, though narrowly, both Cambridge and his home base of Watertown.

By contrast, the 1998 primary was a tamer affair, but with Cambridge still the battleground. Three strong candidates had bases outside the city: Mayor Michael Capuano in Somerville, former Mayor Ray Flynn in Boston, and Bachrach in Watertown. Meanwhile, the campaign of the Cambridge candidate, the environmental activist John T. O'Connor, sputtered like Roosevelt's in 1986. And in the end it was a move to Capuano by some core Cambridge political figures that put him ahead of O'Connor in the city's vote and contributed to his solid win in the district. Capuano ended up swamping the Republican, Philip Hyde III of Somerville, and two minor candidates, winning 74.4 percent of the vote in the final.

"What's in a Name?" or "Is This the First Garden Club?"

ANNETTE LAMOND

AN UNUSUAL THING HAPPENED in a pastoral corner of Cambridge in January 1889: A passion flower bloomed, profusely according to legend, at Havenhurst, the Coolidge Hill home of Mrs. John Lord Hayes. The Hayes family was known for its love of gardening,[1] and Mrs. Hayes for her particular success with houseplants, of which she had many. Even so, the passion flower's many blossoms—sixty that winter, according to a report some twenty years later by one of Mrs. Hayes's daughters—caused much interest among the family's visitors. Their questions regarding its cultivation gave Miss Carrie Hayes, the youngest of three daughters, the idea of forming a club.

Known for her enthusiasm, Miss Hayes consulted with other plant- and garden-loving friends, and on the twenty-eighth of the month a club was founded by some twenty ladies of varying ages. On that day, a name—the Floricultural Club—was selected, by-laws drafted, dues established, officers elected, garden periodical subscriptions selected, and a schedule of bimonthly meetings set, decisions duly recorded in a volume of minutes that now resides in the Schlesinger Library at the Radcliffe Institute.

The organization, which was renamed the Plant Club at its second meeting, thrived from its beginning in that auspiciously mild winter. It soon became known for educational lectures, some by local professors, some by its own learned members. The members also enjoyed informal discussions

Susan "Susie" Hayes with her brother (William Allen Hayes) at Havenhurst on Coolidge Hill, ca. 1920. *(Records of the Cambridge Plant Club & Garden Club, Schlesinger Library, Radcliffe Institute, Harvard University)*

on a variety of subjects: Did professional gardening require too much physical effort for women? Could flowers have a moral influence on prisoners? The topic of favorite plants came up often and in detail. Another feature of meetings was the trading of helpful horticultural hints, including recipes for fertilizers, planting tips, soil preparation, the care of particular plants, propagation methods, and treatments for pests. Members often brought plants and flowers to show and share, and they enjoyed visiting one another's gardens.

By the turn of the century, the club had developed an interest in garden design. In 1904 Mrs. Sarah Warner Brooks, a member who supported herself as a garden "manager" and writer, published a book at the age of eighty-three: *A Garden with House Attached.* In 1907 a lecture by the landscape horticulturist Warren H. Manning showed—with the assistance of lantern slides—"how the most hopelessly unattractive house may be much improved" by planting the right kind of trees to ensure an air of seclusion.

The members' passion for plants led them to be early conservationists. The club's records show that the ladies soon began to talk about the preservation of wildflowers, and in 1900 all members enrolled their names in the Society for the Protection of Native Plants, a predecessor of the New England

First page of the minutes of the Cambridge Plant Club's first meeting, January 28, 1889. (*Records of the Cambridge Plant Club & Garden Club, Schlesinger Library, Radcliffe Institute, Harvard University*)

Wild Flower Preservation Society, founded some twenty years later. In 1904 Professor George Lincoln Goodale, director of the Harvard Botanic Garden, gave a lecture, "The New Science of Oecology: The Relation of Plants to Their Environment." (The minutes for the meeting helpfully note, "Oecology is a word so new that it is not yet in the dictionary.") Issues ranged from concerns about ash barrels (the subject of a club symposium in 1912) to opposition to highway projects that threatened the city's last remaining urban wilds in the 1950s and the sycamores along Memorial Drive in the 1960s.

Medal presented by the Massachusetts Horticultural Society in 1931 to the Cambridge Plant Club in recognition of being "the first of its kind." *(Records of the Cambridge Plant Club & Garden Club, Schlesinger Library, Radcliffe Institute, Harvard University)*

Gradually, the club added civic planting to its portfolio of interests. In 1917 it undertook its first planting projects: adding beds of bulbs to brighten "the otherwise gloomy surroundings of the playground" at the Margaret Fuller House in East Cambridge, as well as children's "war gardens" in a nearby field. In the 1920s it turned its energy to Cambridge Common, which had lost many trees when it was used as a site for military barracks during World War I. First, trees were planted; then, a twenty-year project designed to screen parked cars with a shrubbery border followed.

The Plant Club voted to join the Massachusetts Federation of Garden Clubs just after the organization was formed in 1928. Contacts with like-minded people in other clubs proved a stimulus to civic projects, as did the friendly competition of flower shows. Membership in the federation also seems to have encouraged some measure of political expression. For example, members joined the opposition to the building of filling stations on scenic highways. Although the necessity of gas stations came to be accepted, one area of concern—a campaign for billboard controls—was a rallying issue for years.

In 1931 the club was proud to receive a medal from the Massachusetts Horticultural Society in recognition of its status as the oldest garden club in the country. However, in 1939—the year in which the club marked its fiftieth anniversary—an unsettling event occurred. The national organization of state garden-club federations conferred the title upon another group, one three years younger. The competing club had waged an aggressive campaign, conducted over several years, to discredit the Cambridge organization, but no one had informed the Cambridge women that the honor, the distinction of being the first, required defense. This paper, more than six decades later, documents the facts of the case. It is offered as both a tribute to the founding members of the Plant Club and proof that theirs was the first women's garden club in the United States.

OCTOBER 1928

"There seems to be some question as to the first garden club ever formed in this country." So begins an item entitled "Garden Club Beginnings," just four paragraphs running alongside advertisements for specimen evergreens, rare cacti, and late-blooming peonies on a back page of the October 1 issue of *Horticulture*.[2]

At the time, *Horticulture* was a semimonthly publication of the Massachusetts Horticultural Society. Although the casual tone of its indirect query was perhaps calculated to avoid controversy, no one could have predicted how contentious the debate would prove to be. The article did not indicate why the issue of identifying the first garden club had been raised, but it is likely that the founders of the state garden-club federations then springing up across the country became interested as they drafted charters for the new organizations.[3]

The magazine piece was sensitive to the possibility that a club's name might be an issue. Noting the "general impression" that The Garden Club of Philadelphia, founded in 1904, was the first,[4] given its leading role in the garden-club movement, the feature revealed that a similar organization, the Minnesota Garden Flower Society, had also been founded the same year. Although the Minnesota group may have been called a "flower society," *Horticulture* observed that it was "to all intents and purposes a garden club."

Horticulture thus allowed that the words *garden club* (capital G, capital C) need not be included in a club's name for it to be so recognized, and it acknowledged the difficulty of naming a new club, especially a group based on a novel concept. The magazine noted that even the Garden Club of America (GCA), founded in 1913, went through a period of indecision concerning a name.

DECEMBER 1928

The December 1 issue of *Horticulture* features a letter, "The Oldest Garden Club," from Miss Fanny Elizabeth Corne, a charter member of the Cambridge Plant Club:

Dear Sir –

In the October 1 issue of *Horticulture*, it is stated that the Garden Club of Philadelphia, formed in 1904, and a similar organization formed in Minneapolis, Minn., in the same year were probably the first garden clubs ever formed in this country. The Cambridge (Mass.) Plant Club, however, antedates these clubs by fully 15 years, since it was started in January, 1889, and is not only still in existence, but is in a very flourishing condition. Several of the original members are still interested and active. Since meetings are held at the homes of different members, a social half hour concluding each, membership is limited to 40, usually with a waiting list. The Plant Club is affiliated with the Garden Club Federation of Massachusetts.

The idea of forming a club was original with the late Miss Caroline Hayes, and was suggested by the numerous inquiries she received concerning the method used in cultivating a passion flower blooming in her mother's sitting-room. With a few friends and neighbors, a club was formed which met periodically [every two weeks for a number of years, then monthly], at first only to exchange opinions and experiences related to house plants. But interest soon extended to all growing green things since different members had their specialties—flower gardens, vegetable gardens, trees, ferns and rock gardens. Lectures by Harvard professors and others interested in horticulture were arranged, while occasional excursions were made to neighboring estates. Friends in neighboring towns, hearing of our novel association, liked the idea so well that they started similar clubs of their own.

Fanny Elizabeth Corne
Charter Member

There is no indication in the Plant Club's archives of how *Horticulture*'s historical inquiry came to the attention of the club, but Miss Corne was an avid horticulturist, so presumably she saw the article in the normal course of perusing the periodical. She was also a writer interested in travel and botanical subjects. From 1924 through 1927, for example, she contributed eleven articles to *American Fern Journal*: "Ferns—Facts and Fancies about Them" (in eight parts) and "A Caribbean Cruise and Some Jamaican Wayside Ferns" (in three parts).

Fanny Corne was eighty-one years old when she replied to *Horticulture*'s inquiry. Although her letter gave a good overview of the club, one statement later clouded its claim to be the oldest: her recollection that the group met "at first only to exchange opinions and experience relative to house plants." The statement was inaccurate, and an advocate for a rival claimant later seized on it. In fact, a copy of the letter is in the archives of that rival club.

If only Miss Corne had first reviewed the club's minutes! If she had, she could have stated in most definite terms that the charter members' wide-ranging, learned, and lively interest in gardens, not just in plants, was clear from its very first meetings. Miss Corne might have written:

> The minutes of the first meeting of the new club, held on January 28, 1889, indicate that there was much discussion about a club name. It was voted to call it the Floricultural Club. Two weeks later at the second meeting, however, it was voted to change the name. Some ladies thought that Floricultural Club sounded too grand, as if the group sought to emulate the Massachusetts Horticultural Society—one of the Commonwealth's leading civic organizations, already sixty years old. Mrs. Hayes—whose passion flower inspired the founding of the club—suggested "The Plant Club," and that name was adopted. Why the Plant Club? After all, it was winter, and all had house plants. And as gardeners in a northerly climate, our thoughts in late January were focused on starting seeds and nurturing plants indoors—most of which would take their places outdoors in the garden just a few months later.
>
> Still, allowances made for climate, why not "The Garden Club"? We know that the women who attended that meeting did have gardens and were known for working in them. But "garden club" was not suggested because there was already a club in Cambridge with *garden* and *club* in its name—the Garden Street Club! In fact, the horticulturally gifted Miss Almira Needham, first president of the Plant Club, lived on the corner of Garden and Shepard streets, and was presumably a member of that club, too. In fact, at the Plant Club meeting of December 1, 1890, the members voted to postpone their next meeting by one week so as not to interfere with the meeting of the other group. Did the Garden Street Club have an interest in gardens? Possibly, given its location. (Garden Street was the route from Cambridge Common to the famed Harvard Botanic Garden.) But interest in that club waned, and it did not survive.
>
> Had it not been for the Garden Street Club, the Plant Club might well have been named the Garden Club, and there would have been no basis for dispute.

And, had Miss Corne reviewed the minutes of the nineteen meetings held during the club's first year, she might also have written:

Following the selection of a name at the club's first meeting, the ladies immediately got down to gardening business. An annual assessment was voted, and it was agreed to spend a portion of that assessment on periodicals, including *The English Garden, The American Garden,* and *Garden and Forest.* Lists of seeds were drawn up, including "hardy" varieties. With organizational matters complete, one young member named Jane Newell reported on snowdrops blooming in her garden since January 18! Another had roses that bloomed through the winter! The season was mild that year with little snow, so thoughts of gardening came early—a factor that likely contributed to the enthusiasm for forming a club in the dead of winter, and to members' being able to traverse the streets of Cambridge for meetings.

At the second meeting, the club voted to invest ten dollars on seeds, an amount that went very far in that category in 1889—so far that members subsequently spent hours sorting their seed orders. At the third meeting, the topic was soil; the minutes include a wealth of information and advice that began with "the desirability of having a compost heap in a retired corner of your yard where you accumulate dead leaves, grass, and all other vegetable matter." Over the club's first year, the members studied and discussed all manner of plants: shrubs, trees, wildflowers, roses, ferns, begonias, bulbs (spring, summer, and for forcing), vines, annuals, house plants (especially those offering winter bloom), and various perennials (poppies, lilies, hellebores, chrysanthemums, asters and more, usually referred to by Latin name). Also discussed were fertilizers, the insects that infect plants, and an abundance of horticultural tips. Some discussions were led by members who read their own papers; others were initiated by reading articles from gardening periodicals to which the club subscribed.

In the spring, hostesses of meetings began to open their gardens following the afternoon's official program. (The minutes refer to the members' pleasure in "going over" a garden on these occasions.) Members also brought specimens from their gardens to show, and at the first meeting in May, offerings were bounteous—gloxinias, bunches of forsythia and Pyrus japonica (now known as Japanese Quince), sprays of Japanese Crab, a bucket of yellow and red Polyanthus and cowslips.[5] As the season proceeded, members brought cut flowers for display.

Sharing, too, was a hallmark of the meetings. At a gathering in June, members adjourned to Mrs. Chauncy Smith's garden, where she generously shared "an unusually fine display of pansies" with her guests, in addition to giving out bulbs of hardy oxalis. In July Miss Carrie Hayes offered twenty plants of *Anthericum vittatum variegatum* to any member who wanted one.[6]

Undated photograph of Mrs. Edwin King Lumpkin, née Mary "Mamie" Bryan. *(Hargett Rare Book and Manuscript Library/University of Georgia Libraries)*

In December 1889, near the close of the club's first year, a meeting was devoted to the subject of gardening, during which members listened to an excerpt from a report of the Woman's Division of the German Academic Association. The minutes record that "the German gardeners opposed the movement on the grounds that gardening required too much physical effort of women, and that the business was already overcrowded." It was noted that an English paper had criticized the opposition in Germany to women gardeners, with the argument that "they did not expect women to be educated to dig, but there were many parts of gardening which they could enjoy and make profitable." Following a discussion of the role of women as garden workers, the club secretary recorded, "The rest of the meeting was passed in talking of the pleasures of gardening."

No one who reads through the minutes of the first year of the Plant Club—twenty-four handwritten pages—could conclude that it was anything but a garden club, though a formidably learned one to be sure. And word of it spread. The minutes for November 11, 1889, refer to an article in the *Boston Advertiser* describing the group, while two months later the annual report for the club's first year records that two other "plant clubs" had been founded in other towns—a fact reported with satisfaction.

When the representatives of the Ladies' Garden Club of Athens, Georgia, rose to claim that their club—founded in 1892—was the first, they argued that the name Plant Club implied a group with narrow botanical interests, not a garden club. In reply, the Cambridge ladies might well have sent them copies of the Plant Club minutes of 1889, 1890, and 1891. Indeed, by February 3, 1892—the date of the Athenian club's first gathering—the Cambridge group had already held sixty "garden club" meetings.

FEBRUARY 1929

A prominently placed article in *Horticulture*'s February 15, 1929, issue informs readers that several clubs have claimed precedence in point of age over those in Philadelphia and Minneapolis. No mention is made of the Cambridge club or any of the other "several" clubs but one—the Ladies' Garden Club of Athens, Georgia. *Horticulture* cites the authority of Mrs. E. K. Lumpkin, a woman possessed of a famed Georgia political name, who happened to be a charter member of the Ladies' Garden Club and a president emerita.[7] According to the article, the club was the idea of Dr. E. D. Newton,[8] a philanthropist in Athens and a man of varied achievements, who "consulted several prominent women of the city and then formed a garden club, the first regularly organized and authenticated one of its kind in the South, so far as can be ascertained."[9] Another Athenian distinction was the promulgation of club rules "governing the members" and "for judges to follow in awarding premiums." The rules [drafted by Mr. P. J. Berckmans of "national fame" in 1894] were sent to friends in other cities and "resulted in almost every town of any size in the state having a garden club."[10]

Although the *Horticulture* article did not quote Mrs. Lumpkin directly, it reads as if the magazine's editors relied closely on her communication. In addition to her distinction as a gardener (she had "perhaps the finest collection of iris in the South"), Mrs. Lumpkin clearly knew how to write a successful club press release. Whereas Miss Corne's letter had focused on the Plant Club's horticultural interests, Mrs. Lumpkin established that the Athenian club was a force in the larger community. Beyond flower shows (thirty since the founding of the club), it was busy in other areas. Its activities had included war work (raising money for wool used by the "Gray Knitters" as well as for a liberty bond), planting trees and shrubs in cooperation with city authorities, working in the schools, petitioning to restrict the use of billboards, and encouraging the preservation of native trees, especially the holly and dogwood. It also played an active role in establishing the state federation of garden clubs in June 1928.

Mrs. Lumpkin made an impressive case for the Ladies' Garden Club. But a Plant Club partisan would immediately observe that the founding date of the Athenian club followed the Cantabrigian one by three years. Moreover, the idea that led to the founding of the Georgia club was a man's. In fact, *Horticulture*'s account—based on Mrs. Lumpkin's communication—states that Mr. Newton "founded" the club. In contrast, the women who formed the Cambridge club had the idea themselves. Further, once they determined to create a club, they wrote the by-laws and established their own organizational structure. They did not seek the assistance of an outside authority in the matter of governance.

Another irony: despite the Ladies' Garden Club's name, the importance of judging rules to the Athens club suggests that it was initially more of a plant society—based on growing plants for prizes—than a garden club in the modern sense of the term. Indeed, the 1929 *Horticulture* article omitted the fact that members discussed plant cuttings and experimented with plants at their bimonthly meetings. According to coverage in the *Athens Banner* in the spring of 1892, the Athenian club's first "flower show" was more of an agricultural fair featuring prizes for well-grown vegetables.[11] Premium lists from subsequent flower shows in the 1890s also included prizes for "pot plants" or houseplants. (In Athens as in Cambridge, begonias were a favorite.)

The Cambridge Plant Club made no reply to *Horticulture*'s feature. Why the silence? Perhaps because, despite the title—"Is This the Oldest Garden Club?"—the article referred to the Athens club as the first "of its kind in the South" and did not call it the oldest in the country. The archives of the Cambridge Plant Club do not reveal whether any member saw the piece. It is not in the club's archives, nor is there any reference to it in the club's minutes or other files. Nevertheless, it is unlikely to have escaped the notice of the Cambridge gardeners, as the next item suggests.

NOVEMBER 1931

The November 1 issue of *Horticulture* features an article on the Cambridge Plant Club, "Forty Years of Garden Club Work." It reports that the Massachusetts Horticultural Society has just awarded a medal to the Cambridge Plant Club "in recognition of the distinction which it can boast of being the oldest garden club in America."[12]

Much has been written about the origin of the garden club movement but there is no record of any such organization having been formed previous to 1889, which was the year in which the Cambridge Plant Club came into existence. This club has carried on its various activities with unabated enthusiasm through all the subsequent years and is functioning actively at the present time. It is a member of the Garden Club Federation of Massachusetts and has exhibited at the Centennial Exhibition of the Massachusetts Horticultural Society. [In 1929, the club won a first prize for its exhibit—a reproduction of a flower window in the home of Mrs. Elmer H. Bright of 165 Brattle Street.] Several members of the original group are still taking part in the work of the club.

This organization was considered a novelty when it was formed and a number of similar clubs were started in neighboring cities soon after. They, however, lasted for only a short time. The first meeting of the Cambridge Plant Club was held on January 20 [sic], 1889, at the home of Mrs. John Hayes with about 20 persons present. The purpose of the club was stated to be the exchange of experiences and a discussion of the best methods of cultivating house and garden plants. The name of the club was suggested by Mrs. Hayes. In 1929 the club celebrated its fortieth anniversary with several of the original members present.

Like Miss Corne, the *Horticulture* article describes the club's original focus narrowly, in terms of plant cultivation—another lost opportunity to describe the true breadth of the club's interests at the time it was founded. The article went on to recognize the Ladies' Garden Club of Athens as the second oldest club in the country, followed by the Minnesota Garden Flower Society and the Garden Club of Philadelphia, both founded in 1904. The article also contained a note about names: "This organization [the Minnesota Garden Flower Society], in spite of its name, was a garden club in the commonly accepted sense and is still alive, with a membership of 400 and with much excellent work to its credit."

June 1932

The National Council of State Garden Club Federations meets in Boston for its fourth annual meeting.[13] At the opening session, following welcoming addresses by the presidents of the Garden Club Federation of Massachusetts and the National Council, Miss Fanny Elizabeth Corne is introduced to the delegates as a charter member of the Cambridge Plant Club, "the oldest garden club in America." Later in the week, members of the Plant Club entertain the meeting delegates in Cambridge.

Miss Corne's introduction to the National Council was reported in the June 15 issue of *Horticulture*.[14] The delegates' subsequent visit to Cambridge—a tour of the Longfellow House followed by tea "served in the garden of the charming old Colonial home, known as Larchwood, of Mrs. Henry D. Tudor"—was described in the Council's July *Bulletin*, which noted that the

Plant Club had been awarded a medal for "being the oldest garden club in this country."[15]

MARCH 1936

Mrs. M. R. Redwine, president of the Ladies (now without the apostrophe) Garden Club, writes to the president of the National Council of State Garden Clubs, asking the organization to publish a history of the Athens club in its bulletin. She suggests that the publication's readers would find it interesting to know something of her club. Further, she argues that it would be "only correct" for the national organization to recognize that the Ladies Garden Club was "the first garden club in America."

March 9, 1936
My dear Mrs. Scruggs,

As president of the Ladies Garden Club of Athens, Georgia, I am asking you if you will give us space in the next issue of the bulletin for a brief history of our club. Since the Ladies Garden Club is undoubtedly the parent club of the garden club movement, we feel that it will be of interest to the entire membership to know something of its interesting organization. We feel, also, that it is only correct that the Garden Club, as an organization, should give recognition to the fact the Ladies Garden Club of Athens, Georgia, is the first garden club in America—that it has existed since 1891, and that it is to-day, and has always been a GARDEN CLUB, organized for the same purposes and maintaining the same ideals that the members of the National Council maintain in the good year 1936.

We feel that a distinction should be made between a plant study club or horticultural study club and a garden club, as the term is defined in our organization. There have been numerous horticultural and plant study clubs in our own and in other communities, many of them existing prior to the year in which the Ladies Garden Club came into existence. Some of them are still flourishing in their original state; others, with the passing years, have felt the more human spirit of the real garden club and have accordingly grown away from their original purpose of organization and have become bona fide garden clubs. This does not imply, however, that they were bona fide garden clubs at the time of organization, and they cannot therefore claim to have been such when they organized.

Please bear in mind, dear Mrs. Scruggs, that the Ladies Garden Club was not a haphazard organization. It did not come into being by mere chance, nor was it the outgrowth of any other organization. It was organized as a GARDEN CLUB, under the name of the Ladies Garden Club, with constitution and by-laws setting forth its purposes. As early as the year 1892, this club was giving a flower show, the rules and standards for which would be acceptable for judging any flower show of today. These rules for exhibiting and judging were drawn up for the Ladies Garden Club by the well known horticulturalist [sic], P. J. Berckmans, Sr., of Augusta, Georgia. Copies of some of these old schedules are still in existence to-day.

Have you—has anybody heard of a bona fide garden club prior to the year 1891? Have you—has anybody heard of a GARDEN CLUB FLOWER SHOW prior to the year 1892? I daresay not. Those twelve women who organized the Ladies Garden Club of Athens, Georgia, were pioneers in their own right. They gave to their community and to the nation something new and something worth while, and, as time revealed, something of vital and lasting worth. It is naturally a matter of pride to us, and we feel that it is pardonable that we of the Ladies Garden Club should seek recognition for so valiant a contribution. We also feel that it will be a matter of equal pride, as well as a gracious gesture, for the National Council of State Garden Clubs to accord such recognition.

We shall be grateful indeed to you for any assistance that you may give us, either by giving us space in the bulletin, or through personal effort. Many of us, including myself, are the daughters of the charter members of the Ladies Garden Club, and one of the original members is still an active member, so you may be assured of more than perfunctory thanks.

With very best wishes, and the assurance of our loyalty,

I am
Sincerely

Mrs. M. R. Redwine
President of the Ladies Garden Club
Athens, Ga.

Thus began the Athens club's campaign for national recognition. Would that Mrs. Scruggs of the National Council had asked the Cambridge Plant Club to comment on Mrs. Redwine's letter. The Cantabrigians could have addressed the letter's questionable propositions—for example, the assertion that some plant or horticultural study clubs, feeling the "more human spirit of the real garden club," had grown away from their "original purpose." Certainly this statement did not apply to them. If Mrs. Redwine was referring to other clubs, what were their names and what was her evidence?[16]

Mrs. Redwine's letter also contained misleading statements that the Cantabrigians were not in a position to correct. For example, a reader might well infer that the rules and standards for judging a flower show were developed for the Athens club's first show; they were actually developed two years later.

A more important matter concerns the original constitution and by-laws of the garden club in Georgia, which faced a serious problem in making the claim to be the oldest in America: namely, it had no official records earlier than 1913. A fire had destroyed the home of a longtime club secretary, and with it, the minutes book containing the club's by-laws. Although Mrs. Redwine had referred to the group's "constitution and by-laws setting forth its purposes," they were long gone, their words a matter of conjecture.[17]

APRIL 1936

The southern club's campaign for recognition has immediate positive results close to home. In early April, the Garden Club of Georgia—the state federation—passes a resolution at its annual convention to establish a "national shrine" in Athens as a memorial to what they say has been "long considered the first garden club of America." It further resolves to make "every effort" to have the National Council of State Garden Clubs officially declare such status at its annual convention later in the month. Despite the Georgia federation's endorsement, the ladies of Athens continue to recognize the Cambridge club as a rival claimant to be vanquished. Preparing for the annual meeting of the National Council, the Athenians attack the northern club by name:

> The difference in a garden club and a horticultural study club, according to two eminent national authorities on garden club matters, makes the Athens club the first garden club, organized under the name of garden club and functioning in the modern sense of the term, the first such club in America.
>
> While there is another older than the Athens club, the Cambridge Plant Club, organized in January 1889, it seems that some of the garden club authorities consider this distinguished club more on the order of a horticultural study club than a garden club in its original organization.

One reads these paragraphs and wonders, Who were the "eminent national authorities" consulted by the Athens ladies? What was the basis of their opinion that the Plant Club was "more on the order of a horticultural study club than a garden club" when it was founded?

Beyond theorizing about the origins of the Cambridge club, the ladies of Athens began an effort to fill in the lost history of their club's beginnings, gleaning information from articles in the *Athens Banner* and making certified copies of a number of 1892 articles. Similarly, affidavits from charter members were taken. Mrs. Lumpkin had died in 1932, but her husband, Judge E. K. Lumpkin, gave a witnessed statement. Another statement was made by one of Mrs. Lumpkin's daughters, Louise Lumpkin Upson, who had been present "assisting" her mother at the formal organizational meeting of the club in December 1891. Although Mrs. Upson's recollection was not witnessed, she closed by declaring in an underscored hand, "I know these facts to be true."

MAY 1936

The *Athens Banner-Herald* publishes a letter from three members of the Ladies Garden Club (including two nieces of Dr. Newton's) who wish "the recorded facts concerning the organization" of their club to "be known by the public":

1. That the Lady's Garden Club was organized in the Seney-Stovall Chapel Feb. 3rd, 1892.

2. That its name when it was organized was the Lady's Garden Club of Clarke County. If there has been any change in its name it was made since its organization.

3. That the idea of organizing this Garden Club originated entirely with Dr. Edwin D. Newton, and he is entitled to the credit for it, and he gave it its name, viz: 'The Lady's Garden Club of Clarke County.'

They also cite the *Athens Banner* of February 9, 1892, as verification of the club's organizational meeting six days earlier. The article's headline:

THE LADIES MEET

And Perfect the Organization of Their Garden Club

TWO SPLENDID LECTURES

Delivered by Drs. Lane and Davis

Officers of the Club — The Work They Propose To Do

The authors of the letter note that these "facts, and many other interesting ones, about this Garden club" are on record in the clerk's office of the Superior Court, Clarke County, Georgia.

Indeed, the article is interesting; judging from it, vegetable gardening was to be the primary focus of the Ladies' Garden Club. At the February 3 meeting, Dr. Newton, serving as the club's spokesman, described the purpose of the new organization and introduced the speakers. First, Dr. Lane spoke about the evolution of garden vegetables and fruit; then, Dr. Davis addressed the topic of insects as both friends and enemies. Following "the class in botany," Dr. Newton explained that the Ladies' Garden Club—being an auxiliary to the Farmers' Club—was entitled to all the privileges and advantages of the experiment station and the state department of agriculture.[18]

Documents in the club's archives at the University of Georgia also make interesting reading. In "Some Facts about the Ladies Garden Club," Mrs. Redwine offered more facts—and some speculation—on the club's early history. Indeed, she quibbled a bit with two of the points in the letter to the *Banner-Herald* quoted above. On the matter of the club's creation, she sifted again through articles, announcements, gossip columns, and reports in the *Athens Banner* from December 1891 through 1892 to divine a founding date. Although she conceded that the exact day of the club's organization was "a matter of conjecture," she maintained that the date must have been before the *Banner*'s February 2 announcement of the first open meeting because the newspaper stated that the club "has been organized." She inferred that the founding date may have been as early as the mid-December 1891 meeting in Mrs. Lumpkin's parlor.

With regard to the role of Dr. Newton in founding the club, Mrs. Redwine acknowledged his "ingenious" mind but suggested that he may have had the idea for "an enlarged organization" after a small garden club had already been established. (The archival record offers no evidence of an earlier club.) Also, in her recitation of "facts," Mrs. Redwine omitted the one about Dr. Newton suggesting the new club's name.[19] Although she gave him credit for his "intense interest in horticulture," she made much more of his sister, Mrs. Cobb, the club's first president, whom she called "one of Athens' best gardeners [a great distinction in those days of horticultural experiments]...a person of dignity, poise and ability...a good looking woman with a keen intellect and a ready wit...a member of one of Athens' old established families, the wife of a prominent lawyer, and...quite capable of presiding over any organization with ease and charm." Mrs. Lumpkin, chairman of the first executive board, "to whose untiring zeal and interest the club owes its life to-day," was also lauded for laboring "to preserve the organization."

Mrs. Redwine was on a campaign; the earlier the founding date, the better. It was preferable, too, to minimize the role of the man who founded the club and elevate the contributions of the founding women.

August 1936

In August 1936, Mrs. Redwine submits a nine-page, legal-sized notarized brief in support of the Ladies Garden Club's claim to be "America's first Garden Club."[20] Again, she opens with an attack on the Cambridge club—though an indirect one. Her argument ("the members of the Ladies Garden Club feel that a distinction should be made between a plant study club or an amateur horticultural society and a GARDEN CLUB") proceeds almost verbatim from her earlier letter to the president of the National Council of State Garden Clubs. Again, she refers to horticultural groups that had felt "the more human spirit of the real GARDEN CLUB" and altered their course. Still, she asserts, these groups cannot "claim to have made any definite original contribution to the Garden Club movement." Following this dismissal, she then provides a definition of a true garden club:

A GARDEN CLUB as the name implies, concerns itself with practical gardening, as well as horticultural study, which it embraces; with home and civic beautification; with correct display of the fruits of the garden; with the encouragement of gardening and garden activities within and beyond the club's own circle; and with educating the public and raising the standards of horticulture in the community by means of correctly staged flower shows.

"It is in this latter category," Mrs. Redwine continues, "that the Ladies Garden Club belongs, and it is in this field that it was a pioneer. The Ladies Garden Club, be it known, was not a haphazard organization, nor did it come into existence by mere chance. It was organized as a GARDEN CLUB and was so named; its purposes were clearly set forth from the beginning." She goes on to describe how the group functioned as a garden club *within the first year of its existence* [emphasis in original]. She cites programs (those lectures on vegetables, fruit, and insects held on February 3, 1892); the procurement of horticultural bulletins; the ordering and distribution of seed; the sharing of cuttings, plants, and home-grown seed; member experiments and reports; and the reports of the club's "civic usefulness" in the Athens newspaper. According to Mrs. Redwine's historical reporting, discussions of flowers and vegetables were a feature of meetings, and members worked for improvement in various lines of plants—strawberries (for the club's president, Mrs. Cobb) and roses (for the chairman of the first executive board, Mrs. Lumpkin).

Mrs. Redwine attributes a high level of self-consciousness to the founders of the club. She states that they "knew clearly that they had created a new and unique organization." On this point, she cites Mr. P. J. Berckmans

Sr., who formulated the club's rules for exhibiting and judging. Recalling his words some forty years after the fact, she reports that he *"stated at the time* [emphasis in original] that this was the only organization of the kind in existence, so far as he knew." She continues, "Mr. Berkmans [*sic*], being a horticulturalist [*sic*] of national and international repute, was well conversant with the situation at the time, and his testimony may therefore be given much weight."

Mrs. Redwine's submission stresses the importance of the club's public flower shows, the first held in May 1892. She notes with pride, "These shows were held with the same precision of exhibiting and judging that governs the flower shows of to-day."

Only five pages into the petition to the National Council does Mrs. Redwine mention the fire that destroyed the club's early records and the recent effort to "reconstruct" its by-laws from affidavits of charter members and articles in the *Athens Banner*. She cites the issue of March 22, 1892, regarding the club's mission:

> The object of this club is two-fold. The ladies wish to exchange ideas and information regarding the best practical methods for treating seeds and plants. Also to make thorough investigation as to the best places to purchase their garden and flower supplies, and the purity and freshness of seeds and plants, and to this end reports will be kept, and submitted to the club from time to time.

The National Council did not send a copy of this brief to the Cambridge Plant Club for a reply. If it had, an advocate for the Cantabrigian gardeners could have responded as follows:

> First, regarding the charge that the Plant Club was not a garden club from the beginning, on what authority did Mrs. Redwine describe horticultural and plant study clubs as being "numerous" before 1891? Further, where was the evidence that any other garden club existed in Athens before the founding of the Ladies Garden Club? Similarly, regarding her statement that some clubs "are still functioning" in their original state while others "have...grown away" from their original intent, what was her evidence? Did she canvas plant study clubs around the country? Did she review the objectives stated in their by-laws? Did she peruse their minutes to determine that meetings had stayed the same or changed over the decades? Finally, on what basis did she determine that plant study clubs had not made "any definite original contribution to the Garden Club movement"?

Second, regarding the objective of the Ladies Garden Club, there is a discrepancy between Mrs. Redwine's ideal standard and the one actually attributed to her club in the *Athens Banner* of March 22, 1892. As the reader will note, the *Banner*'s statement places the focus on exchanging information to promote better plant cultivation. According to the *Banner*, in early 1892, the Ladies' Garden Club was seeking members interested in learning "to grow anything from a carrot to a chrysanthemum." Although the affidavits and statements collected some forty years later from charter members of the club include the words *garden* and *gardening*, the contemporaneous newspaper accounts do not, except narrowly in reference to vegetable gardens. Like the founders of the Plant Club, the women of the Ladies' Garden Club were interested in growing plants well. Gardening, circa 1890, was very much a matter of growing plants from seeds and cuttings.

The Cambridge club would also have raised a question concerning the statement that Mrs. Redwine attributed to Mr. Berckmans around the time of the club's founding, that the Ladies' Garden Club was "the only organization of the kind in existence, *so far as he knew*" [emphasis added]. Yes, perhaps he uttered these words. But could even the most knowledgeable horticulturist of the 1890s be so confident of developments beyond his home territory of north Georgia? The age of easy communication was still far in the future. Indeed, in 1892, the founding of *Horticulture* magazine was twelve years away.

In fact, evidence in the archives of the Ladies' Garden Club indicates that Mr. Berckmans did say something worth quoting about the new club, which Mrs. Redwine likely read but did not report accurately. A "little sketch" of the organization, written by Mrs. E. K. Lumpkin in 1895 for the premium list distributed at the club's fourth annual chrysanthemum show, begins with a reference to the eminent horticulturist: "Our next door neighbor and friend, Mr. P. J. Berckman's [*sic*] of Augusta, Ga., tells me that *so far as his observation extends*, this is the only organization of its kind in the State, and probably in the South…" [emphasis added].[21] So, Mr. Berckmans's statement was not general, but qualified. Perhaps he did know of the existence of a certain northern plant club.

Finally, the Cambridge ladies would have applauded the public flower shows of the Ladies' Garden Club—with rules and regulations that anticipated modern ones—as a major innovation showing great civic spirit. But they might have asked, Is holding an annual flower show a requirement of garden club status?

For Athenians, the horticultural sharing of flower shows is natural, encouraged by their southerly climate. Spring comes early to Georgia. Azaleas bloom in March, and camellias are not greenhouse plants. The growing season is long. And in 1892, Athens was still in touch with its agricultural roots. The city's Farmers' Club was a prominent civic organization, and the Ladies' Garden Club was conceived, according to the *Athens Banner*, as an auxiliary of the group. According to newspaper accounts of the garden club's first flower show, the event seems to have been as much about "best" vegetables—with prizes awarded for tomatoes, cabbages, corn, Irish potatoes, celery, lettuce, and strawberries—as it was about flowers.

By 1892 Cambridge's pastoral age was receding into memory. Since the mid-1800s, developers had been filling plots of open land with houses. Waves of immigrants had settled in Cambridge. The cityscape was changing, and suburbs were spreading beyond the city's borders. Though an amateur flower show could be a major civic event in Athens, such was not the case in Cambridge. Still, was the Plant Club less of a garden club than its southern sister?

OCTOBER 1936

A committee of the National Council of State Garden Clubs appointed to decide which garden club was the first in the country reports its findings to its executive board at a meeting in White Sulphur Springs, West Virginia. The findings: The first garden club was organized in 1884 in Eufaula, Alabama, but soon after changed its work to that of a civic organization; the second was the Plant Club of Cambridge, Massachusetts, organized in 1889 and still active in garden club work; the third was the Ladies' Garden Club of Athens, Georgia, organized in 1891 and also still active.

It was surely disappointing news for the Ladies Garden Club after the effort that had gone into its appeal for recognition. Unaware that the question was under investigation, the Plant Club had put up no defense, yet it had prevailed. Why did the National Council judge the Plant Club to be the earlier one? The council's records are unavailable, so the answer is a matter of conjecture. But some of the executives of the council in 1936 likely recalled having been entertained by the Plant Club at their national convention in Boston four years earlier. Moreover, Mrs. Thomas Motley Jr., of Milton, the first president of the National Council, had also been a founding light in the establishment of the Massachusetts Federation of Garden Clubs and would have known members of the Plant Club. She may well have spoken up on behalf of the Cambridge club.

NOVEMBER 1936

The November 1 issue of *Horticulture* revisits the controversy with a lead article: "Again—The First Garden Club." It reports that a special committee of the National Council of State Garden Clubs has been investigating this question: "For several years an effort has been made to determine which was the first garden club to be established in this country. Claims for this honor have been made by various organizations in different states." Noting that the Cambridge Plant Club was generally believed to be the oldest in continuous existence, the article reports a surprise concerning another club not far from Cambridge—the Lexington (Massachusetts) Field and Garden Club, continuously active since 1876 (electing officers, holding meetings, and open to men and women).[22] Not only was the Lexington club founded earlier, it was also the first to hold a flower show—with prizes and certificates—in the fall of 1881.

Clearly a garden club by purpose—"the care and protection of trees and shrubs in the public places of Lexington, the improvement of the town by planting of additional trees and ornamental plants and the cultivation of taste in arboriculture and horticulture"—the Lexington club's claim on the title of first garden club seems indisputable. It is surprising that the ladies of the Cambridge Plant Club did not know of the nearby club. After all, Lexington Center is less than ten miles from Harvard Square, but towns were more insular in those days. In any case, the existence of the Lexington Field and Garden Club now known, the Plant Club could only claim to be the first women's garden club, not the oldest.

Why didn't the National Council's special committee revise its report and recognize the Lexington group? A hint to the answer may be found in a May 1963 letter from Susan B. Goodale of the Cambridge Plant Club to the editor of *Horticulture*. Goodale notes that the Lexington Field and Garden Club was founded in 1876 but apparently was not considered to have "continually" fulfilled its function because some years' minutes of meetings had been lost, though the group had an unbroken line of presidents. The *Horticulture* article made no reference to this gap, nor does any information in the Plant Club's archives shed light on it. A trip to the Lexington Public Library, repository of the Lexington club's archives, showed the following: There are some years without minutes (1898–1902, 1910–1919, and 1927), but the club has continuous financial records since 1876 as well as a continuous line of presidents.

Indeed, one may ask whether the Ladies Garden Club itself had "continually" fulfilled its function as a garden club. Given the loss of its early records, the question cannot be definitively answered. The group's archives, housed at the Hargrett Rare Book and Manuscript Library at the University of Georgia in Athens, include fourteen boxes, but most of the material is from the last thirty years. Minutes begin only in 1913, correspondence files in the 1930s. The earliest items are newspaper write-ups dated 1891–1892. The only other documents from the 1890s are "premium lists" from 1894 to 1912 and a scrapbook dated 1897–1933 (the only piece of information in the scrapbook from the 1890s concerns the cost of flowers).

Based on archival records, the Ladies Garden Club would seem to be short on proof that it functioned continually during its first two decades. Why disallow the claim of the Lexington Field and Garden Club on the basis of gaps in its minutes when the Athens club has no minutes from its first twenty-one years? In contrast, the Cambridge Plant Club has minutes going back to its first meeting as well as a wealth of companion material—papers, journals, scrapbooks, photographs—accumulated thereafter.

1939

The National Council of State Garden Clubs officially recognizes the Ladies Garden Club in Athens as the first such organization in America. With this recognition, the Georgia state garden club federation—the Garden Club of Georgia—begins a fund to create a living memorial to the twelve founders of the Athens club.

The Cambridge Plant Club is not informed that the National Council had reopened an inquiry into the question of the first garden club. Nor is it told of the council's changed opinion.

SEPTEMBER 1940

Senior members of the Cambridge Plant Club are jolted at the end of the summer by a lead article in the September 1 edition of *Horticulture*: "Athens, Georgia, Claims the Country's First Garden Club." The news: The National Council of State Garden Clubs determined in 1939 that the Ladies Garden Club was "the first group organized in the United States for the sole purpose of forming a garden club." Further, a six-thousand-dollar garden, "a masterpiece in design and content," is reported to be nearing completion in Athens as a living memorial to the club's charter members, sponsored by the clubs of the Georgia state garden federation and the University of Georgia.[23] The article provides a lengthy description of this garden, actually a series of four gardens, around an antebellum smokehouse transformed into a museum and haven for garden club members and a laboratory for the university's landscape students.

One can imagine the shocked silence in Cambridge as the Plant Club members read this news—a judgment made without any request for informa-

SEPTEMBER 1, 1940   VOL. XVIII. NO. 17

HORTICULTURE

Better Gardens Make Better Homes

HORTICULTURAL NEWS-LETTER

A $6000 garden, a masterpiece in design and content, is rapidly nearing completion in Athens, Ga., where it will stand as a living memorial to the 12 charter members of the Ladies' Garden Club of that city, the first group organized in the United States for the sole purpose of forming a garden club. In December 1891 these women assembled to collaborate their efforts in gardening and exactly 48 years later, 1939, the National Council of Garden Clubs recognized their efforts.

Athens, Georgia, Claims the Country's First Garden Club

For four years the Garden Club of Georgia which is composed of 215 clubs throughout the state has been perfecting plans for the series of four gardens which will form the memorial. Under the direction of the landscape architecture department of the University of Georgia, co-sponsor of the project, the memorial has reached the laying out of the gardens around a museum and trophy room made from an ante-bellum smokehouse.

Carved into the white wooden panel above the doorway are the words "Garden Club of Georgia" flanked by small white Doric columns and espalliered jasmine. On the pale lemon-colored walls inside hangs an oil painting of the twelve founders who will look down in the future on countless garden schools, receptions and flower shows made possible by their initiative. A bay window has been draped and cushioned by a club in Augusta. Colonial furniture has been donated by members of pioneer Athens families.

The trophy room opens into a courtyard garden of cut stone and brick shaded by an aged oak and surrounded by an old-fashioned pierced brick wall. Later, white azaleas will stand out against the yellow jasmines and clematis vines are being trained over the walls which are enhanced by three hanging gates of Williamsburg green.

A bay window looks out on the opposite side at an old-fashioned boxwood garden. Four flower beds radiate from a central sundial and in each is to be a Georgia product outlined with boxwood. An Atlanta club has already supplied the 2000 boxwoods. Against the white gravel will be a conventionalized Cherokee rose, a watermelon, a peach and a cotton boll will stand out effectively.

Old brick is used for all the walks as well as a circular path separating the four central beds from the outer ones which will be filled with pinks, asters, narcissi and lilies. Two mimosa trees in the outside corners and a surrounding white picket fence will close off this area from the trophy house. An espalliered pear tree and a white camellia, trained fan shape, will decorate the north and south walls of the trophy house.

The terrace garden with its gravel surface shaded by flowering dogwoods is intended as an outdoor classroom, for the entire project will be not only a haven for garden club members and their guests but also a laboratory for the university's landscape students. The university will assume responsibility for the garden's protection and upkeep after its completion.

The lower garden will be devoted to perennials and is the most ambitious part of the development. Here will be two six by 100-foot beds surrounded by a white picket fence and fed by underground irrigation. The choicest Spring and Fall flowering perennials will be used and at the end of the plot will be a pool with a stone coping.

The remaining portion of the land will be used for a col-

This garden in front of the new museum of the Garden Club of Georgia is in the process of making. A sundial is to be surrounded by four beds, each featuring a Georgia product done in boxwood— a watermelon, a peach, a cotton boll and a Cherokee rose.

355

Lead article in Horticulture, September 1, 1940, claiming the Ladies' Garden Club of Athens, Georgia, as the country's first garden club. The photograph shows a view of the garden planted by the Georgia state garden club federation in honor of the Ladies Garden Club's twelve charter members. *(Records of the Cambridge Plant Club & Garden Club, Schlesinger Library, Radcliffe Institute, Harvard University)*

tion from them, a trial in absentia. Also stunning: The six-thousand-dollar memorial garden, which no doubt produced a twinge of jealousy, described in glorious detail. Two photographs accompanied the text, one of the garden, the other—the pièce de résistance—an oil painting depicting the founders of the Ladies' Garden Club at their first meeting in Mrs. Lumpkin's parlor. The painting of the imagined scene was displayed inside the garden club museum "on a pale lemon-colored wall."[24]

On September 4, stunned though she may have been, Miss Corne writes to Lois Lilley Howe, president of the Plant Club and a noted architect:[25]

17 Hilliard Street
Sept 4

Dear Miss Howe

As I have unsuccessfully tried several times to get you on the telephone I conclude that you are still away, and so am writing—hoping that you will be able to read my crayon scrawl—Have you yet seen *Horticulture* for Sept 1 with its interesting article about a wonderful garden being built by the Garden Club of Athens Georgia and *claiming again* in large first page letters to be the "Country's First Garden Club."—We have had trouble with this Club before—perhaps because we are not *called* a garden club, they won't believe figures, and were reported to have said that we were "only a *sewing* club, any way"—They have naturally been disappointed to learn of an older club but would you not think that they would be too proud to claim an honor which belongs to others and now hundreds who read *Horticulture* will believe it—Won't you please write to Mr. Farrington [editor of *Horticulture*] and ask him to try and correct this. It was chiefly through his kind interest in us that ten years ago the Mass. Horticultural Society "after *careful investigation*" bestowed a silver medal on the Cambridge Plant Club for being "The *first* Club of its kind in the Country." He can surely not have forgotten....I will try to write a few lines as a Charter Member—but writing has become a punishment rather than a pleasure since my eyes have misbehaved. An early Athens Club member may even have copied us—as did others, having heard through friends in Cambridge, one in Germantown, Pa. and another one in a little town in Maine were started before many months passed—But whether they continued or not I do not know—Perhaps Mrs. Moore our other Charter Member would write too—The more the better—I enjoyed your call so much—and this wonderful iris came out beautifully the next day. I had never seen anything like them. I went to Rockport for a few weeks and it did me good—though I can't walk very far yet. I would not care if only I could see to read and write but it is a cataract you know—and without an operation—about the advisability of which the doctor is not decided, I will never be better. I am sorry to inflict such a letter upon you but it is the best I can do at present—Hoping that you have had a pleasant summer and that you can do something about this Athens club's claim.

Very sincerely,
Fanny E. Corne

Miss Corne's letter is a bit difficult to read in spots (all underscoring is in the original) but is still amazingly clear for a woman of ninety-three. Despite her problems with her eyesight, her interest in horticulture remained strong. In January 1940, for example, she contributed questions to an "Information Please" program hosted by the Garden Club Federation of Massachusetts for some 350 garden club members in Horticultural Hall. The questions, "fired right and left in quick succession," sometimes "baffled" a panel of experts, including the directors of the Arnold Arboretum and the Harvard Botanic Garden. According to an account in the *Herald*, Miss Corne was one of seven members of federated garden clubs whose questions stumped the experts, for which achievement they were awarded packages of seeds.

Miss Howe received Miss Corne's letter at the Philbrook Farm Inn in Shelburne, New Hampshire—a small town at the northern end of Mount Washington Valley—where she was vacationing. On September 10, she sent a letter to Mr. E. I. Farrington, whose acquaintance with members of the Plant Club went back at least as far as the 1920s.

September 10, 1940
Dear Mr. Farrington:

Why does the Athens Georgia Garden Club claim to be the oldest garden club in America?

The Cambridge Plant Club has the medal awarded to it for that honorable position by the Horticultural Society.

Could you not make a statement—quite pointedly—to this effect in the next number of "Horticulture"? I should have written before but failed to see my September number in this summer period of flitting.

The Cambridge Plant Club had its fiftieth anniversary in January 1939—an account of this was given in "Horticulture." It is well-known & active & has taken prizes at various of the shows. Being far from home, I can look up no dates but they could easily be found.

Please straighten this out for us.

Yours very sincerely,
Lois Lilley Howe
President of the Cambridge Plant Club

Mr. Farrington's reply, dated September 16, shows his surprise:

Dear Mrs. Howe:

I found your letter on my return from vacation and well understand the way you feel about the claim made by the Garden Club of Athens, Georgia.

I will, of course, publish something setting forth the position of your organization. I am rather surprised that the National Council did not investigate this matter more fully before recognizing the claim of the Athens club.

Very truly yours,
E. I. Farrington
Editor

OCTOBER 1940

A letter from Fanny Elizabeth Corne appears in the October 15 edition of *Horticulture* under the title "Cambridge Plant Club's Protest."

Dear Editor,

Horticulture for September 1 has an interesting article about a wonderful garden being created by the Garden Club of Athens, Ga. The article, however, reiterates the mistaken claim of the Athens club that it is the oldest club of its kind in the country.

About ten years ago, the Massachusetts Horticultural Society, after careful investigation, bestowed upon the Cambridge (Mass.) Plant Club a silver medal in recognition of its being the first club of its kind in the United States.

This club held its first meeting, which I attended, in January, 1889. About this date there can be no mistake. The Athens club, according to its own statement, was not organized until nearly three years later in December, 1891. These dates speak for themselves. We celebrated our 50th anniversary about 20 months ago. It will be 15 months before the Athens group can celebrate its own.

The Athens club will deservedly receive much honor and renown for the beautiful garden it is creating, but the honor of being the oldest club of its kind in America still belongs to the Cambridge Plant Club.

Fanny Elizabeth Corne
A Charter Member of the Cambridge Plant Club

Although Miss Corne's letter is gracious in referring to the Athens club's memorial garden, a tone of impatience comes through. Why don't the ladies of Athens simply recognize that the Cambridge Plant Club is a garden club and that it predates theirs?

February 1941

A dueling correspondence in *Horticulture* continues as Nina Scudder of the Ladies Garden Club replies to Miss Corne in the magazine of February 1. Miss Scudder's missive uses Miss Corne's own words against her:

Dear Editor,

Horticulture's October 15 issue contains a letter from a charter member of the Cambridge (Mass.) Plant Club which protests the statement that the Ladies' Garden Club of Athens, Ga., is the oldest club of its kind in the country. That the Cambridge Plant Club is an older organization is understood but a distinction exists between a plant club and a garden club. Founded in 1891, the Ladies' Garden Club has had an uninterrupted record. Some of the early rules for flower shows and judging drawn by P.J.A. Berckmans form a pattern for those of the present time. It is also fitting at this season to recall the club's first chrysanthemum show held in 1892. Furthermore, the National Council of State Garden Clubs of America passed a resolution which awarded the honor of being the first garden club in the country to the Ladies' Garden Club. As Fannie [*sic*] Elizabeth Corne states, the Cambridge Plant Club is the first of its kind in the United States but it must be remembered that the Ladies' Garden Club is the first and oldest garden club in America.

Nina Scudder
Athens, Ga.

One can only imagine how the ladies of the Plant Club received Miss Scudder's communication. A high level of irritation, if not distress, is reflected in a letter from Miss Corne to Miss Howe. Reconsidering how to argue the case, the nonagenarian charter member asks Miss Howe and Mrs. J. Lowell Moore (another charter member) to reply to Nina Scudder.[26] (Miss Howe and Mrs. Moore, at ages 76 and 83, respectively, were a bit younger than Miss Corne.)

Feb 11
Dear Miss Howe,

I have been reading Nina Scudder's letter over again, and do hope that both you and Mrs. Moore have or surely will reply. She is so smugly satisfied with herself and so inconsequential. She has to concede that we are the older "organization" but "a difference exists between a plant club and a garden club"—perhaps so, but we don't happen to be a plant club—but *the* one and only Plant Club—so named for reasons of our own before any other club of its kind existed any where in the United States, the country or even in Europe. In so far as we ever heard, and my sister and I lived abroad many years—You know—She says they were organized in 1891 [and] have an unbroken record ever since. [What a pity that Miss Corne did not know about the Athenian club's missing records!] We have an unbroken record since January 1889— Three years earlier—Yet they are the oldest club of its kind in the country—a bit mixed up isn't she? One can't help being rather sorry for them, having been led to believe by the Federation of Garden Clubs [National Council of State Garden Club Federations] that they were the first—Yet when the Federation met in Boston it was taken for granted that we of course were the Mother Club—Mrs. Moore and I as Charter Members were invited to their banquet with seats of honor at the 1st table...I had to rise and make my little bow. The Plant Club has been too modest—On receiving our medal 8 or 9 years ago if some one had only written a note at once to Horticulture proclaiming the honor done us then this trouble would have been prevented—Why did no one think of doing so!! There is another matter I want to write you about but have inflicted enough of my hieroglyphics upon you for this time. I can only follow what I am doing by using a strong magnifier and following a thin gray line—

Very sincerely yours,
Fanny E. Corne

Although Mrs. Moore did not rise to the defense of the Plant Club's claim,[27] the archives do include rebuttal notes in the hand of Miss Howe. Her points are as follows:

The Ladies Garden Club of Athens, Georgia, still considers itself the oldest garden club & we must allow it to be the oldest club to be called a Garden Club.

The Cambridge Plant Club was founded in 1889 before anyone had thought of a garden club. [Like Miss Scudder, Miss Howe overlooks the Lexington Field and Garden Club and the club in Eufaula, Alabama.]

Its most important members were three ladies who had notable gardens [Miss Howe refers to Mrs. Hayes and her daughters] in which they worked themselves. One of them suggested that it should be called the Floricultural Club. Could this [be] more suggestive of a garden club[?]

And if the Athens Club is the oldest, what is the Cambridge Club going to do with the medal given to it in 1931 as the oldest garden club? It has been for many years a member of the Garden Club Fed of Massch & thru that of the Nat Fed has entered flower shows and taken prizes as a Garden Club.

The archives also contain notes for a draft letter to Arno H. Nerhrling, executive secretary of the Massachusetts Horticulture Society. Undated and unsigned, it is in the hand of Miss Howe.

Dear Mr. Nerhrling,

What is the definition of a Garden Club?

 Does it exist merely on its name or by its role?

 In 1889, a group of plant and flower lovers met at a friend's house to admire her blossoming passion flower. All having gardens, they decided to form a club to enable them to talk over experiments & successes in their gardens.

 This organization has continued to the present day. They had much discussion as to its name, one suggestion being "The Floricultural Club." The Cambridge Plant Club—that was its final decision.

 It is a member of the Garden Club Federation of Massachusetts and as such has exhibited in 15 Flower Shows, received prizes and moreover the Massch Hort Society has awarded it a medal as the oldest Garden Club in America—in spite of this claim of the Athens Garden Club of Georgia that it cannot be a garden club because it is a Plant Club.

 May we suggest that the Athens Club might call itself the oldest so-called Garden Club?

Miss Howe might have added, Can a person engaged in the study and cultivation of plants remain aloof from gardening? Even if one's first love was a houseplant, isn't it natural for that love to spill out of doors to gardens and the surrounding landscape? Clearly, Miss Howe was exasperated that the matter of which club was the first *garden* club was turning on semantics— namely, the breadth of interpretation that might be allowed the word *plant*. Miss Scudder of Athens held fast to the argument that the Plant Club began as a plant society—a group with narrow botanical interests, not a garden club. Had they wanted to play with words, the Cambridge side might have contended that the name Plant Club suggests a broader range of interests than does the name Garden Club.

April 1941

Miss Corne still awaits a reply in *Horticulture*. She writes again to Miss Howe.

> Dear Miss Howe,
>
> As yet I have seen no answer to "Nina Scudder's" snippy note in *Horticulture* from Feb 1st. So as I think it a pity to have the readers of *Horticulture* in doubt as to which club is really the older one, and as also I know that the name Plant Club does puzzle people, I have written an answer myself which I include. Please use it as you think best, as "Fanny Elizabeth Corne Charter Member" like the last letter. I thought that you might prefer to have some one else write—or sign this one—I have such difficulty with writing that I had our student type it for me—and he has made mistakes I think—but you will understand.
>
> > Very Sincerely,
> > *Fanny E. Corne*
> > April 20

A letter from Miss Corne to the editor of *Horticulture* is set forth below. It was not published. Did the editor choose not to publish it, or did Miss Corne decide not to send it? [This question cannot be answered. The magazine does not have old correspondence files relating to articles. Another possible repository of old correspondence is the Massachusetts Horticultural Society, though an archivist who looked for files in the spring of 2004 found none.]

Dear Mr. Editor,

The Cambridge Plant Club hoped that the Athens Ladies Garden Club, when confronted with the authentic dates of the founding of the two clubs, would yield to the inevitable and allow that we started nearly three years before them. But Nina Scudder in *Horticulture* for February first, while conceding the undeniable fact, asserts that there exists a distinction between "a plant club and a garden club." But we are not a plant club (if any such exists). At a time when there were no other such clubs in existence, it made no difference what we chose to call ourselves. The idea of these clubs was original with us—a sudden inspiration of the founder, Miss Caroline S. Hayes....

We could indeed sympathize with the Athenians for their disappointment, aggravated as it must have been by the singularly unfortunate oversight on the part of the Federation, and the consequent mistaken resolution on the part of the Council. But we did not start three years before them in order to aggravate them, as they seem to think, judging from the tone of their letters; that was Fate pure and simple—and nothing that they or we can say or do can alter the fact that The Cambridge Plant Club is the pioneer Garden Club of America.

Under a column entitled "Readers' Questions Answered," the April 15, 1941 edition of *Horticulture* includes the following item:

Which is the oldest garden club in America?

After careful consideration the committee of the National Council of State Garden Clubs, Inc., came to the conclusion that the Ladies Garden Club of Athens, Ga., is the first club, so far as can be ascertained, to have been organized under the name of a garden club and to have continuously fulfilled its functions as a garden club to the present time. Also, after careful consideration the Cambridge (Mass.) Plant Club which is still older was determined to be the first club still existent to be organized for amateur plant study.

Miss Corne and Miss Howe's appeals were thus summarily dismissed. The Plant Club had in effect lost before the highest court in the land—the National Council of State Garden Clubs. Worse still, the Cambridge ladies had not known when the trial was being conducted. Not knowing that the matter was under review, the Plant Club did not represent itself before the council—an unfortunate omission because they could have made an irrefutable case. In contrast, the Ladies Garden Club had a strong, well-connected advocate in its state federation, the Garden Club of Georgia.

Nevertheless, the war in Europe placed the dispute in perspective. Indeed, a letter from an English garden club in the April 15 *Horticulture* made concern over a title seem a vanity.

Appeal from an English Garden Club
Dear Editor—

As you are aware, we island dwellers are now faced with a time when, for our health and very existence, we must depend largely on home-produced food. All of us who cannot fight are digging for our lives, and in the game we are playing "Spades are Trumps."

At some seasons of the year we have a glut of fruit and vegetables which, unless we can preserve them quickly, must be wasted. The most satisfactory way of preservation is by canning but so far we have not been able to purchase over here a fool-proof machine. The only safe one is made in your country.

It has struck me that as all keen gardeners are brothers at heart, some of this family on your side of the Atlantic may be willing to stretch out their hands to their brethren over here and suggest some plan by which we can obtain the canners and steam pressure boilers of which we are in such urgent need.

A friend sends me copies of *Horticulture* twice a month and I feel a word in your paper will call public attention to the matter and do a lot to help us in doing what we mean to do—WIN THE WAR.

Yours faithfully
Mrs. Alan Gardner
Surrey Ladies' Gardening Club
Worplesdon, Surrey, England

In 1942 the Plant Club began a Seeds for England project, which continued through 1950. Miss Howe's presidential papers contain a file of poignant thank-you letters that report successes with these seeds as well as wartime life in England.

December 1943

Miss Corne—aged ninety-six years, four months, and twenty-nine days—dies.

MAY 1945

Presiding at a meeting on May 7, Miss Howe notes that "possibly some of the newer club members [are] unaware of the distinction of the Cambridge Plant Club as the oldest in America," showing the silver medal presented in 1931 by the Massachusetts Horticultural Society, with the dates 1889–1931 inscribed on it and the legend "First of its kind in America."

Miss Howe makes no mention of the controversy with the Ladies Garden Club.

JULY 1945

Jane Newell Moore—aged eighty-eight years, one month, and three days—dies.

Mrs. Moore's obituary reports that she had been a charter member of the Plant Club of Cambridge, "the oldest garden club in the nation."

JANUARY 1948

At a meeting on January 5, Miss Howe brings to the attention of members an article in *Horticulture* that describes a club in Athens, Georgia, as "the first garden club organized in the United States." [28] The author of the item, Dorothy G. Jarnagin of Athens, provides this informative tidbit: "Back in those days [1891] when 'women's place was in the home,' gardening was perhaps not so fashionable as it is now but was looked upon more as a part of the business of homemaking. Those early members met for the purpose of swapping plants and information."

The minutes for the meeting record that Miss Howe would send *Horticulture* a photograph of the medal given to the Plant Club by the Massachusetts Horticulture Society to commemorate its status as the "first of its kind." Did Miss Howe ever send the photograph? Why didn't she tell the club about the earlier articles? The archives do not provide an answer. It is at this time, however, that Miss Howe begins to research her history of the Cambridge Plant Club.

JANUARY 1949

The Plant Club celebrates its sixtieth birthday with a program prepared by members, including a "brief informative and witty history" of the club by Lois Lilley Howe. Following Miss Howe's reading is a charade in three scenes, the first of which represents two ladies of Athens, Georgia, in January 1892. The skit offers a theory that one of those ladies had traveled north and attend-

Photograph taken at a party marking the sixtieth anniversary of the Cambridge Plant Club, January 1949. Lois Lilley Howe (club president, 1938–47) is seated in the first row, fourth from the left, flanked by two senior members of the club: Mrs. L. Eugene Emerson (club president, 1926–38) and Mrs. Edward S. King (author of an article in vol. 31 of the *Proceedings of the Cambridge Historical Society*). Mrs. Thorvald S. Ross (club president, 1947–1950) is kneeling at the right front. *(Records of the Cambridge Plant Club & Garden Club, Schlesinger Library, Radcliffe Institute, Harvard University)*

ed a meeting of the Plant Club, started on account of "a little old potted plant of Passion Flower." Her incredulous friend cries, "What do you mean!—a May Pop—that little old weed that grows in our fields?" And the traveler replies, "May Pop to us"—"*Passiflora*" to them![29]

Although the skit was based on the hypothesis that an Athenian lady had journeyed to Cambridge, it was a member of the Plant Club—its president, Mrs. Nathaniel Southgate Shaler—who traveled to Georgia with her husband, the eminent Harvard geologist, during the winter of 1891–1892. Is it possible that she gave Dr. Newton the idea of a garden club for ladies?[30]

The same month as the Plant Club's sixtieth anniversary celebration, an article in *House & Garden* features the garden at the University of Georgia honoring the Ladies Garden Club. It describes the plan for a parterre—an ornamental arrangement of flowerbeds—in the eighteenth-century manner as one of the gardens celebrating the founding of the first garden club in America.

MARCH 1949

The *Christian Science Monitor* of March 19, 1949, features an article, "Garden Club in Cambridge Oldest in U.S." Did the ladies of Athens see it?

1950

The Ladies Garden Club presents a historical marker at the Founders' Memorial Garden, S. Lumpkin and Bocock streets, University of Georgia North Campus, Athens. The text is as follows:

1891

FIRST GARDEN CLUB

FOUNDERS' MEMORIAL GARDEN WHICH
COMMEMORATES THE FOUNDERS OF AMERICA'S FIRST
GARDEN CLUB, THE LADIES GARDEN CLUB
ORGANIZED IN 1891, ATHENS, GEORGIA.
THIS GARDEN WAS DEVELOPED ON UNIVERSITY OF
GEORGIA CAMPUS BY UNIVERSITY'S LANDSCAPE
ARCHITECTURE DEPARTMENT AND
THE GARDEN CLUB OF GEORGIA.

PRESENTED BY LADIES GARDEN CLUB.

1950

MAY 1953

Lois Lilley Howe, then eighty-nine, reads her paper "History of the Plant Club" to the Cambridge Historical Society on May 28. The report of the Society's council for the year refers to this paper and four companion essays on the club's civic projects as "The Story of the Oldest Garden Club in the United States and Its Service to Cambridge."

Miss Howe's account of the Plant Club's sixty years of history—the first meeting, the development of traditions, notable members, broad interests, and civic projects—makes no reference to the painful correspondence concerning the "oldest" garden club. Still, it cannot be mere coincidence that her essay manages to report Plant Club activities in all the areas described as interests of the Ladies' Garden Club in the 1929 *Horticulture* feature article: war work, flower shows, civic planting, opposition to billboards, preservation of native plants, and the club's role in the founding of the state garden club federation.

Miss Howe's essay does not explicitly claim the title of first garden club in the country for the Plant Club, but she creates the impression that it is. She makes clear through well-chosen details that the club was a garden club in the fullest sense of the term from the beginning. Writing the paper must have been satisfying, making a case for the club and laying the ground for an appeal by a future club historian.

MAY 1954

On May 1, the National Council of State Garden Clubs presents a garden sculpture to the Founders' Garden at the University of Georgia in recognition of the Ladies Garden Club. A bronze plaque on the base of the statue bears the inscription:

A TRIBUTE
FROM THE NATIONAL COUNCIL
OF STATE GARDEN CLUBS
ON ITS 25TH ANNIVERSARY
APRIL, 1954
PRESENTED TO
THE FOUNDERS GARDEN
ATHENS, GEORGIA
"FOR EVERY GOOD THING HAS A BEGINNING
– AND THE BEGINNING WAS HERE"

MAY 1963

The Letters to the Editor section of this month's *Horticulture* (by now a monthly periodical) includes a communication, "Which Came First?" from Susan B. Goodale, a member of the Cambridge Plant Club.

Dear Editor –

The National Federation of Garden Clubs annual meeting in Athens, Ga., in April was of special interest because (quotes its magazine, "National Gardener"), the garden club of Athens, Ga., (founded December 1891) was "the first club to have been organized under the name of garden club, and to have continually fulfilled its function as a garden club up to the present time." We, in Massachusetts, also find it interesting to remember that the garden club movement started in this state with the founding of at least two clubs before that date. The Lexington Field and Garden Club was founded in 1876. Although perhaps it cannot be called "continually" fulfilling its function as a few minutes of meetings are lost, it has an unbroken line of presidents. The Cambridge Plant Club, founded January 1889, was never organized "under the name of garden club" but has continually fulfilled the function of one since its beginning. In 1931, this club was awarded a Silver Medal by the Massachusetts Horticultural Society as the "first club of its kind in America."

Susan B. Goodale
Cambridge, Mass.

Mrs. Goodale, who joined the Plant Club in the 1930s, served as president from 1956 to 1959.[31] In preparation for the club's seventy-fifth anniversary, she reviewed the club's file on the dispute with the Ladies Garden Club—her notes on the matter are in the archives—and offered the salvo printed above.

JUNE 1964

Lois Lilley Howe dies, twelve days short of her one hundredth birthday.

1968

The Ladies Garden Club is recognized with a Georgia Historical Commission marker on the front lawn of the house where the club's first meeting was held. The text of the sign reads:

AMERICA'S FIRST GARDEN CLUB

In 1891 at this site, the Ladies Garden Club was founded by twelve Athens ladies in the home of Mrs. E. K. Lumpkin. Mrs. Lamar Cobb was the first president. Beginning as a small neighborhood group, the club extended membership to all Athens ladies interested in gardening in 1892.

In the spring of 1892, the group presented its first flower and vegetable exhibition. By 1894 a set of standards, similar to those of today, had been drawn up to make the shows as professional as possible.

*In 1936 [sic] the National Council of State Garden Clubs recognized
the Ladies Garden Club as America's first garden club.*

Did the ladies of Athens see Mrs. Goodale's letter and respond by apply-
ing to the Georgia Historical Commission for permission to install a plaque?

AUGUST 2002

The dispute between the two clubs has long been forgotten in Cambridge. Indeed, members of the Cambridge Plant & Garden Club, who regularly refer to the Plant Club as the oldest in the country, are quite unaware of
the Ladies Garden Club. Then, in August 2002, *The Garden Club of America Bulletin* publishes an excerpt from an address by Ann S. Frierson, president
of the GCA and a member of the Junior Ladies' Garden Club of Athens,
Georgia.[32] Her speech refers to the founders of the oldest garden club in
America—the Ladies Garden Club—and the garden that memorializes them:

> In mid-January I was walking through the University of Georgia campus
> and wandered through the Founders Memorial Garden. This garden is
> dedicated to the members of the Ladies Garden Club, who, in 1891,
> formed the first garden club in America....I noticed for the first time that
> there was a plaque on a statue in the garden, and I walked over. It read:
> "For every good thing there is a beginning, and the beginning was here."

Certainly an innocent mistake, the Cambridge club's historian assumes.
Preparing to write a letter that will (gently) inform Mrs. Frierson that the
Cambridge Plant Club was an older garden club than the Ladies Garden
Club, the historian reviews her club's archives at the Schlesinger Library and
finds a thin file labeled "Material re: Age of club, 1929–1963."[33]

Since the summer of 2002, I, as that historian, have combed through the
issues of *Horticulture* magazine from the 1930s and 1940s (at the Boston
Public Library), the archives of the Cambridge Plant Club and other organizations to which members of the Plant Club belonged (at the Schlesinger
Library), the papers of Lois Lilley Howe and her architecture firm (at MIT),[34]
material held by the Hargrett Rare Book Library (the repository of the
archives of the Ladies' Garden Club and information related to Dr. Edwin
Dorset Newton, central figure in the founding of the Athens club), the
archives of the Lexington Field and Garden Club, a collection of personal
papers held by the grandsons of Mrs. J. Lowell Moore (née Jane Hancox
Newell, a charter member of the Cambridge Plant Club), and assorted historical and biographical sources of information on the town of Athens, Georgia,

prominent Athenians of the 1890s, and distinguished Cantabrigians of the period as well.

All this material provides a fuller picture of the dispute. In laying out the facts, I hope to give the reader a sense of two unique women's clubs, both ahead of their time. Does either one deserve the title of the first garden club in America? In fact, the Lexington Field and Garden Club— still an impressive and active club—was indisputably the first. But as far as the first *women's* garden club is concerned, the Ladies Garden Club may have been the first to have been organized under the name, but the Cambridge Plant Club was a garden club for nearly three years before Dr. Newton began to promote the idea in Georgia.

A debate turning on the breadth of definition allowed the word *plant* vis-à-vis *garden* has its ironies. The name "garden club" belies the range of interests that members of garden clubs pursue—from horticulture and garden design to civic planting, plant conservation, and landscape preservation. Few people who are not members of a garden club—or related to a member of one—appreciate how much good garden club members do. In that spirit, let the ladies of Athens, Georgia, put aside their misconceptions concerning the Plant Club. Similarly, let the ladies of Cambridge, Massachusetts, recognize the innovation of the Athenian flower shows. Let both clubs salute the Lexington Field and Garden Club. And let the National Garden Clubs—the umbrella association of state garden club federations—give proper recognition to the two oldest continuous garden clubs in the country: The Lexington Field and Garden Club and the Cambridge Plant Club.

AFTERWORD

OCTOBER 2005

In September 2005, just as the Society's centennial book was going through the final editing process, I made a chance discovery of the records of a women's garden club older than either the Cambridge Plant Club or the Ladies' Garden Club. Ironically, on a research trail full of small ironies, this discovery was made close to home. Thanks to the Cambridge Historical Society's Summer 2005 newsletter, I had learned about the newly processed papers of Sara Thorp Bull (1850–1911). This was an intriguing item to me, because Mrs. Bull was a charter member of the Plant Club, known in club history for her hospitality (she was the first hostess to offer club members a cup of tea after a meeting).[35]

Excited at the possibility of finding new material on the early years of the Plant Club, I made an appointment with the Society's archivist, Mark Vassar, to review the Bull papers in the Brinkler Library. When I arrived, I told

Mark a bit about the "first garden club" controversy. He pointed to a shelf on the other side of the room and mentioned the Society's collection of the Garden Street *Garden* Club's records. Imagine a moment of silence as I absorbed this information. Turn back for a moment, dear reader, to the entry for December 1928. You will be reminded that the minutes of a Plant Club meeting on December 1, 1890, contain a reference to an intriguingly named club—the Garden Street Club—and the information that the Plant Club's next meeting would be postponed "so as not to interfere with the meeting" of the other club. Presumably the postponement was necessary because Miss Almira Needham, director of the Plant Club, who lived at 47 Garden Street, was a member of the Garden Street Club as well.

The archives of the Plant Club provide no further information about the other club, except for a passing reference in a fortieth anniversary paper—written by none other than Miss Corne—that its members' interest had apparently waned. Throughout the course of my research, I had wondered, Was the Garden Street Club a social club for people who lived in the Garden Street neighborhood? Were its members connected with the Harvard Botanic Garden, bordered by Garden and Linnaean streets? Was the existence of a neighborhood club named the Garden Street Club, even if not a garden club, the reason the name Garden Club had not been chosen—or even mentioned—when the founders of the Plant Club were considering names?

The purpose of the Garden Street Club had seemed maddeningly unknowable, so I offered my speculations in a tentative way. Still, the existence of the other club would seem on its face to explain why The Plant Club had not been named The Garden Club. How gratifying to learn by chance, more than a year after finishing my paper, that my suppositions were correct. Indeed, the Garden Street Club was not a neighborhood social club, but an actual garden club—whose full name turned out to be the Garden Street Garden Club. And, yes, Miss Needham of the Plant Club was also a member of the older garden club—a charter member recommended by none other than Mrs. Asa Gray.

Why was the Garden Street Garden Club forgotten? There is no record of when the club's archives were given to the Cambridge Historical Society, or by whom (though one likely candidate is Mrs. Swan, a member of both clubs as well as of the historical society). Until the Cambridge Public Library on Broadway was closed for renovation, the collection of the Garden Street Garden Club was held in what had become the inaccessible recesses of the library's Cambridge Room, and no one was aware of it. Early in 2005, the Society retrieved the collection and processed it that spring.

Not only was the Garden Street Garden Club a garden club, its records—five bound volumes of minutes from 1879 to 1895, with inserts for annual reports dated 1896 and 1897—are a treasure. The first meeting of the club was on March 24, 1879, at the home of Mrs. Marcou of 42 Garden Street.[36] Membership was small (only eleven ladies were at the first meeting), but the club elected a president and a secretary. Subscription for membership was one dollar. Meetings were on Monday afternoons at four (a potential for conflict with the Plant Club's meetings, also on Monday afternoons). The minutes of the club include tips, facts, and personal stories about gardening, chronicle field trips to local greenhouses and gardens, and record the sharing of plants and flowers at meetings and various exhibitions. They note that at the first meeting, Asa Gray kindly offered the club *The Gardener's Monthly*.[37] Also recorded was the date of the first crocus at the Botanical Garden (March 16, 1879), and this maxim from Miss Howe: "No seeds so good as your own seeds." And at the club's meeting (its 329th) on October 26, 1891, members offered appreciations of Miss Needham, who had passed away since the last meeting.[38] Meetings continued to be recorded through 1895, and annual reports for two more years, but the archives give no information as to why the club disbanded.

Where do things stand in 2005 on the issue of which is the oldest women's garden club in the country? For over seventy-five years, Cantabrigians have supported the claim of the Cambridge Plant Club and Athenians, that of the Ladies' Garden Club. The unearthing of the records of the Garden Street Garden Club reveals the surprising news that neither was first. The Garden Street Garden Club, founded in 1879, was first by a substantial margin—nine years, ten months, and four days, to be precise. The Plant Club must accept second-place status and a qualification on its title, granted by the Massachusetts Horticulture Society, as "the first of its kind."

At the same time, the new knowledge of the existence of the Garden Street Garden Club clarifies the Plant Club's choice of name; the word *plant* in the younger club's name cannot be taken as a descriptor suggesting a limited focus. The Garden Street club aside, the records of the Plant Club, which document the breadth of the club's garden interests, are indisputable on this point. The evidence is both ample and clear: The Ladies' Garden Club, which has no official club records before 1913, must acknowledge not just one, but two, Cambridge clubs as earlier women's garden clubs.

ENDNOTES

1. The Hayes family—father, mother, two unmarried sons and three unmarried daughters—settled in Cambridge in the late 1860s. They were reportedly so outspoken and frank that at first their more reserved neighbors misunderstood them—perhaps because they had lived more in the world than most Cantabrigians.

Born in 1812, the Honorable John L. Hayes had a remarkably varied life in business and politics, even for a Dartmouth graduate and Harvard-trained lawyer. As a young man, he organized the Katahdin ironworks in Maine, then served as a counsel for the Canadian government in

Washington, D.C., negotiating reciprocity treaties. Stirred by the nation's debate on slavery, he called for the first convention of Independent Democrats. Later, he organized and served as secretary of the Mexican, Rio Grande, and Pacific Railway Company (obtaining a charter from the Mexican government that authorized the construction of a railroad across Mexico). In 1860 Dartmouth College honored him with an LL.D degree. From 1861 to 1865, he was chief clerk of the U.S. Patent Office, and in later years, until his death in 1887, he served as secretary of the National Association of Wool Manufacturers.

John Hayes was also a student of natural history. He collected and mounted a complete cabinet of birds, made a herbarium of flora, and studied geology in both the library and the field. He became a member of the Boston Society of Natural History in 1845 and was also connected with other scientific associations in the United States and Europe. His writings, devoted mainly to legal, political, and scientific subjects, included over sixty titles, among them, "The Iron Mines of Nova Scotia," "Jackson's Vindication as the Discoverer of Anaesthetics," "Reminiscences of the Free-Soil Movement in New Hampshire," "The Hudson Bay Question," "The Protective Question Abroad and at Home," "Sheep Industry in the South," and many articles and pamphlets on wool production. A paper on glaciers that he presented in 1843 was regarded as an important contribution to the history of glacial phenomena in relation to geology.

The Hayeses drew friends easily into their family circle. The three Hayes sisters in particular were noted for their devotion to home and family, loyalty to friends, and love of gardening. Indeed, the whole family was fond of gardening and did much of the work on their several Cambridge acres themselves. The two sons were lawyers like their father, but before and after office hours during the growing season, they worked in the family garden. The sisters also did their share. In the summer, visitors were apt to be met at the door with the request to "please walk 'round to the garden, the ladies are there," and rarely did a guest leave without a gift of flowers or fruit.

2. Founded in 1904, *Horticulture* is the country's oldest gardening magazine. Started as a weekly trade journal for florists and estate and greenhouse gardeners, it was purchased by the Massachusetts Horticultural Society in 1923 and turned into a publication for members. In the late 1970s, new editors began to transform the magazine into a national publication. Since 1981 it has had a series of owners (including *The New Yorker* and White Flower Farm). Despite these changes, *Horticulture* remains a serious magazine for people interested in plants and gardens.

3. In 1924 the Massachusetts Horticultural Society (MHS) called a meeting to encourage the commonwealth's garden clubs to form an affiliation. The Plant Club sent two senior members—Miss Peabody and Mrs. Drinkwater—as delegates. For three years, the resulting group was a "very loose" organization. Then, in March 1927, twenty-seven garden club presidents from various corners of the Bay State gathered at the MHS's annual spring flower show to discuss a more formal federation. This time the Plant Club was represented by Jane Newell Moore, a charter member of the club and its immediate past president. A committee was formed to recommend by-laws, and the Garden Club Federation of Massachusetts was established later in the year.

The Plant Club was not a charter member of the federation; some members were cautious about accepting the new idea. But the hesitation was short-lived, and the club voted to join the organization in November 1928—a decision that was a stimulus to civic projects, horticulture, conservation, and the friendly competition of flower shows.

4. According to *Horticulture*, the Garden Club of Philadelphia had often been cited as the first garden club, likely because of the important role it had played in the garden club movement. Such was the encouragement of the club's first president, Mrs. Stuart Patterson, that she came to be known as the "beloved 'mother of garden clubs.'" In fact, it was Mrs. Patterson who, in 1913, proposed a national organization of garden clubs—an idea that led to the founding of the Garden Club of America (GCA). So important was Mrs. Patterson that the GCA's founders elected her honorary president before they had even settled on a name for the organization.

5. The Polyanthus and the cowslip are hardy perennials, both members of the Primula family.

6. *Anthericum* is a genus of bulbous perennial plants in the Lily family. Species have rhizomatous or tuberous roots as well as long narrow leaves and branched stems of starry white flowers. Not many are grown in cultivation. Was Miss Hayes's offering a rare plant? Possibly. But some *Anthericum* species of old are now included in the genus *Chlorophytum*—notably, the spider plant, a very familiar and popular houseplant.

7. Born Mary "Mamie" Bryan Thomas in 1857, Mrs. Edwin King Lumpkin married into an eminent Georgia family that traced its roots back to the arrival of one Jacob Lumpkin in Virginia around 1670. Her husband's grandfather was Joseph Henry Lumpkin, the first chief justice of the Supreme Court of Georgia and a founder of the University of Georgia's School of Law. A granduncle was Wilson Lumpkin, who served in both Georgia state houses, then as governor, a U.S. representative, and a senator. He was honored by the naming of Lumpkin Street in Athens and Lumpkin County in North Georgia. Atlanta was briefly named Marthasville for his daughter, Martha Atalanta, until her goddess-inspired middle name (minus an a) was chosen for the honor (another example of the difficulty of naming a new entity); the renaming seems appropriate, for the town was the terminus of the Western and Atlantic Railroad, of which her father was then president.

Mrs. Lumpkin's father-in-law, William Wilburforce Lumpkin, was a scholarly man, a lawyer, planter, and teacher (for several years a professor of English at the University of Georgia). Her mother-in-law, née Maria Louisa King, was a member of a prominent Alabama family. Her husband, Edwin King Lumpkin, received a degree in civil engineering from the University of Georgia in 1873, but the law was his vocation, and he came to be known as "one of the most able lawyers in the state of Georgia." Mrs. Lumpkin's own fame was guaranteed when, in December 1891, she invited eleven ladies to her antebellum home to organize a garden club.

8. Edwin Dorset Newton (1835–1917)—a person who can be Googled more than 170 years after his birth—still figures in the chronicles of Athens, his native city. A physician, he was also an avid horticulturist and began to promote the idea of a ladies' garden club in 1891.

A personal recollection of Dr. Newton is included in a history of the University of Georgia, written by Thomas "Tom" Walter Reed, the university registrar for many years. Upon his retirement in 1945, Reed began a history of his alma mater. As luck would have it, he came to know Dr. Newton (University of Georgia, Class of 1856) just before the Ladies' Garden Club was founded. In his entry on the Class of 1856, Reed notes that as a young man, he enjoyed "the intimate friendship" of Newton, and perhaps the doctor's portion is longer than some others as a result. According to Reed, Newton studied medicine after graduating from the university, served in the War Between the States as a surgeon in the Confederate Army, and later "manifested great interest in the horticultural and agricultural development of Georgia."

Says Reed, "On one fact my memory is quite clear....In the fall of [1891], Dr. Newton was very much interested in having a Garden Club organized among the ladies of Athens." Apparently, he talked about such a movement until he got his sisters and other ladies interested. He even suggested the name, the Ladies' Garden Club of Athens. His sister, Mrs. Lamar Cobb, became the first president. Another sister, Mrs. H. H. Carlton, was also a member.

Reed's description of Dr. Newton's role in founding the Ladies' Garden Club is supported by the reminiscence of Mrs. Florida C. Orr, a charter member, published in the *Athens Banner-Herald* in February 1920: "The Garden Club idea was born in the heart of the late Dr. Edwin D. Newton. From his knowledge as a physician, he observed that women stayed indoors too constantly; that to freshen and invigorate the mind, rest tired nerves and create a real, worthwhile interest, women should be out of doors more. So, he talked his idea over with his sisters, Mrs. Lamar Cobb and Mrs. H. H. Carlton Sr. They cordially entered into his thought and in the pioneer days of the Garden Club nobody did more for the actual working out of the idea than these two charming ladies."

Whether Dr. Newton was present at the club's organizational meeting at Mrs. Lumpkin's home in December 1891 is not indicated in the record. However, he was the spokesman at the meeting in February 1892, when the club was opened to all interested ladies of Athens.

As vice president of the Georgia State Horticultural Society for the Eighth Congressional District of Georgia, Dr. Newton subsequently organized ladies' garden clubs in other cities. His efforts in promoting garden clubs were assisted, too, by the daughters of the founding members as they married and moved to other states and wrote home for information about organizing a garden club and staging flower and vegetable shows.

As Reed portrays him, Dr. Newton was certainly a man of enthusiasm: "Back in the early nineties he was a contributor to the *Athens Banner*, of which newspaper this writer was then editor. If one of Dr. Newton's manuscripts were shown me today at a distance of twenty feet, I could identify it. He used more capital letters than any man whose writings have come before my eyes. About ever[y] other word was underscored, not once but twice and sometimes three times."

In 1981, the Ladies' Garden Club (now with the apostrophe again) honored the memory of Dr. Newton with a donation of $1,000 to provide for the perpetual care of his burial plot in Oconee Hill Cemetery.

9. How did Dr. Newton happen upon the idea of a ladies' garden club? By some chance, might he have heard of the Cambridge Plant Club? After all, the Cambridge club reportedly received some attention in the press during its first two years. And it is possible that Dr. Newton actually made the acquaintance of a member of the Cambridge Plant Club in 1891. The minutes of a Plant Club meeting held on February 29, 1892, note that the president, Mrs. Nathaniel Southgate Shaler, spoke about Spanish moss and shared samples collected on a visit to Georgia. Although her itinerary is not reported, one may speculate: Did she and her husband, the Harvard geologist Nathaniel Southgate Shaler, visit Athens? Did they meet Dr. Newton? Did she speak of her club? Given his varied interests and affiliation with the *Athens Banner*, Dr. Newton would have been likely to seek out a distinguished visiting scientist. (Coincidentally, both Professor and Mrs. Shaler were Southerners by birth and manner.)

What might have taken the Shalers to Georgia? It is interesting to note that in February 1891, the state's new geological bureau had received some unfortunate publicity. In its wake, the editors of the *Athens Banner* called on the geological bureau, which it described as being in a state of "innocuous desuetude," to make progress in documenting Georgia's mineral resources. The editors (Dr. Newton was one) noted that Georgia possessed "more variety of soil, more diversity of mineral ores and richer deposits of precious metals than any State east of the Mississippi river," and urged that the "people of Georgia are anxiously awaiting some good results of the geological department." The Georgia geological bureau might well have called Nathaniel Shaler for advice. He was an eminent geology professor, the author of several textbooks, and had devoted nearly a decade to mapping and documenting the geologic resources of Kentucky, his home state. In addition, he regularly contributed articles to popular journals such as *Scribner's Magazine* and *The Atlantic Monthly*, so his name would likely have occurred to people in Georgia's geology bureau.

Speculation about the Shalers aside, an item in the *Athens Banner* of June 7, 1892, establishes that another member of the Harvard faculty—one with close ties to the Cambridge Plant Club—was in communication with a University of Georgia professor in the early 1890s. An article on a proposed summer school reports that Professor J. P. Campbell had been told by Harvard's professor of botany of the good results at his summer program in Cambridge. The Harvard man was Professor George Goodale, who would have been well known to the ladies of the Plant Club. Not only was he a Cambridge neighbor (on Sparks Street), but Jane Newell, one of the charter members, had also taken his summer course. Through Miss Newell, Professor Goodale knew of the Plant Club early on; the minutes record that he lent illustrations for a paper presented to the group by Miss Newell in March 1890. The next year he sent the club a letter on the plants of Australia and the botanic garden at Adelaide and a paper entitled "Some of the Possibilities of Economic Botany," and in succeeding years he spoke to the club on various subjects. Perhaps Dr. Newton learned of the northern club through the Goodale connection.

10. P. J. Berckmans was a pioneering horticulturist in Georgia. Some of his papers, including the manuscript of an orchard handbook, are in the Hargrett Rare Book and Manuscript Library at the University of Georgia. In her 1920 article in the *Athens Banner-Herald*, Mrs. Orr referred to Mr. P. J. Berckmans as the longtime and "beloved" president of the state horticultural society, who also "gave the Garden Club the benefit of his sympathy and advice."

11. One of the prizes (a "premium, handsome Jardimiere [*sic*] for finest decorative plant") at a subsequent flower show in November 1894 was donated by Mr. A. H. Hews & Co. of North Cambridge, Massachusetts.

12. An entry for November 2, 1931, in a club member's notebook records that Mr. E. I. Farrington, editor of *Horticulture*, had sent advance word of the medal. The minutes for the meeting on the same day report the honor was given in recognition of "our being the oldest garden club in the United States."

13. The National Council of State Garden Club Federations was formed in May 1929 by representatives of thirteen state federations. (The organization's name has been shortened twice—to National Council of State Garden Clubs in 1935 and to National Garden Clubs, Inc. [NGC] in 2001.) The first president was Mrs. Thomas Motley Jr., who had been a leader in the formation of the Massachusetts federation. She was determined that the collective energy of garden clubs should make a difference. Regarding the Massachusetts federation, she said: "We will show those men on Beacon Hill that we are more than a social club." By 1931 the national organization included seventeen state federations, representing 1,000 individual clubs and a membership

of 50,000. Sixty-five years later, the NGC is the largest volunteer organization of its kind in the world, representing over 7,000 garden clubs (with more than 220,000 members) in each state plus the District of Columbia, as well as nearly 500 affiliate (national and international) clubs.

14. A clipping from *Horticulture*'s report on the fourth annual meeting of the National Council of State Garden Club Federations was saved in a scrapbook kept by Plant Club member Katharine L. Storer.

15. The *Bulletin* article was preserved in the club's minute book, entry dated June 10, 1932. The personal notebook of Miss Christine Farley, a charter member of the Plant Club, provides a further description of the delegates' visit to Cambridge: "It was a lovely day, just warm enough to enjoy being out in the garden, where Roses were blooming—many varieties—& the ladies seemed most happy to see such a lovely place, where hospitality took the form of a long table spread on the lawn with refreshment for the travellers. C.P.C.'s had a Badge to wear for the 1st time in its history of forty odd yrs—a pleasant memory for us all to share & remember."

16. There is no evidence in the archives of the Ladies' Garden Club to support Mrs. Redwine's assertions.

17. The loss of the records has also led to differing opinions on the club's founding date, which is variously given as December 1891, January 1892, or February 1892 (depending on which meeting date is accepted as the starting point). See "Is This the Oldest Garden Club?" *Horticulture*, February 15, 1929; "The Ladies' Garden Club will hold an interesting meeting next Wednesday," *Athens Banner*, February 2, 1892; and "The Ladies Meet and Perfect the Organization of Their Garden Club," *Athens Banner*, February 9, 1892.

The confusion regarding the founding date was compounded by a *New York Herald Tribune* article in March 1934, which incorrectly cited January 1891 as the birth month of the club. This error made its way into later newspaper articles and the club's own publications. It has been perpetuated most recently in *Fulfilling the Dream: The Story of the National Garden Clubs, Inc., 1929–2004*, by Mary Leffler Cochran.

18. The resolution of the Farmers' Club, reported in the *Banner* on January 26, 1892, gives further insight into Dr. Newton's goal in the founding of the Ladies' Garden Club:
"Whereas, the garden as well as the farm can be utilized in raising food products for the wants of the people of our State, promoting thereby true home economy and commercial independence for the same, Be it resolved, that we beg the earnest co-operation of the fair women of Georgia in the organization of Garden Club[s] (as auxiliary clubs to the Farmers' Clubs)...not only on the farms...but in each village, each town and amongst the suburban residents of our cities....Resolved, that the Ladies' Garden Club be granted every privilege enjoyed by the Farmers' Club of Georgia, and receive all the literature published by above mentioned departments [the state agricultural commission and the experiment station] relative to the culture of the kitchen garden, the flower garden and the orchard."

Further, an editorial in the February 2, 1892, *Banner*, which announced the public meeting of the Ladies' Garden Club, made clear that the call to women "interested in the matter of gardening" referred to growing fruit and vegetables: "The Ladies' Garden Clubs all over Georgia will do much towards solving the question of home supplies being raised on the farm, and the Ladies' Garden Club of Clarke County will accomplish much good if its members take a proper interest in it. It has been said that a large garden and a good cow will furnish a living to a family of five members if properly attended to. The movement started in Athens at the last meeting of the Agricultural Society organizing these clubs is sure to result in great benefit."

The article in the same issue notes that it had been suggested that the "movement" be advanced by "a hand-book for the children of all of our female colleges and public schools of Georgia, said hand-book containing the botanical names of each food and plant of the vegetable garden, its nativity, its migrations, methods of culture and commercial value."

19. After the Ladies' Garden Club was formed, Dr. Newton continued to take an active interest, "keeping in touch with its affairs, sending material for lectures, obtaining seeds, insecticides, and so forth for the members' use."

20. Many of club's charter members were the sisters, daughters, or wives of lawyers. Whether such extensive legal connections still characterized the club in 1936 is not certain, but a tone of lawyerly advocacy is apparent in the documents prepared for submission to the National Council of State Garden Clubs.

21. The archives of the Ladies' Garden Club include two copies of Mrs. Lumpkin's description, one from 1895 and the other from 1897. Both cite Mr. Berckmans's belief that the club was "the only organization of its kind in the State, and probably in the South." The latter one is in a scrapbook presented to the club in 1930 by the charter member herself. It is not likely that Mrs. Redwine would have failed to read these documents as she prepared her submission to the National Council of Garden Clubs.

22. The idea that led to the founding of the Lexington Field and Garden Club grew out of the town's preparations for celebrating the centennial of the American Revolution. As the town readied itself for important visitors, including President Ulysses S. Grant, some residents noted the need for attention to Lexington's civic spaces, particularly to a shabby area by the train station. A continuing result of those preparations was a garden club that has been a vital part of the town for 130 years.

It is interesting to note that the founders of the Lexington Field and Garden Club had no difficulty in establishing their goals and by-laws. However, the choice of a name was more difficult. The minutes of the meeting on May 17, 1876, leave a space in the first article of the by-laws after "This Association shall be called." "Lexington Field and Garden Club" was inserted —in a different hand—after a decision was made on May 30.

The inclusion of the word *field* in the name reflects the interest that gardeners then had in "botanizing" expeditions. *Horticulture* reported that the club's records showed that many excursions were made to different points "where living plants and especially ferns were sought, identified and discussed." For example, in June 1881, 130 people went on a field trip to Greenfield, New Hampshire, in special railcars. Laurel excursions were an annual flower-gathering event for several years.

Even rock gardens were studied by members of the Lexington club as far back as 1876. One of the early records reads: "Some inquiries were made, and a discussion was had, relative to the growth of lichens on rocks and the construction of artificial rock works." So ahead of its time was the club that, in 1881, it held a flower show. According to the records of this event, it was "voted that the secretary be instructed to call a meeting to discuss the desirability and feasibility of having a floral exhibition in the Fall, with certificates and prizes."

Finally, acknowledging the club's claim to garden club status, *Horticulture* concluded: "Considerable attention was given to botanical subjects, specimens which had been collected being examined and reported upon. It is true that attention was also given to geological formations and to kindred matters, but apparently the interest of the members lay especially in matters pertaining to plants."

23. The $6,000 that created the Memorial Garden in 1939 translates into nearly $90,000 in 2006 dollars. An index gauged to the costs of plant material and stonework would likely produce a still higher figure. Consider the scope of the garden (summarized from *Horticulture*): Central was a courtyard of cut stone and brick shaded by an aged oak and surrounded by an old-fashioned pierced brick wall, white azaleas against yellow jasmine and clematis vines being trained on the walls, an old-fashioned boxwood garden with four flowerbeds radiating from a central sundial. In each central bed, a Georgia agricultural product (Cherokee rose, watermelon, peach and a cotton boll) was outlined with boxwood (2,000 boxwood plants to be donated by another garden club). A brick circular path separated the central beds from the outer ones, which featured pinks, asters, narcissi and lilies. Two mimosa trees in the outside corners and surrounding white picket fence were planned to close off this area from the terrace garden. An espaliered pear tree and a white camellia, trained in fan shapes, would decorate the north and south walls of the museum's trophy room. The terrace garden with a gravel surface shaded by flowering dogwoods was intended as an outdoor classroom. The lower garden would be devoted to perennials—the most ambitious part of the development, with two 6-by-100-foot beds filled with choice spring and fall perennials, surrounded by a white picket fence and fed by underground irrigation. Other plans: At the end of the plot would be a pool with a stone coping. The remaining portion of the land would be used for a collection of wildflowers, all properly labeled, planted beneath mature oak trees and around small native trees and shrubs.

24. This painting was done by Calvert Smith, a New York artist, who claimed to have southern roots. Specializing in pictures for publications as well as paintings that recreated historical events, Smith contacted the Ladies' Garden Club in 1932 after seeing a reference to its age in a newspaper article. He exhorted the club to gather the facts relating to its origin and expressed an interest in making a painting that would depict its founders.

25. At the time of this crisis, Lois Lilley Howe, age 74, a senior member of the Plant Club, was recognized in the world beyond Cambridge as a distinguished architect. Still active in the field, her career had already spanned five decades. An 1890 graduate of an MIT architecture program, Miss Howe received early recognition with a second-place prize of $500 in a nationwide design competition open to women architects for a "Woman's Building" at the Chicago Columbian Exposition—an enormously important cultural event celebrating the 400th anniversary of Columbus's voyage to the New World. Her first commission to design a house followed in 1894. By 1900 Miss Howe had established her own firm, and thirteen years later she formed a partnership with another MIT-trained woman. The firm was eventually joined by a third woman, also with an MIT degree. The firm—Howe, Manning and Almy—was one of the most successful women's architecture firms of the time, specializing in domestic architecture (especially in "renovising," a term the women coined), though they also designed commercial spaces, professional clubs, and public housing. The partners closed the firm in 1937, but Miss Howe continued to practice architecture until the end of her life. In addition to writing articles and a book about her work, she was active in many architectural and arts organizations and was one of the first women admitted to the Boston Society of Architects. In 1931 she was elected a Fellow of the American Institute of Architects, the first woman so honored.

Miss Howe was also active in Cambridge life. A lifelong Cantabrigian, she was treasurer of the Old Cambridge Shakespeare Association, vice president of the Cambridge Historical Society (for which she wrote at least ten essays), and a member of the Cambridge Social Dramatic Club and various Unitarian clubs. She joined the Cambridge Plant Club in 1933 and became president in 1938, a position she held until 1947. She was old enough to have been a charter member, albeit a young one, but in 1889 Miss Howe was otherwise engaged, embarking on her pioneering career in architecture. If any woman could set straight the record concerning which garden club was the first, surely it was Miss Howe.

26. Mrs. J. Lowell Moore (née Jane Hancox Newell) was born into a family of teachers, writers, and ministers. In 1857, the year of her birth, her father ("second scholar" of his Harvard class) had been minister of the First Parish Church in Cambridge —one of the most historic churches in America—for twenty-seven years. His line of Newells traced its origin in America to one Andrew Newell, who arrived in Charlestown around 1630. Miss Newell's mother, Frances Boott Wells, was also a Bostonian, though the Bootts had arrived in America later than the Newells. Her maternal grandfather, William Wells, was born in England, but came to America as a boy in 1793 and finished his education (with high honors) at Harvard. A literary man, he became a partner in a publishing company and bookshop in Boston. After a fire destroyed the bookshop, he purchased (with the assistance of friends) a Tory mansion on Brattle Street (the Ruggles-Fayerweather House) and opened a boys' school known for its English discipline and its pupils, including James Russell Lowell and Oliver Wendell Holmes. This house, with its large gardens, was a "paradise" to Miss Newell as a girl.

A friend who came to know Miss Newell in 1878 described the family as "very world conscious." Besides Mr. Newell, who was interested in everything, the eldest brother was a great reader who became a noted American folklorist. Another brother, Robert, became a lawyer after serving with the 54th Massachusetts Regiment in the Civil War (Robert's letters are in the Boston Public Library). A third brother, Kirke, became a businessman in Philadelphia. Visiting the dinner table at the Newells' was to discover "what good family conversation" could be like. All loved to talk. Young Jane was a poet, both writing and memorizing poems easily. Nature was one of her inspirations—she loved rowing on the Charles and wandering in the fields that still surrounded Old Cambridge in the 1860s. In her twenties, she studied Italian on a European trip and translated the sonnets of Michelangelo.

The youngest child of older parents (her mother was forty-two when she was born, her father fifty-three), Jane had a heavy portion of sorrows early in her life. As a young girl, she was affected by her two brothers' service in the Civil War and then, in 1870, by the family's grief—especially her mother's—over the deaths of two sisters that occurred four months apart. Newell's teenage years and early twenties were much given to the care of her elderly father, mother, and aunts. One of her brothers would also die young—at 36—in 1883.

Despite her family responsibilities, Jane was a member of the Basket Club, a group of ladies who did sewing for the sick, and she worked enthusiastically with the underprivileged at a social center in Boston. She is said to have found many of these people more interesting than acquaintances in her own social circle.

As busy as she was, Miss Newell pursued further coursework after her studies at the Berkeley Street School. A remembrance written by her future sister-in-law describes Jane's interest in a summer class at the Harvard Botanic Garden, where the two young women worked under the supervision of Professor Goodale, examining specimens as well as plants in the six-acre garden. Jane later studied botany, chemistry, and mineralogy at MIT, from which she received a degree in 1882. Subsequently, she wrote three books on botany: *Outlines of Lessons in Botany, Part I: From Seed to Leaf (1888)*, *A Reader in Botany, Selected and adapted from well-known authors*, and *Outlines of Lessons in Botany: For the use of teachers or mothers studying with their children* (1893) As a member of the Plant Club, she shared her learning. Her name appears regularly in the minutes, and in 1898–99 she gave a series of five talks, "The Purpose of the Flower," which demonstrate the depth of her knowledge, the seriousness of purpose of the club, and its members' willingness to be "informed."

For Newell, 1895 was a momentous year. At the age of thirty-seven she married James Lowell Moore, the brother of a longtime friend. One year later Mrs. Moore gave birth to a son, and six years later, to a second son. For a time the Moores lived on a dairy farm in Wayland, but the education of their sons brought them back to Cambridge. Despite her varied interests, including women's suffrage and later the League of Women Voters, the Cambridge Plant Club was dear to her. On trips to California she pressed flowers to share with the club. When she could not attend a meeting, she sent a postcard to be read in her absence. From 1921 through 1926, she served as president. When Mrs. Moore and her husband returned to Cambridge, they lived in a smaller house and garden than the ones she had known as a girl, but they also had a house with a beautiful seaside garden on Cape Elizabeth, Maine, photographs of which she shared with the club. In later life, Mrs. Moore shared her memories of the Cambridge of her girlhood in papers for the Cambridge Historical Society and the Plant Club. ["Flower Memories" was written for the fiftieth anniversary of the Plant Club. A profile of her mother included in Julia Baynard Pickard Bailey's "The Distaff Side of the Ministerial Succession in the First Parish Church in Cambridge" (1933) and "The Fayerweather House" (1939) were both written for the historical society.]

Although Mrs. Moore was the corresponding secretary of the Plant Club at the time of the controversy with the Ladies' Garden Club, there is no record of her thoughts on the matter. Letters in the possession of two of her grandsons indicate that, in the 1930s and early 1940s, she was writing about interests other than gardening, such as telepathy, the conception of man as a microcosm embodying the macrocosm, manifestations of the divine, and whether the universe was shrinking or expanding. Indeed, in April 1942, she sent a treatise, "Mind and Spirit," to Gustaf Stromberg at the Mount Wilson Observatory after reading his book *The Soul of the Universe*. An earlier letter (1938) to Edwin Hubble explained that she had been thinking of the universe since she began to study the "new theories of matter and energy" fifteen years earlier. An Easter letter to her grandchildren during this time suggests that her scientific interest in the universe sprang from her love of nature: "Here is Easter and the spring festival, the flowers are springing and the birds are coming and it is easy to believe that life is beautiful and eternal." Mrs. Moore's may not have engaged in the debate with the Ladies' Garden Club, but her obituary in July 1945 states that she was a charter member of the Plant Club, "the oldest garden club in the nation."

The Newell-Moore spirit of inquiry continues. One of Mrs. Moore's grandchildren is the prolific author Robin Moore, whose books include *The Green Berets*, *The Devil to Pay*, *The French Connection*, *The Happy Hooker* (with Xaviera Hollander), *The Accidental Pope* (with Ray Flynn), and *Task Force Dagger: The Hunt for Bin Laden* (with J. K. Idema and Chris Thompson).

27. The club's archives do contain a note written by Mrs. Moore to Miss Howe in February 1941, but it concerns new members and arrangements for a club speaker. In her note, Mrs. Moore indicates that she did not have her usual energy, and she resigned from the club in the spring of the year. As a charter member, it was fitting that the last meeting she attended was one she arranged. Her daughter-in-law, Mrs. Robert L. Moore, invited the Plant Club to her house and garden at 26 Elm Street in Concord on May 26. The minutes read: "We first inspected the unusual Chinese garden in the rear of the estate and sat awhile in the tea-house while Mrs. Moore [the younger] told how it came into being. Then we gathered in the large Studio and held the business meeting." It is recorded that Mrs. Moore's resignation was accepted with regret.

28. The *Horticulture* article in question, "A Floral Menagerie," appeared in the January issue. It featured a one-woman flower show by the president of the Ladies Garden' Club that was

"unique for its originality and represented an achievement in horticultural research...a floral menagerie," for which she assembled seventy-nine specimens of plants whose names contain the name of an animal—such as catnip, dogwood, and tiger lily, to name only a few of the more familiar—each tagged with a card bearing its botanical name, the family to which it belonged, and many of its common names.

29. The Plant Club adopted the passion flower (genus *Passiflora*) as its symbol in 1912. Most species of the passion flower are tender evergreen tropical vines native to South America. An exception found in the southern part of the United States, the *Passiflora incarnata* (commonly known as the May Pop) is deciduous and can survive winter freezes.

30. For more on this possibility, see endnote number 9.

31. Susan B. Goodale was a granddaughter-in-law of George Lincoln Goodale, the Harvard professor whose summer school program was a subject of interest to Professor Campbell of the University of Georgia in the early 1890s. Professor Goodale spoke to the club a number of times in its early decades. Some of his topics: "Principles Which Underlie Improvements in Native Plants" in 1892, "The Water-Hyacinth Menace" in 1899, and "The New Science of Oecology—The Relation of Plants to Their Environment" in 1904. As head of the Harvard Botanic Garden, Professor Goodale, was responsible for Harvard's purchase of the Blaschka glass flowers.

32. In 1940, four members of the Ladies' Garden Club founded the Junior Ladies' Garden Club, a club with the same ideals as the senior club but with a smaller membership that could meet in members' homes.

33 The Plant Club file on the dispute contains four letters addressed to Lois Lilley Howe, some notes and a draft letter in Miss Howe's hand, and the notes of Susan B. Goodale. In addition, the archives include seven issues of *Horticulture* magazine: December 1, 1928, containing "The Oldest Garden Club," Letter from Fanny Elizabeth Corne, 546; November 1, 1931, containing "Forty Years of Garden Club Work," 462 [including the excerpt, "The Massachusetts Horticultural Society has just awarded a medal to the Cambridge Plant Club of Cambridge, Mass., in recognition of the distinction which it can boast of being the oldest garden club in America"]; November 1, 1936, containing "Again—The First Garden Club," 424 [a profile of the Lexington Field and Garden Club]; September 1, 1940, containing "Athens, Georgia, Claims the Country's First Garden Club," 1-2; April 15, 1941, containing "Readers' Questions Answered: Which Is the Oldest Garden Club in America?" 191; January 1948, containing "A Floral Menagerie," 16 [a feature on a one-woman flower show by the president of the Ladies Garden Club of Athens, Georgia]; May 1963, containing "Which Came First?" Letter to the Editor from Susan B. Goodale, 249.

34. The Howe, Manning and Almy files (including personal papers) at MIT are divided among the Institute Archives, various department libraries, and the MIT Museum (personal photographs).

35. Sara Bull was perhaps better known to the larger world as the beautiful second wife of famed Norwegian violinist Ole Bull and later as a follower of Swami Vivekananda, who introduced the Vedanta movement to this country in the 1890s.

36. Mrs. Marcou's husband was Jules Marcou (1824–1898), a French-American geologist and paleontologist who assisted Louis Agassiz in founding Harvard's Museum of Comparative Zoology.

37. Considered the most important American botanist of the nineteenth century, Asa Gray (1810–1888) devoted a lifetime to identifying and cataloguing the flora of North America. *His Manual of the Botany of the Northern United States* went through numerous editions and remains a standard. (A correspondent of Charles Darwin, Gray also provided information for the development of Darwin's theory in Darwin's Origin of the Species.) Professor Gray built a major herbarium (now the Gray Herbarium) at Harvard and is credited with founding the college's botany department. The minutes of the Garden Street Garden Club refer to him frequently, describing plants and specimens that he offered to club members through his wife ("Dr. Gray expressed a wish that the ladies would perpetuate some of these in their gardens"). He seems to have joined the ladies when meetings were held at the Grays' home, offering facts and tips on gardening as well as books and journals. In the ninth annual report of the club, the secretary expresses the women's feelings of deep loss occasioned by the death of Dr. Gray.

38. The minutes for the meeting describe Almira Needham as a kind and generous woman with an extraordinary gift for growing things: "Her house in winter and her garden in summer were literally crowded with flowers whose luxuriant growth filled us all with wonder and admiration. She had a desire that all should share in the great delight of her life....She scattered her flowers far and wide with liberal hands."

Literary Cambridge: The Passage from the Past

MICHAEL KENNEY

the Cambridge ladies who live in furnished souls
are unbeautiful and have comfortable minds
...they believe in Christ and Longfellow, both dead...
— *E. E. Cummings*[1]

BY 1905, CAMBRIDGE'S LITERARY grandees were long gone—or would soon be so.

Longfellow had died in 1882 and James Russell Lowell in 1891. William Dean Howells had left for New York in 1881. Of the Jameses, Alice, the poet, had died in 1892, and William, the philosopher, would be giving his last lecture at Harvard in 1907. Henry, the novelist—long an expatriate in Europe—would come back to Boston in 1904 and retrace the walks through Cambridge that he had taken with Howells so many years before, but he would soon return to England and die there in 1916.

Speaking at Harvard's commencement the previous June was a local boy, Edward Estlin Cummings, class of 1915, who had attended the Agassiz School when Maria Baldwin was its principal and then the Cambridge Latin School, a few blocks from his family's house on Irving Street. Cummings was soon off to France as a wartime ambulance driver, and he spent most of his life away, in Paris, New York's Greenwich Village, and New Hampshire. He returned to Harvard in 1952–53 to give the prestigious Charles Eliot Norton Lectures—under the title of "i: six nonlectures"—and recalled a day from his Cambridge childhood when a neighbor, the philosopher Josiah Royce, hailed him:

> "Estlin" his courteous and gentle voice hazarded, "I understand that you write poetry." I blushed. "Are you perhaps," he inquired, regarding a particular leaf of a particular tree, "acquainted with the sonnets of Dante Gabriel Rossetti?" I blushed a different blush and shook an ignorant head.... Shortly thereafter, sage and ignoramus were sitting opposite each other in a diminutive study...the ignoramus listening, enthralled; the sage intoning, lovingly and beautifully, his favorite poems.[2]

And, said Cummings, "very possibly (although I don't, as usual, know) that is the reason—or more likely the unreason—I've been writing sonnets ever since."

No one could confuse the E. E. Cummings of the 1923 mocking jab at "the Cambridge ladies" of his youth with Rossetti's elegant lyrics. But in an appreciation written at the time of Cummings's death in 1962, the critic Malcolm Cowley—a lifelong admirer a few years below Cummings at Harvard—wrote that "for all his rebellions and innovations, Cummings was, in another sense, the last and youngest in [the] rich tradition" of what he termed "the Harvard dandies."

These poets—Cowley includes Edwin Arlington Robinson, Wallace Stevens, Conrad Aiken, and T. S. Eliot—"weren't dandies in the sense that they dressed or acted with any precious sort of refinement. The dandyism went into their poems, which were as proudly discriminating and as free from vulgarity (except of a deliberate sort, introduced for effect) as the costume of a Regency gentleman." All, but certainly Cummings, "had a cold, dry, sharp New England wit of the kind that stabs you with icicles." And of them, Cowley writes, Cummings was the last "because the Great War changed the literary atmosphere at Harvard and elsewhere."[3]

THE HARVARD CONNECTION

The one inescapable element in the Cambridge literary scene is Harvard—so often a literary scene of its own. Foremost come the poets, and one has to be struck not only by their importance but also by the cross-generational mentoring by which they nurtured their art. On the "importance" point, they were that: Robert Frost, Archibald MacLeish, Robert Lowell, Pulitzer Prize winners who taught or lectured at Harvard and who also were established members of the local literary scene.

Among the other major poets of the last hundred years, both E. E. Cummings and T. S. Eliot attended Harvard but left Cambridge, returning only for events like the Norton Lectures and Eliot's Sanders Theatre reading, occasions recalled with awe a half-century later by those in attendance. More recently, Seamus Heaney has moved between Cambridge and his native Ireland.

Curiously, as the novelist and longtime Harvard writing instructor Monroe Engel noted in an interview, there is no comparable group of "Harvard novelists." Writers as disparate as John Updike, John Hawkes, Alice Hoffman, and the critic John Simon have attended the university. But many, such as Thomas Wolfe, who was working on *Of Time and the River* when he was at Harvard in the 1920s, and Updike, who was a fixture at the *Harvard Lampoon* in the early 1950s, left soon after commencement. Vladimir Nabokov's connection is even more tenuous: he was a part-time researcher at the Museum of Contemporary Zoology while living on Craigie Circle in the 1940s.

In more recent years, Engel's students have included the novelists Jay Cantor and Jonathan Strong, both of whom went on to teach writing at Tufts University; Melanie Thernstrom, whose *Halfway Heaven* dealt with a murder-suicide involving Harvard roommates; and the novelist and medical essayist Perri Klass. For star power, there is Dennis Lehane, who was teaching a workshop in Harvard's Extension School in 2003, the year his novel *Mystic River* made it to the screen. But, said Engel, it seems that at least as far as Harvard is concerned, "poets are more acceptable in the academic community than novelists."4

It is on the "mentoring" point that the role of Harvard poets like Frost, MacLeish, and Lowell takes on the greatest significance in the literary scene. Although Robert Frost is usually associated with upcountry New England, he bought a house at 35 Brewster Street in 1941 and lived there for several months a year until his death in 1963. The late editor and poet Peter Davison wrote that, well into his eighties, "the old man, still working at his poems, always thinking aloud, welcomed company in Cambridge, and held court for one or two or three friends, or sometimes even a whole class of schoolboys in his parlor." And, since Frost was "a notorious night owl," there was a company of young poets entrusted with the difficult task of "Getting Frost Home Before Midnight."5

In the postwar years, Davison wrote, poets of that generation, like John Ciardi, Richard Eberhart, May Sarton, and Richard Wilbur—and occasional-

Poet May Sarton, photographed at her home in York, Maine, 1992. Sarton is seated below a portrait of her painted in 1937, eight years after she graduated from Cambridge High & Latin School, where she wrote for and edited *The Cambridge Review*. *(The Boston Globe)*

ly older poets, like John Holmes, Edwin Honig, and Archibald MacLeish— "would come together of an evening at one person's house...and share their poems."[6] Sarton, who had written for Cambridge High and Latin School's *Review* while a student there, dreamed of a theatrical career and went to New York after graduating in 1929. She returned to Cambridge after serving in the Office for War Information and was a part-time instructor at Harvard, Radcliffe, and Wellesley. Wilbur came to Harvard as a graduate student after the war, and according to Davison, "a special personal interaction" developed between the MacLeishes and the Wilburs—"a social poise they had in common.... [T]hough they saw many things differently, [they] enjoyed the worldliness and the bonhomie of each other's company."[7]

MacLeish was very much a public figure, with a Pulitzer Prize (his first of three) in 1933 for *Conquistador*, a narrative poem pegged to the Spanish conquest of Mexico. A former librarian of Congress, he had performed wartime service with the Office for War Information, was a former assistant secretary of state, and wrote the preamble to the United Nations charter. According to MacLeish's biographer Scott Donaldson, the poet's recruitment to Harvard's Boylston professorship of rhetoric and oratory in 1949 reflected his dual careers; after receiving the offer, he consulted Supreme Court Justice Felix Frankfurter, his teacher at Harvard Law School, who urged him to accept it.

MacLeish would recall the thirteen years he spent at Harvard up until his retirement in 1962 as the happiest period of his life. There were the dinner parties that May Sarton remembered as "dazzling," with guests drawn from MacLeish's many public worlds—a practice he continued on a more informal note for students in Eliot House during a year as acting master in the mid-1950s. And there were the students in his English S: George Plimpton and Charles Bracelen Flood, Edward Hoagland and Jonathan Kozol, Donald Hall and Robert Bly, and William Alfred, himself to become a legendary mentor of young writers, who recalled MacLeish as "the best teacher of writing" he had known.[8]

"Sometimes," Donaldson wrote, "he made mistakes." A major one was turning down John Updike, not once but twice, for English S. Updike recalled going to MacLeish's office in Widener Library on one of those occasions to see if he had been admitted. There, he said, he found that "my poor play was lying in a scattered heap of other manuscripts, all of which except mine had a few comments scratched on them. On my play, not a word." Donaldson said that "over time [MacLeish] was able to persuade himself that Updike had never applied. 'If only I could have had him in English S,' he remarked in 1980."[9]

The occasion of the publication of Robert Lowell's *Collected Poems* in 2003 prompted similar recollections from poets of the current generation who took Lowell's poetry seminar in the 1960s. Following family tradition, Lowell had entered Harvard as a freshman in 1935 but left for Kenyon College the following year. Yet as the critic Adam Kirsch wrote in *Harvard Magazine*, "The end of Lowell's undergraduate career was just the beginning of his relationship with Harvard. Throughout his life, his poetry remained preoccupied with questions of family, inheritance and history; and in all these connections, Harvard was an inevitable subject"—appearing by name, by Kirsch's count, in at least twenty of his poems.[10]

When he returned in 1963 to teach creative writing and literature, Lowell was one of the most distinguished and best known of American poets, and the poems of the years before his death in 1977—like "Thanksgiving 1660 or 1960"—reflect the turbulent college life of that time, so changed from the privileged years when he had been at college: "the young are mobile, friends of the tossed waste leaf,/bell bottom, barefoot, Christendom's wild hair—/words are what get in the way of what they say."[11]

Lowell's weekly office-hours-turned-seminars became Harvard—and literary—legends. Lloyd Schwartz, the poet and Pulitzer Prize–winning music critic, described them in the *Boston Phoenix* as "a kind of open workshop—and not just for students. Anyone who had a new poem and brought copies of it could come—people off the street, famous poets who happened to be passing through Cambridge." Schwartz recalled one session when a Radcliffe undergraduate brought in a poem about a statue in Mexico: "Lowell was struck by this student's poem, and it was exciting to see him get excited about something of 'ours.'" Lowell's "jubilation" sparked a lively discussion about the poem and prompted an undergraduate who was on the *Harvard Advocate* —which had not accepted Lowell in the 1930s—to say that the magazine "would be interested in considering" the Radcliffe student's poem. "Without missing a beat," Schwartz wrote, "Lowell waved away the invitation and said [to the young woman]: 'Oh, you can do better than that.'"[12]

Just as MacLeish had headed over to Jim Cronin's on Dunster Street for beef stew and twenty-five-cent beer with his acolytes after English S, Lowell would lead the way from his basement seminar room in Quincy House to Cafe Iruña with a select group of students trailing after him—including, at various times, Schwartz, Gail Mazur, and Frank Bidart, co-editor of the *Collected Poems*, "like ducklings after their mother," as Schwartz put it. Those processionals were memorable even for those who were not included. "I was hardly alone in my hunger for Lowell's attention," recalled the poet and biographer James Atlas. "Everyone clamored for a share: the Brattle Street ladies who invited him to dinner; the undergraduates who clustered around him after class on the thinnest excuse...the graduate students and tutors who accompanied him to the Faculty Club for a drink. Nothing dejected me more than to watch Lowell moving off down the sidewalk surrounded by his coterie."[13]

"Once, after lunch," Schwartz wrote in his *Phoenix* appreciation, "I walked with him back into Harvard Square. He wanted an ice cream at Bailey's, where I ordered a vanilla malt with an egg in it (a Bailey's specialty). He'd never heard of putting an egg in a milk shake and had to try one too. He was so excited, he wanted to take a long walk, and we strolled all the way up Brattle Street to Sparks Street and back. It was, I think, the longest time I'd ever spent alone with him."[14]

But for all that conviviality, there was also a loneliness, which Lowell writes of in "Eating Out Alone": "The loneliness inside me is a place, /Har-

Poet Robert Lowell, right, takes a note from poet supporter and confidant Gordon Cairnie, owner of the Grolier Book Store, July 1968. *(Photograph by Elsa Dorfman/The Boston Globe)*

vard where no one might always be someone."[15] In the early 1970s, the poet Gail Mazur was turning the corner from Church Street onto Brattle to open one of the poetry readings at the Blacksmith House when she glimpsed Lowell "through the front window of Reading International, browsing through the poetry magazines. He seemed so lonely," she remembers, "and I just never felt I could go and speak with him."[16]

Stopping to speak with William Alfred was never a problem. As the *Boston Globe* wrote after his death in May 1999, Alfred "often strolled around Putnam Square [and] his daily walks were punctuated by a tip of the hat and a smile."[17] The recipients of those greetings could be students, present and former, Harvard colleagues, American Repertory Theatre patrons, fellow parishioners at St. Paul's Church where he attended Mass every day, and his neighbors from Kerry's Corner. Tutorials held at his house on Athens Street are remembered as "a famously unique mixture of conversation, dramatic and poetic readings, reminiscences of [growing up in] Brooklyn, avuncular wisdom and Irish jokes."[18] And his Beowulf course was remembered for the vivid way in which he conjured up a legendary world.

Alfred's first love was the theater—the source of his friendship of four decades with the actress Faye Dunaway. As he told a *Globe* interviewer, "I'll

Professor William Alfred
with actress Faye
Dunaway. *(Harvard
University Archives)*

never forget the day she came in to audition" in September 1965 for *Hogan's Goat,* Alfred's play about Irish American politicians. "It was," he recalled, "as if the goddess Aphrodite had appeared in the rehearsal hall."[19]

But what was perhaps most remarkable about Alfred was that he could connect not only with Broadway stars and Harvard intellectuals but also with the city's poor. As the *Globe's* obituary noted, "Each day, the dispossessed would show up at [his] house, where he would ask how their evening had gone and whether they'd like some tea. Then he'd reach into a jar he kept by the door and hand over a dollar or two."[20]

The Varieties of the Local

When the novelist Anne Bernays arrived in Cambridge in 1959 and settled on Francis Avenue with her husband, the biographer Justin Kaplan, her first reaction, she recalled in an interview, was that "it wasn't New York."[21]

And it wasn't Boston, either, as William Dean Howells had found a half-century or more earlier, nor "sinful Somerville," as the youthful E. E. Cummings would put it—although the Cambridge ladies Cummings had derided are later described by Marian Cannon Schlesinger as "passionate lady lecturegoers" in her *Snatched from Oblivion*, an account of growing up in Cambridge in the early years of the twentieth century.[22] What Bernays said she and Kaplan found after the "feverish life" in New York, with its round of literary events and parties, was not only a one-restaurant, one-dress-shop town but also a spot where there were "no events, no readings, no place for writers to meet, except in each other's houses."

Peter Davison wrote that it was gatherings of local poets—Donald Hall, Robert Bly, Frank O'Hara, Edward St. John Gorey, John Ashbery—at Richard Eberhart's house that led to the founding of the Poets' Theatre, which flourished on Palmer Street in the 1950s. "They amused themselves," Davison said, "by writing and performing plays that, at the outset, only poets could abide."[23] On a more formal note, he went on, "this was the era of the urban, academic dinner party, a formidable and deeply entrenched institution of the 1950s and 1960s," hosted often by senior faculty members like MacLeish or Harry Levin.[24]

Also flourishing in equally private settings were reading groups, which like women's groups have become so popular in recent years. A paper read at the Cambridge Historical Society in 1942 marked the centenary of the Cambridge Book Club, founded in 1832 "to promote and circulate private reading"; it was believed to be "the first of the now innumerable book clubs." The paper noted that of the twenty people present at the club's first meeting, eleven were professors or tutors at Harvard.[25]

Recalling her efforts in the 1970s to foster a more public literary scene in Cambridge—close to twenty years after she arrived in town—Bernays was surprised at "why I waited so long." Remembering an institution in New York, she proposed a New England chapter of PEN, the national poet-essayist-novelist group, which she and a group of literary friends put together around her kitchen table. The first public meeting—held, inauspiciously, outside of Cambridge at the Boston Athenaeum on the night after the February 1978 blizzard—took up the subject "Why I Live Here and Not There," "a way," said Bernays, "of saying that it's not New York." As a variety of events took place—panel discussions, "Discovery" parties at which established writers presented fledglings, parties to honor members who had published during the year—a local scene developed. "I was looking for the company of other writers," Bernays recalled. "That was why I started it."[26]

The bookstores of Harvard Square—at least before their decline toward the end of the twentieth century—had always fostered a kind of clubby-groupie scene. Gordon Cairnie's Grolier Poetry Book Shop was a notable "gathering place for writers," said his successor, Louisa Solano, with "some heavy drinking parties" after hours.[27] Irwin Rosen's Mandrake Bookstore, when it was on Boylston Street, was a hangout for English department graduates and undergraduates; there was always a new shipment of books from England. And from its opening in 1983, Kate's Mystery Books in a landmark Victorian on Massachusetts Avenue was a mecca, not just for mystery fans, but also for mystery writers, including Robert B. Parker, the author of the bestselling Spenser detective novels, who built for store owner Kate Mattes some conspicuously wobbly shelves.

Those years in the late 1970s and early 1980s—following what Bernays called "the chaos theory"—also saw the development of what has become another fixture of the Cambridge literary scene: author readings at bookstores. As Frank Kramer of the Harvard Book Store put it, the readings sponsored by his store, WordsWorth, and the Harvard Coop were "something that was waiting to happen." He remembers that when the Harvard Book Store readings began—initially in Boston in 1980 and then, when the Harvard Square store expanded in 1987, in Cambridge—"all the local authors who had signed books for me, after having a signing at the store, would write things like, 'Thanks for bringing us together.' I think they had a sense of not being connected." And, he said, in a view echoed by Bernays and others, "as [readings] have become a part of what the city is, they have added to its culture."[28]

Predating these events by a half-dozen years were the poetry readings Gail Mazur began in 1973 at the Blacksmith House (of Longfellow's "spreading chestnut tree" and "village smithy" fame). And after Solano took over the Grolier from Cairnie, she instituted the shop's poetry readings. It was here that Allen Ginsberg was arrested, according to the poet William Corbett, while "[standing] on a table hawking copies of *Big Table*," a magazine banned in Boston for printing chapters of William Burroughs's *Naked Lunch*.[29] [The Grolier was bought in 2006, by a new owner Ifeanyi Menkiti, also professor of philosophy at Wellesley College. Editor]

Ginsberg and the other Beat Generation writers were an elusive part of the Cambridge literary scene during the 1950s and early 1960s. Ginsberg and his friends stayed with the photographer Elsa Dorfman on Flagg Street, and Gregory Corso crashed in one of the Harvard houses for a year or so.[30] Solano remembers a crowded reading by Jack Kerouac at Lowell House and her being "dragged in by poet [Desmond] O'Grady before they shut the doors."[31] But "they were only here for a few nights or so, just came and went," Dorfman recalls. "So, really and truly, there wasn't a beat scene."

Throughout, Cambridge has been a breeding ground for literary magazines. Many were short-lived, like *Halcyon* in the late 1940s, which despite publishing the poetry of Cummings, Richmond Lattimore, James Merrill, and L. E. Sissman, lasted for just two issues. Still thriving into the new century are several that found academic homes—The *Harvard Advocate* and *Harvard Review*, along with AGNI at Boston University, *Boston Review* at MIT, and *Ploughshares*, now at Emerson College but founded, according to its editor Don Lee, by a group of young writers and political activists who gathered in the early 1970s with its first editor, DeWitt Henry, at the Plough and Stars pub.[32]

Henry dubbed his *Ploughshares* colleague James Randall "the unofficial pope of Cambridge literary life." Randall, who died in March 2005, taught at Emerson College for twenty-nine years; with his wife, Joanne, he operated the small Pym-Randall Press, which published early works of Kenneth Rexroth, Richard Eberhart, and Robert Lowell. Later, the couple ran Ahab Rare Books, an antiquarian bookstore in Harvard Square.[33]

Harking back a half-century to the days of the academic dinner party— but liberated from faculty dining rooms to an expansive porch on Avon Hill— is the Porch Table, a gathering of writers convened by the novelist Elena Castedo. It has been meeting weekly on her porch since 1995.[34] Just past its tenth anniversary, the list of "porchers," as they call themselves, is a veritable *Who's Who* of writers living in the area, including Ann Beattie and Alice Hoffman, Jill McCorkle and Sue Miller. The only requirements for membership are to have published a piece or two of fiction and to be invited by a "porcher."

Now a regular, Mameve Medwed had just published her first novel, *Mail*, and was barely known beyond the neighborhood when she started attending. She noted at one gathering that with two novels set in Cambridge, "there are too many restaurants I can't go into anymore." Now, with her third novel, she said, "there'll be some new places I can't go."[35]

Not surprisingly, the Avon Hill writers have been good observers of the local literary landscape, acknowledging, like Bernays, its limits when compared with New York. In the latter, noted the novelist Elizabeth Benedict, "There are people who make the scene at magazine parties at *Vanity Fair* and the *New York Observer*, [and] the whole media world is there." By contrast, she said, "This is a smallish town, a university town."[36]

Monroe Engel had observed the local scene as a Harvard undergraduate in the 1940s, then returned to teach in the English department in the mid-1950s. Reflecting that Cambridge is indeed a university town, he noted that there have been a fair number of novels connected to Harvard—May Sarton's *Faithful Are the Wounds* (1955) Anne Bernays's *Professor Romeo* (1989), and John Kenneth Galbraith's *A Tenured Professor* (1990), for example—with Margaret Atwood's dystopian *The Handmaid's Tale* (1986) in a category all its own. But, said Engel, "There hasn't been a lot of 'townie' literature."[37]

A major exception is Engel's own 1981 novel, *Fish*. Its central character, the eponymous Fish, "vagueing" through a Cambridge summer, is as much a part of the Cambridge scene as the panhandlers and hawkers and "extraordinary range of people...selling salvation or seeking it in this city at all times."[38] Fish thinks of the city's squares as many of its residents—and all its urban planners—do, "as informing nodes distinguishable from each other not only architecturally and by what they offer in the way of commerce and entertainment, but also by the expectations they arouse and the consequent life they attract."[39] And however gentrified, Fish's Cambridge can still be "rank as an old shoe" on a humid summer evening.[40]

Other exceptions include Medwed's *Mail* and possibly Eric Segal's *Love Story*, which although remembered primarily as a "Harvard novel," featured the former Midget Restaurant on Massachusetts Avenue and has prompted the occasional tourist to seek out "the Love Story house" on Oxford Street. Further, there is *Central Square* (1998), by George Packer, who remarked that while the novel's "big themes"—loneliness, anomie—might be "geographically transferable, the atmosphere is absolutely rooted in this neighborhood right here."[41]

Packer—staff writer for *The New Yorker*, columnist for *Mother Jones*, and author of the highly acclaimed *Assassin's Gate* about the war in Iraq—lived in Central Square long enough to be part of the neighborhood and absorb the atmosphere. That is felt most strongly, he said, during the late afternoon, the going-home time, when "accidental encounters" occur on the streets. "You've got to get your characters out on the street where there are strangers around. That's where you witness the romance of a city."

Into the Future

Observant readers of *The Harvard Book of Contemporary American Poetry* will note that, at one point in the anthology, the world changes. From Wallace Stevens through Robert Lowell and Richard Wilbur, to Donald Hall and John Ashbery, the poets themselves had direct Harvard connections—as students or teachers or in some cases both. But then those connections diminish and fracture.

What happened, said the poet David Gewanter, was a reflection of what Cambridge had become: "It's a change in its profile, the kind of writers and the 'imaginative presence' that you find in Cambridge now."[42] In the old Cambridge, he said, "that 'imaginative presence' derived from New England, Emersonian transcendentalist backgrounds. . . . [Now] it seems an imaginative worldscape imported by each writer, and producing a kind of lapidary sense of 'everywhere is here.'" The old center, said Gewanter, "was probably

Longfellow's house, and things, ideas, padded back and forth along Brattle Street. [But he] has become antiquarian, a kind of local writer now." And although Longfellow's classic Dante translation has been "stepped over by Robert Pinsky's," Longfellow's furnished the inspiration for the 2003 literary whodunit *The Dante Club*, by the Cambridge writer Matthew Pearl.

After Longfellow and his circle were gone, there was Cummings's "mythical domain of semiwilderness," Norton's Woods, on an axis leading along Francis Avenue into Harvard Yard. And well into the middle of the last century, the focus was still the old Harvard ties, the old New England spirit. But in the new Cambridge, the perspective shifted outward, said Gewanter, "turning [the city] into a world literary center, a Paris for international writers." Now, he continued, "you come to this place to write about where you came from"—Frank Bidart from California and Pinsky from New Jersey, Seamus Heaney from Ireland, Stanislaus Baranowski from Poland, Jamaica Kincaid and Derek Walcott from the Caribbean. That trend is perhaps seen most vividly in the collection of writers from afar that Henry Louis Gates Jr. assembled for Harvard's Afro-American Studies Department.

Gewanter, co-editor of Robert Lowell's *Collected Poems*, taught writing at Harvard before moving to Georgetown, where he is an associate professor of English. He sees Harvard today as less of a training ground for poets and writers than it was in the past, instead focusing "on creating a professional class of literary critics." And, he said, "the next Updike might not even think of going to Harvard" and might not stay in Cambridge afterward.

Cambridge "is still interesting," said Gail Mazur, "because of the college, and what it brings, the sophistication, but also the commercialization...I know it's a very unromantic explanation, but I attribute a lot of the changes in the literary scene to the end of rent control."[43] Poets with jobs as adjunct writing teachers and young writers working on a first novel "can't live here anymore." There was an apartment building on Massachusetts Avenue, Mazur recalled, "that with its $180, $200 rents used to be favored by young writers, and where the superintendent was frequently a young writer himself." Now, she said, "they're all gone. Not one stayed in Cambridge."

"I've thought about it a great deal," said Bernays. "Perhaps Cambridge was always a state of mind, rather than a physical thing."[44] And now "it's coasting. It's become a place where ideas are hatched, but then [writers] go to New York or Hollywood to be produced."

ENDNOTES

1. E. E. Cummings, *Poems*, 1923–1954 (New York: Harcourt, Brace, 1954), 58.

2. Cummings, "i: six nonlectures," (Cambridge: Harvard University Press, 1953), 26.

3. Malcolm Cowley, *New England Writers and Writing*, ed. Donald W. Faulker, (Hanover, N.H.: University Press of New England, 1996), 200-201.

4. Monroe Engel in an interview with the author, Cambridge, Mass., May 3, 2004.

5. Peter Davison, *The Fading Smile: Poets in Boston from Robert Lowell to Sylvia Plath* (New York: W. W. Norton, 1994), 15–16.

6. Ibid., 64ff.

7. Ibid., 67.

8. Scott Donaldson, *Archibald MacLeish: An American Life* (Boston: Houghton Mifflin, 1992), 405.

9. Ibid, 409.

10. Adam Kirsch, "The Brahmin Rebel," *Harvard Magazine*, May–June 2004.

11. Robert Lowell, *Collected Poems*, ed. Frank Bidart and David Gewanter (New York: Farrar, Straus, 2003), 557.

12. Lloyd Schwartz, "Memories of Brattle Street and Lowell," *Boston Phoenix*, December 19, 2003.

13. James Atlas, "Lord Weary: Robert Lowell in Cambridge," *Atlantic Monthly*, July 1982.

14. Schwartz, *Boston Phoenix*, December 19, 2003.

15. Lowell, *Collected Poems*, 577.

16. Gail Mazur in an interview with the author, Cambridge, Mass., May 12, 2004.

17. Joseph P. Kahn and Michael Blowen, "William Alfred, 1922–99: Playwright, Teacher, Inspiration," *Boston Globe*, May 21, 1999.

18. "William Alfred: Memorial Minute," *Harvard Gazette*, April 3, 2003.

19. Carol Flake, "William Alfred's Whimsy and Wisdom," *Boston Globe*, May 16, 1989.

20. Kahn and Blowen, *Boston Globe*, May 21, 1999.

21. Anne Bernays in an interview with the author, Cambridge, Mass., April 28, 2004.

22. Marian Cannon Schlesinger, *Snatched from Oblivion: A Cambridge Memoir* (Boston: Little, Brown, 1979), 73.

23. Davison, *Fading Smile: Poets in Boston from Robert Lowell to Sylvia Plath*, 24.

24. Ibid., 66.

25. "Introduction to the Centenary of the Cambridge Book Club," *Proceedings of the Cambridge Historical Society*, 28 (1942): 105-09.

26. Bernays in interview with author, April 28, 2004.

27. Louise Solano in an interview with the author, Cambridge, Mass., May 7, 2004.

28. Frank Kramer in an interview with the author, Cambridge, Mass., May 10, 2004.

29. William Corbett, *Literary New England: A History and Guide* (Boston: Faber and Faber, 1993), 108.

30. Elsa Dorfman in a telephone interview with the author, Cambridge, Mass., May 7, 2004.

31. Solano in interview with author, May 7, 2004.

32. Michael Kenney, "The Little Journal with the Big Names," *Boston Globe*, February 7, 1996.

33. Avi Steinberg, "James Randall, Literary Critic, Mentor, Teacher," *Boston Globe*, March 22, 2005.

34. David Wildman, "Writers' Bloc," *Boston Globe*, December 17, 2001.

35. Mameve Medwed in conversation with the author, Cambridge, Mass., May 5, 2004.

36. Elizabeth Benedict in conversation with the author, Cambridge, Mass., May 5, 2004.

37. Monroe Engel in interview with author, May 3, 2004.

38. Monroe Engel, *Fish* (New York: Athenaeum, 1981), 12.

39. Ibid., 41.

40. Ibid., 114.

41. Michael Kenney, "Packer's Novel of Strangers," *Boston Globe*, December 7, 1998.

42. David Gewanter in a telephone interview with the author, Washington, D.C., May 22, 2004.

43. Mazur in interview with author, May 12, 2004.

44. Bernays in interview with author, April 28, 2004.

Looking Backward: Club 47 and the 1960s Folk Revival in Cambridge[1]

MILLIE RAHN

WHEN A VIRTUALLY unknown folksinger from Cambridge named Joan Baez stepped onstage at the first Newport Folk Festival in 1959—at the invitation of Chicago's Bob Gibson—the nascent folk music scene took notice. Back home, the young singer had been setting the stage for rising national prominence at her Tuesday-night gigs at Club 47, and the rest, as they say, is folk music history.

The forty-seventh anniversary of the founding of Club 47 coincides with the centennial of the Cambridge Historical Society, both serving as markers for assessing local history and calling attention to one aspect of it: the story of Club 47 and what is commonly called the folk revival, verbal shorthand for the mid-twentieth-century folk music revival. This piece looks at Club 47 from a folklorist's perspective and places it in its socio-cultural context.

Club 47 is central to any study of the Cambridge music scene—and the folk revival—in part because eastern Massachusetts was one of the major centers of nineteenth- and twentieth-century cultural revivals. Moreover, today Club Passim, the legendary music club "between the Coops" on Palmer Street, is the successor to Club 47 and thus carries the distinction of being the longest-running folk music venue in the country.

An early performance by Joan Baez at the original Club 47, 1962. *Time* magazine featured her in a cover story, dubbing her "Girl with Guitar."

Club 47's story epitomizes the golden age of the New England music scene of the mid-twentieth century. Dubbed the home of "the power elite of the folk revival," the club was the epicenter of musical activity on both sides of the Charles River during the "great folk boom" of the late 1950s and 1960s.[2] For the ten years that it existed, between 1958 and 1968, the club helped to create a community and a market for folk music. In each of its two locations—first in the storefront at 47 Mount Auburn Street, from whence it took its name, and then in the subterranean room on Palmer Street that is now Club Passim—most folk music enthusiasts, this author included, would claim that Club 47 showcased the best *music* the revival had to offer.

Besides Baez, Club 47 launched local and regional performers such as blues singer Eric von Schmidt from Connecticut; the Charles River Valley Boys (CRVB), one of the first urban bluegrass groups to combine traditional musicians and revivalists and made up mostly of Harvard students from Oklahoma, Texas, New York, and Massachusetts; Tom Rush, a Harvard student from New Hampshire whose eclectic repertoire came in part from nineteenth- and early-twentieth-century academic song collections; and, later, Radcliffe dropout Bonnie Raitt, Peter Wolf, Peter Rowan, and many, many others. Jackie Washington and Taj Mahal drew on their families' respective African-American and Puerto Rican and Caribbean traditions. Arlo Guthrie's "Alice's Restaurant Massacree" chronicled a Thanksgiving in the Berkshires along with commentary on Vietnam War draft resistance. The Jim Kweskin Jug Band, composed entirely of northeasterners, reinterpreted 1920s Memphis jug band songs with jugs, kazoos, washtub bass, and conventional instruments, and took the revival into folk rock and psychedelia before the boom ended. All of these performers also played the Newport folk festivals and recorded and toured nationally, but that came later.

In addition to local talent, the club featured legends of blues, bluegrass, early country, and old-time music, some of them the first generation to record on vinyl. These included Maybelle Carter of the Carter Family, bluesman Mississippi John Hurt, Bill Monroe and the Bluegrass Boys, flat-picking guitarist Doc Watson, and others who found the new, and younger, audiences of the sixties literally sitting at their feet. Club 47's bookings also influenced and mirrored changes at the Newport folk festivals and on the national revival circuit, and helped assure the folk boom's place in popular culture.

The mid-century folk revival began amid the political tensions of an international Cold War combined with social and political conservatism in the United States. The country was on the brink of a war in Southeast Asia while experiencing social and political movements at home about racial desegregation and civil rights, women's rights, sexual freedom, and recreational drugs. These were uncharted waters, and popular folk music provided the soundtrack to the times.

Songs reflected, and even changed, attitudes: ballads were cautionary tales about life and love; blues and gospel woke up suburban kids to the realities of another America and went hand in hand with the civil rights movement; "topical" songs echoed nineteenth-century broadside commentaries on everyday injustices and social and political events, including an unpopular war; and old-time music and bluegrass got people dancing. When all was said and done, coffeehouses and festivals were about rites of passage as a generation came of age, literally and figuratively. Song texts, tunes, styles, musical instruments, and their cultural contexts opened up an imaginative world and enabled a privileged generation to assemble and transport their own canon of historical and contemporary American music into a new cultural realm called the folk revival.

Almost from the beginning, Club 47 audiences were card-carrying members (or guests) of a nonprofit educational institution incorporated in the Commonwealth of Massachusetts, a unique model for coffeehouses at the time. Anyone could join Club 47 by paying a nominal one-dollar membership fee. The creation of "The Club Mount Auburn 47, Inc." skirted the city's arcane blue laws that put the coffeehouse in the same category as boozy cabarets and kept the peace with the local constabulary—sort of. Although it was started by recent Brandeis graduates Paula Kelley and Joyce Kalina as a coffeehouse and jazz venue patterned on European models popular at the time, the organization was soon run by a board of directors.

That board included Betsy Siggins, who also booked the club and ran the kitchen; Jim Rooney, a graduate student in classics and a bluegrass musician who later managed the club and served on the Newport Folk Festival board; the late Manny Greenhill, manager, impresario, and surrogate father to many members; and others involved in local business and artistic pursuits. The longtime board president Nancy Sweezy, whose children introduced her to Club 47, found the Palmer Street space when the club had to move from Mount Auburn Street. She was a potter, token "grownup," and club chatelaine, and her house north of the Square became an informal bed-and-breakfast for multigenerational visitors. Sweezy also ran an Appalachian crafts cooperative in Harvard Square called Country Roads with the late Ralph Rinzler, a talent scout for Newport who went on to create the Smithsonian's Festival of American Folklife, and Scottish singer and weaver Norman Kennedy.

MUSIC AT CLUB 47

Music was the core of Club 47. Classical ballads and blues were introduced in the late 1950s by predominantly local white solo singers, both female and male, including Baez, von Schmidt, Debbie Green, Carolyn Hester, Rolf Cahn, and an occasional visitor from New York named Bob Dylan. Ultimately, however, blues and bluegrass became the most popular genres.

Memorial Day weekend in 1962—a good example of how the genre's growing popularity featured some of the best of the 47's regular musicians and visitors—was devoted to bluegrass. From New York, two of the Greenbriar Boys, John Herald and the aforementioned Rinzler, joined the CRVB on Friday night; Bill Keith and Jim Rooney, like the CRVB virtually a house band, played on Saturday; and the Gray Sky Boys, "bluegrass from Yale University," as the *Boston Broadside* described them, played on Monday. That was months before bluegrass hit network television and Middle America on

Menu for the Club Mt. Auburn 47, which took its name from its address. The club was opened by Brandeis graduates Paula Kelley and Joyce Kalina as a European-inspired jazz coffee house in January 1958.

a new show called *The Beverly Hillbillies.* Grand Ole Opry stars Lester Flatt and Earl Scruggs, already heroes to many Cambridge folks through their recordings and Scruggs's Newport appearances, wrote and played the show's theme song and sometimes made cameo appearances. A subculture was invading the mainstream.

Most weeks in the mid-1960s followed a pattern at Club 47. Sunday night "hoots" were hosted by local folks, including Taj Mahal, current Newport Folk Festival impresario and former ballad singer Robert L. Jones of Boston, Harvard undergrad Paul Arnoldi from Wyoming, and individual members of the CRVB and the Jug Band. Monday nights were more or less devoted to Tom Rush and Tuesday nights to Jackie Washington, with the CRVB filling in when needed, which could be up to five times a month. Weekends were reserved for folk stars—regulars *and* visitors—who until the late 1960s usually appeared for only one night at a time.

The roster of who played at Club 47 in the course of ten years is a revivalist's and collector's dream. The calendar for July 1963, the last summer on Mount Auburn Street and the first year of the revived and reorganized Newport festivals, exemplified the eclectic bookings when the revival was hitting its stride. In addition to the regulars already mentioned, visitors were

Scottish singer Jean Redpath; West Virginia coal miner and five-string banjo player Dock Boggs, who had recorded in the 1920s; ballad singer Rita Weill from Berkeley and Ramblin' Jack Elliott from Brooklyn; New Lost City Rambler and old-time musician Mike Seeger; and singer-songwriter Tim Hardin. In between were locals Don MacSorley doing English and Irish songs, blues singers and guitarists Mitch Greenhill and Rick Lee, and country and ballad singers Dayle Stanley and Carol Langstaff.

By 1966, bands were the thing at Club 47. The Paul Butterfield Blues Band stimulated interest in urban, Chicago blues when it appeared in August 1965 following its controversial electrified set with Bob Dylan at Newport the previous month, Muddy Waters's band, the first African-American Chicago blues players at the club (except perhaps for Pops Staples), and the Junior Wells Blues Band became frequent guests. By fall 1967, electrified groups were booked for four to six days at a time, their music often closer to folk and psychedelic rock than roots. Admission was still just a few bucks.

But the party was soon over. Club 47 closed in late April 1968 the way it had begun—among a circle of musicians and surrogate family. Its last week was a microcosm of its, and the revival's, short history; stars, quasi–house-bands, local amateurs with name recognition, and spin-off bands were all represented.

Its demise reflected the swiftly changing tastes and the growing sophistication of the music business, and the coming of age of a largely core college crowd ready to be grownups. Many members moved to new cities and towns to pursue jobs, rear families, and begin the lives for which they were, often perfunctorily, educated when they were not making music.

In many ways Club 47 succeeded too well, literally bursting out of its tiny premises as a force to be reckoned with on the musical scene. Still, changing tastes and economics took their toll. Music fans wanted to hear louder bands in larger spaces like the Boston Tea Party across the Charles, where they could dance—and drink—to the music of such groups as Peter Wolf's new outfit, the J. Geils Band (which was reinterpreting old blues for rocking audiences) or Peter Rowan's Earth Opera (which was taking the Jug Band's psychedelia to new heights).

CLUB 47 AT NEWPORT

All the while, Club 47 had been developing a symbiotic relationship with the annual Newport folk festivals in Rhode Island that by 1963 were the gathering place of the folk communities of Cambridge and New York. No other scene contributed as much to Newport as did Club 47. Well-known artists who had established their reputations and drew fans to "the 47" appeared to even larger audiences at Newport and on its festival-related recordings. For others, especially non-performers, Newport was the musical and social event of the summer. Folk "enthusiasts," as the media called them, volunteered for hospitality work to get free passes and meet and interact with the stars. Others went simply to soak up the music.

Many "Cambridge people" played Newport. The Kweskin Jug Band was among the most acclaimed acts at its first appearance in 1964 and played annually until 1967. By 1968 the group had disbanded, but several former members appeared in new configurations. Jim Kweskin, who by then was a member of the Newport board, appeared with the Lyman Family, Geoff and Maria Muldaur performed as a duo, and Bill Keith played solo. The CRVB appeared as a group only at the 1965 festival, although banjo player Bob Siggins and mandolin player Joe Val returned individually in 1968. Other well-known Cambridge folks at Newport were Jackie Washington (1963 and 1968), Eric von Schmidt (1965 and 1968), Tom Rush (1966), and Jim Rooney (1968 and as a guitarist with the CRVB in 1965). Bill Keith also appeared in 1963 as a member of Bill Monroe's Bluegrass Boys before he joined the Kweskin band.

The summer programming at Club 47 often piggybacked on the Newport schedule to take advantage of distant performers who were already in New England. A survey of mid-1960s bookings shows that traditional and revival artists were booked before and after the festival. In July 1964 these appearances included the Kentucky Colonels, a California bluegrass band with roots in Maine and the Canadian Maritimes; the home-grown Kweskin Jug Band, which essentially "rehearsed" and honed their material onstage for an entire week before their first Newport gig; Mike Seeger; and the revival blues trio Koerner, Ray, and Glover from Minneapolis. Those who played the following summer before or after Newport were bluesman Lightnin' Hopkins, Doc Watson, Irish "tinker" Margaret Barry, and fiddler Michael Gorman, as well as revivalists Hamilton Camp, the Paul Butterfield Blues Band, Eric von Schmidt, and the California duo Kathy and Carol.

Besides club gigs, Club 47 sponsored a series of concerts in Harvard Square halls by more traditional performers before the summer festival in early 1965. The series was run under the auspices of the Newport Folk Foundation, a spin-off of the festival that located and produced more grassroots talent. Performers were Bessie Jones and the Georgia Sea Island Singers; Bahamian guitarist Joseph Spence; and Grand Ole Opry stars Maybelle Carter, Sam and Kirk McGee, and old-time fiddler Arthur Smith. The series also included Kentucky guitar and banjo player Roscoe Holcomb, North Carolina ballad singer Dillard Chandler, and the Galax String Band from Virginia, as well as Ed Young, a fife player and dancer from Mississippi, and blues singer and guitarist Fred MacDowell.

During 1966 and 1967, a number of artists—some local, some not—who had been at Newport were featured at concerts produced by Club 47 at large halls in Boston. Among them were Tom Rush, Doc Watson, Tom Paxton, Pete Seeger, and the Paul Butterfield and Otis Rush blues bands. Spring 1967 featured what was billed as "the country music show of the year," with Buck Owens and His Buckaroos and Bill Monroe and His Blue Grass Boys. Monroe held a special place in the hearts of Club 47 audiences; their own Bill Keith, Peter Rowan, and Richard Greene had all been Blue Grass Boys, among the first urban revivalists to join that legendary band, which came through the club regularly.

An equally ambitious schedule for the fall of 1967 had concerts by Joan Baez, Arlo Guthrie, Patrick Sky, and the Chambers Brothers, and return engagements by the Butterfield Band and Buck Owens. Like the previous lineup, many of these musicians were fresh from recent Newport festivals, and by then each had established some sort of connection to Club 47, usually having appeared there more than once. Guthrie, for instance, made his Club 47 debut in April 1966, but it was his first Newport gig a year later that gained him national attention for "Alice's Restaurant," his anti-draft, anti–Vietnam War talking blues that started over a Thanksgiving dinner in Stockbridge, Massachusetts. Despite the stellar lineups and outward success, Club 47—and the revival itself—was losing its edge and would close within the year.

Newport held the last of its old festivals in 1969 and did not reappear until the mid-1980s. The bigger party was over, too, as Woodstock would confirm a month later, despite the size of its audience, the juxtaposition of folk stars like Baez and Guthrie with rockers like Janis Joplin and Jimi Hendrix, and its success in capturing the national imagination.

Venues such as Club 47 and the Newport folk festivals—and a phenomenon like the revival—are artifacts of their time and place and, like many things in American culture, are generally short-lived. Before Club 47 is consigned to the cultural attic, however, it should receive its well-deserved due for having moved beyond its four walls to influence the folk scenes in Cambridge, Boston, and eastern New England, the Newport festivals, and the popular music industry nationwide.

THE FOLK REVIVAL

Folklorists believe that one cannot tell a story properly without putting it into its socio-historical context. The folk revival of the late 1950s and 1960s was a brief cultural phenomenon. The word *revival* implies a sense of rebirth, of resurrecting items from the past to suit the needs and sensibilities of the present. Revivals often come at a time when a culture perceives itself under threat of major change. Ozzie and Harriet may have romanticized the late 1950s, but the United States was on the brink of a Cold War with the Soviet Union as well as a simmering war in Southeast Asia and social and political unrest at home. Times weren't like they used to be, and popular folk music gathered a generation of mostly young, well-educated, middle-class consumers together into one community and provided a sound track to the era, all the while creating a popular music genre that was an alternative to mass entertainment.

New England was at the center of the folk revival in part due to its many colleges and universities. Along with the surrounding coffeehouses, folksong societies, contra dance groups, and music stores selling instruments and recordings, they were the vital centers of youth culture. Amherst College students Bill Keith and Jim Rooney and University of Massachusetts student Taj Mahal organized the Pioneer Valley Folklore Society in the late 1950s to put on concerts by popular folksingers, an activity echoed on other campuses and by folksong societies throughout the region. Soon after graduation they gravitated eastward and themselves became popular performers in Cambridge. By contrast, other organizations formed at the same time, such as the Folk Song Society of Greater Boston, were more insular and reflected the progressive politics and social activism of earlier revivalists, particularly those in New York in the 1940s. Again, part of the uniqueness of the revival in New England—and in Cambridge in particular—was that music and musicianship, rather than political activism, were firmly at its hub.

Directly and indirectly, the folk revival was part of a long tradition of interest in folk music in New England, both inside and outside the academic milieu. Founded in 1888 in Cambridge, the American Folklore Society (AFS) included many independent scholars and antiquarians, particularly folksong collectors, such as Francis James Child, a medievalist at Harvard and the organization's first president. Child's six-volume ballad collection provided texts for songs that revivalists sang half a century later at coffeehouses, festivals, concerts, and on recordings.

Country music also influenced the later revival. In 1948, a decade before the coffeehouse boom, the radio show "Hillbilly at Harvard" started life as "Barn Howl," a closed-circuit country music broadcast heard by the college community on Harvard's radio station, WHRB, which began transmitting publicly in 1957 and continues today. Commercial shows such as WCOP's "Hayloft Jamboree" began broadcasting in Boston in the early 1950s and organized Grand Ole Opry–like revues at Symphony Hall, with touring country acts. Bars such as the Hillbilly Ranch in Park Square and the nearby Mohawk Ranch catered to the thriving live country music scene supported by military personnel stationed nearby and the many southerners who had come north to work or study. Banjo whiz Don Stover and fiddler and then MIT graduate student Tex Logan, whom many local musicians credit as major influences, played with groups like the Lilly Brothers from West Virginia. Moreover, Everett Lilly had recorded with Flatt and Scruggs and played the Opry, and his son Everett Alan contributed his traditional music-making credentials to the Charles River Valley Boys.

All of these artists, venues, and activities influenced the revivalists, who went on to become performers, record company and festival producers, agents and managers, and fans. Rounder Records, now in Burlington, was founded by several music enthusiasts in 1970 as a direct result of the revival and continues to record roots musicians from many traditions. Passim, the successor to Club 47 run by Rae Anne and Bob Donlin (both deceased) as a coffeehouse and gift shop, persevered during the lean years of the music business in the 1970s and 1980s. It was a major force in developing and supporting the singer-songwriter phenomenon that contributed to the region's rich community-based coffeehouse tradition. Now Passim's successor, Club Passim, has come full circle and been reincorporated as a nonprofit like Club 47. Club Passim combines traditional, or roots, and multicultural performers with newer contemporary genres, as well as running a music school and cultural outreach programs under the banner of the Passim Folk Music and Cultural Center. The Newport Folk Festival, which paralleled all these developments and ran from 1959 to 1969, was revived in the mid-1980s and continues to thrive today.

By 1969, with the last Newport festival and the first Woodstock event in nearby New York, the revival was in decline. Fans and scholars both have attributed the beginning of the end to Bob Dylan's "going electric" at Newport in July 1965, although he was not the first to do so. Rather, a new generation of performers and genres was attracting its own following. But the question remains: Why was Cambridge the epicenter of the great boom, and why the late 1950s?

Cambridge, Harvard, and Nineteenth-Century Influences

From the beginning, Club 47 had a unique cultural, historical, and intellectual context that set it apart from other local—and even national—revival venues. It was situated in Harvard Square, in the midst of an environment that was (and is) highly cognizant of its academic, political, and social history. Cambridge and its foremost educational institution, Harvard University, share a distinguished, interdependent relationship as centers of academic and popular interest in folklore, while Cantabrigians have historically supported and participated in avant-garde cultural movements that directly or indirectly influenced activities at the club.

Early on, many (if not the majority) of the 47's core members were Harvard and Radcliffe students, alumni, or followers of the area's scholarly and cultural milieu and thus inherently part of the intellectual and social tradition of Cambridge. To understand the relationships among revivalism, the search for identity within a generation, the processes resulting in the formation of communities and subcultures like that at the 47, and the creation of new musical traditions and performance aesthetics, we must first look at the confluence of the cultural, historical, and intellectual contexts in Cambridge, which gave the revival its unique cachet.

Again, two elements are generally common to cultural revivals: the appropriation of perceived portions of an older culture in order to adapt them to contemporary needs, and the leisure time use of such cultural products as a consumable commodity. Idealized influences are drawn from the past or from romanticized concepts of contemporary life, such as pastoral images of rugged mountaineers in the southern United States or of rural peoples struggling to adapt to urban life.

These notions themselves are historical and cultural constructs. In nineteenth- and twentieth-century North America, ideas of purity and authenticity usually were rooted in some form of belief that pre-industrial rural cultures held symbolic values, clues to, and/or mechanisms for purifying the present and enhancing the postindustrial quality of life. The three periods of heightened revival activity that exhibited such sentiments and were reflected in Cambridge are those dating to the turn of the twentieth century, during the 1930s, and the great boom of the late 1950s and 1960s, of which Club 47 was a part.

The City of Cambridge had a long and dynamic historical tradition that often intersected with scholarly pursuits at Harvard, particularly in the field of folkloristics. To distinguish it from its subject matter, folkloristics is the formal study of folklore (intangible songs, stories, legends, customs, and beliefs) and folklife (material culture such as buildings, domestic and occupational crafts, costumes, and foodways—what European folklorists call ethnology).

More than most American cities, Cambridge has usually looked to Britain, especially England, for its cultural models, and it continues to nurture its connections to the mother country in its customs, mores, and even haberdashery. New England's Cambridge is named for Cambridge, England, a shire town in the East Anglia fens along the river Cam, which like the Charles, is a topographic feature that helps define the literal and metaphorical boundaries of local life. As with C.A.W. (Cambridge Across the Water), the local term for its North American namesake, Cambridge, England, is a city whose identity

Francis James Childs, president of the American Folklore Society. *(Houghton Library, Harvard University)*

is linked to its preeminent university.[3] Cambridge University's graduates are well represented among the ruling classes of England, where their successes in the larger world reflect well on their alma mater.

Harvard College, America's oldest and best-known educational institution, is modeled after Cambridge University.[4] Harvard's founders and early faculty were predominantly Cambridge graduates, and its first students were generally descendants of the East Anglian Puritans who settled Massachusetts Bay. Harvard sits literally in the middle of Cambridge, Massachusetts, reaching from the banks of the Charles River well into the heart of the city at Harvard Square. Its alumni are likewise well represented among the ruling classes of the United States.

Just as there is a strong affinity between Cambridge (Massachusetts) and its university, there are also strong links connecting Cambridge, Harvard, and folkloristics. The AFS was founded in University Hall in 1888, ten years after the Folklore Society was founded in England, and for many years the American society, its journal, and some of its officers were based in Cambridge. It was at Harvard that Francis James Child—a founder of the AFS, its first president, and a medievalist specializing in Chaucer—conducted the research that culminated between 1882 and 1898 in his multivolume publication, *The English and Scottish Popular Ballads*.[5] Child's legacy as a ballad scholar was the founding of an academic dynasty of literary folklore studies that reached well into the twentieth century, extending through the 1960s to the members of Club 47 and other revivalists.

During the first half of the twentieth century, Harvard had a profound impact on folklore studies, particularly literary genres, beginning with the international attention generated by the publication of Child's ballad canon. For more than a generation after the collection appeared, a stream of students attended Harvard to study folklore, many of them supervised by Child's protégé, George Lyman Kittredge.[6] Kittredge was another literary scholar who, like Child, grounded his students in the classics, English literature, and ballads; he also edited the remainder of Child's work after his mentor's death in 1896.

It was Kittredge's protégés, such as Stith Thompson, Archer Taylor, Francis Lee Utley, Milman Parry, and later Albert Lord, who were among the Harvard alumni who helped establish and perpetuate what is primarily a literary approach to folkloristics in the United States. They continue to influence the field to this day, having produced fundamental works of their own.[7] Parry and Lord remained at Harvard to pursue their academic careers while their colleagues established folklore curricula at Indiana University, the University of California system, and Ohio State University, among other institutions.

Later, Richard Dorson, a product of Harvard's history and American civilization programs and heir to Thompson's mantle at Indiana, alluded to Harvard's approach to folkloristics in terms of preservation and classification. His historical approach to studying what he considered America's unique folklore encompassed the literary folklorists' perspective and the paradigms put forth by interdisciplinary scholars in the history of American civilization and American studies movements that were taking shape at Harvard and other institutions during his student days.[8]

Outside the academy, Benjamin Botkin, Robert Winslow Gordon, and John Lomax were folksong collectors and archivists who applied their Harvard training at federal agencies and programs to establish a tradition of research, collecting, and publishing (including sound recordings) that paralleled the academic process with which they were familiar as students of Kittredge and his colleagues. Gordon is best known as the founder in 1928 of the Archive of American Folk Song in Washington—now the Archive of Folk Culture at the American Folklife Center at the Library of Congress—an agency in which both Botkin and Lomax worked periodically for the next two decades. The three men also worked on various research projects commissioned by the Works Progress Administration (WPA) during the New Deal, as did many other folksong collectors, both academic and commercial, around the country.

Gordon's experiences served as exemplar for the prototypical activities that combined the academic and popular traditions later emulated by the members of Club 47. In 1906 the Bangor, Maine, native began his undergraduate studies at Harvard with Kittredge and the Americanist Barrett Wendell. Encouraged by his mentors, he began teaching in 1917 at the University of California at Berkeley, where he collected the songs of workers on the Oakland and San Francisco waterfronts. Gordon was particularly interested in the influences of African-American traditions and minstrel shows on sea shanties. He worked under the premise that he was collecting the "vanishing remains"—as the AFS defined them—of American folklore, ironically from other occupational groups, such as the multicultural cowboys that Lomax was studying in his native Texas, whose music and songs threatened the cultural hegemony of the Establishment.

Gordon's and others' collections were gathered in regions beyond the domination of the East and included items from African-American and Latino traditions. As such, they challenged the Anglo-American focus of literary and field collectors like Child and Cecil Sharp, Child's nonacademic English counterpart whose own work on folksong came to prominence almost immediately on Child's death and who later was involved with early-twentieth-century revival endeavors in Cambridge. Unlike Child and Sharp, who institutionalized British and Anglo-American texts and items, collectors such as Gordon helped to shape a body of *American* texts and a respect for indigenous folk music from occupational and non-Anglo traditions.

While Gordon pursued his ethnographic work out West, the United States was accommodating on both coasts a massive influx of immigrants from non-British and non–northern European cultures. As one method of assimilating these new settlers, "American" folk music derived from previously infused traditions was becoming an egalitarian cultural force in social reform projects such as settlement houses, festivals, and public schools—all ironically geared to defining, nurturing, and homogenizing a new popular culture through folksong, dance, and crafts.[9] Soon, in the third and fourth decades of the twentieth century, the interaction and exchange between narrowly defined tradition bearers and cultural consumers was possible in ways that had been unheard of when folksong collectors began amassing song texts, even among those using new technology and instruments to record both words and tunes.

Throughout much of the last century, lines became blurred between strict definitions of what constituted "traditional" materials and to whom they belonged, as recording technology and marketing forces came to dominate the entertainment industry. The standardization of these materials saw a rise in the number of professional performers whose sole occupation was to perform and record some of these works and who often traveled a circuit of bookings around the country. Beginning in the 1920s, factors such as the popularity of commercial recordings; the proliferation of regional radio broadcasts; the professionalization of the music, recording, and publishing industries; and a climate of economic prosperity all contributed to the process of equalizing access to cultural products. While details of these trends are far too complex to do more than allude to here, all these activities had an audience in Cambridge, with its predisposition toward new ideas as well as its predilection toward the past.

Meanwhile, public sector collectors like those commissioned by the New Deal's WPA continued to espouse pluralism in American culture through their work in governmental agencies. The folklorist Botkin, for instance, was an early advocate of the scholarly study of revivals that used American songs. His work also challenged the establishment worldview, but from a different perspective. Born in Boston, Botkin was a first-generation American of Lithuanian-Jewish descent. By the 1930s he was able to articulate his pluralistic vision of American culture, challenging the dominant Anglo-American worldview that prevailed in places like Cambridge, where he was educated. Yet, in a different voice, he echoed generations of foreign and domestic romantic nationalists and antimodernists by expressing "a hope that somehow folklore will furnish insight into the past as the key to the present and that folk culture...will provide a corrective for the sterility of our national culture."[10]

By arguing that "folksong could be a 'cultural force' as well as a 'cultural expression,'" Botkin could well have been a spokesperson for the members of Club 47 as well as for an earlier generation. As one of the folklorists who realized that the 1960s revival could have important implications for both folkloristics and popular culture, Botkin provided continuity between the past and present and between academic and popular folksong enthusiasts.

Closer to Harvard Square, the extent of the influence of ballad and folksong scholars associated with Harvard is sometimes evident and sometimes not. Pete Seeger, for instance, was well established by the boom years, having been an active performer in the early 1940s, traveling on his own or singing and recording with the Almanac Singers and with the Weavers. While he did not play at the 47, he was well known to many of its patrons as a performer and author of the much-reprinted 1950s' book, *How to Play the 5-String Banjo*, and the companion Folkways record. He also gave concerts regularly in Boston in the 1950s and 1960s. Before his musical career, Seeger had enjoyed his parents' musicological association with both Harvard and the Lomax family during his Cambridge days. Abandoning his undergraduate studies at the college in the late 1930s and moving to New York to pursue his song and political interests, Seeger did not graduate with his fellow classmate and future U.S. president John F. Kennedy.[11] Similarly, Seeger's sister, Peggy, left Radcliffe in the mid-1950s before graduation but returned to Cambridge as a singer, often accompanied by her husband, the late Scottish revivalist Ewan MacColl.[12]

Directly and indirectly, then, Club 47's members were part of the long, local tradition of exploring folksong inside the academy or within its shadows, whether they were aware of it or not. Some of the club's performers knew of Harvard's history of folklore studies. Others benefited from access to the print collections and field recordings—often gathered and supervised by Gordon and his colleagues—reissued to general consumers in the 1950s and 1960s by the Library of Congress, as well as to the anthologist Harry Smith's influential and quirky 1952 Folkways collection, *Anthology of American Folk Music*, a three-volume compilation of commercial songs released during the 1920s and 1930s.[13]

Regardless of their awareness of Cambridge and Harvard's traditions, many Club 47 members were well educated and well heeled enough to have the research skills and the means to locate and acquire historic folksong collections and recordings, many from public and academic collections. For these nonspecialists, lesser-known printed and aural collections directly expanded their knowledge of folksong. In addition, academic and popular collections—frequently organized by state or region, occupation, subgenres, or a combination of these—often formed the basis for enthusiasts' repertoires, whether sung actively and avocationally in groups, later played onstage, or known but not performed. More than one musician has spoken of the thrill of finding what they considered esoteric folksong collections, unlike those in the popular commercial songbooks of the 1940s and 1950s that were readily available to the general public.[14] By meshing the old and the new, local revivalists were very much part of the contemporary popular culture of their times. This was particularly true of the counterculture of the mid- to late-1960s, which—however liberated from convention—focused on historical and cultural antecedents, and engaged in the New England cultural tradition of looking backward.

LOOKING BACKWARD

Using romanticized images of the past to create a culturally unified American mythology apparently resonated in Cambridge to a greater extent than in other centers of revival activity. In Cambridge and sometimes at Harvard, traditions were largely Anglophilic, despite the city's and the university's multicultural populations, reflecting a long history of involvement with the avant-garde social, political, and humanitarian causes of the day. Such a reformist response, paradoxically, was highly intellectual and drew its inspiration from eighteenth- and nineteenth-century European romanticism. In fact, the notions of communal values, cultural homogeneity, and even pastoralism were at the heart of the intellectual history and evolution of the field of folklore. The application of these ideas to nineteenth-century academic reform, for example, particularly in Germany, created several disciplinary foci on which Child and his colleagues modeled their work and which became part of the folkloristic legacy they bequeathed to their students and followers along with their collections.

This marriage of romantics and reformers was characterized by an anthropological urge to collect and classify items of culture, particularly items perceived to be threatened with extinction, and many early fieldworkers followed the urge. In keeping with the growing emphasis on preservation, late-nineteenth-century academic efforts to collect and preserve items from the folk cultures of North America were expressed in new undertakings in the United States that benefited later folklorists and revivalists. In addition to the founding of the AFS, these included the creation in 1879 of the Bureau of American Ethnology to study Native Americans and in 1899 of the American Anthropological Society, which also studied native peoples. Implicit in these institutional ethnographic efforts was what became a longstanding tendency in urban, industrial American culture to romanticize rural life and values. In fact, much of the mid-twentieth-century Arcadian romanticism expressed during the 1960s folk revival in the United States—and particularly in Cambridge—was rooted in the nineteenth-century movement that the cultural historian T. J. Jackson Lears called "antimodernism." He defined it as

> not simply escapism; it was ambivalent, often coexisting with enthusiasm for material progress. And it was part of a much broader quest for intense experience which ranged from militarism and "progressive" social reform to popular occultism and the early fascination with depth psychology. Far from being the nostalgic flutterings of a "dying elite," as historians have claimed, anti-modernism was a complex blend of accommodation and protest which tells us a great deal about the beginnings of present-day values and attitudes.[14]

Lears added that historical advocates of antimodernism were primarily from "the educated strata of the Northeastern elites," the ruling class, if not always the actual individuals who "ruled" American society. His observations could easily serve to describe the prevailing people and attitudes in Cambridge for most of the last four centuries: "[O]ld-stock, Protestant...the moral and intellectual leaders of the American WASP bourgeoisie, who joined their British counterparts in shaping a transatlantic Victorian culture and who helped (sometimes unwittingly) to maintain dominant norms and values."

Clearly, the members of Club 47 who spoke of continuity with the past were not idly inventing those notions; many had family and community links to that very "transatlantic Victorian culture." Unlike the dynamic affecting the 47's heyday, earlier revivalism supported the status quo during periods of great social and cultural change. Expressions of cultural nationalism that celebrated a consensus view of American history became even more prominent in the late nineteenth century, after the centennial celebration of the Declaration of Independence, and lasted well into the twentieth century, when they remained part of the local consciousness. Consensus views were expressed subsequently in attitudes toward song collections like Child's, which supported the dominant structure, and Gordon's and Lomax's, which did not.

This period, known as the Colonial Revival, lasted into the 1920s and was paradoxically an era of great change rather than preservation, particularly in the Northeast. Like the earlier European romanticism, the domestic Colonial Revival foreshadowed the boom activities at Club 47. This half century saw massive domestic and foreign immigration to coastal cities, the growth of urbanism, the apex of the Industrial Revolution, and the emergence of the United States as a world power, with expanded roles for Washington and New York's centers of political and financial power. It also was a period that codified and homogenized the cultural canon, in part to "Americanize" immigrants by instilling in them a common amalgamated heritage in their new country, even if this "heritage" often ran counter to their own experiences and was at odds with the customs and traditions of their homelands.

The era was commemorated in Cambridge with public and vernacular architecture that is still extant and with public celebrations that are still enacted. Ironically, the Colonial Revival heralded a twentieth-century pluralism that proved to be the swan song of ideas about monolithic Anglo-Saxon hegemony—progressive ideas, again, that later were literally played out on Club 47's stage.

In keeping with its avant-garde bent, Cambridge in the 1910s was one of the first sites of the English-inspired dance and song revival in America, a fad that further influenced the folk revival community indirectly. While the English revival may seem to have only a tangential connection to Club 47, revivalists repeated legends about the English folksong collector Cecil Sharp finding unchanged "Elizabethan" ballads in the southern mountains, versions of which they sang or heard even before they got to the 47. Others spoke of his more direct influence on their lives, through their or their family members having attended "Robin Hood festivals" at a museum in a town where Sharp and his dancers held some of their most popular classes.[16]

That early-twentieth-century revival activity was also influenced, in part, by the Harvard playwright and director George Pierce Baker and the playwright Percy MacKaye, a student of Child's, both of whom were associated with Sharp when he was visiting Cambridge during the 1910s. Given Cantabrigians' history of interest in folklore, Sharp perhaps encountered more ready support in Cambridge and its environs than anywhere else for his civic and academic collecting projects. One such instance was his founding in 1911 of the Country Dance and Song Society of America, a branch of the English Folk Dance Society.

When Sharp came to the United States in 1914, preceded by one of his dance instructors, leaders in Cambridge were already involved in sponsoring historical pageants that combined social reform, dance, and revitalization impulses. Popular during the late Colonial Revival just after the turn of the century, these pageants were dramatic productions based on historical themes that romanticized and idealized political events and peoples. Not surprisingly, many of them were organized by the same people who led the local dance revival. Harvard offered a summer course in pageantry and held in its stadium in 1917 a performance of *Caliban*, MacKaye's classically draped Shakespearean tercentenary pageant for which Sharp helped script the "Elizabethan" dance interlude "Sumer is y-cumen in."[17] Women's colleges, such as nearby Radcliffe, were also involved in pageants, using them either to dramatize political issues like the campaign for woman suffrage or to entertain, as when celebrating romanticized versions of calendar customs like May Day.

In keeping with the sense of continuity, these historical pageants were themselves descended from the commemorative reenactments of the eighteenth century. Since the latter part of that century, people in Cambridge and surrounding towns had been reenacting events like Patriots Day, which commemorated the battles of Lexington and Concord in 1775 that began the war of independence from Britain.[18]

Thus, Cambridge had a direct claim on activities that led to the manufacture of an American mythology, often commemorated in military events. Many of the scenes that twentieth-century pageants symbolically glorified had transpired in and around Cambridge during the American Revolution, such as both British and American forces passing through en route to Lexington and Concord; the colonial militia's encamping on Cambridge Common; and national heroes such as George Washington basing his campaign headquarters on Brattle Street while commanding the Continental Army during the siege of Boston.

Partly as a reaction to the influx of non–northern European immigrants in the first quarter of the twentieth century, however, the pageants were an extension of then politically correct, almost reactionary themes celebrating a revisionist and even propagandistic view of the Anglo roots of American culture. During the period of political isolationism and xenophobia before World War I, these activities used tradition to buttress the modern. Often, in Cambridge, reenactments reinforced the It-Happened-Here-First theme that so pervades the local worldview and helped to create an awareness—or tradition—of homogenizing American values. Later, as individuals, these same forces were at play at Club 47, usually opposing homogenization and choosing what to reinterpret and what to jettison from their personal and cultural heritage, often highly influenced by romanticism.

Not surprisingly, given the intellectual traditions of Cambridge, a renewed interest in folksong emerged along with the dance revival and dramatic pageantry. In sharp contrast to the homogeneity and scope of the pageants was a less formal and more intimate interest in the songs of pre-industrial peoples. Much of that interest was expressed first by antiquarian and academic folksong collectors and ultimately by urban, often university-based revivalists nearly half a century later. Sensitivity to the past and a love of tradition often go hand-in-hand with a preoccupation with establishment values. This process of exchange and synthesis—of borrowing, imitating, and interpreting—lessens distinctions between classes and experiences, an exchange that was very much in evidence during the revival. Yet by adapting something perceived to be old, revivalists actually created something new. That was the principal paradox of Club 47, and of the folk revival, short-lived as they were.

Ultimately, at Club 47 as elsewhere, the folksong revival was more than a passing cultural phenomenon. Some participants were aware of their heritage and capitalized on it; others may have been unaware of—or rejected—historical and cultural antecedents. The fact remains, however, that the revival came to have a profound effect on the lives of many of those involved, something that continues to this day. Influences in Cambridge at the time, combined with the traditionalizing urge behind cultural revivalism, set the intellectual and historical scene in which Club 47 opened in 1958.

Bob Dylan, who performed informally and unofficially at the 47 and is often credited with being a spokesperson for the great baby-boom generation, integrated several strands of revivalism in his talking-blues introduction to the song "Baby, Let Me Follow You Down."[19] He learned the song, he said, from the New Englander Eric von Schmidt, another white blues revivalist who was one of the patriarchal figures at the 47. Indeed, it may have been the outsider (Dylan came from Minnesota via New York) who could best observe and articulate a fitting tribute to Cambridge, tradition, and the pastoral aspects of revivalism. His decision to include his spoken comment on his early 1962 recording served to broadcast the news about the Cambridge folk scene to thousands of record buyers, perhaps an indication of just how avant garde

Cambridge was in looking backward. "I first heard this from, uh, Rick von Schmidt," Dylan drawled. "He lives in Cambridge. Rick's a blues guitar player. I met him one day in the green pastures of, uh, Harvard University."[20]

CONCLUSIONS

The folk music revival of the late 1950s and 1960s left an important legacy in Cambridge and the surrounding region. Cultural connections inspired by the music made in coffeehouses such as Club 47 and at festivals such as the Newport Folk Festival literally changed individual lives, public policy, and the course of American history in the second half of the twentieth century. The revival helped to change notions about the nature of American culture and raise questions about its ownership as well as to create new models of social and political interaction, where the prevailing ethos can be—as it was in the 1960s—inspired and united by music.

Today's popular culture, examining its own roots and continuity with the past, regularly calls on elders from the 1960s, and those who once sat at the feet of *their* heroes during the revival are now the ones at whose feet young followers are sitting. In its way, the folk revival lives on to influence new generations shaping the city, the region, and the world in the twenty-first century. Who could possibly have imagined in 1958 that the daughter of an MIT science scholar, singing Child ballads and gospel songs to college kids on Tuesday nights in a storefront coffeehouse on Mount Auburn Street, would have such a profound effect half a century later, far beyond the banks of the Charles?

ENDNOTES

1. © 2004 by Millie Rahn. All rights reserved.

2. Neil Rosenberg, ed., *Transforming Tradition: Folk Music Revivals Examined* (Urbana: University of Illinois Press, 1993). Folklorist Rosenberg, who first dubbed Club 47 "the power elite of the folk revival," also coined the term "the great folk boom" for the 1960s folk revival.

3. I draw on personal experience for these observations.

4. Harvard traditions modeled after Cambridge University are evident in ritual language, academic dress, and other features of the ceremonial procession and subsequent commencement rites of passage that are re-enacted in Harvard Yard every June.

5. Child was born in Boston of working-class Irish American parents. He was educated at Boston Latin School and, with the help of a patron, at Harvard. He married into a "proper" Boston family; his daughter, Helen Child Sargent, published an abridged edition of his works in 1904, aided by George Lyman Kittredge. See also Abrahams, "Rough Sincerities."

6. The list of folklorists connected to Harvard during this period is seemingly endless. Among those not already mentioned in the text, this list-in-progress includes ballad scholar Francis Barton Gummere and Fred Norris Robinson in Celtic studies, who were members of the faculty; and Phillips Barry, H. M. Belden, S. B. Hustvedt, AFS cofounder William Wells Newell, E. C. Perrow, Franz Rickaby, and Charles Seeger. Among the teachers and students in related humanities dis-

ciplines were poet Conrad Aiken, humanist Irving Babbit, educator and Radcliffe president LeBaron Russell Briggs, literary scholar Charles T. Copeland, novelist John Dos Passos, poets T. S. Eliot and E. E. Cummings, historian John Fiske, psychologists and philosophers William James and Hugo Münsterberg, historian Francis Parkman, literary historian and editor Bliss Perry, journalist John Reed, philosophers Josiah Royce and George Santayana, and historian Frederick Jackson Turner. See Kodish, Wilgus, and Zumwalt in works cited.

7. These works include Thompson's six-volume *Motif-Index of Folk Literature* and his revisions to Antti Aarne's *The Types of the Folktale*, Utley's writing on medieval literature, Taylor's work on proverbs and riddles, and Lord's expansion of Parry's studies of oral formulaic theories in *The Singer of Tales*.

8. See Dorson, *American Folklore*.

9. See Whisnant, *All That Is Native and Fine*.

10. See Hirsch, "Cultural Pluralism and Applied Folklore."

11. From conversations with Seeger and Bess Lomax Hawes, daughter of John Lomax, before their concert at the Museum of Our National Heritage in May 1989; and with Seeger in June 1990 at the Massachusetts Maritime Festival in Salem, just before he attended his fiftieth class reunion at Harvard.

12. Other Radcliffe alumnae who were involved in song revival activities in the 1940s and early 1950s included the late Beth Best Milton, who co-edited the 1955 revised edition of *Song Fest* with her then-husband, Dick Best, a Cornell alumnus. *Song Fest* was published by the Intercollegiate Outing Club Association, of which Radcliffe, Harvard, and MIT students were members.

13. Independent collectors included Phillips Barry, Fannie Hardy Eckstorm, Helen Hartness Flanders, and Mary Winslow Smyth. The Folkways collection is now owned by the Smithsonian, which issues releases under the Smithsonian/Folkways label. The Anthology of American Folk Music was reissued on CD in 1997 (SFW CD 40090).

14. Recordings were far less available at the beginning of the revival. Often they could be found only in the back of secondhand bookshops such as Pangloss, or in the record bins at Briggs and Briggs and the Coop, before shops like New England Music City capitalized on the youth market.

15. See Lears, *No Place of Grace*.

16. One of Sharp's American supporters was Helen Osborne Storrow of Lincoln, a friend of George Pierce Baker's who introduced her to Sharp and his dancer, Claud Wright. She subsequently endowed the Storrow Room in the Cecil Sharp House in London in the 1930s, still the home of the English Folk Dance and Song Society. Baker is usually remembered for his theatrical work with Eugene O'Neill in Radcliffe's Agassiz Theatre. His correspondence with Sharp and Wright is archived in the Baker papers in the Harvard Theatre Collection.

17. See Glassberg, *American Historical Pageantry*.

18. Patriots Day itself is a reinterpretation of an earlier religious fast day that became a feast day. Shortly after the Revolution, days like these were re-appropriated to celebrate national events and renamed founders' or forefathers' days. Celebrations were based in community gatherings, not unlike the customary Thanksgiving celebration that began in the Plymouth Colony south of Massachusetts Bay and eventually became an official national holiday. Perhaps the most spectacular Patriots Day pageant was the one staged on Lexington Green in 1925 to celebrate the 150th anniversary of the battle. Materials documenting that event are in the collections of Lexington's Cary Memorial Library and the Massachusetts Historical Society.

19. Dylan's involvement at Club 47 and with many members of the community is discussed throughout von Schmidt and Rooney's book (see bibliography). According to various people I interviewed, he performed informally at the club during billed acts' breaks and mixed with club members, but I have found no evidence of Dylan being billed as a performer at the club, although admittedly records of the early years are at best scant, or nonexistent. In *Bob Dylan: Behind the Shades* (New York: Summit, 1991), Clinton Heylin wrote that Dylan repeatedly was refused bookings because management preferred "the dulcet tones of Joan Baez or Carolyn Hester" and that his only appearances were informal at the invitation of other performers.

20. Transcribed from Dylan's version of "Baby, Let Me Follow You Down," released on the Columbia LP Bob Dylan in March 1962. According to notes with the 1986 collected vinyl edition of Dylan's songs, Biograph (Columbia C5X-38830), the song was taped during his first recording session on November 20, 1961, in New York, where he "sounded witty and worldwise far beyond his twenty years. It had been only twenty months since he left Hibbing [Minnesota]." Dylan himself wrote in the Biograph notes:

That's the way Eric von Schmidt played the song. I think it's a Reverend Gary Davis [black blues/gospel singer who later came to Cambridge and Club 47] song. He used to sing it 'Baby Let Me Lay It on You.' Strange, he used to sing 'Twelve Gates to the City,' 'Yonder at the Cross,' and then 'Baby Let Me Lay It on You. . . . Dave Van Ronk [a New York revivalist] might have played it too [Side 1 notes].

BIBLIOGRAPHY

Abrahams, Roger. "Rough Sincerities: William Wells Newell and the Discovery of Folklore in Late-19th–Century America." In Folk Roots, New Roots: Folklore in American Life, edited by Jane C. Becker and Barbara Franco. Lexington, Mass.: Museum of Our National Heritage, 1988.

Dorson, Richard M. American Folklore. 1959. Reprinted with revised bibliographical notes. Chicago: University of Chicago Press, 1977.

Glassberg, David. American Historical Pageantry: The Uses of Tradition in the Early Twentieth Century. Chapel Hill: University of North Carolina Press, 1990.

Hirsch, Jerrold. "Cultural Pluralism and Applied Folklore: The New Deal Precedent." In The Conservation of Culture, edited by Burt Feintuch. Lexington: University of Kentucky Press, 1988.

Kodish, Debora. Good Friends and Bad Enemies: Robert Winslow Gordon and the Study of American Folksong. Urbana: University of Illinois Press, 1986.

Lears, T. J. Jackson. No Place of Grace: Antimodernism and the Transformation of American Culture, 1888–1920. New York: Pantheon, 1981.

Rosenberg, Neil, ed. Transforming Tradition: Folk Music Revivals Examined. Urbana: University of Illinois Press, 1993.

von Schmidt, Eric, and Jim Rooney. Baby, Let Me Follow You Down: The Illustrated Story of the Cambridge Folk Years. 1979. Amherst: University of Massachusetts Press, 1994.

Whisnant, David. All That Is Native and Fine: The Politics of Culture in an American Region. Chapel Hill: University of North Carolina Press, 1983.

Wilgus, D. K. Anglo-American Folksong Scholarship since 1898. New Brunswick, N.J.: Rutgers University Press, 1959.

Zumwalt, Rosemary Levy. American Folklore Scholarship: A Dialogue of Dissent. Bloomington: Indiana University Press, 1988.

Coolidge Hill in the Past Century[1]

BARBARA R. DEMARNEFFE

ELLEN G. MOOT

"I'VE ALWAYS thought of Coolidge Hill as an island," says a current resident who grew up there, "and if you think of it loosely as a square, its houses sit on a low hill permanently bounded by the two major roads and the river on three sides and restricted on the fourth side by the Cambridge Cemetery. Furthermore," she says,

> "the large Mount Auburn Cemetery is another wide boundary on the far side of Coolidge Avenue. In geologic terms, our hill is a perfect example of a glacial drumlin. To those who live outside Cambridge and to many within it, Coolidge Hill is a small and obscure enclave. Taxi drivers have a terrible time finding addresses, especially in the dark, as the streets wind around and are all named some variation of *Coolidge*, and the numbers are barely visible and some are not sequential."[2]

EARLY HISTORY

From the early seventeenth to the early twentieth century, Coolidge Hill was active farmland. In the summer of 1630, John and Mary Coolidge arrived from England with Sir Richard Saltonstall on the *Arbella*. Most of the settlers, including future Bay State Colony governors John Winthrop and Thomas Dudley, disembarked near the present Harvard Square, but the Coolidges and Sir Richard went a mile farther and landed at the base of Coolidge Hill.[3] By

The original Coolidge Hill farmhouse is the oldest house on the Hill, built in 1822 by farmer Josiah Coolidge. *(Photograph by Jennifer F. Diener)*

1642, Deacon Samuel Thatcher had occupied his grant, which included most of the Hill. He built a house by the road leading to the Charles River, near the present corner of Coolidge Avenue and Mount Auburn Street, where his heirs lived for over 150 years. In 1793, Elbridge Gerry[4] bought that property from Colonel Samuel Thatcher[5] and held it until 1811, when he sold it to Thomas Melville, a grandfather of Herman Melville,[6] who held the property for ten years.

In 1821, Josiah Coolidge and his wife, Mary [Hastings], from Watertown, bought the Thatcher house and farmed its land, as did their descendants for over one hundred years. Tearing down the old house, Josiah built a new one in 1822 along with farm outbuildings, all facing Mount Auburn Street on the lower part of the Hill. Living in that yellow farmhouse (later called both 14 Coolidge Avenue and 24 Coolidge Hill Road, depending on its orientation[7]), Josiah acquired land on Coolidge Hill as far as what is now the Cambridge Cemetery, through the marshes to the river, as well as a strip up from the river on the far side of the path to the Landing.[8]

In 1847 Josiah gave some land to his son Joseph Grafton Coolidge and his wife, Emily [Griggs], who built a handsome house in 1856 up the hill, facing Coolidge Avenue. It was later given the number 34 Coolidge Avenue, but

Once the Widow Orne's storage house, 10 Coolidge Hill Road has undergone much remodeling. Now "Havenhurst," it was moved from a location near the Cambridge homes on Mt. Auburn Street. *(Photograph by Jennifer F. Diener)*

when its entrance was changed to face south by Dr. John C. Coolidge in the mid-twentieth century, it became 141 Coolidge Hill.[9]

A dozen years later, Josiah Coolidge, then sixty-nine, sold his lower house to the H. W. Muzzey family, but in 1886 the Coolidge family bought it back. (In 1901, Helen Keller and her companion, Miss Annie Sullivan, rented it while Helen [class of 1904] was studying at Radcliffe). Some land on the lower Hill was sold for development in 1910 and 1915, but most of the upper Hill continued as the active Coolidge farm.

Meanwhile, going back to the early years of the nineteenth century, a second residential house (now 10 Coolidge Hill Road) appeared on the Hill. While Josiah Coolidge was adding new lots to his farm in the 1820s, he also sold one in 1825 to the "Widow Orne" (Sarah Gerry Orne),[10] a small strip on the side of the Hill facing north toward today's Elmwood Avenue, which Sarah added to a strip she had bought fourteen years earlier from her uncle Elbridge Gerry.

It seems that back in 1807, Orne's son, John Gerry Orne, had also bought a small piece of land from Gerry near the Landing, on which he built a store or storehouse. In 1809 his enterprise failed, and John sold the land back to his great-uncle but reserved the right eventually to remove his store-house and its shed. In 1825 or shortly thereafter, his mother moved John's storehouse to her newly purchased hillside and had it remodeled into a comfortable residence.[11] Members of the Orne family (including Sarah's daughter and her husband, Loring Austin) lived there until the 1850s.

After a succession of owners, including George P. Baker, Harvard Business School dean, it is now the home of Richard and Priscilla Hunt.[12] Previous owners named it Havenhurst, the name carved on one of the three stout granite posts marking the drive to the house's former entrance, which faced north toward Mount Auburn Street. In the 1930s, its southern kitchen wing was lopped off by the Bakers, moved to the east beside the larger house, and made into a separate residence, 8 Coolidge Hill Road, where James "Jim" and Eliza Borland lived for many years. It is possible that this section was Mrs. Orne's original early-nineteenth-century house.[13]

Havenhurst's stable, now 6 Coolidge Hill Road, was converted into a pleasant large house by the well-known architect Ralph Adams Cram, probably late in the second decade of the twentieth century. It saw many residents, including the Robert F. Bradfords (before they moved up the Hill), the Arthur Comeys, the Charles H. Taylors (he was a Harvard history professor), Sheila G. Cook, and David Forney. It is now owned by Jill Forney Gates.

In 1910 Browne & Nichols School purchased a lower cow pasture from the Coolidge farm for a playing field, which included a small hill. The hill was later leveled and used to fill in the lowland. And in 1910 Edward W. Forbes (later the director of Harvard's Fogg Art Museum)[14] and his sister, Mrs. Kenneth G. T. Webster, bought the fields and lower slopes of the Hill nearest the river, naming the property Gerry's Landing, as it was so close to the traditional landing area. They built two large houses there: Forbes's handsome brick Colonial Revival house, now owned by Maurice and Kitty Pechet,[15] and Mrs. Webster's large stucco nearby, since 1971 the home of J. Malcolm "Jock" and Ariadne Forbes.[16]

In 1948 Rosamond Coolidge, the great-granddaughter of Josiah, wrote:

When the houses were built, it became immediately and painfully apparent that the days of pig-raising on the Coolidge Farm were over. The pig pens were under the hill, exactly where the main building of Shady Hill School now stands, and the southwest wind which so frequently prevails blew gently and persistently right up to the houses of the new neighbors.

The pig pens had long been a landmark and were the destination of a favorite walk for children in this part of the city. My father spent hours on weekends and during school vacations just patrolling. The boys from the 'Marsh,' which in my childhood meant the crowded neighborhood

Edward Forbes' brick mansion at Gerry's Landing. *(Photograph by Jennifer F. Diener)*

from Willard to Lowell Street along Mount Auburn Street, knew every fruit tree on the farm and spent hours trying to evade my father or the watchman and to throw rotten apples at the pigs.[17]

Coolidge further explained that, in 1915, the parcel of land along the bottom of the Hill by Mount Auburn Street, from Coolidge Avenue to Havenhurst's driveway was sold to a development company that had also purchased the huge Larchwood estate. Both properties were divided up and sold as small house lots. The Coolidges' old yellow farmhouse was turned around to face Coolidge Avenue and moved one hundred feet west. Though seventeen house lots were squeezed into the lower Hill area, only six houses were built between 1915 and 1917 on the new Coolidge Hill Road. Rosamond Coolidge continued:

There now began to arrive the swarm of dogs and small children which are still two of the chief characteristics of our neighborhood. As children, my sister and I had had the rich and rare experience of farm life in a city. We had learned about flowers, vegetables, cows, and pigs and

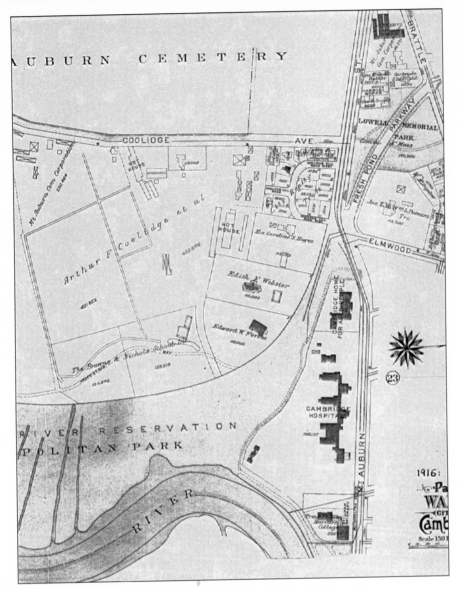

A 1916 map of Coolidge Hill.

chickens; we had played in a big barn; we had ridden behind the farm horses; we had learned that people who work all day in the fields are kindly, simple people, and—at that time—usually came here from Italy; but we never had many children friends near enough for neighborhood playing. Now we could see lights in our neighbors' windows, where once we had been able to see the State House dome ablaze with light when looking out our bedroom windows.

Farm workers became increasingly difficult to hire and a farm within a city became a luxury. It required skilled helpers to raise greenhouses full of violets, carnations, geraniums, and chrysanthemums. It was equally a tremendous job to raise fields and greenhouses of lettuce, cucumbers, tomatoes, corn, and, down in the meadow, wonderful celery, all to be sent to Faneuil Hall Market. My father, who had always driven horses, now learned to drive his own truck, but the war years after 1914 put a staggering load on men past middle age.

In 1924, Mr. Alva Morrison and Mr. Arthur Nichols bought the rest of the farm, and they were responsible for the attractive development of the top of the hill. The house lots were sold to families who built their own houses, not as in the 1915 purchase to contractors who built for the most part to sell again. Shady Hill School bought the remainder of the meadowland. The big barn, stables, carriage house, the greenhouses, the two great chimneys and the boiler rooms were taken down, and the last bit of rural Cambridge became residential.[18]

Morrison and Nichols formed the Coolidge Hill Associates in 1924 to further develop the top section of the Hill. The Associates' plan consisted of thirty large house lots with certain deed restrictions: that they be single-family residences at least two stories high, that they have garages for no more than two cars and setbacks for siting the houses, and that the houses be designed by an architect and have slate roofs. Furthermore, all utilities were to be placed underground. These stipulations ensured a development of good taste and looks that would appeal to residents who wanted an environment of high quality.

At the same time, in 1925 Shady Hill School purchased ten and a half acres of land on the south slope of the Hill, the last of the Coolidge farm's fields. In 1926 the school moved from Shady Hill Square, off Holden Street near the Norton-Sachs estate, into its new campus.

Many houses were built on the Hill over the next few years. By 1929 only two house lots were vacant. But not all the houses had been built on their sites. The present 144 Coolidge Hill was built in 1801 on Appian Way and, untouched through the Victorian era, retained its original beauty. It had housed many illustrious individuals in the nineteenth century, including Elizabeth Dana (the sister of Richard Henry Dana), Albert Bushnell Hart (an American historian and confidant of Theodore Roosevelt's), and Arthur Hugh Clough (the English poet). But the Appian Way location was obstructing Radcliffe College's building plans. So in 1929 it was moved to Coolidge Hill by its new owners, the Reginald Hulls, in line with the good New England custom of relocating houses. Rosamond Coolidge described its journey:

A good example of the Colonial Revival style, 15 Coolidge Hill Road was part of the lower hill development of the 1918-25 era. *(Photograph by Jennifer F. Diener)*

The moving was a major operation....It began in late June. The house remained in Brattle Street one whole month. The most dramatic episode in the trip was the midnight progress along Mount Auburn Street from Elmwood Avenue. Trolley and other important wires had to be cut or taken down at a time when traffic was least likely to be impeded. The flare of torches, the clang of iron bars, the shouts of the men working made the scene both colorful and memorable. The little house then made its dignified way up Coolidge Avenue to its present site. A service wing was added, and Mrs. Hull made a beautiful garden as an appropriate setting for this lovely example of late 18th-century architecture.[19]

From the 1950s to the early 1990s, John and Gibby Ferry and their children lived at this delightful house.[20]

Outside the boundaries of the Coolidge Hill Associates, three additional "modern" houses were built from 1935 to 1948, all on the northeast slope of the Hill on the land of Edward W. Forbes, for members of his family. One of the buildings, at 197 Coolidge Hill—later a Pechet house—was built in 1935 for Forbes's daughter Rosamond Bowers. She lived there for a short time and was succeeded by several owners, most recently Elwood Henneman

The house at 144 Coolidge Hill was moved there from its original location on Appian Way. *(Photography by Jennifer F. Diener)*

and his wife, Karel. The structure was notable as the first prefabricated modern house in Cambridge, designed by Edward T. Fisher of General Houses Inc., Chicago. In 2006 it was demolished by its owners. The two other modern houses were designed by Carl Koch in 1946 and 1948. Both were bought by Buckingham Browne & Nichols School, but the first, used as an art studio, was torn down in 1997.

HOUSES AND PEOPLE

A great joy for the residents of Coolidge Hill has been getting to know— or know about—this community of varied and interesting people. In 1924 Lydia Storer Hall built her house at 154 Coolidge Hill, with her brothers, Robert and Theodore Storer, across the road at numbers 133 and 139, respectively. Bob Storer's house until recently belonged to the Frank Brownings, whose daughter Holly and son-in-law Edward White are the new owners. Ted Storer, a principal of R. M. Bradley Real Estate, was a prime mover in the Hill's development. Also a squash player, he had a court built into the basement of his house, now owned by Anita Wyzanski Robboy, a lawyer. Henry

Hall, Lydia's husband, was a lawyer, a Himalayan climber, and a president of the Appalachian Mountain Club.

Beginning at the west entrance to Coolidge Hill, at number 141, were for most of the last fifty years John and Melba Coolidge, where Fred Wang now lives. John, a psychiatrist, was a cousin of the Coolidge farmers.

Next, 151 Coolidge Hill—one of the last houses to be built—was sited on the farm's former orchard,[21] and occupied by Perry and Euretta "Rettles" Rathbone during Perry's long term as director of Boston's Museum of Fine Arts. It was then owned by Peter and Mary Lee "Widgie" Aldrich and has just been bought by Charles and Ashley Cherington.

Next door is 157 Coolidge Hill, built by Francis Cleveland, the son of President Grover Cleveland and the legendary founder of the Barnstormers Theatre in Tamworth, New Hampshire. Later owners included the Paul Means family and the Harold I. Pratts. The house is now owned by Molly Miller and Bob Rodat, screenwriter for the Oscar–nominated *Saving Private Ryan*. Molly was a film director for television movies before becoming a full-time mother.

In 1929 a handsome brick house was built on the corner at 134 Coolidge Hill, modeled on Westover, the Governor's House at Williamsburg, Virginia. For a time it was owned by Gerald Blakeley, a principal of Cabot, Cabot & Forbes, who helped make Route 128 famous as a mecca for major technology companies in the 1950s and 1960s. In 1971 the house was bought by Darcy and Howard Fuguet; Howard is a partner at Ropes & Gray, and Darcy is a social worker and teacher in early childhood education.

In 1970 Francis de Marneffe and his wife, Barbara ("Bobbie"), bought number 126, a two-story gambrel house around the curve, designed by Stanley B. Elwell for his wife, Gladys, and her sister, Miss Hildreth, and probably built in 1928. Elwell was an architect at Royal Barry Wills Associates, which specialized in this Colonial style. Francis de Marneffe's career as a psychiatrist has spanned more than fifty years at McLean Hospital, Massachusetts General Hospital's psychiatric wing, twenty-five as its director. A rower since childhood, he stroked the crew that won the Wyfold Cup at Henley in 1946 and rows regularly from the Cambridge Boat Club. Bobbie chaired the successful effort to restore The Mount, Edith Wharton's house in Lenox, Massachusetts, which opened to the public in 2002.

Across the street at number 127 is the home of James W. "Jim" Wallace and his late wife, Linda. This house has had a series of interesting previous owners, including the Winthrop Browns; Jerome Bruner, the Harvard cognitive psychologist; John and Elizabeth Freeman; and Emily McFarland.

Next door, in the classic brick house at 125 Coolidge Hill, Daniel and Prudence Steiner lived for more than thirty years. Daniel served as general counsel and vice president of Harvard under three presidents and was president of the New England Conservatory of Music from 1999 until his death in 2006. Prudence taught in Harvard's English Department and founded the expository writing center at the Extension School. Number 125 is now home to Christopher and Heidi Legg.

In 1932 Leonard "Andy" and Cornelia (Balch) Wheeler bought the Tudor-style brick house at 123 Coolidge Hill, which was built in 1927. Andy was a lawyer with Goodwin, Procter and participated in the Nuremberg Trials of Nazi war criminals. Cornelia was an outstanding citizen and an able civic leader; she served six terms on the Cambridge City Council and took on numerous other volunteer commitments. She moved off the Hill in 2004, after seventy-two years in her house.

Next door, number 115, was until recently Bill and Julie Shelmerdine's house, a copy of a well-known manse in Pepperell, Massachusetts, built by Count Rumford (born Benjamin Thompson), the renowned eighteenth-century physicist, inventor, and master designer of fireplaces. (The Pepperell house was demolished some years ago to allow for the Burlington Mall.) Most of the roof slates for the house came from the pre–Revolutionary King's Tavern on Boston's State Street, which was torn down in the 1920s.[22]

On the other corner, 111 Coolidge Hill was designed by the architectural firm of Howe, Manning and Almy (Mary) for Charles and Elizabeth Almy. It occupied the site (some believe) of an old "star fort" from the period between the Revolutionary War to the War of 1812.[23] Its granite battlements were reportedly uncovered during the Almys' 1926 cellar excavations, along with an ancient cannon with which "Farmer Coolidge" is reputed to have made off, saying it was his property! The cannon has not been seen since.[24] More large granite blocks were discovered in situ when the road was recently torn up, deeply excavated for water pipes, and repaved. A granite wall still exists under the road at the Shelmerdines' driveway, says resident archaeologist Cornelius Vermeule, who watched the excavations carefully with his wife, Emily (also a renowned archaeologist), and he confirms these discoveries. One such block is visible by Vermeule's steps to the street at 47 Coolidge Hill Road, and others are built into the house's original foundations (ca. 1895), visible on the front corner by the driveway·

Elizabeth Almy was long a respected presence on the Hill. Her husband, Charles, started the Cambridge firm of Dewey & Almy with Bradley Dewey and was also involved with the development of synthetic rubber, an important contribution to the war effort in the 1940s, when the Japanese took over the rubber plantations of Southeast Asia. When Elizabeth Almy moved, she gave the house to Buckingham Browne & Nichols (BB&N) as the residence for the school's head. Mary Newmann, with her husband, Ted Smith, president of the

Kendall Foundation, lived there for ten years. In 2002 the house was sold to its present owners, Leonard and Chris Bierbrier.

John and Ellen Moots' stucco house (ca. 1915) at 44 Coolidge Hill Road predated the Coolidge Hill Associates development. From 1921 through 1923 the poet Archibald MacLeish lived there. In the 1930s and 1940s it belonged to the George R. Hardings and then to Talcott "Ted" Banks, president of the Boston Symphony. When the Moots bought the house in 1968, Banks had two grand pianos (and little else) in the living room and an organ in the dining room, powered by a vacuum cleaner in the basement. The Moots, like others on the Hill, have been politically active in the community and involved with a number of social service agencies. John helped to save the sycamores (in fact, Oriental plane trees) on Memorial Drive in 1962 and has worked to preserve the quality of life in Cambridge neighborhoods.

Opposite, at 45 Coolidge Hill Road,[25] for many years lived Richard and Suzie Kirsch, Czech refugees from the Nazis, who bought their house from Rosamond Coolidge in the 1940s. Richard, a lawyer, had served as an officer in the Austro-Hungarian cavalry in World War I. In the 1960s and 1970s, Suzie had a shop in Harvard Square on Church Street, where the Cambridge Artists Cooperative Gallery is today.

Another former Coolidge house is that of the Vermeules, number 47, which they bought in 1963 from Helen Coolidge von Snydern, Rosamond's sister. Like Rosamond's own house "over the fence" (16 Coolidge Avenue), it had been rented earlier to many people, notably Professor and Mrs. Mason Hammond, Mr. and Mrs. Royal Little,[26] Ernest and Elizabeth Begien, and John and Sylvia Constable.

In the 1960s Carroll "Curly" Bowen, who headed the MIT Press, and his wife, Alice Wick Bowen, lived at 16 Coolidge Avenue. Later, Theodore "Ted" and Mary Gene Myer were there for many years.

Back on the upper Hill, 116 Coolidge Hill was for decades the home of John and Kay Cushman and is now owned by William "Bill" and Irene Marsh. It is a recognizable copy of Salem's House of the Seven Gables.

Next door are William and Sally Fay Cottingham, at 110 Coolidge Hill. Bill is the senior executive director of Sotheby's, and Sally is a writer, director, and actress, when she isn't being a mother or community volunteer.

Their house, which was built in 1928, was previously owned by H. S. Payson and Florence Rowe, who lived there for forty-eight years. Payson was a vice president of John Hancock and then president of the Brookline Savings Bank. He and Andy Wheeler, across the street, were classmates at Harvard (1922), and in 1956 Payson was elected president of the Harvard Alumni Association.

Florence Rowe was one of four friends who helped to change history during the civil rights movement in 1964 by marching for integration in St. Augustine, Florida, for the Southern Christian Leadership Conference. The others were wives of Episcopal bishops: Mary Peabody (whose son Endicott "Chub" was then the Massachusetts governor); Hester Hocking Campbell (whose parents founded Shady Hill School); and Esther Burgess (the wife of the first black suffragan bishop of Massachusetts). As Mrs. Rowe's daughter, Barbara de Marneffe, said of her mother,

> For a shy Victorian lady and housewife, she had great courage to make the trip to a place so full of danger, tension, and hostility. My father tried to dissuade her from going, but she was determined to go and believed deeply in the cause. Mike Peabody [Endicott's brother, who is married to Pamela Rowe] says today [2004] that that march and the huge publicity it generated featuring the governor's mother was a major turning point in the civil rights movement. We were very proud of her for making this stand for integration.[27]

Next to the Rowes' is 106 Coolidge Hill, built in 1928 by Robert F. Bradford (later governor of Massachusetts) and his wife, Rebecca. They lived there for many years, Rebecca for over fifty. Bob had graduated from Browne & Nichols, and the Bradfords were benefactors of the school, though their children all went to Shady Hill. Later long-term residents were Maren and Tim Robinson, and its current owners are Charles and Susan Longfield.

At 102 Coolidge Hill, on the corner of Coolidge Avenue, lived Sam and Rebecca Leland,[28] preceded by Addison and Fabia Closson. Across the street, at 24 Coolidge Avenue, were Cornelia Wheeler's brother and sister, Franklin Balch (known by the Wheeler children as "Uncle Punky") and Lucy Balch Putnam. Punky's cello would have combined nicely with the piano of the next occupant, Rowland Sturges, and his able wife, Heddy, who was the treasurer for many nonprofits in town. The current owners of the house are Richard and Martha Wagner.

Until recently at 105 Coolidge Hill were Barbara Haviland and her husband, Field, a retired professor of international affairs at the Fletcher School of Law and Diplomacy at Tufts. Earlier, the house had belonged to the John Middletons.

In 1947 Richard and Janet Elliott Hobart moved into 44 Coolidge Avenue, near the Shady Hill gym driveway. Richard was a banker, collector, and scholar of Chinese art. Janet was previously married to Frederick Wulsin, and in 1921 and 1925 they were early explorers of Inner Mongolia and northeastern Tibet under the auspices of the Peabody Museum at Harvard. As the first woman to take part in such an expedition, Janet wrote copious notes and took photographs of arduous and often dangerous treks that are described in a recent book[29] by the Hobarts' daughter, Mabel H. Cabot, who spent her youth on Coolidge Hill.

Following the senior Hobarts, Jane and Jeremy Knowles lived at 44 Coolidge Avenue. Jeremy, a biochemistry professor at Harvard, completed ten years as dean of the Faculty of Arts and Sciences in 2002 and in 2006 returned as acting dean until a new Harvard president was appointed. Jane directs the Radcliffe Archives and for a time managed the Schlesinger Library. Ford and Phyllis Goldman are the current owners.

The Frederick Websters[30] lived next door, at 62 Coolidge Avenue, for many years until 1971, when Shady Hill bought the house for its director's residence.[31] Before World War II, Fred was involved in research on bats—for which, his neighbor Jane Williams[32] tells us, he kept a house below his garden, likely the Quonset hut that was long there. His work with bats contributed to the development of radar. Jane also remembers that Fred had a giant trampoline in his backyard and could sometimes be seen bouncing almost to the tree line.

Jane's parents, John and Jessie Williams, built their house at 148 Coolidge Hill on land that Jane said had been the Coolidge farm's dump.[33] Jane's father was a Harvard economics professor, dean of the Littauer School of Public Administration,[34] and vice president of the New York Federal Reserve Bank. In the late 1970s Frederick Bruck, an architect, and his wife, Phoebe, a landscape architect, bought the house and stayed for many years. More recently the late Adam B. Ulam, the eminent Harvard Sovietologist, rented the east wing of the Brucks' house.

Across the street, at 141 Coolidge Hill, Jane would see Albert Sprague Coolidge playing his oboe in the cupola on top of his house, which had a blue light at night. She said the Coolidges also had a roller coaster in their backyard.[35] John Coolidge, Sprague's son, grew up in that house and lived there until recently with his wife, Melba. Melba single-handedly got UPS to ban its trucks from using Coolidge Avenue as the access road to its warehouse and persuaded Mount Auburn Hospital to find another route for its shuttle buses.

Jane Williams reported, too, that "the Hinton kids[36] rode their horses to Shady Hill from Belmont and hitched them up in the apple orchard" (in the Meanses' lot, which was later to contain the Rathbones' house). She also recalled "the sound of the cattle at the abattoir in Brighton and the smell from the abattoir and the dump on lower Coolidge Avenue beyond the Cambridge Cemetery when the wind changed." Those smells are also remembered by many Shady Hill students on the school's playing fields.

Reminiscences from Binda Payson Parra capture her happy youth on Coolidge Hill with warmth and delight. Her family, the William Paysons, built and lived for more than fifty years at 173 Coolidge Hill, across from Shady Hill:[37]

> Coolidge Hill in my day [1930s and 1940s] was a magic place in which to grow up. The golden rule for us was to stay on the Hill. With that restriction, we were allowed total freedom. We were in and out of all the houses. Some of my happiest memories were playing dolls with Polly Brown at number 127. The Coolidge Hill gang loved above all playing Kick the Can until late on spring evenings, or coasting down the Hill after school in the winter—not many cars then. We were safe and happy as long as we stayed on the Hill....I often heard Uncle Dodo—Theodore Lyman Storer—talking about how Coolidge Hill was developed. I know he made some of the detailed decisions about how the lots were designed.[38]

Parra also remembered during World War II "the Chopin funeral march with much tuba, as the dead were brought to be buried in the soldiers' lots in the Cambridge Cemetery." Ellen Moot recalls the frequent "Taps" on the bugles wafting in the open windows of the Shady Hill ninth-grade classroom in Building H.

On the lower half-circle of the Hill, Professor and Mrs. Richard D. Fay bought the brick house at 20 Coolidge Hill Road in 1921. He was at MIT and helped to develop sonar for detecting submarines underwater during the war. Later, number 20 was the home of the much-respected anthropologist Cora Dubois, who held the only women's chair at Harvard, the Zemurray-Stone Radcliffe professorship. She would be followed in that chair by Emily Vermeule, her almost next-door neighbor at number 47 and a celebrated Classicist.[39] "Ironic," comments Emily's husband, Cornelius, "that Harvard searched the world and found the successor almost over the back fence!"

Around 1930 the Fays moved across the Hill and built the large stucco house at number 177, across from Shady Hill, where they lived for several decades. John and Sylvia Constable bought it from them in 1962. John was an eminent plastic surgeon at Massachusetts General Hospital and, with Sylvia, an inveterate leader of Harvard Natural History Museum travel expeditions. The house now belongs to Tiron and Marie Pechet.

Across the street, number 170 was built by the George Macombers.[40] Later inhabitants included Robert "Bob" and Theodosia "Teddie" Bowie. Bob was the first director of the Harvard Center for International Affairs in the early 1960s, with Henry Kissinger as his assistant.

Like the Bowies, Kate Benedict lived on the rise overlooking Shady Hill at number 162. Benedict's residence of forty years is now home to Kristen Wainwright and Rick Harriman.

On the half-circle of Coolidge Hill Road, on the lower north slope, have lived a number of well-known academics and faithful activists in community projects: George W. Mackey, the Landon T. Clay Professor of Mathematics and Theoretical Science at Harvard; Silvio "Skip" Onesti with his wife, Jean, and George Vaillant, both respected psychiatrists; Professor Victor Brudney and his late wife, Juliet, a *Boston Globe* columnist; Henry and Katherine Winslow, Cambridge community leaders; Porter Gifford, a fine photographer, and his wife, Serena, a popular Shady Hill teacher; David Osonoff, an environmental scientist at MIT; the artist Jill Slosberg-Ackermann and her husband, James Ackermann, a retired Italian Renaissance art professor and scholar at Harvard; and Ginny Dyer, Beverly Evans, Alice Mackey, Debby Barry, Rita Cherington, Judy King, Priscilla Hunt, Betsy van Buren, and Joanne Bauer—all willing, able, and reliable doers for whatever needed doing, political or otherwise. There was once a sports hero, too. Sixty years ago Jimmy Foxx, the great first baseman for the Boston Red Sox, lived at number 4, later the home of Greg and Sandy Downes.

OTHER INHABITANTS OF THE HILL

Over the years there have been numerous canine residents worthy of recognition, but first we should mention the famous pigs of Coolidge Hill, so often cited for what they bequeathed to later generations—the Hill's fine, rich soil. John Cushman, later the owner of number 116, told a tale of his youthful encounter with the pigs when he was a Harvard undergraduate in the 1920s. One dark night he was hurrying to get back from a party in Brookline to Harvard Yard before the gates closed. Taking a shortcut on foot through the Hill, he fell into the pigpen, which, he said, was located where the de Marneffes' house is now. Cornelius Vermeule adds that these pigs seemed to move around a lot, or perhaps the neighborhood supported both "home pigs" (to be baked) and "lowland pigs" (to be sold).

As for the dogs, for years Vermeule himself was a familiar sight, walking his several dalmatians during the day and sometimes in the evening. He tells of a policeman on the Hill beat during this period, Officer Mahoney, who, aided by the sharp eyes of Kay Cushman at number 116, spotted and eventually apprehended a burglar, whom he chased down the road. The suspect tried to cut through Vermeule 's driveway to reach Coolidge Avenue and then the relative safety and anonymity of Mount Auburn Street. But scaling the fence, he ended up in the dalmatians' dog pen and was forced up a tree, where Officer Mahoney found him. Later, the same dogs scared off other thieves going after Ted and Mary Gene Myer's rugs at 16 Coolidge Avenue, in back of the dog pen.

These dalmatians—Gaius Valarius Diocletianus (known as Sheepie), Tina (from her real name, Rogue's Little Miss Nicotina), Max, Marcus Aurelius, Mattie, and Val, among others, most with the names of Roman emperors—led the dog population of the Hill, usually at least three of them together, down to the "dog club" gatherings on the Shady Hill fields in early morning and again in late afternoon. Also in the pack were Richard Kirsch's Tuley; Jim Ackermann's dalmatian, Tosh (Max's brother and Sheepie's son); the de Marneffes' Dublin; the Moots' Sophie; Jim Wallace's dogs; and the Forbeses' golden retriever Maya—the only dog known to have graduated from Shady Hill (with Blakey Vermeule's and Lydia Forbes's class in 1981)—all chasing one another while their owners exchanged local gossip.

John Williams's wife (at number 148) owned an unspayed canine bitch whose friendship Max was determined to win. One day Max (who could leap to six feet) found the Williamses' Dutch door wide open and leapt in, to find the lady in question on Mr. Williams's lap as he sat in his living room armchair—and Max leapt again.

Cornelius Vermeule relates also that the house at 125 Coolidge Hill, then Charles and Winifred "Winnie" Chatfield's, was known to have housed dogs in volume: English sheepdogs and Jack Russells—at one time twenty-five of the former and one hundred of the latter—which Winnie showed at Boston dog shows.

Coolidge Hill is surrounded by two lovely cemeteries (Mount Auburn and Cambridge City), full of lush vegetation, ponds, and streams, which has both pluses and minuses. The latter are the "wild" animals. In 2000 the Hunts saw a fox in their front yard, and in the past three years a coyote has been seen on the road, suggesting that pets might be in danger after dark. Skunks, raccoons, and rabbits roam the gardens and stalk the trash, and squirrels abound.

The trash has been stalked by less-than-wild beasts as well. Vermeule admits that Tina (Sheepie's wife) sometimes rooted in the trash by the Shady Hill parking lot and near the Websters' Quonset hut. She found little of canine interest but did discover a Franz Kline painting and also a William Harnett (a nineteenth-century American still-life painter).[41] Cornelius later gave the Franz Kline to the Yale University Art Gallery when he was teaching in "Bulldogtowne."

THE TENNIS COURT (AND SKATING RINK)

The clay tennis court, a hidden but important element of life on the Hill, was built soon after the upper part of the Hill was settled. In December 1935, four neighbors combined adjoining pieces of their backyards in the center of the Hill and created a tennis court for interested residents and Shady Hill School. Robert Bradford, later a governor of the Commonwealth, drew up the document that gave the tennis court to the school. The deed stipulated that Hill residents could use the court whenever the school was not using it. Donors included George P. Baker, the Leonard Wheelers, Robert B. Owen, and Charles Taylor. Though it belonged to the school, the court's maintenance was the responsibility of the neighborhood group later known as the Coolidge Hill Tennis Association (CHTA), which managed and regulated the court and its membership at no cost to the school.

Every year, families came out in force on the first nice Saturday in April to remove winter leaves and twigs, cut back vines on the chainlink fence, score and rake the surface, spread clay or Har-Tru as needed, nail down the wandering lines, and generally prepare for the season. The event was also a social one, giving neighbors a chance to either meet or catch up with one another. Since 2004, however, in a new agreement with the school, the court has been prepared and maintained by professionals for the CHTA, reducing residents' labor but eliminating the opportunity to mingle and strengthen the sense of community.

To the delight of the children, the court was sometimes the site of a makeshift skating rink in winter. The Wheelers made ice in the early years, simply hosing down the bare frozen court with successive layers of water, and John and Ellen Moot did it again in the late 1960s and early 1970s. As Ellen recalls:

> We covered the court surface with a huge plastic sheet, with low boards up around the sides, and water from a hose out of the Wheelers' basement. There were many nice nights of walking back and forth, spraying the court in the moonlight, hearing airplanes overhead, the whine of cars down below, and occasional crashes at the intersection. In those cold winters, we got good skating and occasional pickup hockey for our kids. We even hosted the Shady Hill Hockey Program once or twice when the BB&N rink was out of action.[42]

Supporters and skaters included the Wallaces, Moots, Wheelers, Steiners, Hunts, Clossons, Forbeses, Downes, and Kings.

About the same time in the early 1970s, a number of Coolidge Hill women engaged in a unique sporting venture that lasted for more than ten years—an early women's ice hockey group. Jealous of their children's fun, the group rented evening ice at BB&N and played a nonchecking but energetic game among themselves and sporadically against outside teams. Almost half of the women lived on Coolidge Hill: Robin Ackroyd (23 Coolidge Hill

Road), Rita Cherington (number 9), Fay Closson (number 102), Gibby Ferry (number 144), Frances Pratt (number 157), Karel Henneman (number 197), Priscilla Hunt (number 10), Judy King (6 Gerry's Landing), Ellen Moot (44 Coolidge Hill Road), and Betsy van Buren (number 19). The captain and organizer was Shady Hill grad Betsy Myer Dunn, who lived elsewhere in town. The BB&N rink was partially open to the night air and often mighty cold. Gibby, the goalie and a grandmother, sometimes played in a fur coat with a goalie pad strapped over it.

Known officially as the Ms. Sticks and informally as the Mother Puckers, the group first played (and beat, 11–2) the Brown Grizzlies from Providence in 1973, organized by a former Coolidge Hiller, Neely Wheeler Lanou. They defeated the Harvard Business School Bladettes twice and succeeded in squeaking by (3–2) the Harvard women's squad, then in its second year of existence. But the team later lost badly to the women at Boston College, who nevertheless saluted them as "awesome."

Neighborhood Schools

Though the residential buildings on Coolidge Hill were substantially completed by the late 1920s, the two schools on its edges have continued to add buildings and expand existing ones up to the present day. The largest new building was BB&N's Nicholas Athletic Center facing the river, which replaced the old gym and 1960s ice rink and tennis structure. Shady Hill will likely demolish its own gym and create a larger one in the near future.

Browne & Nichols School began in 1883 on Garden Street as a boys' day school. Almost one hundred years later, in 1974, it merged with Buckingham School, an independent girls' school with facilities at two locations in Cambridge.[43] Renamed Buckingham Browne & Nichols, the school is now coeducational. Although the merger did not affect residential Coolidge Hill, it was apparent that the school's buildings were expanding and its athletic facilities changing. BB&N did buy two former Forbes houses and east slope acreage.

Shady Hill School has been a welcome and integral part of the community since it moved into its modest one-story wooden buildings in 1926. It has continued to thrive, becoming one of the most sought-after elementary schools in the area. As the school developed, its curriculum and enrollment grew, its buildings aged, and occasional flooding disrupted the use of its playing fields and sometimes damaged the buildings. Much relief was achieved a few years ago when the stream from the Mount Auburn Cemetery to the river, through Shady Hill's swamp, was channeled under the fields through huge culverts.[44] A year later, the level of the fields was also raised. Nevertheless, the increased demands of growing numbers of students have required some buildings to be repaired, renovated, or replaced and new buildings to be constructed.

From its start Shady Hill was a neighborhood school—and a good reason to live on Coolidge Hill—but in recent years its demographics have changed. It no longer serves primarily Cambridge residents, and few students now walk or bike to school or use the MBTA. A huge increase in morning and afternoon carpool traffic induced the school, the neighborhood, and the Cambridge Traffic Department to work out a system that substantially reduced congestion and improved safety, though traffic and safety problems persist. Most agree that Shady Hill has been a good neighbor, contributing to the liveliness and dynamic atmosphere of the Hill and, with the occasional turnover of houses to young families, encouraging a healthy influx of new residents.

COMMUNITY TRADITIONS

In December the Christmas caroling tradition continues, with all ages participating. As Betsy van Buren writes,

> The history of caroling goes back to the fifties. It began with three couples, the Squibbs (23 Coolidge Hill Road), the Biddles (number 40), and Sheff and I (at number 19). We loved to sing, and we gathered at the Biddles' once a week. A year or so later, we took a lantern and went around the Hill at Christmas, singing carols. Sometime later we joined with John and Melba Coolidge and children and even practiced beforehand! Gibby and John Ferry began having us in afterward for refreshment, and it just grew. For a number of years, families took turns entertaining the singers: I remember the Wallaces, Brownings, and Wheelers, among others. Jim Wallace led the singing for years. Children grew up, and enthusiasm dwindled. For a while the Sturges, Rita Cherington, and I took turns with hosting and kept the tradition going. However, the singing took on a whole new life when a rash of young families with children moved onto the Hill, and enthusiasm revived. Now Jim Garabedian[45] leads the singing. That's the ebb and flow of its history, as I remember.[46]

Starting in the mid-1990s, Coolidge Hill became host to a block party held one Sunday in September, the inspiration of Sally Cottingham and Kristen Wainwright, both relatively new residents. The street named Coolidge Hill is closed to traffic from Coolidge Avenue to the junction at Coolidge Hill Road, with residents gathering in front of the Cottingham house. Three or four long tables covered with red-and-white-checked tablecloths are

Coolidge Hill residents Bob Rodat and Molly Miller get ready for a street picnic. *(Photograph by Sally Cottingham)*

placed end to end down the middle of the street and spread with a potluck lunch for scores of neighbors. So far, the sun has shone brightly on this enterprise.

Sally Cottingham has also compiled and printed a booklet—updated every so often—of the names of all Coolidge Hill residents, their children, and their pets. Complete with addresses and phone numbers, it has been an invaluable tool for keeping the community together. More recently, a Coolidge Hill website has been created for further information sharing.

The Hill is also a popular place for ghosts and goblins (some over 6 feet tall) who dare to come calling at Halloween and who are rewarded with an abundance of treats. In the 1960s Ridgeway Banks created an ingenious chute from a second-story window at 40 Coolidge Hill Road that would dispatch candy into the hands of delighted beggars every time the doorbell rang.

The Hill has even had its own haunted house, at number 127, which was at one time the home of Jack Freeman and his wife, Elizabeth. When Elizabeth died, her ashes were spread in her beloved garden. Over the next two decades the subsequent owners, Jim and Linda Wallace, claimed they heard Mrs. Freeman walking around the house at night. Other unexpected events occurred, like a strange bottle mysteriously appearing in the sink or a light spontaneously turning on.

Jack Freeman had been an executive at Houghton Mifflin, and for exercise he would cut firewood (with permission) in the Cambridge Cemetery—much to the delight of the local "Yoricks"—and perhaps also in the jungle of Hell's Half-Acre by the river. In his youth, he had rowed along with Dr. Benjamin Spock on the famous Yale crew that won the gold in the 1924 Chariots of Fire Olympics.

Memorial Day has been a special day of celebration for the Hill, when residents gather on Coolidge Avenue or Mount Auburn Street to watch the parade pass by.[47] Addy Closson says he will never forget a band named the Gates of Heaven Rockettes marching by, incongruously playing and singing "Love for Sale" to a march rhythm. He also remembers the gun salutes at the cemetery unleashing veritable clouds of birds from the trees.

Barbara de Marneffe describes the events in 2004, when the day was sunny and clear and Hill folk joined the public as usual to cheer the marchers on:

> We are so lucky to be almost at the parade's end (it terminates at the Cambridge Cemetery) to view the marching veterans, Scouts, sport teams, bands, waving flags, fire and rescue trucks, and gleaming police motorcycles rolling by. On Coolidge Avenue there is a reviewing stand full of city dignitaries, opposite the field of veterans' graves, marked with American flags fluttering gently, row upon row. This year the fire department attached a huge flag atop their fully extended ladder, and a soft breeze filled it with air and then released it in a beautiful wave, over and over again, high against the blue sky streaked with faint white contrails and wispy clouds, creating a beautiful tribute to their comrades. The words of remembrance were heartfelt, touching, and especially moving this year marking the sixtieth anniversary of D-Day.[48]

It is next to impossible to capture in a few pages the variety and excitement of the many interesting lives lived by those who resided on the Hill in some sixty different houses over the last hundred years. This narrative has undoubtedly missed some special people, for which the authors apologize. As residents, we treasure the Hill's inhabitants and are grateful for the accident of geography that allows this oasis of relative peace, tranquility, green space, and color where the flowers grow. Special thanks are due to the Coolidge farm families and the Coolidge Hill Associates for their foresight and planning. They were ahead of their time in urban residential design. We are the grateful inheritors of their enlightened legacy.

ENDNOTES

1. The authors of this essay gratefully acknowledge the valuable assistance of Cornelia B. Wheeler, Edith Hall Overly, Anne Storer Lyons, Richard M. and Priscilla S. Hunt, James W. Wallace, Elizabeth P. van Buren, Jane Williams, Binda Payson Parra, J. Malcolm Forbes, Addison Closson, Bruce Shaw, and Susan E. Maycock and Charles M. Sullivan (both staff at the Cambridge Historical Commission). Most especially, we appreciate the willing and spirited help of Cornelius Vermeule.

2. The resident quoted here is Barbara de Marneffe, one of the authors of this article, in 2004.

3. The site was therefore called Sir Richard's Landing, a name that lasted for almost two centuries until it was renamed for the eighteenth-century inhabitant of Elmwood, Elbridge Gerry. The Landing, with all the land west of today's Sparks Street, was part of Watertown until 1754, when it became part of Cambridge. Into the early twentieth century, ships and barges brought cargoes upriver to the Landing and carried farm produce from western towns downriver to city markets.

4. A signer of the Declaration of Independence, Gerry was later Massachusetts governor, U.S. vice president, and architect of redistricting as a political tool (i.e., *gerrymandering*). He was also owner of Elmwood, near the Landing—subsequently home to James Russell Lowell and now the Harvard president's official residence.

5. A man of importance, Samuel Thatcher was a frequent representative to the Massachusetts General Court, a Minuteman, and a commander of Cambridge men at Lexington and Concord and at the battle of Bunker Hill.

6. As mentioned on ehistorybuff.com, Thomas Melville was also a participant in the Boston Tea Party and a Revolutionary War veteran.

7. When split into two houses, Coolidge's farm kept both addresses. It is now one house and owned by Alex MacDonald and Maureen Stafford and faces Coolidge Hill Road.

8. Since the name Gerry's Landing had temporarily disappeared, the site was then known as Willis Court. Much of this early history and later quotations come from "The History of Coolidge Hill," an essay read to the Cambridge Historical Society in 1948 by Rosamond Coolidge, daughter of Arthur F. Coolidge, the last "Farmer Coolidge."

9. Dr. John Coolidge was not an immediate relation to the farmers Coolidge but a cousin. His father, Albert Sprague Coolidge, bought the house in the early twentieth century. It is now owned by Fred Wang, son of An Wang, inventor and developer of the electronic word processor. Fred put the front door back at its original location, on the house's west side.

10. Sarah's husband, Azor Orne, was a friend and companion of Elbridge Gerry in the 1770s and '80s. Azor and Gerry were at the meeting of the Committee of Safety on the road to Lexington in April 1775. Hearing that the British were coming, they warned Hancock and Adams, who were sleeping nearby, enabling them to escape.

11. John Orne's storehouse has been remodeled many times since to become the handsome house it is today.

12. The former marshal of Harvard and long "the voice of Harvard Commencement," Rick Hunt taught modern German history in the social studies department. Priscilla Stevenson Hunt, a former trustee of Oberlin College, is active with many community groups, especially Travelers Aid and the Harvard Art Museums.

13. Such was suggested by the Cambridge Historical Commission's Charles M. Sullivan in a letter to the Hunts, April 12, 2003.

14. Edward Forbes was later honored by Harvard with the naming of Forbes Plaza in front of Holyoke Center in Harvard Square.

15. Dr. Maurice Pechet is a renowned medical researcher who founded the Research Institute for Medicine and Chemistry and who, through the Pechet Family Foundation, has been generous as well to other science and arts organizations.

16. Jock and Ariadne Forbes followed their cousins, the Greggs, in the house, buying it from Edith Webster Gregg, daughter of Mrs. Webster, who had built the house. Mrs. Gregg was the niece of Professor Forbes, and great-granddaughter of Ralph Waldo Emerson. Jock Forbes has worked hard to promote international peace through the United Nations Association and World Federalists, and Ariadne has been active in supporting the classical and chamber music world of Boston and Cambridge.

17. Rosamond Coolidge, "The History of Coolidge Hill," 99.

18. Ibid., 99-100.

19. Ibid., 100-101.

20. John Ferry was a Boston lawyer and Elizabeth "Gibby," his wife, an artist who taught at Buckingham Browne & Nichols. The house is now owned by Sam Spektor and Ann Berman, who did a major renovation in the 1990s. In the course of the renovation, it was discovered that the house had actually been doubled in size at some time after the move.

21. The Coolidge farm's former orchard was where the Hinton children would tether their ponies during school. One apple tree is still visible in the back corner of the yard of the Closson/Leland house, 102 Coolidge Hill, along the original farm's stone wall.

22. According to Cornelius Vermeule, the slate tiles appear in Paul Revere's engraving of the Boston Massacre.

23. A "star fort" has bulwarks in the form of a five-pointed star. Cambridge's official historian, Charles Sullivan, doubts that this is a likely location for a fort. But another theory holds that the construction was the site of a beacon gun, to warn of hostile activity on the river or of a threat to one of the major overland roads to the northwest from Boston.

24. The information on the discovery of the cannon came to Cornelius Vermeule from Elizabeth Almy in the 1960s.

25. Both houses, number 45 (the Kirsches) and number 47 (the Vermeules), similar in style, were built by Coolidges around 1895.

26. Royal Little was a president of the Textron Corporation.

27. Hester Campbell wrote a book about their experiences, *Four for Freedom*, 1969.

28. Sam Leland is deceased. Rebecca, now remarried to Bob Swiggett, still lives at 102 Coolidge Hill.

29. Mabel H. Cabot, *Vanished Kingdoms*, 2003.

30. Fred Webster was a son of Edie (Mrs. Kenneth Forbes) Webster, the sister of Edward W. Forbes, who had together with her brother built the large houses at Gerry's Landing in 1910.

31. The current residents are Shady Hill's director, Bruce Shaw, and his wife, Sandy.

32. The information in these pages attributed to Jane Williams came in a handwritten memorandum from Williams to the de Marneffes in May 2004. Jane lived on the rise above the Webster house at 148 Coolidge Hill, which was more recently Fred and Phoebe Bruck's house.

33. Opinions differ concerning the location of the old dump or pigpen. Much of the Hill, however—geologically a drumlin—appears more fertile than most Cambridge land.

34. The Littauer School of Public Administration predated the Kennedy School of Government.

35. Ellen Moot also remembers a week in the 1970s when John and Melba Coolidge "babysat" a grandchild's pony in the same yard, quite illegal by Cambridge ordinance but nicely hidden by a thick evergreen hedge.

36. The "Hinton kids" were the children of the formidable Carmelita Hinton, a Shady Hill teacher and later founder of The Putney School in Vermont.

37. Later Dick Belin's and Rosann O'Brien's house, 173 Coolidge Hill now belongs to John Gates.

38. Binda Payson Parra's reminiscences are contained in a memo she wrote to the de Marneffes, May 2004.

39. Emily Vermeule was also one of Harvard's most popular lecturers.

40. President of the Cambridge Trust Co., George Macomber was also a leader in the Cambridge community.

41. Vermeule hung the small Harnett in his study until the early 1990s, when he was teaching in Scotland and gave it to the Aberdeen Art Gallery.

42. Ellen Moot, 2004.

43. While rows of these culverts were waiting to be dug under, the Vermeule dalmatians would venture inside and get disoriented, requiring Cornelius to crawl in after them.

44. Garabedian lives at 416 Mount Auburn Street and is the music master at the Armenian Holy Trinity Church at Brattle and Sparks streets.

45. Elizabeth P. van Buren's memories are recorded in a letter she sent to the de Marneffes, May 2004.

46. When they lived at 412 Mount Auburn Street, Jim and Linda Wallace would host Memorial Day martini parties. Addy Closson says that from 1958 to 1977, he and Fay commemorated the day with a party at their house (at the corner of Coolidge Hill and Coolidge Avenue), serving drinks in official funereal flower pots with plastic linings.

47. Barbara de Marneffe to Ellen Moot, 2004.

BIBLIOGRAPHY

Blue Book—Cambridge (1900–1928). Cambridge, Mass. A street directory available at the Cambridge Historical Society library.

Cabot, Mabel H. *Vanished Kingdoms: A Woman Explorer in Tibet, China, and Mongolia, 1921–1925*. Cambridge, Mass.: Aperture, in association with the Peabody Museum of Archaeology and Ethnology, Harvard University, 2003.

Cambridge Historical Commission. Cambridge, Mass. Archival maps, memoirs, and other materials.

Campbell, Hester Hocking. *Four for Freedom*. New York: Carlton Press, 1969.

Coolidge, Dr. John C. "The Woolly Mammoth and the Ambiance of Coolidge Hill." Manuscript of a 1990 lecture.

Coolidge, Rosamond. "The History of Coolidge Hill," *Proceedings of the Cambridge Historical Society for the Year 1943*. Cambridge, Mass.: Cambridge Historical Society 32 (1948): 96–103.

Coolidge Howe, Rosamond. "Reminiscences." 1942. Manuscript in the possession of Cornelius C. Vermeule.

Gozzaldi, Mary Isabella. "Gerry's Landing and Its Neighborhood." *Proceedings of the CHS for the Year 1918*. Cambridge, Mass.: Cambridge Historical Society 13 (1925): 81–88.

Morison, Samuel Eliot. *Builders of the Bay Colony*. Cambridge, Mass.: Riverside Press, 1930.

Nylander, Richard H. Handwritten notes collected in 1968 on the history and ownership of 10 Coolidge Hill Road from nineteenth-century Cambridge records; also notes on the relationships between the Gerry and Orne families.

Parra, Binda Payson. Correspondence with the de Marneffes, 2004.

Sullivan, Charles M. Correspondence with the Hunts, April 2003.

Van Buren, Elizabeth P. Correspondence with the de Marneffes, 2004.

Vermeule, Cornelius C. "One Family's View: Coolidge Hill, Cambridge, 1963–1990." Monograph from the author, 1990.

Williams, Jane. Correspondence with the de Marneffes, 2004.

Yeomans, Edward. *Shady Hill School: The First Fifty Years.* Cambridge, Mass.: Windflower Press, 1979.

Growing Up
on Worcester Street

SUZANNE R. GREEN

JUST BEFORE THE beginning of the twentieth century, my nanna's husband-to-be bought a house on Worcester Street as a wedding present for his bride. It was especially good for him because the barn behind the house would be fine for his horse and wagon. He was a dealer in fruits and vegetables.

My mother had grown up on Worcester Street and had graduated from the Harvard Grammar School, which is now the City Hall Annex at the corner of Broadway and Inman streets. Her next graduation was from English High, later Cambridge High and Latin and now Cambridge Rindge and Latin School. She had attended Sunday school at the Harvard Street Methodist Church, now St. Bartholomew's Episcopal Church, only a block and a half away from where she lived. When she married, her husband, my father, lived on the North Slope of Beacon Hill, but they decided to make their home on Worcester Street also, and they moved into their three-room apartment.

I was their first child and grew up in a friendly, mixed neighborhood. My mother, who stayed at home, often made hats and dresses for her friends and neighbors. There were many children in the neighborhood, and we spent many hours playing together. With the help of our next-door neighbor, a retired Irish carpenter, my father built me a playhouse in our yard. Parts of its construction came from the demolition of some beautiful old houses on Norfolk Street, where new apartment houses were being built. As a little girl, I can also remember standing in our bay window at dusk to watch the lamplighter ride up the street on his bicycle to light the gas lamp at the corner of Norfolk and Worcester streets.

Suzanne's mother, Ruby Higginbotham Revaleon, left, with Suzanne and baby brother, Paul, outside a playhouse in the backyard at Worcester Street. The house was built by Suzanne's father with the help of an Irish neighbor, ca. 1920.

Early one February morning in 1918, when I was six years old, the stork brought me a new baby brother. After a frantic telephone call made by my father, Dr. Lockhart arrived quickly from his home on Massachusetts Avenue, near Bigelow Street.

I walked to the Fletcher School on Elm Street each day and went home for lunch, returning to school within an hour for the afternoon session. We all attended our nearest neighborhood schools. At the Fletcher School, the auditorium was on the top floor, and for my first two years, during World War I when coal was often hard to get, the building was not warm. Students from all the classes climbed the stairs to the auditorium to sit together on wooden benches, to sing songs and feel warm.

The day the Armistice was signed was a wonderful day. We went up to the auditorium, sang one or two patriotic songs, pledged allegiance to the flag, sang "The Star Spangled Banner," and were dismissed early.

Suzanne Revaleon
(Green), age 7, in 1919.

When I was in the third grade, my teacher was Miss Gertrude Baker, the second African American teacher in the Cambridge schools. She followed the renowned Maria Baldwin, who in 1882 had been appointed a teacher and in 1889 became headmaster at the Agassiz School, which was recently renamed the Maria Baldwin School in her honor. In 1937 I became the seventh African American teacher in the Cambridge schools with an appointment at the Houghton School, now the Reverend Martin Luther King Jr. School on Putnam Avenue.

There were so few cars and so little street traffic on Worcester Street that our quiet one-block, tree-lined street was a safe playground for our after-school play. We all had metal roller skates that we clamped onto our shoes with a metal key. Up and down the street we'd skate, sometimes with a best friend, sometimes with a group. Then, often, we'd put the skates away and play Hide and Seek. The telephone pole served as "home." The last person to call out a name would be "it." While that person closed his or her eyes at the post and counted, perhaps to twenty, everyone else would run and hide, behind fences, trees, steps, wherever, hoping to have a chance to dash over to tag the pole before being tagged themselves. The last person caught became "it" for the next game.

The boys liked to play marbles, and they usually kept a supply of the many-hued glass orbs available. Down on their knees or crouched over a little hole in the ground, they would aim to knock the others' marbles out, thereby increasing their own holdings.

On a warm summer's day, many of the boys and girls walked down for a swim at Magazine Beach, not far from Brookline and Magazine streets on the Charles River, where there was a sandy bank. Everyone could enjoy a swim. The Magga, as it was called, has been closed now for years because of the pollution in the river. But cleanup efforts are under way.

Mid-day on Saturdays, neighborhood boys and girls would be found lined up in Central Square waiting for the movie theater to open. For an entrance fee of ten cents, they would see the news of the day, sports, a cartoon, and the movie, which was usually a serial that left the heroine in a most life-threatening situation. The next week, however, she would be back, hale and hearty, to carry on until the next week's climax.

The Central Square was the largest neighborhood theater, with padded theater seats and a large balcony. Sometimes in the evening there would be a stage show and free dishes or other gifts to encourage attendance. A much smaller movie house stood near Lafayette Square. The Olympia Theatre, better known as the "Olymp," was opposite the police station in Central Square, in a long, narrow block. It was not considered clean and well-cared-for, but it showed serials and westerns and had its own regular patrons.

During the month of May—and only during May—there were May parties. The child giving the party would be the Queen, her best male friend the King, or the other way around. Tissue papers in pastels, a bit heavier than the tissue paper now used for wrapping, was sold at our corner stores for a penny a sheet. That, cut and braided with streamers, became our May Party headpieces. The girl hostess wore a gold paper crown, as did her escort. Often a half-circle hoop, covered with pastel papers and with streamers, provided an arch under which the children paraded around the block followed by their friends, all wearing headpieces, singing—or chanting, really—all the way:

May Party, May Party

Rah, Rah, Rah,

Who are we?

We are the Worcester Streets

Don't you see?

Are we in it?

Well, I guess we are

Two, four, six, eight

Who do we appreciate?

Mary, Mary, Mary (the name of the hostess)

Rah, Rah, Rah.

At their return to the yard of the hostess or host, games were played, punch and cookies were served, and the May Party was over.

Days before the Fourth of July, my brother and I would walk with my father to the little store on Essex Street to buy firecrackers, sparklers, and Roman candles. The tiny firecrackers and the sparklers would satisfy me. My brother usually chose the big firecrackers and the Roman candles that shot off like rockets. Only later did I realize how dangerous they were and how much safer it was for everyone when fireworks were made illegal. Picnics became a much more enjoyable means of celebrating the national holiday.

Often our street would become a baseball field, with several rocks providing bases. A bat, a baseball, and a few gloves were all that were needed. The constant hope was that no neighbor's front window would fall victim to a strong hitter.

The girls liked hopscotch. We would draw a diagram of the hopscotch boxes on the pavement with a piece of chalk, which probably had come from school. Turns were taken tossing the little stone and hopping through, skipping designated squares. Even mothers joined in once in a while.

One noisy sport enjoyed by the boys required the acquisition of a wooden orange crate and roller-skate wheels. The addition of a handlebar provided a means of steering and called for a bit of engineering.

In the winter, snow usually stayed where it fell, and we'd all bring out our sleds. Smaller children were pulled around on their little sleds by indulgent older brothers and sisters. Flexible Flyers were the favorites of the older boys and girls. If you ran fast enough and fell down fast enough onto your Flexible Flyer, the moment carried you several yards, with the steering bar making it possible to choose your course.

All our news came in print. Along with the regular morning edition of the newspaper, there was an afternoon edition for later news. If there were some really noteworthy happenings, an extra edition would be published quickly. Then newsboys would go through the community shouting, "Extra, Extra," to sell the later edition. Thus on April 19, Marathon Day, we would await the extra edition to learn the name of the Marathon winner, which for a number of years always seemed to be Clarence De Mar.

Loaves of bread wrapped at the bakery could be bought at the grocery store and brought home to be sliced. It was an exciting time when the bakeries began to provide loaves already sliced.

Exciting, too, was the discovery that ice cream could be bought in packages at the grocery store, made possible by electric refrigeration. Before that, ice cream could be had only at the ice cream store, kept cold by means of real ice. As the packaging got better, the taste and quality improved.

Few families had radios, and television was yet to be invented, so there was little to keep us in the house after we'd come home from school and finished our homework. On stormy days, our only means of discovering whether or not there would be school was to listen for the big fire whistle to blow at 7:30 a.m. Somerville had the same method, and since the two cities are so close, by agreement both closed on the same stormy days.

We were all so proud when our father, following the directions he had, made a radio by winding small wires around a big round oatmeal box. There was a special spot where one wire had to be touched by another wire called a cat's whisker. We put on our earphones and could hear music for fifteen minutes, followed by a pause of five minutes, then fifteen minutes more of music. The source of this magic was the old Shepard Store on Tremont Street in downtown Boston, the location of Boston's first radio station, WNAC.

In the 1920s the horse and wagon were an important part of life in Cambridge. That was how we received our daily supply of milk and cream early each morning, left on our back doorstep. If the day was very cold and we were slow in taking it in, the bottle of milk might have a stovepipe hat; the cream would rise to the top, freeze, and push the cap up. Homogenized milk had yet to be invented.

The ice man brought huge cakes of ice on his wagon. His nine-by-nine-inch card in our front window would tell him the size of the pieces we needed by its position. He would cut the piece, carry it on his back into our kitchen or pantry, and use his huge tongs to place in the top of our oaken ice chest.

The fresh fish man came on certain days, and always on Fridays. The vegetable man also had a regular schedule. But most spectacular of all was the ragman, who rode through the streets calling, "Rags, rags, any old rags." He bought old newspaper, too, paying a few cents a pound for each.

In the winter, since it was before the days of snow plows and plowed streets, the wagons with wheels were put away and out came the pungs, wagon bodies with sleigh runners. Snow and ice was then no obstacle.

Angelina was a man most eagerly watched for in the summer. He was short and brown-skinned and wore a big straw hat and a white coat and

Suzanne R. Green, at 90.

sang his song of cold ices. He had a big cake of ice and many bottles of colorful fruit syrup on his little pushcart, from which he would add your choice of syrup to a cup of scraped ice. It was a refreshing break on a hot summer day.

The coal stove that provided heat for the kitchen and for all our cooking was shiny black. In the winter the fire was kept burning night and day. It also heated the handsome, tall copper boiler that contained our hot water supply. The boiler was kept polished to a shine, along with the brass faucets and the piping over the sink and washtub.

Our regular schedule called for fish for Friday night supper. On Saturday, it was baked beans, brown bread, and frankfurts. Except in the summertime, the brown, glazed-clay bean pot spent the entire day in the oven, having been put there in the morning by my nanna, who filled it with parboiled navy beans, molasses, a piece of salt pork, and spices. The flour, molasses, raisins, and spices for brown bread were placed in the round metal container with the tight top and boiled for hours in a pot of water on top of the stove.

Central Square was once the focal point of Saturday night shopping, not only for Cambridge residents, but also for those from neighboring communities.

There were large stores and small stores. Our big market was the owner-operated Manhattan Market, with a sales person behind every counter to bag your purchase and accept your payment. Grants, the Lincoln stores, Enterprise, Kresge, Woolworth's, and others supplied the needs of our households over the years. Woolworth's, which had started as a five-and-ten-cent store, was the last to leave.

Many small stores lined Massachusetts Avenue and the small adjoining streets. There were bakeries, barber shops, confectionery stores, butter and egg stores, fish markets, florists, tailors, shoe stores, jewelry stores, even a furniture store. Saturday night shopping ended quickly with the advent of motor cars and the attraction of the new shopping center.

These are my early memories of growing up on Worcester Street.

A Cambridge Memoir[1]

MARIAN CANNON SCHLESINGER

SOME TIME AGO, I happened to run into the eminent Harvard psychologist B. F. Skinner at a gathering on Cape Cod and we fell to discussing my father, Dr. Walter B. Cannon, who had been for many years professor of physiology at the Harvard Medical School and whose student he had been. My father had been a friend of Ivan Pavlov, the great Russian physiologist, and there was some discussion as to whether there existed any photographs of the two men together. I recalled having seen in the family album a snapshot of the two men taken when Pavlov came to this country for the International Physiological Congress that was held in Boston in 1929. I promised to go back to Cambridge and look it up.

A few weeks later I was idly examining some framed photographs on the wall of my sister's house in New Hampshire and saw there an enlarged photograph of Pavlov and my father and the whole family taken against the hills of New Hampshire so many years ago. The thing that struck me was how Russian it looked. It might have been from an album from Yasnaya Polyana, Tolstoy's country estate, and used as an illustration in the biography of the famous writer. Even a clump of gray birches and the grayness of the print gave it a feeling of authenticity. Pavlov stood in the middle, his arms linked to those of my father and my ancient grandfather, who might have been an old retainer on the Tolstoy estate with his white, muttonchop whiskers and quaint air of nineteenth-century gentility, and who happened to be exactly the same age as Pavlov. My father, who had a wide, round face and an expression of open simplicity and kindliness, seemed close kin to Pavlov himself, who in turn radiated a feeling of gentleness and high intelligence. They both had a fresh, almost childlike, "born yesterday," air about them that is so often present in men of imaginative genius. My oldest sister sat in front, very spiritual and Chekhovian. As I remember, she was in love for the first time with some forgettable young man, I suppose, and dreaming of the world beyond the confines of rural New Hampshire and even provincial Cambridge. The NKVD man, or whatever he was called in those days, the official informer who accompanied distinguished Russians traveling abroad when they were allowed out at all, lolled beside my lovesick sister, and Pavlov's son stood next to his father. My brother, at that point a first-year medical student, in white plus fours, with his hair parted in the middle and slicked down in an unwonted way, was obviously impressed with the seriousness of the occasion. We three younger girls, in our lumpish adolescence, looked as though we had just come out of the hay fields with our sunburned faces and lank hair cut in boyish bobs. We wore hopeless, shapeless, homemade shifts, run up, no doubt, by our mother on the old pedal Singer sewing machine with its lock stitch, which, should the thread snag, could result in a complete parting of the seams. It might happen anywhere, and often did, much to our excruciating humiliation. My mother, plump, vigorous, and pretty, with a black band around her forehead, Indian style, her hair done in a no-nonsense bun at the nape of her neck, and dressed in her cotton long-waisted shift, completed the family picture. She believed in plain living and high thinking and was of an iconoclastic turn of mind that would have fitted in well with the teachings of Tolstoy (minus the mysticism, since she was an implacable agnostic) and the mores of Yasnaya Polyana; and from the looks of the photograph, so would the rest of us.

Many interesting people passed through the family farmhouse in Franklin, New Hampshire, over the years but no one more lovable or distinguished than Pavlov. Had he stayed awhile he would no doubt have recalled some simple dacha, surrounded by woods and meadowlands, in his native Russia. Years later, when my mother and father traveled to Russia on the Trans-Siberian Railway from China in 1935 on the way to the International Physiological Congress in Leningrad, my mother wrote to comment on the scenery along the way that reminded her of the stands of birch and the rank fields of New Hampshire. Even the weathered wooden village houses were not unlike some of the tumbledown farm buildings falling into their cellar holes that dotted the back roads of our neighboring countryside.

It was here that we came every summer after we escaped from school in Cambridge, which as children we regarded as a place of temporary incarceration to which we were banished for nine long months of the year. Each June when we returned to our beloved hillside, it was as if life had begun again.

Our old, deserted farm had been bought by my parents in 1910 when my father was a young professor in the Harvard Medical School. They spent the vast sum of $1400 on sixty acres "more or less" (as the deeds always read) of rocky hillside and stony hay fields. The place fulfilled all the requirements they had set themselves; it had a view, a barn, and a stream, but most significant of all, it demanded enormous amounts of ingenuity and human labor to set the whole place to rights. The house and barn sat high up on a ridge commanding a sweeping view of the Pemigewasset valley, with Mount Kearsarge in the distance to the west, and to the north, the silhouette of Cardigan mountain with its distinctive granite peak. There was a dilapidated orchard, a falling-down hen house, and some tottering outbuildings, and in late June fields were red with wild strawberries and bluebirds rested in the empty barnyard. The smell of the clover in the mowing fields was intoxicating and the steady hum of the bees in the hot early summer sun called up fantasies of pancakes running with honey and melted butter. At the foot of the lower field was the stream where random trout idled and, bordering it, granite ledges in whose crevices mayflowers sprouted in the early spring. The neighboring farmer's cows browsed in the boulder-strewn pasture at the bottom of the slope in front of the house and the jingle of their bells was one of the first sounds I remember as a child.

Alas, this is not where real life was led. That was reserved for the old house on Divinity Avenue in Cambridge. Here we lived in an extended family that would have met the requirements (or perhaps the misgivings) of modern psychiatrists lamenting the nuclear family. Nine permanent members —five children, two maiden aunts, my mother and father—and any number of transients—visiting physiologists, homeless students, neurasthenic relatives, old Radcliffe classmates of my mother, and hordes of "best friends" of my brother and sisters—made up the enormous household.

The ancient house, which belonged to the University, is still standing, still the sensible muddy gray that was the prevailing color of all respectable arks in the old days. Like so many other Cambridge houses, it was uprooted in the late 1920s from its original site, winched on large wooden legs, and dragged by heavy draft horses across the street to a new location behind the Busch-Reisinger Museum. Some wit is said to have remarked on this peculiarly Cantabrigian habit of dislodging its domiciles, "One has to get up early in Cambridge before the houses begin to move."[2]

An ugly cinder-block office has been stuck on the back of the house off the kitchen and three or four generations of academic committees and bureaus have been housed there since the family moved out in the late thirties.

In a rash of nostalgia, I went to see it a few months ago, fearful that the old house might be torn down before I could once again explore it. The house looked much the same, though the pressure of stark office furniture and steel filing cabinets in the downstairs rooms struck a mournful note. The dining room with its charming large bay window had been the scene of tumultuous talk and laughter in our youth. It had once held a generous dining table that had accommodated a basic family of nine and more often than not had been stretched out for the stream of extras dropping in for meals. A self-portrait of my portrait painter great-grandfather once hung over the black-painted onyx fireplace and under the bay window curved a window seat, with cushions upholstered in green velvet. There we children used to linger on Sunday mornings surreptitiously reading the funnies after my father had removed himself to sit by the living room fireplace and smoke his morning cigar. Funnies were anathema to him though as I look back it seems that nothing could have been more harmless than "The Katzenjammer Kids" or "Moon Mullins." My mother merely threw up her hands in resignation.

Beyond the dining room was the butler's pantry with its copper sink and deep built-in drawers that used to contain geologic ages of linens; tablecloths that had not been seen, much less used, for decades; Irish linen napkins elaborately initialed in Baroque script, ironed, folded, and forgotten. Topping them all was a yearly gross of embroidered runners and doilies that my mother always bought from the Armenian refugee woman who, with the first breath of spring, arrived on our doorstep, two ratty suitcases of linens in her hands and the glint of a fanatic in her eye. She would tear her hair and wail, shedding copious tears over the fate of her countrymen, much to our fascination as children, for being little New Englanders, we were not often exposed to such emotional storms. More interesting still was the sight of my mother melting before the steamy tempest and each year piling up a new mound of *unwanted things. Unwanted things* were anathema to her, her philosophy being rather austere, not to say un-American; not "Do I want it?" but "Do I need it?"

To the left of the door was the long living room, which ran the width of the house. Four large windows reaching from the ceiling to the floor flooded the room with light and bookcases lined three sides. On the fourth side was the fireplace, its elaborate Victorian mantel embellished with a mirror, convenient for last minute primping in our adolescent days. When my mother and father moved into the house in 1910, they were at a loss as to how to fill the yawning bookshelves and Dr. Crothers, the Unitarian minister, is reputed to have suggested that he lend them a few bushels of theological texts. Whether they took him up on his offer, I don't know, but the bookcases were soon overflowing. One corner, seemingly the darkest, was given over to the children's books. On snowy or rainy afternoons, or on Sundays, when the adults were "taking their naps," we children used to repair to this cozy nook. It was often so dark on a really stormy day that we had to find our favorite books by feel. Electric lights were sparse and at any rate, we knew where they were by heart. The Red and the Blue Fairy Books had a certain smell that identified them; the spine of the Howard Pyle *Robin Hood* was broken and binding frayed; the Twin books were all in a row and it did not matter which volume one came away with, the plot and the illustrations being virtually interchangeable. The feast, though, was the volume illustrated by Edmund Dulac or Arthur Rackham, whose *Ring of the Nibelungs*, which some indulgent uncle had given us one Christmas, fixed in my mind forever the brooding strangeness of the German myths.

At the far end of the front hall was the beautiful circular staircase curving up three stories to the top of the house, down whose mahogany banister we children slid for years from the third floor to the first in one mighty swish. No self-respecting child would have deigned to use the stairs, and I am surprised that no one was killed, or even toppled off, nor did the banister collapse under the strain. My mother, whose desk was under the stairs on the first floor, seemed to be hardened to living bodies landing at her feet, though startled guests were often alarmed by small forms whizzing past them on the staircase. No habits were ever changed just because there were guests in the house.

My sisters and I used to occupy two rooms high up under the eaves, and when I saw them again, they seemed small and cramped. I remembered them as huge, with dark corners and hidden cubbyholes. How fearful we were of the shadows, cast on the slanting walls by the gas street lamp, of the leafless limbs of the elm tree towering outside our window and of the sound of its creaking and swaying in the wind! The floors were splintery under our bare feet and the walls were papered in a gruesome gray floral pattern left over from the previous tenants. These had been servants' rooms, so naturally no provision for heat had been made. And it was bitterly cold in that great ill-heated house, when a northeaster swirled about and the snow sifted onto the floor through the window cracks, for no child could sleep with the window not open whatever the weather. Fresh air was *all*, in those days, taking the place of antibiotics, psychoanalysis, and health foods, so that the thought of denying one's child its benefits would have marked any parent as irresponsible if not criminal in his neglect. So we froze and were healthy.

When spring thaws came in late March and early April the windows would be thrown open, and if the wind blew from the west, the fetid odors of the abattoir in Brighton mingled with the delicious smell of damp earth; if it blew from the east, it carried a bizarre mix of other odors, the fat being rendered in East Cambridge at the Lever Brothers' soap factory and the tantalizing flavor of chocolate from the Necco factory in Cambridgeport. As spring progressed and the days became longer, when the six o'clock bells rang from the Divinity School's gothic tower at the end of the street, we children went to bed when it was still light outside. I used to think the lines from *A Child's Garden of Verses*, "In summer, quite the other way, I have to go to bed by day," had been written about me personally. I recall looking out from our third-floor aerie at the sun bursting through the clouds after a late afternoon shower, making the drops of rain sparkle on the purple blossoms of the lilac hedge, and hearing those bells and longing with all the keenness and poignancy of a child who has no sense of future time for the day when I should be grown up and the tolling of the bells would no longer fill me with such a sense of desolation. I don't think the bells will ring, but if they do, they could never carry for me such intimations of despair.

The varsity tennis courts were situated on the velvety green lawn that stretched away from the gothic pile of the Divinity School toward Norton's Woods, and I remember, as I grew older, sighing over the beautiful white-clad, long-limbed Apollos of the tennis team as they passed our house on sunny spring afternoons. I used to know their names, and follow their careers, and later in life, read of their deaths, respectable brokers and businessmen in old age, unaware of the swooning glances and unspoken passions that were expended on them in their youth.

From time to time President Lowell would take his solitary afternoon walk with his cocker spaniel past our house, swinging his cane as he surveyed his demesne with a proprietary air; but the traffic usually consisted of professors and graduate students, their book-filled green baize bags slung over their shoulders, walking to and fro from the science laboratories and the museums that lined the street.

Our house was surrounded by other Harvard buildings. On one side was the old Harvard University Printing Office, an elegant neo-Georgian edifice (long since demolished to make way for the William James behemoth), with its wooden platform at the back where heavy horse-drawn drays delivered enormous rolls of paper. It was, I think, the scene of my first childhood memory, a team of white fire-horses hitched to a flaming red fire wagon galloping in to the staging area beyond our gray board fence. It is a memory as vivid as yesterday and perhaps foreshadowed a lifelong fascination with horses.

Just across the board fence that lined two sides of our yard was a three-story tenement housing a number of young Irish girls, fresh from the old country. They worked for a pittance cleaning the "young gentlemen's" rooms or waiting on tables in Memorial Hall, where most of the undergraduates ate their meals. For some reason we children always referred to them as the "Dirty Dozens," an unattractive nomenclature bristling with childish hostility, and as I remember, we never exchanged a word with them. However, on warm spring days, we used to enjoy showing off to them as we climbed to the topmost limbs of the maple tree in the back yard. They would sit at their windows and register highly satisfactory wonder and fear at our daring but not a breath of recognition ever passed between us.

On this side, at least, there was a species of life and commerce markedly lacking in the Semitic Museum on our other side. It was a ponderous structure built of the depressing dark red brick popular with architects of the mid-nineteenth century, constructed with a variety of ledges and projecting masonry. We children used to compete fiercely with one another as to who could climb completely around the building clinging to the jutting brickwork of the ledges without falling the seeming killing distance to the ground. This was apt to be an autumn project, and if anyone slipped, there were piles of leaves to soften the fall. The museum was a place of mystery to us, its interior dark and somber as seen through the dusty windows as we clung perilously to its granite sills, our eyes peeping just over the tops. It seemed to be inhabited by enormous stone figures of animals and men with bit ornaments or crowns on their heads but it was so dim inside, with a single bulb hanging from the middle of each ceiling, that in our fleeting glances we never really got a good look. We must have been lamentably incurious children, for never in our wildest dreams would we ever have dared venture inside. It would have been as unimaginable as a trip to Persia itself. Not until I grew up did it occur to me to enter the museum, only to discover that it was just as gloomy and spooky as I remembered. The figures we had seen were indeed colossal plaster casts of Assyrian lions and Babylonian kings, and a few years ago, when I traveled to Iran and saw Persepolis, I realized that along with the others we had glimpsed through the streaked windows were huge replicas of the reliefs on the stairway of the Palace of Darius.

In recent years, the sleepiness of the erstwhile Semitic Museum was for a time rudely interrupted. The ancient building was refurbished and for some years served as the Center for International Affairs, once a realm of Henry Kissinger. During the late sixties and early seventies it became the scene of periodic bombings by anti-Vietnam War protesters, thus adding an exotic note heretofore lacking in this particularly dry and dusty corner of academia.

The Semitic Museum was just the beginning of our institutional entrapment. Across the street, the Germanic Museum, renamed the Busch-Reisinger, was peopled in its turn by a huge plaster cast of Barbarossa on horseback, an enormous stallion, with its back in the cathedral-like window, which became a fascinating bit of source material to us puritanically raised children. As if this were not enough, a compound of chemistry buildings stood opposite, and up the street the dour and forbidding Zoological Museum, whose occupants were, to be sure, genuine, if stuffed, completed the encirclement.

Wedged between the Chemistry Laboratory and the Germanic Museum, however, was the only other habitation containing live, breathing householders, though it must be said that the Misses Peirce and their mother, a ramrod-backed horsy-cheeked Scottish old lady, the widow of a professor of mathematics, were of such quaintness and such perfect specimens of nineteenth-century gentility as to be worthy themselves of being encapsulated and preserved for posterity. They lived in a clapboard house of the usual Cambridge gray full of antiques, old china, and cats. From time to time, all three would wait upon my mother, like characters out of *Cranford*, bearing gifts of calves'-foot jelly and broth in times of family illness. Whenever they came to call, there always seemed to be more noise and numbers around the house than usual, and I can remember having the feeling that Mrs. Peirce, a most gentle and proper lady, thought it rather vulgar of Mrs. Cannon to have so many children. The effect of their calls on my mother was remarkable. She, who not particularly sensitive to atmosphere, would temper her verbal sallies with unusual constraint, sit almost as straight in her chair as Mrs. Peirce, and rather than direct the conversation, which was her wont, follow the bland lead of the unexceptionable Mrs. Peirce. I recall it was quite a strain for all of us, but of interest to see my mother cast in a role unusual for her.

Many years later, after their mother had died, the Misses Peirce, who had stayed on in the house, used to summon my father to "sniff the air for gas," which they were sure was poisoning not only themselves but their more than half-dozen cats. Although weary representatives of the gas company had already paid numberless visits, summoned from their beds, no doubt, in the middle of the night, they had found no leaks.

There was something reassuring to the old ladies about pronouncements based on evidence collected by my father's olfactory nerves. For, after all, he *was* a full professor and they were rather intellectual snobs. He was even asked to prescribe for their cats. The fact that he should be called on in the face of their knowing that many of the experiments in his physiological laboratory were conducted on cats was discreetly overlooked, showing a touching faith in his forbearance and humanity. Even my father's reassurance that there was just as much oxygen in the air in our house as in theirs could not persuade them that it was safe for them to come to my sister's wedding. They feared that smoke from candles on the table would poison the air.

As time went on, they virtually withdrew from the world, barricading themselves and their cats from the exhaust fumes in nearby Kirkland Street, ahead of their times in recognizing the perils of pollution. But not before Miss Emily had one day rushed to my mother, wringing her hands in horror, to report that if she knelt down and peeked through one of the third-story dormer windows she could see a distinguished professor of chemistry kissing his female assistant in the laboratory across the way. It seemed to have been one of the few signs of life among our institutional neighbors and it was good to think that something besides flasks and retorts was bubbling in those austere buildings. My mother's advice to Miss Emily has not been recorded, though she was rather good at handling neurasthenic females. She understood the pleasure that both sisters took in Emily's "highstrung" and delicate constitution. It was one of the last times that Miss Emily was ever seen outside her house. As for the cats, they went on to a certain kind of fame. At one point, while canvassing for votes, I saw listed the name "Peirce, Oliver—Independent" on the voting list along with those of the Misses Peirce, all three of the same address. Oliver was indeed the old tiger cat saved from the nonexistent fumes by my father's sniffing and the first cat registered to vote in Cambridge.

The Agassiz and Peabody museums were great resorts of our childhood, years before modern showcase designing had transformed museums into "educational experiences." On dreary Saturday afternoons we would troop off to look at the stuffed giraffes and rhinoceroses in their dusty glass cases or delight in the models of the Ute Indians' Great Hall or the undifferentiated mélange of Indian artifacts that jammed the cases of the remote third floor. I can still smell the pervasive odor of formaldehyde, feel the gloom of the enormous, echoing, dark rooms, and hear the ring of our shoes on the iron stairways with the terrifying space between each lift down which we feared to slip. They contained (and still do) a unique jumble of treasures from priceless Mayan gold ornaments to a stuffed dodo bird, but perhaps the greatest prize of the Agassiz museum was the collection of the Glass Flowers. They were housed in ill-lit, grimy, glass cases with unreadable Latin-German-English identifying legends, and were visited sparingly in those days, being better known to visitors from abroad than to local museum-goers.

My father was a research physiologist and teacher who had many foreign students. It was often the fate of these scholars when my father and mother would "have them around" for Sunday dinner to be asked if they would like "to go and see the Glass Flowers." This suggestion was always greeted by us children with inward groans. We recognized it as a sign that conversation, apt to be about the "exports or imports of Chile or Hungary," or wherever the students came from, had run dry and we were about to be drafted to conduct them through the midwinter slush and snow whether they wished it or not.

My mother usually bore the brunt of such social intercourse, for outside his laboratory my father was apt to be diffident and shy. She was a woman of endless curiosity who liked a well-rounded, concrete fact, and she genuinely wanted to know about imports and exports and other solid statistics she

Sledding on the Sachses' Hill. *(Drawing by Marian Cannon Schlesinger)*

could get her teeth into. But it took me a long time to get over the idea that this was the only form of "conversation." It was always such a relief to have her "in charge"; no dreaded hiatuses ever yawned no matter how boring the company. It seemed to me as a child no one could be more skilled or gifted in the art of social intercourse than she, though as I grew older I did think that subjects more soul-searching, like art or music, or more worldly, like politics, might be more edifying.

Opposite the Zoological Museums and behind the drab brick dormitories where the theological students lived stood three wooden gothic houses, their pointed gables festooned with Baroque scrollery, on sweeping lawns that were dotted with snowdrops and daffodils in the spring. They belonged, like our house, to the University and therefore did not "count," in our minds, as houses. The occupants, being academics, too, somehow lacked validity. It was only over the back fence that the real world began, where people lived in huge houses and had uniformed maids and Irish gardeners; where fathers went to work downtown in Boston and all the children were having their teeth straightened. It seemed a no-man's land of wealth and privilege and as remote from our lives as the corridors of the Semitic Museum. In actual fact, it was in this part of Cambridge that William James lived and the families of E.E. Cummings and of the philosopher Josiah Royce and other distinguished members of the Harvard faculty in comfortable houses that had been built in the last decade of the nineteenth century on land originally belonging to the Norton estate. A scattering of lawyers and judges and businessman or two lived in this area, too, but as far as we children were concerned they were like creatures from another sphere and we kept a wary eye out for their Irish maids when we climbed their fences and sprinted through their gardens on mysterious errands that took us through the neighborhood. It was an accept- ed fact that we never walked on sidewalks ("step on a crack and break your mother's back" was the couplet for cement sidewalks) but always took short- cuts through other people's back yards. Once when my nine-year-old sister Helen and a "best" friend were stopped by one of the "college cops" on their way home from school, cross-country, they expostulated in self-righteous indignation. "Our fathers are Harvard professors and we can do anything we want!" This magnificent bit of priggishness was our shield against the world; it would never do today! Nor would the remark reported by a neighbor of another "college cop," a philosophical red-faced Irishman who used to keep a solicitous eye on us as children. "It takes these Italians and furriners a long time to learn that Cambridge is not a place but an opportunity!"

ENDNOTES

1. Reprinted with permission from Marian Cannon Schlesinger, *Snatched from Oblivion* (Boston: Little, Brown, 1979) 3-16 .

2. Some wit was right! Since this was written, the house has again been moved to a new site, making it the most peripatetic house left in Cambridge.

The Register Forum:
A Treasure
and a Record

STEPHEN G. SURETTE

THE *REGISTER FORUM* is a treasure. Established in 1891 as the *C.M.T.S. Register* and later rechristened the *Rindge Register*, the official student newspaper of Cambridge Rindge and Latin School is one of the oldest continuously published high school newspapers in the country. Renamed in 1977 after a reorganization of high schools in the city,[1] the *Register Forum* has spanned the entire twentieth century and more, providing a firsthand look at the lives of Cambridge teenagers generation after generation.

In 1888 Frederick H. Rindge built the Cambridge Manual Training School (CMTS), later renamed Rindge Technical School to better reflect the nature of the curriculum and to honor Rindge. It offered an alternative to the classical education of Cambridge Latin School (CLS), which had split off from Cambridge High School in 1886.

The Latin School immediately embarked on a student writing project called *The Latin Review*. Known also in its early years as *The Latin and High School Review*, it promised to "chronicle all events, athletic and otherwise, which pertain to the school" and quickly gained a solid reputation as a student newspaper. The Manual Training School subsequently saw a need to come up with a newspaper of its own. Its first headmaster, Harry Ellis, wanted to instill in CMTS students Rindge's concept that "work is one of our greatest blessings," and he saw the printing program as a natural for producing a student publication. George W. Wells, John W. Wood Jr., and Webster T. Rich,

Logos from the different incarnations of what is now Cambridge Rindge & Latin Schools' *Register Forum*, the student newspaper.

members of the class of 1893, put out the first *Register* on February 1, 1892. Commenting years later, Wells said, "It was an experiment, this idea of teaching boys how to use hands as well as head, and educators came from all parts to see our work."[2]

The newspapers of both schools captured the attention of their students. Both charged five cents per issue, seventy-five cents per subscription, and people were purchasing them. The schools prided themselves on teaching good communication skills, and the *Review* and *Register* were the perfect venues for demonstrating students' abilities. *Vita Sine Literis Mors Est*, "life without literature is death," soon became the motto of the *Review*, as its beautifully presented pages contained short stories, essays, and poetry as well as news.

The *Register* tended to encourage news from around the school and appropriately adopted the slogan "If it happened at Rindge, you'll see it in the *Register*." The *Review* ended its run during the 1950s and was eventually replaced by Cambridge High and Latin School's tabloid newspaper, the *Latin Forum*, published throughout the 1960s until 1977. Today, the *Register Forum* draws on the heritage of both schools and continues the mission

Unidentified participants in an early printing class at Cambridge Manual Training School.

that Wells, its first editor, stated long ago, to be "devoted to the interests of students."[3]

The merger of the former Cambridge High and Latin School (CHLS) and Rindge Tech in September 1977 challenged the continuance of the veritable "old" school newspaper. Most of the Rindge building was closed during substantial remodeling, and the majority of students were either placed in the CHLS building or scattered around the city at various satellite locations. The creation of eight distinct "houses" (A, B, C, D, E, Fundamental, Pilot, and Occupational Education) within the larger Cambridge Rindge and Latin School caused Henry Lukas, the assistant headmaster, to initially encourage eight newspapers.

Amazingly, however, the entire staff of the *Rindge Register* found itself assigned to House C, and all were ready and willing to resume production of a paper. Acknowledging the amount of energy needed for such an endeavor and realizing that House C's might be the only group capable of it, Lukas asked the veteran Rindge staff to consider producing a school-wide paper. Everyone agreed, and co-adviser John Rutter (CHLS 1968) suggested a nom-

John W. Wood Jr., headmaster, with students in 1932.

inal merger of the *Rindge Register* and the *Latin Forum*. Thus, the *Register Forum* was born.

The schools have always supported such extracurricular activities through their sponsorship, the provision of space and equipment, and the assignment of excellent faculty advisers to teach and inspire those in their charge. Two names in particular jump to the top of the list.

As mentioned, John W. Wood Jr. (CMTS 1893) was one of the original team of three to "experiment" with the idea of a school newspaper. He began teaching at Rindge after graduating from MIT in 1898 and served as head-master for forty-three years (1907–50). Wood was loved by all of his students, who seemed to equate a love of school with a love for its headmaster, and he received countless letters and postcards from alumni serving in embattled countries during the wars who wanted, Wood said, "just to say hello." His interest in the newspaper was never small, and his support as headmaster was vital. Long after his retirement, he observed that "the *Rindge Register* had a rather difficult existence for many years [though it became] one of the outstanding school papers, unique in that [the students] carried on all phases of its production."[4]

Yet Wood gave much of the credit for the success of the *Register* to his former student Walter H. Gomes (Rindge 1911). Although Gomes's title for thirty-nine years was faculty technical adviser, he was affectionately called "Mr. Rindge Register." Wood remarked that "this was a misnomer, for Mr. Gomes was . . . actually the *Rindge Register*. The *Register* would never have been produced without his able, expert knowledge, his untiring energy, and his abiding devotion to the Rindge Technical School."[5]

Many other faculty advisers have bolstered the *Rindge Register* since the 1920s, among them Henry Lynch, M. H. Cunningham, Michael Skinner, J. J. Garvey, Gunard Haugh, Pierce Fitzgerald, Harry Eaton, William Mahoney, Larry O'Brien, George McMahon, Wendell Fogg, Edward Correia, Francis McCarthy, Andrea Romagna Ciccolo, Michael Corless, Jane Kervick, Edward Bullock, John Rutter, and Stephen Surette. From the 1920s until the 1950s, when it ceased publication, the *Review* received guidance from Mary Hardy, Mary Bligh, and Alice Kelley. Elizabeth Grady was the last adviser for the *Forum*, and the *Register Forum* has previously had three advisors: Stephen Surette (1976–99), assisted by John Rutter (1976–78) and Karen Davis (1979–80).

Today the *Register Forum* continues under the capable direction of Paul Burke (CHLS 1970), its current faculty adviser. A veteran English teacher at CRLS, Burke moved the newspaper from a club-only operation in 1999 to one run in tandem with a journalism course. His students now master page-layout software on Macintosh computers instead of the Linotype machines and Compugraphic typesetting equipment of previous generations, performing all pre-press design and composition tasks before sending the paper to an outside commercial printer. And his staffs continue to receive acclaim, winning annual awards for excellence from the esteemed Columbia Scholastic Press Association.

The participation of an estimated three thousand editors and staffers from 1891 to the present have accounted for no fewer than one thousand individual issues of the *Register* and *Register Forum*, constituting 118 volumes, most of which are bound in hardcover and kept in a permanent collection in Cambridge Public Library. One can double that figure if counting the staffs of the *Review* and the *Forum*.* A perusal of mastheads shows that the *Register*'s original staff of three grew to more than a hundred regular staff members and contributors in 1979.

It is difficult to tell whether periodic calls for more student participation on the editorial pages of the school papers had any real impact on the success of subsequent issues. Given what a 1928 editorial suggested, the editor did it all by himself, causing one to wonder if a staff was needed at all. "An editor should be a superman endowed with the patience of Job, the editorial ability of Horace Greeley, the managing and directing abilities of Charles Schwab, the diplomacy of Woodrow Wilson, the judicial qualities of Chief Justice Marshall," the editorial read. "[H]e should be absolutely foreign to the needs

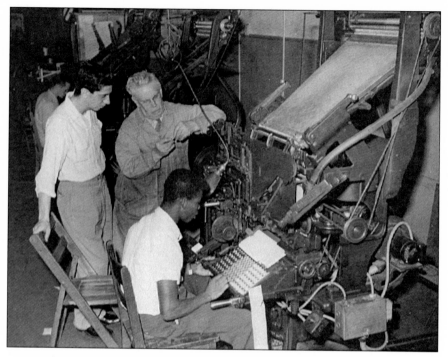
Walter Gomes and students at the linotype, ca. 1953.

of rest, sleep, eating, recreation, and love of society, the inclination for glory in athletics, and love."[6]

In truth, all kinds of people have aided the editor. In 1944, for instance, an editor-in-charge stepped in for Walter Stotik, the editor-in-chief, who entered the armed forces before the year ended. And while editors doubtless put their personal imprints on each volume, they have been encouraged by an army of co-editors; assistant editors; associate editors; club editors; freshman, sophomore, junior, and senior editors; class editors; page editors; literary editors; alumni editors; social editors; and publicity editors. Reporters of all descriptions, too, have continued to pound out their stories and meet their deadlines while trying to remain typo-free.

More than, say, the president of a club, an editor has to mix organizational and leadership skills with a nose for news, an eye for attractive design, and—in the modern era—a knowledge of relevant software. The editors of Cambridge's school newspapers have tended to be active in school life, and their appointments or elections have often been considered prestigious, impressing college admissions officials. Howard Shaw (RMTS 1903), an editor-in-chief of the *Register*, became a rear admiral in the U.S. Navy. Francis Duehay (CHLS 1951), editor-in-chief of the *Review* from 1950 to 1951, later served as mayor of Cambridge. Kathia Manzi (CRLS 1986), who joined the *Register Forum* staff as a freshman declaring that she wanted to be a television news anchor someday, succeeded in achieving her goal. She has been a radio and television news personality in Worcester and Springfield since graduating from college. Ned Colby (CRLS 1998), who as *Register Forum* editor helped direct Cambridge Rindge and Latin's 350th Anniversary movie, became an editor of the *The Harvard Crimson*. And former editor Jessica Rubin-Wills (CRLS 2002) served on the *Crimson* staff in 2005. An unofficial count of editors of the past two decades shows that all have gone on to good colleges and universities, taking with them a valuable high school experience.

THROUGH THE YEARS

Because Cambridge Public Library houses an archive of the school newspapers, students and others can easily obtain a glimpse of the past century's technological innovations. In 1889 the *Review* covered the installation of electric lights at Cambridge Manual Training School by its second headmaster, Charles Morse, and his students. The first volumes of the *Register* covered the activities of the fire brigade, when hand pumping was the newest invention, and in 1896 the paper featured the introduction of x-ray technology. One reporter spoke of being able to make radio broadcasts in 1924, and another wrote of how the radio club of 1928 piqued student interest in the "possibility of TV" and "remote control." An early photograph used by the newspaper shows a Navy Boeing seaplane being delivered to Rindge for a new "aeroplane" maintenance and repair course.

Readers were also informed about refrigeration, which had been newly installed in the school kitchen, thus allowing the kitchen staff "to keep food from day to day." Elsewhere an article described telephotography, a novel science that allowed photos to be transmitted between cities. By 1940, readers were learning about the full-credit Public Safety and Automobile Driving class, though, oddly, there was no mention of the passing of the horse-and-carriage era.

During the next half century, stories about moon landings, MX missiles, and nuclear disarmament took center stage, morphing into a concern today with the growing sciences of incendiary devices and weapons of mass destruction.

A LOCAL PERSPECTIVE DURING THE GREAT DEPRESSION

Eliot Spalding, former editor of the *Cambridge Chronicle*, once remarked that a community needs a paper that will report stories about youngsters receiving their scout medals. The *Register* has done that and more.

From the beginning, its stories have announced the activities of teams, clubs, and organizations, given coverage to new programs, classes, and courses, and recorded the names of students and teachers who have involved themselves in school life. In 1929 a policy decision mandated an extra forty-five-minute period in the school schedule "in which no actual school work is done but in which we carry on various clubs," the start of a bonanza of news that continues to hit the pages of the school paper in great detail.

Although the late 1920s and the 1930s saw a country in the throes of the Great Depression, the pages of the *Register* were uplifting. Inside lay news about the ongoing Ski Club and the popular Dance Class, as well as highlights of the new Airplane Model League (1928), the regional championship of the Checker Club (1929), the introduction of a senior class yearbook (1931), the Camera Club (1933), the Symphony Band (1937), and the Golf Club (1940). Also covered were the activities of the Chemistry Club, Bowling League, Tennis Club, Harmonica Club, and Travel Club. The last, established in 1929, boasted having "the largest membership in school," though its members did not actually travel. Instead, they watched films and listened to lectures—exciting goings-on in the days before television. Distracted by such flurries of activity, the students failed to mention the Depression until 1937, when they cited the fourth anniversary of Franklin Roosevelt's "Bank Holiday."[7]

THE BIGGEST EVENT: WORLD WAR II

No event in history came alive on the pages of the *Register* as did World War II. America was at war, and the students and teachers of Rindge were made aware of the fact in part through articles in the school newspaper. The entire country was focused on the monumental struggle, and young people were clearly going to be instrumental in saving the day. Rindge students, teachers, and staff did their part, from conducting scrap metal drives and war stamps sales to enlisting in the armed forces.[8]

Most of these firsthand accounts about life on the home front were reprinted in 2000 in a separate book published by the Rindge Alumni Association for use by social studies teachers and students at CRLS. (A similar booklet was prepared in 2003 using student writings about World War I from the pages of the *Review*.) Since many boys were leaving school to go into the service, the *Register* gave explicit instructions on how to register under the Selective Service Act and reported on a school committee decision in 1942 to combine the athletic teams of Rindge Tech and CHLS in order to save resources.

Although the paper reported a demand by seniors for an early graduation in February 1944, an editorial called on junior males to continue to study hard and not think of enlisting in the military. "They don't want you now," read the editorial. "Next year, when you've finished your school training...you will be welcomed with open arms....Make the most of extra advantages you have in attending a technical school. Your chances of becoming an officer when you do join the Service are actually twice as great as those of the common high school student."[9]

In May 1945 the *Rindge Register* reported that V-E Day was "the day that everyone has been waiting for." One anonymous student, no doubt expressing sentiments common to the entire student body, wrote in a letter to America: "I want to go to college. I want to get a good job after I graduate and I want to get married and raise my children. I want to spend my few years on this earth on the simpler, glorious ways of peace."[10]

THE 1950S AND 1960S

The time between wars is often a more innocent time, and later historic events received less attention from student writers. Sputnik garnered a mention in 1957—on page 8—prompting an alumnus to repeat former headmaster Wood's admonition: "America needs trained scientists and mathematicians." John F. Kennedy's assassination on November 22, 1963, was termed "The Day America Trembled" but did not make it into the paper until the spring of 1964. The civil rights movement, however, occasioned several articles, one of which reminded readers that an African American had died for his country in Cambridge on April 19, 1775.[11]

THE 1970S AND 1980S

In the decades that followed, a discernible "maturity" swept over the *Register Forum* as students placed major issues—school vandalism, tax-related Proposition 2 1/2, the refugee crisis in Haiti, the death of John Lennon, nuclear madness—on the front page with large headlines. Coverage of the Law Club's early morning "Breakfasts with the Judges" showed students and staff asking tough questions of real judges, two of whom were alumni Lawrence Feloney (CHLS 1939) and Severlin Singleton (Rindge 1966).

During a faculty meeting in 1981, one teacher wondered whether students weren't mixing emotions and opinions in front-page stories and on editorial pages, thereby "inciting" fellow students, and asked if anyone was censoring what the students wrote. Assistant headmaster Lukas, a staunch supporter of student journalism, replied that restricting student reporting would inhibit student expression. On another occasion, a local television news crew visited CRLS to interview the *Register Forum* staff about a U.S.

Supreme Court decision that outlined the role of school principals in censoring students. The television reporter, perhaps expecting a bit of a sensation, heard headmaster Edward Sarasin defend the rights of student writers and speak in favor of responsible student journalism.

DRAMA

Dramatics maintained its popularity throughout the century, with one or more productions each year. The early plays were presented in a number of places: the old Washington Hall, Sanders Theatre, and for a number of years, Brattle Hall. *The Ghost Train,* the senior drama of 1933, was the first to be given in the new Rindge auditorium, which helped to counter the building's image as a prison.[12] Often the frequency of each edition of the school paper allowed for a top-of-the-page headline announcing the opening of a play that evening, something the school committee in 1896 apparently took exception to. A letter to the editor argued against "dramatic performances by the classes of the High Schools [interfering] with the study for which the High Schools were formed." Further, a decision was made to deny the use of the high school hall "for the presentation of the base-ball trophy."

Over the years, however, numerous Rindge and Latin students have become professional actors. And during the last three decades, the *Register Forum* has faithfully covered the school's many entries in the Massachusetts Drama Festival. (The most recent production, *Assembly Line,* reached the semifinals.) The school newspapers have opened readers' eyes to the art, poetry, literary works, reviews, and dramatic and musical performances that are emblematic of CRLS's art, music, and drama departments.

ATHLETICS

Sports have also drawn readers in since the first school newspaper rolled off the press, with box scores, game highlights, and the names of countless participants filling innumerable personal scrapbooks. Only a few headlines have extended across the entire front page since the tabloid format was adopted in 1919, and some of these were indeed about sports victories and championships. "R.T.S. Surprises Newton" was one of the first (1928), in a major sports upset victory. "Jenkins is National 440 Yard Champion for the Second Year" (1953) was another. In 1981, "Patrick Ewing, All American Leads No. 1 Team" accompanied a full-body photograph extending down the entire right side of the front page, thus accentuating Ewing's height and his stardom. Jenkins and Ewing would become Olympic gold medal winners, and their stories would grace the pages of future issues as well.

Speaking Directly to the Reader

On many occasions, school editors have felt a need to speak directly to readers, as in a 1938 editorial that addressed an entire class with the opening sentence, "If you are a senior, don't read this." Another piece targeted a single subscriber with the message, "If the student wearing a bogus "R" on his sweater doesn't cease doing so, the *Register* will be compelled to expose him." And when grass was newly planted around the school that same decade, the editor wrote of his hope that every fellow in the school would comply with a request to stay off it.

More broadly, in 1939 the editors reminded their readership that "the good reputation of our school depends upon the good and proper conduct in public and private of each from the tiniest Freshman to the largest Senior and Post Graduate," a theme that resurfaced the same year when a particular student in the orchestra was asked to "quiet down and not drown everyone else out." By 2004, editorial admonitions had been extended to include adults as well as students, as in the one that declared, "There must be mutual respect, there must be mutual consideration, and there must be mutual understanding."

Visitors

The newspapers have covered visits to the school by the famous and the interesting, people such as President Karl Compton of MIT, who spoke to the students in 1933 on "Engineering, A Changing Art," and the actors Janet Leigh and Walter Brennan, who appeared on the high school stage in the 1950s. Senator John F. Kennedy met with students and staff in 1946; Senator Edward M. Kennedy did the same in 1975. The Reverend Jesse Jackson gave an impassioned speech during the 1980s, and in the 1990s William Weld, then governor of Massachusetts, visited during the years his daughter attended CRLS. In 2002 Eric Cornell, who won the Nobel Prize in Physics, returned to thank his teachers.

Photographs

Before photos were in vogue, cartoonists would illustrate the highlights of various events on campus, but photography soon played an increasingly important role in news coverage. In 1932 a hockey game was the theme of one of the *Register*'s first action shots. The paper's photos became progressively more creative thereafter, as in a 1980 demolition view of CHLS after sunset, the silhouette of a crane both serene and haunting. Later, shots of a student demonstration depicted a new era of activism. Today, digital cameras have made it even easier to accompany any given article with high-quality pictures.

ADVERTISERS

Long a fixture in Harvard Square, Brine's Athletic Equipment, now in Belmont, was among the first businesses to advertise in the school newspaper. Advertisers were the lifeline of the paper for much of its existence, and they tried to appeal to young people. The University Theater in Harvard Square boasted "continuing showings," while the Central Square Theater spoke of "a sacred obligation" and "confidence entrusted in them by the people." The Broadway Pharmacy, opposite Felton Street, advertised "the best frappes in town," and William McAdoo Milk Company advertised "the milk you drink in the Rindge lunch room." D. A. Ravanis Typewriters, on Western Avenue, suggested that students should use a typewriter "for better marks" while another ad tried to convince Rindge boys that "Your Girls will be pleased with a corsage from" Galgay Florist. In recent decades, East Cambridge Savings Bank not only has supported the school newspaper with a full-page ad in each issue but also has set up a full-fledged branch at CRLS so that students can use its services while others train as interns in the banking operations course.

KEEPING UP TO DATE

In the late 1970s, graphic arts students were using the industry-changing Compugraphic typesetting machine, which allowed the operator to key in text and correct errors on a small screen before collecting all the data on a tape that could be turned into sheets of film. These film strips had to be photographically processed using a chemical mix, dried, and affixed to a board using printer's wax before a negative of the entire page could be shot in preparation for offset printing. The process was quicker than the old Linotype process but more cumbersome than modern desktop publishing techniques.

The latter was introduced to CRLS in 1987 by the *Register Forum* staff. When the school's Compugraphic equipment broke down and no money was to be had for expensive repairs, the editor, Beth Auterio, saved the day by bringing together the faculty adviser, Stephen Surette, and a freshman staff member, Derrick Doyle, whose parents were well versed in desktop publishing. Bob Doyle, Derrick's father and a principal of Boston Software, Inc., had developed MacPublisher, one of the pioneering desktop programs, and he lent his generous support to the paper's staff. As each year went by, the student body grew increasingly proficient with Macintosh computers and desktop publishing procedures, until every submission arrived on a floppy disk. Today it's e-mail.

A New Century

What do we have to look forward to? If recent editions of the *Register Forum* are any indication, the paper will try to engage students in topics of national and international interest. In a page-one news article covered Secretary of State Colin Powell's 2003 presentation on Iraq before the United Nations; another followed the 2004 Democratic primary elections with statistical detail. In fact, a new motto adorns the nameplate of the newspaper: "Listening to every voice, printing what you need to hear." Those needs have been deemed of late to include such issues as genetically engineered food, reality television, obesity among the young, and gay marriage. As one boldly honest editorial declared, "We believe what we believe. The RF staff is predominantly liberal. You, as a Cantabrigian reader, probably are too."[13]

It is probably unnecessary to state that the pages of the *Review*, the *Register*, the *Forum*, and the *Register Forum* constitute "a journal of events and personalities that have made the school great." Guided by caring adults, the student staffers have been the beneficiaries of a valuable learning experience. The student body at large has enjoyed the sharing of news and ideas with their peers. The *Register* expressed this thought in a June 1928 editorial, saying farewell and "hoping that you leave benefited by its influence."[14]

Editors-in-Chief (1891-1979)

1891–92
GEORGE W. WELLS

1892–93
GEORGE W. WELLS

1893–94
JOHN F. MARSHALL

1894–95
JOHN FITZGERALD,
ALBERT HARRIS

1895–96
WALTER DOHERTY,
AUGUST GUTHEIM

1896–97
WILLIAM J. GREENE

1897–98
VINCENT M. FROST

1898–99
CARLTON WILBY

1899–00
CARRIER LANG

1900–01
FRANCIS B. ELLIS

1901–02
UNKNOWN

1902–03
HOWARD R. SHAW

1903–04
WILLIAM C. GLASS

1905–14
UNKNOWN

1914–15
F. CARLETON TURNER

1915–19
UNKNOWN

1919–20
LOUIS M. CAMPFIELD

1920–21
THOMAS LOWE

1921–22
LAWRENCE R. CLARKE

1922–23
WILLIAM H. DOHERTY

1923–24
JOSEPH A. O'HEARN

1924–25
LEON CAMPBELL JR.

1925–26
JAMES E. McCABE

1926–27
THOMAS BERENSTEN

1927–28
GEORGE A. LINCOLN

1928–29
O. WILLIAM WHITE

1929–30
J. B. SKINNER

1930–31
F. J. GRAZULIS

1931–32
N. E. BATTIT

1932–33
N. E. BATTIT

1933–34
F. J. BROWN

1934–35
ROBERT CALVERT

1935–36
FRANK A. CHANCE

1936–37
ROBERT BEMIS

1937–38
KALMAN NOVAK

1938–39
ESAU VERGE

1939–40
ESAU VERGE

1940–41
FRANCIS WISHAM

1941–42
CLYDE HANSON

1942–43
PAUL DYER

1943–44
WALTER W. STOTIK

1944–45
WILLIAM FLANAGAN,
HENRY HAYES

1945–46
ROGER M. LANOUE

1946–47
NICHOLAS GIANACOSTIS

1947–48
ARTHUR R. MAHON

1948–49
PAUL KING

1949–50
WILLIAM R. BOUDREAU

1950–51
JOHN BISIKIRSKI

1951–52
WILLIAM SULLIVAN

1952–53
HENRY DIESELMAN

1953–54
PAUL E. DiBENEDETTI

1954–55
DAVID R. McPHELIM

1955–56
ROBERT A. WALSH

1956–57
ROBERT F. HUDSON

1957–58
JOSEPH F. MAGNO

1958–59
RICHARD PARKHURST,
EDWARD DOOKS

1959–60
ROBERT J. AYERS

1960–61
JOSEPH L. BOURNE

1961–62
ROBERT L. GALVIN

1962–63
NORMAN R. SABBEY

1963–64
FRANCIS T. DiPACE JR.

1964–65
RICHARD BARRELL,
DAVID HOLWAY,
PAUL ST. GERMAINE,
PEDRO SILVA

1965–66
RONALD R. IPPOLITO

1966–67
GEORGE F. LONGO JR.

1967–68
ANTHONY JORGE

1968–69
FRANCIS ACCARRINO

1969–70
RUPERT G. MARGETSON

1970–71
JOHN SPINETTO

1971–72
JOHN SPINETTO

1972–73
RICHARD SARNO

1973–74
RICHARD STAREK

1974–75
NONE CHOSEN

1975–76
MICHAEL F. STANLEY

1976–79
TONY FIGUEREIDO

REGISTER FORUM EDITORS-IN-CHIEF

1977–78
CRAIG SISCO

1978–79
PAUL LOWE

1979–80
MARIA SEQUEIRA

1980–81
PAMELA CYR

1981–82
JOSE INVENCIO

1982–83
MELISSA SAWYER

1983–84
NORMAN SMITH,
LAUREL STROHMAN

1984–85
CECILIA AKUFFO,
KATHIA MANZI

1985–86
KATHIA MANZI

1986–87
BETH AUTERIO

1987–88
BRIAN SULLIVAN

1988–89
ROSEANNE AMORE

1989–90
MARIA AMORE

1990–91
BEN SCHLAVER

1991–92
ETHAN NASR

1992–93
CHRISTINE JAMIOL

1993–94
SAMANTHA SPITZER

1994–95
KAYA STONE

1995–96
KAYA STONE

1996–97
KEVIN SANGUDI,
NED COLBY

1997–98
NED COLBY

1998–99
BUSHRA MAKIYA,
LEAH BEEFERMAN

1999–00
LEAH BEEFERMAN

2000–01
REBECCA MOTHERWELL-SWANSON

2001–02
PAUL HEINTZ,
JESSICA RUBIN-WILLS

2002–03
JEFF BARNES,
JONATHAN MAYNARD

2003–04
JEN ATHANASIADIS,
KAISEY PAJA

2004–05
DAN RUBIN-WILLS,
GENEVRA PITTMAN

PRODUCTION

For much of the paper's existence before the computer age, the production process remained unchanged. Two students, Richard Barrell and Paul St. Germaine, described that process in a 1965 article.

The edited story is typed on one side of the paper, double-spaced, and sent down to Mr. O'Brien. In the print shop it is referred to as 'copy.' Mr. O'Brien gives the copy to one of his students to set on the Linotype machine. This is a machine with a typewriter-like keyboard, containing little brass units called matrices, which in turn carry letters in reverse. When the letters and other characters for a line of print have been assembled, the line is justified, or spaced out to fit the width of the column.

Mr. Larry O'Brien and students at the linotype.

The line is then cast in type metal and the casting, called a slug, is ejected into a rack called a 'stick.'

Next the slugs are assembled into a column, placed in a galley or shallow tray, and laid in a proof press; inked; then a roller presses a sheet of paper down on the inked slugs to make a proof, which shows what the page will look like. The job is proofread, or the proof is compared carefully to the copy; at first by the boy who set it, secondly by Mr. O'Brien, to see that it follows the copy exactly, and finally by Mr. Fogg for a final check. Any errors are corrected on the Linotype, and another proof is taken and read.

When the proofs of the stories for one page have been approved as correct, they are assembled in a frame called a form, and locked in with wooden blocks called furniture and interlocking metal wedges called quoins (pronounced coins).

Two pages are actually printed at one time....The printing is done under Mr. McMahon's direction.

In the final stage of production the printing class as a unit folds and assembles the paper and counts out the completed paper in bundles of 50 for the convenience of the sales staff and the mailing editor.

The assembling and production of a school paper involves many trades, occupations, and learning situations. Adequate mastery of such subjects as English composition, spelling, reading, and mathematics is essential.[15]

ENDNOTES

1. John Langone, *The Cambridge Rindge & Latin School: Yesterday and Today* (Cambridge, Mass.: Cambridge Historical Society, 1998).

2. George W. Wells. "Wanted: A Rindge Paper," *Rindge Register*, June 1936, 1.

3. *The C.M.T.S. Register* 1, no. 1, February 1, 1892, 2.

4. John W. Wood, "Testimonials," *Rindge Register*, October 24, 1962.

5. "Our 'Mr. Rindge Register' Passes On," *Rindge Register*, October 24, 1962.

6. "Ye Editors," *Rindge Register*, November 27, 1928, 8.

7. Joseph X. Cochrane, "Facts and Comments," *Rindge Register*, May 13, 1937, 7.

8. Stephen Surette, *World War II through the Files of the Rindge Register* (Cambridge, Mass.: Rindge Alumni Association, 2000), 5.

9. "The Juniors," *Rindge Register*, April 16, 1943.

10. "Please Keep This Peace, Mr. America," *Rindge Register*, June 15, 1945.

11. "Crisis in the South," *Rindge Register*, April 7, 1965, 2.

12. "The Old 'Ghost Train' Packed the New Rindge Auditorium to Capacity," *Rindge Register*, March 17, 1933, 1.

13. "Not as Tolerant as We Thought," *Register Forum*, October 2003, 2.

14. "Farewell, Seniors," *Rindge Register*, June 13, 1930, 2.

15. Richard Barrell and Paul St. Germaine, "Producing the Rindge Register," *Rindge Register*, April 7, 1965, 7.

*Very few issues of the *Forum* were saved for archival purposes. Contributions of individual issues are welcomed from private collections. —S.S.

A Landscape History of the Hooper-Lee-Nichols House in the 20th Century

KAREN FORSLUND FALB

TODAY, the Hooper-Lee-Nichols House at 159 Brattle Street is one of only two historic properties in Cambridge open to the public as a museum. Unlike the more renowned Longfellow National Historic Site at 105 Brattle Street, the Hooper-Lee-Nichols House is not recognized for any outstanding event or person. It is, however, many decades older than the Longfellow House and is significant for being a property whose development can be documented from 1684 onward.[1] Furthermore, the history of its landscaping over the last century shows a pattern typically seen in other older properties in Cambridge and is helpful in portraying the evolution of designed residential landscape in the Cambridge area.

Until quite recently, interest in the Hooper-Lee-Nichols property centered mainly on its architecture and owners, and not on its landscape and land usage. Nevertheless, enough documentation exists to piece together the evolution of its landscape features over the last century, including since 1957, when it was bequeathed to the Cambridge Historical Society.[2] Visual documentation from the 1870s forms a major part of the early record but does not tell the whole story, as initial photographs show primarily the front of the house. Recent photographs and plans, as well as oral histories, give a more complete account, producing a history of the landscape that is not only interesting but also useful for making future landscape-treatment decisions.

The Hooper-Lee-Nichols House and landscaping in 2004. The 1916 gate system of the Colonial Revival period complements the balustrade, which was added to the roof in 1853. The tree to the left is the lone survivor of a row of horsechestnut trees planted by the Lee family in the early Federal period.

In 1905, the year the Cambridge Historical Society was founded, ownership of the Hooper-Lee-Nichols House returned to the Nichols family after a span of twelve years. At the time, the property was the same two-fifths of an acre parcel that the family had sold in 1893 to Henry Lee, a prominent civic leader in Boston, Brookline, and the Harvard College community.[3] It was also the same two-fifths of an acre parcel that remains today.

The Nichols family first lived at the house in 1850, when George and Susan Nichols rented it from Deborah Lee Carpenter, a first cousin of Henry Lee's father. They had six children and enjoyed the benefits of a small suburban farm and its proximity to George's work in Harvard Square.[4] When Carpenter died in 1860, the Nichols family was able to buy the property, which then comprised one and three-quarters acres. At that time they had a milking cow and chickens, and enjoyed gardens, an orchard, and a hay field. It was during their ownership that the Brattle Street neighborhood underwent most of its residential development. On George's death in 1882, the family started subdividing the land and selling off house lots, and right after Susan's death in 1892, the surviving children sold the house on the two-fifths of an acre to Henry Lee. Lee

This 1880s photo, taken at the same angle as the previous photograph, shows the house and landscape in the picturesque style. The horsechestnut trees are in their prime. A grandson of George and Susan Nichols stands by the fence post. A Federal-style carriage barn is in the distance on the left and a garden structure is in the lilac bushes to the right.

was interested in the house because of its long history of ownership by the Lee family, through the Colonial and Federal periods back to 1757.[5]

There were several reasons that the house and landscape did not undergo significant change during Henry Lee's ownership. Lee was in his seventies when he bought the property, and although he wanted to preserve it, he did not invest in many improvements. He also collected rental income from Mary Nichols White, a daughter of George and Susan Nichols, who maintained the house and landscape as it was. When Lee died in 1898, his estate continued to rent the house to Mary White until seven years later, when her brother John Nichols bought the property and then rented it to their sister Harriet Nichols Lamb. From the late 1880s to 1915, the landscape remained essentially the same.

During the 1880s, residential landscaping in Cambridge reflected the change in land use from homestead farming to suburban residential living. First described in the 1840s in publications by Andrew Jackson Downing, this evolving suburban style, also known as the picturesque style, gained momentum in the 1870s with Frank J. Scott's book *Victorian Estates, Part I. Suburban Home Grounds.* It promoted curvilinear drives, walks, and planting beds,

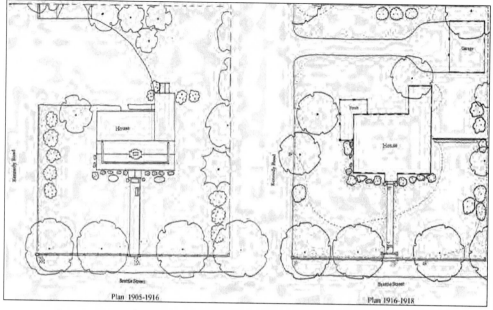

Plan 1905-1916   Plan 1916-1918

A comparison of these plans shows the earlier service courtyard and its replacement by the driveway and garage. It also shows the new side porch and increased private area of lawn at the back. In front, a narrow brick walk and Colonial Revival gate system have been added.

as well as the spatial organization that left the front of the house public and made the sides and back private for service and "pleasure" areas.[6] Ideas on plantings included lawns of turf, flowering deciduous shrubs, and foundation plantings with a shrub or two at the corner of a house. Annuals were chosen for small ornamental gardens. Climbing roses and vines decorated doorways.

Although by the late 1880s the Nichols property had many features of the picturesque style, earlier Georgian features had been consciously retained by both the Lee and Nichols families. They included the house, its relationship to Brattle Street, and its former service drive, which by the 1880s had become Kennedy Road. The Nichols family had even accentuated the Classical features of the house in 1853 by the addition of the roof balustrade. The most significant planting feature was the row of horsechestnut trees at the front of the property, which had been planted some time between 1790 and 1808 by the Joseph Lee family.[7] Lilac bushes, which defined the sides of the property and afforded some privacy, were also valued. Abandoned during the 1880s was the idea of bare house foundations.

The house was remodeled in 1916, when John Nichols sold the property to Amelia White, the wife of Mary Nichols White's son, Austin. The Whites

The back of the house in the 1890s (left) and after the 1916 Chandler remodeling. (Right photo taken in 2003.)

lived in Weston and continued to rely on the property for rental income but wished to update both the house and the landscape in a contemporary suburban style. The architectural style they chose was Colonial Revival, the architect, Joseph Everett Chandler—renowned for his restoration and remodeling of many historic buildings, including the Old State House and the Paul Revere House in Boston and the House of the Seven Gables in Salem.

Major remodeling occurred inside the house and in the back, leaving the front, with its Georgian features, untouched. A new porch was added to the northwest side and back of the building to provide residents a private sitting area. The color of the house was changed from the muddy brown of the Nichols years to a clear tan with off-white trim.

Chandler also thought of himself as a landscape architect. Although he did not change the plantings, he made two major alterations. He emphasized the Georgian features of the front of the house by adding to the existing Greek Revival picket fence an ornate Colonial Revival gate system with wooden urns. This system and the new, narrow brick walk leading to the front door were characteristic of the Colonial Revival period around 1910-1930 and were routinely added to Colonial- and Federal-period houses at that time. He also changed the spatial organization of the service area behind the house by designing a driveway from Kennedy Road along the north property line to a newly built Colonial Revival garage behind the house.[8] A new lawn enhanced the outdoor sitting area of the new porch and provided more outdoor play space.

In 1921 the Austin Whites hired Helen Spalding, a young, unknown landscape architect, to redo the foundation plantings. A 1916 graduate of Cornell University's landscape architecture program and a friend of the better-known Cornell graduate Marjorie Sewell Cautley, Spalding at that time was writing for *House Beautiful*, which frequently published articles by

This photograph, from the February 1922 issue of *House Beautiful*, shows the front foundation plantings chosen by Helen Spalding the preceding year.

Joseph Everett Chandler. He refers to her work at the Hooper-Lee-Nichols house in an article in the February 1922 issue of the magazine. Her plantings were typical of the Brattle Street landscaping of that period, and remnants of these plantings can be seen at houses on the street to this day. She chose primarily evergreen shrubs, such as yews, rhododendrons, and mountain laurels, for easy maintenance and four-season interest. Shrubs at the west corners of the house assured privacy for activities on the porch. A pair of conifers at the front door, which appear to be red cedars, gave vertical interest and winter color. She retained the old lilac shrubs at the sides of the property. Colonial Revival planting ideas about enclosed formal gardens and perennial garden beds were to come later to the property, and even then, gradually.

In 1923, soon after the new landscaping was completed, the house was sold to Frances Emerson, the wife of William Emerson, dean of the MIT School of Architecture from 1919 to 1939. The Emersons had been living across the street at 158 Brattle (built by an Emerson cousin) and had long admired the old Nichols house and loved the many stories handed down about it by the Nichols family.[9]

Since the Emersons spent their summers in France and England, they made few changes to the Spalding landscaping. Photographs during that time show a flagpole at the right of the front door, the two sentinel conifers near-

NICHOLS HOUSE, BUILT IN 1660 BY OLIVER WENDELL HOLMES.
BRATTLE STREET, CAMBRIDGE, MASS.

A postcard dated 1954 and labeled with misinformation shows the front foundation borders widened and flowering herbaceous plants added. By this time, the horsechestnut tree to the left of the front walk had been lost.

by, and the front shrubs growing out of scale. By the early 1950s, changes were taking place, with increased foundation plantings in front of the house and a decline in the row of horsechestnut trees.

In 1957 the Emersons died within months of each other. Frances bequeathed the house and property to the Cambridge Historical Society, with an endowment of twenty thousand dollars for its upkeep. In her will she stipulated that if the Society discontinued its stewardship, the property should be conveyed to the President and Fellows of Harvard College. For the next nineteen years the Society maintained the property with a William and Frances White Emerson Scholar in residence acting as curator of the house, a role filled until 1974 by Professor and Mrs. Sterling Dow.[10] After 1976 the house was used increasingly as a museum and served as the Society's headquarters.

In the late 1950s, members of the Society were excited not only about maintaining the historic house but also about improving the landscaping. They painted the house gray with black shutters and planted a pair of crabapple trees in front to replace two of the horsechestnut trees that had been lost. The front brick walk was widened, and steppingstone paths of bluestone were added to the side and back of the house. A little-leaf linden was placed at the southeast corner as a tree appropriate to a historic site.

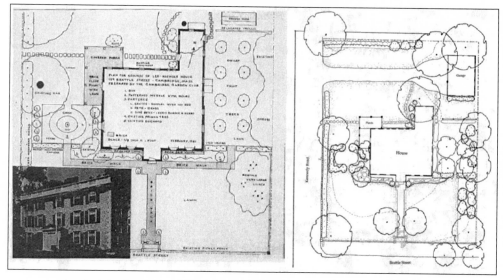

On the left, the 1961 plan by a member of the Cambridge Garden Club; at right, the Conditions Plan of 1988 based on a design by Phebe Leighton. The 1988 plan shows the features and plantings that were carried out by garden club volunteers from 1962 to 1967.

Some women of the Cambridge Garden Club also belonged to the Society, and one, Ruth Cutter, proposed in 1961 to have the club members improve the Hooper-Lee-Nichols landscape in celebration of the twenty-fifth anniversary of the founding of the garden club. At the time, members of the club were interested in gardens of the Colonial Revival period as well as the garden reconstruction at Colonial Williamsburg, and they held a contest in which designs were submitted for improving the landscaping with appropriate plantings.

The winning plan (see left, above) represented Joseph Lee's former large eighteenth-century estate, with its orchards and formal garden reduced to a form that would fit on the now smaller property. This plan also incorporated the idea of a journey or tour around the house. The rectilinear placement of hedges and steppingstone paths returned the landscape to a spatial organization that echoed the Colonial and Federal periods, and its garden rooms were a feature of formal eighteenth- as well as early twentieth-century gardens. The original plan also called for front foundation plantings of myrtle, which are easy to maintain and present the clean look characteristic of the Colonial and Federal periods. Evergreen shrubs were to frame the front door and soften the corners of the house.

Two other members of the garden club, Lizanne Chapin and Erica Payson, joined Cutter in the project. As remembered by Chapin in her talk,

A member of the Cambridge Plant and Garden Club works on the front foundation borders in the spring of 1988.

"The Origin of the Lee-Nichols Garden," given on September 30, 1989, to the Cambridge Plant and Garden Club (the Cambridge Plant Club and the Cambridge Garden Club had merged in 1966), the three women—along with other volunteers—pruned the lilacs and transplanted bulbs to more prominent places. They formed a hedge of yews to enclose and define the property along Kennedy Road and another on the east side of the house to front an orchard serving as a private seating area. On the west side, a small parterre in the shape of a hollow square was formed by planting boxwood. An armillary sundial placed near the roughcast wall of the house functioned as its focal point. The women enjoyed finding appropriate plants, such as four dwarf fruit trees for the orchard and old roses and pinks for the boxwood parterre garden beds. Except during summer vacations, Chapin would mow the lawn every week, after which she and other volunteers would leave for Christ Church and its rectory in Harvard Square to maintain their grounds.

In 1967, in honor of Harvard's Dean Delmar Leighton, who lived across Kennedy Road, the women planted a little-leaf linden and a fringe tree so that he could see them from his house. They also removed every other yew bush from the hedge at Kennedy Road to make a hedge along the driveway on the north side. Chapin's story shows the extent to which the garden club movement, with its philosophy of performing civic-minded service work, contributed to the preservation of historic landscapes and buildings.

A report by the Cambridge Plant and Garden Club later that year states that consistent maintenance of the property was a major problem: volunteering club members were away during the summer when the number of visitors to the house increased. It was, therefore, mutually decided by the garden club and the Society that the latter would take over the care of the grounds. For the next twenty years, maintenance remained the major focus of the Society's stewardship of the landscape. Eventually, residents living on the third floor of the house mowed the lawn and swept the walks, and volunteers from the Society took care of the plantings.

Not only were members of both organizations influenced by the twentieth-century garden club movement, many were also involved with the Radcliffe Seminars Landscape Design Program.[11] Started in the mid-1960s by Diane McGuire, a landscape designer and well-known landscape historian, the program offered courses in garden design and construction as well as garden history. Held eventually in the basement of the Cronkhite Graduate Center at 6 Ash Street, the courses were popular with local women, many doing independent projects on the history of nearby properties, including the Hooper-Lee-Nichols House. One graduate of the program—and an accomplished landscape designer—was Phebe Leighton. After being involved with maintaining the Society's grounds as a member of the plant and garden club, Leighton suggested in 1987 that the Society ask the club to again take on some of the stewardship of the grounds. Esther Pullman, another student in the program and president of the club at that time, urged its members to assume this task.

During the spring and summer of 1988, volunteers replanted the front gardens with flowering annuals and perennials for three-season interest. Pansies, daylilies, snapdragons, delphiniums, peonies, and asters were chosen both for their appropriateness for an old house as well as for the blue, pink, and yellow colors that harmonized with the gray paint. The removal of shrubs kept the front foundation of the house bare in the winter, which was more typical of Colonial and Federal landscaping. The club persuaded Ollie Capizzi of Capizzi & Company to donate a comprehensive cleanup of the grounds. In the fall, all the deciduous trees, shrubs, and hedges were pruned, including the last surviving horsechestnut tree, on the southwest corner of the property.

Over the last decade, the twin issues of maintenance and appropriate design have continued to be the driving force behind changes in landscaping. By 1994, Phebe Leighton and Beryl Beatley had redesigned the front foundation beds in a Colonial Revival style appropriate to the Chandler remodeling of 1916. They chose plants suited to a hot and dry garden that would better attract the attention of passersby. The club financed the new beds, which had

Looking at the front garden in the late spring of 1988 and in the late summer of 2004 (facing page) reveals the increased width and change in plantings.

a front serpentine edge and were twice as wide as the old. New bulbs were planted. Annuals were replaced with perennials such as santolina, heather, catnip, phlox, and beebalm.

During this period, the deteriorating boxwood parterre was another challenge. In decline and unsightly by the mid-1990s, the original boxwood was completely removed by 2003, at which time the Cambridge Plant and Garden Club provided funds for new boxwood to be planted in a semicircle around the sundial.[12] Volunteers from the Society led by Shelagh Hadley cared for the garden for many years. Today the Cambridge Plant and Garden Club provides much of the funding and all of the volunteer labor needed to maintain the grounds.

The ongoing, generous support of the Cambridge Plant and Garden Club has been critical to the landscaping of the Hooper-Lee-Nichols House, and the efforts of both organizations have resulted in the unique appearance of this old property on Brattle Street. Most importantly, together they have continued the tradition first started by the Lee, Nichols, and Emerson families—preserving a historic Cambridge property for the public to enjoy.

ENDNOTES

1. The Hooper-Lee-Nichols House property was originally within the town limits of Watertown and remained so until 1754, when Cambridge annexed land west of Sparks Street. The property began as a homestead in 1684, when Richard Hooper, a physician from Hampton, New Hampshire, bought twelve acres of field and upland and built a house.

2. Much of the history for this article has come from recent research on the property's ownership, land usage, and landscape design. This information is presented in a Cultural Landscape Report by the author, archived at the CHS.

3. Lee, known as Colonel Henry Lee (1809–1898), was an overseer of Harvard College for many years and headed the committee in charge of building Memorial Hall.

4. George Nichols was first a bookseller and then a part owner of the University Press, which printed most of the textbooks used at Harvard College. He was later a well-respected editor of books written by Longfellow, Sibley, Prescott, Sumner, and others.

5. The property at this time was a sixty-acre homestead, one of many in West Cambridge, including the John Vassall Jr. estate at what is now the Longfellow National Historic Site. Judge Joseph Lee of Boston was the first of the Lee family to own the property, and he and his wife, Rebecca Phips Lee, used it as a summer estate during the Tory years before the Revolution. The Lees were one of the few Tory families to retain their estate during and after the Revolution.

6. In late Victorian times, designers planned "pleasure gardens," where one could sit or walk and enjoy vistas and special focal points.

7. Rows of a selected tree type were typical at estates along Brattle Street. Elms were the choice of tree for the Longfellow House, then owned by Andrew Craigie. Other horsechestnut trees planted by the Lees and their neighbors during that time survive today along Kennedy Road and on the neighbors' properties, which were once part of the Lee estate.

8. Designed by Chandler to resemble the former carriage barn, the 1918 garage is one of the few documented examples in Cambridge of a garage that incorporates chauffeur's quarters, a gas tank for refueling the car, and an overhead sprinkler for washing the car. With the exception of the gas tank, all the original features of the garage exist today.

9. A daughter of Mrs. Emerson's, Francesca Wiig, remembered years later a story about the Lee family's involvement with the abolitionist movement and about runaway slaves being hidden in the house. Her reminiscence is archived at the CHS.

10. Sterling Dow was the John E. Hudson Professor of Archaeology at Harvard College, where he taught classics and the history of ancient Greece until he retired in 1970.

11. This program has been known since 2003 as the Landscape Institute of the Arnold Arboretum of Harvard University.

12. Under the leadership of its president Elizabeth Meyer and historian Annette LaMond, the Cambridge Plant and Garden Club was successful in receiving a matching grant from the American Federation of Garden Clubs for the new boxwood.

A History of the Cambridge Historical Society,[1] 1905-2006

GEORGE H. HANFORD

THE WEBSITE OF THE Cambridge Historical Society (www.cambridgehistory.org) notes in the abbreviated style of the Internet that the "org" was founded in 1905 "by a group of historians." They were, for the most part—like this author—amateurs, Cantabrigians with an interest in the history of their city and an urge to explore some facet of it. Less clear is what motivated this group of citizens to associate and why others had not done so before. The answers, I believe, are implicit in the reason other communities chose to establish historical societies around the turn of the century as well: fallout from the Industrial Revolution.

Industry's demands for unskilled labor generated the migration to this country of peoples from a variety of national and ethnic backgrounds. Seeking to maintain their traditions while aspiring to become part of the proverbial American melting pot, these immigrants brought with them or created their own social, fraternal, and church-related (mostly Roman Catholic) societies. Whether inspired by these examples or fearful that "Old Cambridge" might get lost in the mix, societies for the preservation of Puritan-Anglo-Yankee heritage came into being.

Although these considerations may have influenced the founders of the Cambridge Historical Society, the early volumes of the Society's *Proceedings* make it clear that the group's focus was on the history of Old (or west) Cambridge—as differentiated from Cambridgeport, East Cambridge, and North Cambridge, where the new immigrants had settled. (This distinction, not incidentally, was manifested more than half a century earlier when the Massachu-

Richard Henry Dana 3rd, founding president of the Cambridge Historical Society.

setts General Court thwarted Old Cambridge's plans to secede from the city by including it in the incorporation of the municipality in 1846.)

If the Society can be said to have had a founder, he was most certainly Richard Henry Dana 3rd.[2] Dana belonged to a socially prominent Cambridge family whose forebears had played important parts in the first two and a half centuries of the city's existence. "The Dana Saga," by Henry Wadsworth Longfellow Dana, in the twenty-sixth edition of the *Proceedings*, records that Richard Henry Dana 3rd was a direct descendant of one Richard Dana, who migrated from England in 1640 and settled in Cambridge ("Little Cambridge," to be precise—now Brighton). His great-grandfather Francis Dana was a well-known Patriot during the Revolutionary era, a chief justice of the commonwealth, and an ambassador to Russia. According to the "Saga," his grandfather Richard Henry Dana (1st) "was for a time regarded as one of the most important, if not the most important of American poets." His father, Richard Henry Dana Jr., was a minister to England and "an advocate for the poor, the enslaved, and the oppressed," but he is best remembered as the author of *Two Years Before the Mast*. It is not surprising that with this heritage, Richard Henry Dana 3rd had an interest in preserving the record of those earlier years, an interest he shared with the other community leaders involved in the founding of the Society, such as the abolitionist, soldier, and writer Thomas Wentworth Higginson; the Harvard historian Albert Bushnell

The Hooper-Lee-Nichols House—now headquarters of the Cambridge Historical Society—as it looked in 1905.

Hart; the Harvard librarian William C. Hart; Mary I. Gozzaldi, representing the Daughters of the American Revolution; Alice Longfellow; and Oscar F. Allen, the treasurer of the Cambridge Savings Bank.

The Society's history sorts itself out into roughly three eras: the first reflects a lifestyle that remained virtually unchanged for a half century; the second depicts a thirty-year period of change and transition; and the third shows a return to stability, but in a style different from that of those first fifty years. Within these eras, the organization evolved from an exclusive club focused on the history of Old Cambridge into one open to anybody interested in the history of the city's neighborhoods, with all their national and ethnic diversity. In 1957 the Society's nomadic existence came to an end with the gift of the Hooper-Lee-Nichols House, and in 1963 the Cambridge Historical Commission was created. Twenty years later, the Society went from a venture run entirely by volunteers to a staffed enterprise. But perhaps most significant of all is the fact that, over time, the organization has grown from a group whose members explored and recorded history into one that reaches out to the city's community of social and architectural experts.

The Society held its first formal meeting on June 17, 1905, at the Cambridge Social Union at 42 Brattle Street. In accordance with the Articles of Association drawn up by a group of twenty Cantabrigians chaired by Richard

Henry Dana 3rd, it was organized as a private club with a maximum of two hundred elected members. Those members, in turn, elected officers and a governing council to oversee and direct the group's activities.

The Society's members met regularly in different places throughout the city. During the first dozen years, classrooms in the Cambridge Latin School and Emerson Hall in Harvard Yard were the most frequent sites, with Sanders Theatre and the Agassiz House Theatre accommodating larger audiences for special occasions. Later, the Harvard Faculty Club was pressed into service, with the Commander Hotel, Andover Hall at the Harvard Divinity School, the Episcopal Theological Seminary (now the Episcopal Divinity School), and the Unitarian Church occasionally providing space. Otherwise, meetings were held at the homes of members in what are some of today's well-known houses: the Craigie (now Longfellow) House at 105 Brattle Street; Elmwood, at 33 Elmwood Avenue (now the Harvard president's official residence); and The Larches at 22 Larch Road.

The programs at those first gatherings consisted of the reading of members' papers devoted to different aspects of Cambridge history, preceded or followed by brief business sessions, all duly recorded in the Society's *Proceedings*. Most of those early papers came in the form of personal reminiscences about people who lived or had lived in Cambridge, or about events that had taken place there. Their titles included "Reminiscences of Old Cambridge," "Reminiscences of John Bartlett," and "Cambridge Eighty Years Since." But soon papers that required research began to be offered on topics such as "Tudor House at Fresh Pond," "Ancient Fish Weir on Menotomy River," "Adventures of John Nutting, Cambridge Loyalist," and "Elegy on Elijah Culet, the First Schoolmaster of the Town."

As Edward James, editor of the *Proceedings, 1976–1979*, wrote in his introduction, "The first volume, covering the Society's inaugural year, appeared in 1906. Through succeeding decades the giving and publishing of papers on Cambridge history has remained a central activity. In earlier years the papers were fairly formal exercises, written by members and read to fellow members at meetings held during the course of the year. The minutes for 1954, for instance, report that the Society was 'very fortunate in the diversity and quality of the papers presented, all of them by members.'" The *Proceedings, 1973–1975* list some 250 papers that were printed during the Society's first seventy years.

Meetings were regularly held in January, March, June, and October, with the first serving as the annual meeting of the members. Special sessions were occasionally convened to celebrate particular events. Early on, for instance, Sanders Theatre held the Society's celebrations of the one hundredth anniversary of the birth of Oliver Wendell Holmes and the 275th anniversary of the founding of Cambridge. At that latter meeting, Dana noted at one point that "next on our program comes The City of Cambridge—dear, old Cambridge, not dear Old Cambridge"—a recognition by its founding president that the Society's mission encompassed the entire city.

The minutes of the business sessions call attention to the operational matters of the Society. A regular item on the agenda was the election of members, councilors, and officers. Although no actions to reject applicants were recorded, one nevertheless had to be sponsored by a member before one could be elected to membership, a requirement that lent an air of exclusivity to the enterprise. With an authorized membership of two hundred, the actual numbers during these early years varied from 240 down to 147, including associate and honorary members, with attendance at the regular meetings averaging around thirty. The minutes of the fourth meeting, in April 1906, show a membership of 190, with thirty on hand to adopt the Articles of Association. Problems concerning the maintenance of records and archives frequently came up for discussion. One of the Society's missions was and is to collect Cambridge-related memorabilia (for example, documents, photographs, manuscripts, and books). The Cambridge Public Library served as the repository for such items until 1916, when many were transferred to Widener Library at Harvard. Nevertheless, such an arrangement had its drawbacks. Indeed, as early as the fifth meeting of the Society, the problem of housing the archives, including its operating records, was recognized in the minutes in these words: "It is obvious that it would be a great stimulus to the growth of such a collection...if a suitable building should be provided for its sole use and enjoyment." The Hooper-Lee-Nichols House fulfilled that wish forty-one years later.

Reports from the treasurer were regularly on the agenda of the annual meetings, and some sense of the scope of the enterprise during the first half of its existence can be gleaned from the financial statements printed in the *Proceedings*. Membership dues and special donations provided the bulk of the income. The costs of meetings, mailings, and postage, plus those for printing the *Proceedings* or setting aside reserves for future editions, constituted the Society's major expenses, seldom exceeding $2,500 in any given year.

Inevitably other items of business arose. At the tenth meeting, for instance, a design for the association's seal was approved, incorporating "the powers that have made Cambridge history—the Church, the College, and the Press." It depicted the Day Printing Press (the first in America) flanked by both the Fourth Meeting House of the First Church and Massachusetts Hall, Harvard's oldest extant building. And at seven annual meetings between 1908 and 1920, Longfellow medals were awarded to Cambridge high school students in an essay contest sponsored by the Society.

In 1980, at its 299th regular meeting—a celebration of the seventy-fifth anniversary of the founding of the Society—its president Charles W. Eliot 2nd

Charles W. Eliot 2nd,
president, Cambridge
Historical Society
1970-1978. *(Harvard
University Archives)*

presented highlights of the Society's early years. In concluding an overview of his remarks, the minutes read: "Programs of the Society meetings dealt with a variety of topics: famous Cambridge residents; historic buildings; Cambridge institutions, its universities, seminaries, etc.; businesses and industries; and neighborhoods. The Society took an active interest also in the preservation and restoration of historic buildings around the city: in having the Hicks house moved rather than torn down; in repairing the Margaret Fuller house; in having the Dana Palmer House moved; in providing public care for the Old Burying Ground; in the restoration of Fort Washington, etc. Designation of a Brattle Street Historic District was proposed by the Society." The minutes went on to note that "Mr. Eliot ended his talk by some remarks on the gift of the Hooper-Lee-Nichols House by Mrs. Frances White Emerson and the changes within the Society made possible by this circumstance, as well as the responsibilities involved in the ownership of such an historic building."

Built in the late 1600s by a physician named Richard Hooper, the house was typical of dwellings constructed by the wealthier citizens in the early years of the colonial settlement. It passed from Hooper through several owners to Joseph Lee, a wealthy merchant and judge and an English sympathizer at the outset of the Revolution. Like his predecessors at 159 Brattle Street, he sought to enlarge and enhance the house, furthering its transformation from a First Period dwelling into a Georgian mansion. He had the west wall of the house, for instance, coated with "roughcast," plaster scored to look like stone. Today, it remains one of the few examples of this surface in the region. George Nichols, who succeeded Lee's heirs as owner in 1860, installed scenic wallpaper and added a rooftop balustrade made from a church chancel railing. Early twentieth-century owners remodeled and expanded the back of the house to include a library, now called the Chandler Room after Joseph Everett Chandler, the premier restoration architect of the era. The next owner, Frances Emerson, acquired the house in 1923. From her, it came to the Society in 1957.

Frances Emerson's gift was only one of four events that combined to alter significantly the way the Society operated over the next three decades, but it was the trigger for the changes that occurred during the "middle period" of the association's first one hundred years. As it turned out, the acquisition was a mixed blessing. On the positive side, the house accommodated the Society's archives, working files, and library, and provided meeting space for the members. From 1957 to 1974, Sterling Dow, a professor of archaeology at Harvard, and his wife occupied the premises, he as resident curator. The Dows furnished the place with antiques and provided tours twice a week. In 1976 Gerald B. Warden was appointed resident caretaker. Living on the third floor, he began displaying on the first and second some of the objects the Society had collected, and the facility was further opened up for use by other Cambridge organizations. It became a full-time headquarters in 1983 when the Society's first professional staff required that rooms be converted to office space.

On the negative side, however, the gift of the house had one long string attached. Similar to a life estate, it belongs to the Society as long as the Society uses and maintains it; otherwise, title goes to Harvard University. Listed in 1979 on the National Register of Historic Places, the house is a historic treasure to be carefully preserved—a challenge involving time and money. Because the original endowment of $20,000 has proved inadequate, funds to ensure its proper upkeep have to be included in the Society's budgets and annual fundraising drives. With a fine house on Brattle Street as its base, the Society gives the impression of being wealthy while in truth it has to compete with more than a hundred other social service organizations in the city for donations from individuals, businesses, and foundations.

A review of the minutes of the Society and the council during this middle period and after makes it clear that a significant portion of the group's formal deliberations have been devoted to the maintenance of the house. In dollar terms, the annual expenses involved in the stewardship of the property have on occasion amounted to more than all other operating expenses combined. Although it is expensive to maintain, the Society recognizes that the house is one of the most historically significant in Cambridge and one of only two with substantial seventeenth-century building material. It is not only a fine example of a house that has evolved over time but also one that escaped drastic alterations during the Victorian era. For these reasons, the Society is committed to preserving the Hooper-Lee-Nichols House.

The second major development of this twenty-six-year period was the creation of the Cambridge Historical Commission in 1963. A municipally supported entity, its mission was and is to administer Cambridge's historic districts, survey the city's architecture and publish its findings, and to research and mark historic sites and buildings. To support its goals, the commission maintains a public archive of the city's architectural and social history, with staff members presenting programs to schools, organizations, and community groups. In pursuing its work, the commission runs activities that have come to complement those of the Society.

There are, however, differences of scale. While the commission employs multiple staff members, the Society has never had more than one and a fraction full-time equivalent. Financed by tax dollars, the commission has a budget about four times that of the Society, which relies on membership dues, fund-raising activities, and the voluntary largesse of a much smaller constituency. Although one might expect conflict in such circumstances, cooperation has instead prevailed. Charles Sullivan, the commission's director since 1979, has been a staunch supporter of the Society; he has served as a member of the council or as an advisor from 1980 to the present day, and as president from 1985 to 1988.

The Society also works with other historical groups, including the Longfellow House, a National Historic Site, and the Cambridge African American Heritage Alliance. With the Society's executive director Aurore Eaton taking the lead in the late 1990s, the Society, the commission, the Longfellow House, and the African American Heritage Alliance joined with the Friends of Mount Auburn Cemetery and the office of tourism to form the Historic Cambridge Collaborative. Its goal is to cooperate in developing educational programs that promote an appreciation of Cambridge's history.

In the third major development of this period, the Society opened its membership to the general public. The following excerpt from the council's report to the annual meeting in 1977 contains some of the reasoning behind this change: "Concern over the average advanced age of our members—and the need to involve younger people if the Society is to continue—and over the lack of representation in our membership of historically oriented people from parts of Cambridge outside of Neighborhood Ten [the Brattle Street area] has prompted the Council to establish a membership Committee" to address this matter.

As a result, unlimited membership, both geographical and numerical, was unanimously approved at the annual meeting in 1978. Although not explicitly mentioned as part of the rationale for the change, the resulting increase in dues income helped to meet the cost of maintaining the Hooper-Lee-Nichols House. New members continued to be elected for another five years, nearly doubling the membership. Finally, in 1983, elections were abandoned and an exclusive Old Cambridge club became a truly open society. As of January 2005, the Society had nearly five hundred members.

The last of these four major events, and an outcome not surprising after the first three, was the employment of a staff, albeit a small one. The council minutes of November 11, 1982, stated the case: "It becomes obvious the Society needs direction beyond what we and others as volunteers are able to provide." Two months later, the minutes recorded that "the third item of business related to the procurement of a staff person—about which we now seem able to take immediate steps—a half time one for an executive director with administrative and educational responsibility to be in charge of the programs of the Society's activities in terms of how it reaches out to the community and to have supervisory responsibility for the House in consultation with the officers and Council."

After an extensive search, Bettina "Toni" Norton was named the Society's first executive director, taking office on July 1, 1983. Under her leadership, a new modus operandi, which had been emerging in fits and starts, was organized and put in place. Quarterly meetings—except for those in January, which doubled as annual meetings—were abandoned in favor of programs of historical interest offered from time to time. Field trips to other historic venues, the first to Sturbridge Village, were instituted. Educational activities for students were initiated, and walking tours were offered. The role of the resident fellows occupying the third floor was clarified. The concept of corporate membership was also introduced. These and other developments set the Society on a new course.

In 1987 Norton was succeeded by Warren M. "Renny" Little, a veteran museum administrator, who consolidated and refined the procedures his predecessor had developed. In so doing, he brought a sense of stability to the Society after thirty years of slow, constant, and often unsettling change. Some sense of the magnitude of that change can be gathered from the fact that in 1956, the year before the gift of the Hooper-Lee-Nichols House and well before there was a professional staff, the Society's expenses were about $3,000 (including some $2,000 for the *Proceedings*), compared with roughly $42,000 (and $9,000) in 1986, the year before Little's appointment. Over the same period, assets grew from approximately $34,500 to almost $210,000. The equilibrium achieved under Little has continued since his retirement in 1998 through the succeeding tenures of Aurore Eaton, Sally Purrington Hild, and Karen Davis.

Little's stabilizing stewardship heralded the beginning of the Society's third historical period, but the organization began its second century under the leadership of the husband-and-wife team of Karen Davis and Lewis Bushnell, she as executive director and he as associate director, in office since January 2004. Budgeted expenses for 2004 amounted to roughly $87,500, with assets in the neighborhood of $550,000, thanks to wise investment strategy, inflation, and a gift of over $120,000 from the estate of Bartol Brinkler, a volunteer at the Society after his retirement from Widener Library.

One aspect of the new approach that has governed this third period has had to do with publications. The move away from a focus on formal papers at quarterly meetings meant less grist for the *Proceedings'* mill. Whether intended or not, that result proved fortuitous. Publishing the *Proceedings* had become a real chore—an expensive one. The papers collected from 1976 to 1979 were not published until 1985, while the essays submitted between 1980 and 1985 did not appear in print until 1998. The 1998 edition carried the title *Essays on Cambridge History*, with *Proceedings* noted as a subtitle. As with the preceding volume, it did not include the minutes of the Society's meetings for the period covered.

In the 1990s the Society began to produce other types of publications. Most ambitious among them was *The Cambridge Rindge and Latin School: Yesterday and Today*. Others were booklets or pamphlets. "Built by the Anglicans" briefly recounts the history of the houses so built, mostly on Tory Row (Brattle Street). "A Tale of Three Cities in One" celebrated the 150th anniversary of the city's incorporation in 1846. "On the Cutting Edge," recalling many of Cambridge's innovative enterprises over the years, was intended to encourage corporate membership. "For the Entertainment of Strangers," a look at the city's inns and pubs before, during, and after Prohibition, was lighter fare, prepared as background for a fundraising evening of mostly musical and minimally intoxicating entertainment.

More recently, the newsletter has been given new and effective life as *The Newetowne Chronicle*, which carries short articles of current interest and historic note. In 2003 the Society entered the electronic world of the twenty-first century by launching its website, www.cambridgehistory.org. And now comes this centennial volume, invited articles responding to the editor's call for papers that would reflect Cambridge in the twentieth century.

Another aspect of the modern Society has had to do with the nature of its programs. While many of them have been held at the Hooper-Lee-Nichols House, others have met elsewhere around the city. Cruises on the Charles River, for instance, have dealt with such topics as its bridges, its role as the centerpiece of a river park, plans for inclusion in that park of the riverfronts between the Museum of Science and the Zakim Bunker Hill Bridge, and the myth of Leif Ericson's discovery of America—and of Cambridge. Members have gathered at architecturally acclaimed Baker House at MIT, Harvard's restored Memorial Hall, and Polaroid's International-style building on Memorial Drive. There was an evening with the poetry of E. E. Cummings at the Longy School of Music, a tour of Cambridge firehouses, a visit to the Episcopal Monastery of Saint John the Evangelist, near Kennedy Park, and a lecture on the life of Andrew Craigie at the East Cambridge Library. There were two field trips to Fresh Pond, one to tour the new filtration plant and the other to revisit at Kingsley Park the sites of the Fresh Pond Hotel and of the icehouses that in 1836 had helped make Cambridge the nation's largest producer of ice. These places seemed a natural evolution from members' living rooms, where historical sites, events, and individuals were visited orally.

This is not to say that the Hooper-Lee-Nichols House has not lived up to its promise as a convenient venue for gatherings. Meetings of the members, the council, and its committees are normally held there. The Bosphorus Room welcomes frequent informational and educational programs. A series of conversations on Cambridge monuments, for example, turned up little-known facts about their backgrounds. Former councilor and current advisor Karen Falb discussed the history of the house's garden. A paint detective, with the help of slides, orally peeled away the layers of paint on the house's exterior, calling attention to other aspects of the building's history. And my childhood playmate, now U.S. Navy Commander (Ret.) Richard Bennink, shared with the Society the papers of his ancestor, the Civil War general Cornelius Bennink, about that conflict and his own from World War II. In many instances, through the use of audiovisual materials and site visits, these programs have provided hands-on (or "eyes-on" and "ears-on") historical experiences quite different from those available during the Society's first fifty years.

As already noted, some of these programs have served as fundraising events. Although membership and therefore income from dues has increased, other ways of appealing to the largesse of the Society's family have been explored. One positive result was obtained from the establishment of the Dana Fellows. Members whose support exceeds $100 in a given year enjoy the privilege of special programs offered in intimate settings that are typically closed to the public.

Meanwhile, stewardship of the house, grounds, and collections continues to be a financial challenge. The Society is particularly grateful to the Cambridge Plant and Garden Club; its ministrations, both physical and financial, have kept the grounds in excellent condition. Other recent projects have included restoring the fence, repainting the exterior of the house in colors that match those used by Chandler in 1916, conservation of the rough cast wall, and most recently, replacement of all the roofs and restoration of the roof balustrade. Upcoming is replacement of the electrical system.

The Hooper-Lee-Nichols House in winter, 2004. *(Photograph by Lewis Bushnell)*

Funds are also needed to care for the many books, documents, and photographs in the Brinkler Library on the second floor of the house and to make them more readily available to researchers. And additional dollars are required to properly preserve the many objects related to Cambridge history that have been collected by the Society over the years. A recent project, funded in part by the Society of the Cincinnati, involves the conservation of the Rupert Lilly models—extraordinary dioramas of the houses and grounds of four Tory mansions.

Thus, as the Society enters its second hundred years, its most critical need is an effective fundraising strategy, and plans for a capital campaign are under discussion. Outreach constitutes another major challenge. Beginning with Richard Henry Dana's distinction between "dear, old Cambridge" and "dear Old Cambridge" and running through the concern "over the lack of representation in our membership of historically oriented people from parts of [the city] outside Neighborhood Ten" to the opening of membership to all comers runs a thread that begs to be extended. The Society's goal of fully engaging the interest (and attracting the membership) of Cantabrigians everywhere remains a top priority.

Finally, there is the thread of history itself, and the issue of the degree to which the Society should—as called for in its by-laws—"encourage research...by its members" in order "to promote a better understanding of history as an important factor in the everyday affairs of the City and its residents." To what extent should the Society call on outside authorities to help

The Hooper-Lee-Nichols House in spring, 2005. *(Photograph by Lewis Bushnell)*

preserve and interpret items of historical and antiquarian significance? In the beginning, the members did it themselves. Now fewer do. Perhaps the encouragement of Cantabrigians outside Old Cambridge to share their neighborhoods' histories through the auspices of the Society could serve to reinvigorate an exploration of the city's history across the board. There is a lot of it out there yet to explore.

ENDNOTES

1. The A in the title of this piece bears comment. Recorded history is, of course, what the recorder says happened, not necessarily what actually happened. No one knows for sure which side fired the first shot in the Battle of Lexington in 1775; participants in the fray differed in their recollections. This piece is the author's interpretation of the evolution of the Cambridge Historical Society over its first one hundred years. It is based primarily on his reading of what others have recorded about that evolution in the files of the Society and secondarily on his own fallible, biased memory of the last twelve of those one hundred years, during which he was actively involved. Thus, the piece is not the "official" history of the Society but rather one individual's conception of it. —G.H.H.

2. Dana preferred "3rd" rather than "III" for his name.

Thanks are due to Karen Davis, executive director, and Renny Little, former executive director, both of the Cambridge Historical Society, and to Charles Sullivan, executive director of the Cambridge Historical Commission and former president of the Society, for reviewing drafts of this manuscript. Any errors of fact or interpretation, however, are solely the responsibility of the author. And kudos to my late wife, Elaine, for putting up with me while I was in the throes of research and composition.

Appendix

PRESIDENTS OF THE SOCIETY[1]
1905-2006

1905-1914	Richard Henry Dana 3rd[2]
1915-1921	William Roscoe Thayer
1922-1927	Ephraim Emerton
1928-1954	Robert Walcott
1955-1958	David T. Pottinger
1959	Mrs. George W. Howe
1960-1966	William L. Payson
1967-1969	Richard C. Evarts
1970-1978	Charles W. Eliot 2nd
1979-1982	John T. Blackwell
1983-1984	Robert B. Rettig
1985-1988	Charles M. Sullivan
1989-1994	Helen F. Moulton
1995-1996	George H. Hanford
1997-2002	M. Wyllis Bibbins
2003-2007	Theodore L. Hansen

1. Currently presidents are elected for one-year terms and can serve a maximum of six terms. From 1905 through 1922, annual meetings were held in October. There was no annual meeting in 1923. They resumed in January 1924 and have been held in either January or February ever since.

2. Served as chairman from the organizational meeting in June 1905 to the first annual meeting in October 1905, when he was elected the first president of the Society.

Cambridge Historical Society
Councilors & Directors, 1999-2007

Soon after its founding in 1905, the Cambridge Historical Society began to publish *Proceedings*, papers read at the Society's meetings. In 1998 the Society published *Essays on Cambridge History*. Each of these publications lists the council and—after 1983—the directors. To continue the tradition, the present volume includes the council and directors from 1999 to the present. *Scripta Manent!*

1999

President:	M.Wyllis Bibbins
Vice Presidents:	Allison M. Crump, Karen L. Davis, Karen F. Falb
Secretary:	W. David Klempin
Treasurer:	Andrew Leighton
Curator:	Anne M. Donaghy
Editor:	Nancy B. Woods
Council:	Luise M. Erdmann, Shelagh Hadley, Charlotte Moore, Gillian Richardson, Maxwell D. Solet, Maura A. Smith
Executive Director:	Aurore Eaton

2000

President:	M.Wyllis Bibbins
Vice Presidents:	Allison M. Crump, Karen L. Davis, Karen F. Falb
Secretary:	W. David Klempin
Treasurer:	Andrew Leighton
Curator:	Anne M. Donaghy
Editor:	Nancy B. Woods
Council:	Shelagh Hadley, Theodore Hansen, Charlotte Moore, Larry Nathanson, Gillian Richardson, Maxwell D. Solet
Executive Director:	Aurore Eaton

2001

President:	M.Wyllis Bibbins
Vice Presidents:	Karen L. Davis, Elizabeth D. Meyer, Nancy B. Woods
Secretary:	Maxwell D. Solet
Treasurer:	Andrew Leighton
Curator:	Anne M. Donaghy
Editor:	Daphne Abeel

| COUNCIL: | Carol M. Cerf, Lindsay Leard Coolidge, Shelagh Hadley, Theodore Hansen, Larry Nathanson, Gillian Richardson |
| EXECUTIVE DIRECTOR: | Sally Purrington Hild |

2002

PRESIDENT:	M. Wyllis Bibbins
VICE PRESIDENTS:	Karen L. Davis, Elizabeth D. Meyer, Nancy B. Woods
SECRETARY:	Maxwell D. Solet
TREASURER:	Andrew Leighton
CURATOR:	Anne M. Donaghy
EDITOR:	Daphne Abeel
COUNCIL:	Kathleen Born, Carol M. Cerf, Lindsay Leard Coolidge, Theodore Hansen, Chandra Harrington, Larry Nathanson
EXECUTIVE DIRECTOR:	Sally Purrington Hild

2003

PRESIDENT:	Theodore L. Hansen
VICE PRESIDENTS:	Karen L. Davis, Elizabeth D. Meyer, Nancy B. Woods
SECRETARY:	Maxwell D. Solet
TREASURER:	Andrew Leighton
CURATOR:	Lindsay Leard Coolidge
EDITOR:	Daphne Abeel
COUNCIL:	Kathleen Born, Carol M. Cerf, Robert G. Crocker, Chandra Harrington, Ellen G. Moot, Susan S. Poverman
EXECUTIVE DIRECTOR:	Sally Purrington Hild

2004

PRESIDENT:	Theodore L. Hansen
VICE PRESIDENTS:	Kathleen Born, Chandra Harrington, Nancy B. Woods
SECRETARY:	Maxwell D. Solet
TREASURER:	Andrew Leighton
CURATOR:	Lindsay Leard Coolidge
EDITOR:	Daphne Abeel
COUNCIL:	Thomas Bracken, Robert G. Crocker, D. Eliot Klein, Ellen G. Moot, Paula Paris, Susan S. Poverman
EXECUTIVE DIRECTOR:	Karen L. Davis

2005

PRESIDENT:	Theodore L. Hansen
VICE PRESIDENTS:	Kathleen Born, Chandra Harrington, Maxwell D. Solet
SECRETARY:	Thomas Bracken
TREASURER:	Andrew Leighton
CURATOR:	Lindsay Leard Coolidge
EDITOR:	Daphne Abeel
COUNCIL:	Charlie Allen, Robert G. Crocker, D. Eliot Klein, Ellen G. Moot, Paula Paris, Susan S. Poverman
EXECUTIVE DIRECTOR:	Karen L. Davis

2006

PRESIDENT:	Theodore L. Hansen
VICE PRESIDENTS:	Kathleen Born, Chandra Harrington, Maxwell D. Solet
SECRETARY:	Thomas Bracken
TREASURER:	Andrew Leighton
CURATOR:	Lindsay Leard Coolidge
EDITOR:	Daphne Abeel
COUNCIL:	Charlie Allen, Robert G. Crocker, D. Eliot Klein, Paula Paris, Susan S. Poverman, Mary Webb
EXECUTIVE DIRECTOR:	Karen L. Davis

2007

PRESIDENT:	Theodore L. Hansen
VICE PRESIDENTS:	Kathleen Born, Chandra Harrington, Maxwell D. Solet
SECRETARY:	Thomas Bracken
TREASURER:	Andrew Leighton
CURATOR:	Lindsay Leard Coolidge
EDITOR:	Michael Kenney
COUNCIL:	Charlie Allen, Darleen Bonislawski, Robert G. Crocker, Heli Meltsner, Paula Paris, Mary Webb
EXECUTIVE DIRECTOR:	Karen L. Davis

CONTRIBUTORS' NOTES

A City Life and Times:
Cambridge in the Twentieth Century

THE CONTRIBUTORS

BILL CUNNINGHAM moved to Cambridge in 1962 and raised a family in the Riverside neighborhood. He has worked at Riverside Press and at commercial printers in South Boston and Somerville, and has served as a tenant activist since 1969. His essay is dedicated to the memory of his wife, Boston activist Ellen Maguire Al-Weqayan.

BARBARA ROWE DE MARNEFFE moved to Coolidge Hill with her family in 1945. A graduate of Vassar College, she has had careers in teaching, hospital public relations, politics, and the retailing business. An interest in art and architecture has led to volunteer commitments to the Archives of American Art and to the restoration of Edith Wharton's house, The Mount, in Lenox, Massachusetts.

FRANCIS DE MARNEFFE, M. D. was born in Brussels, Belgium, and educated there and in England. He was trained in psychiatry at Massachusetts Hospital and McLean Hospital, where he was CEO for twenty-five years. He is currently general director emeritus of McLean and lecturer on psychiatry at Harvard Medical School.

KAREN FORSLUND FALB has a certificate in landscape design history from the Landscape Institute of the Arnold Arboretum, Harvard University. Her "Cultural Landscape Report" on the Hooper-Lee-Nichols property was completed in 2005. A former vice president, she is an active volunteer at the Cambridge Historical Society.

DAVID N. FIXLER is a principal at Einhorn-Yaffee Prescott Architecture & Engineering, PC, specializing in the preservation of twentieth-century buildings. His numerous projects include the restoration of Alvar Aalto's Baker House at MIT. He has published widely on architecture and preservation and serves as president of the New England chapter of Docomomo/U.S.

SUZANNE REVALEON GREEN was born and raised in Cambridge. She studied at Cambridge High & Latin School and graduated from Salem Normal School in 1933. She taught for many years in the Cambridge public schools and served on the boards of the YWCA, the Margaret Fuller House, the Cambridge Historical Commission, and the Cambridge African American Heritage Alliance.

GEORGE H. HANFORD is a graduate of Harvard College and Harvard Business School. A past president of the Cambridge Historical Society, he is president emeritus of the College Board and Symposiarch Emeritus of the Canterbury Society.

MICHAEL KENNEY is a graduate of Harvard College, class of 1957. He is a retired reporter for *The Boston Globe* and lives in Cambridgeport.

GLENN KOOCHER, whose family immigrated to Cambridge in 1904, is the fourth generation of his family to live in the city. He has written extensively on the politics and political history of Cambridge. He is a graduate of Harvard College and in 1973 was elected to the first of six terms on the Cambridge School Committee.

ANNETTE LaMOND is a member of the Cambridge Plant & Garden Club and has served as its archivist and historian since the club celebrated its centennial in 1989. She served as the club's president from April 2000 to April 2002. A 1971 Wellesley College graduate, she holds a Ph.D. in economics from Yale University and a master's degree in management from MIT's Sloan School. She published a history of the Cambridge Skating Club in 2002.

ELLEN GUILD MOOT trained as a political scientist at Radcliffe College and Yale University Graduate School. She has lived in Cambridge since the 1930s and now resides on Coolidge Hill. She has been active in many community organizations and is a member of the Cambridge Historical Society and the Massachusetts Historical Society.

EVA S. MOSELEY first lived in Cambridge in 1953-55 while studying Sanskrit at Harvard. In 1971 she went to work at Radcliffe's Schlesinger Library on the History of Women in America, becoming curator of manuscripts in 1972 (and acting director, 1994-1995). She has served on the Council of the Society of American Archivists and as president of New England Archivists. Since retiring in 1999, she has helped launch and chair the Cambridge Archives Committee and chaired an oral history project at Cambridge Homes.

LARRY NATHANSON, M.D. graduated from Harvard College in 1950 and from the University of Chicago School of Medicine in 1955. He has taught at Harvard Medical School, Tufts University School of Medicine, and the State University of New York School of Medicine at Stony Brook, where he is professor emeritus. He is the author of several books and numerous articles. He has served on the council of the Cambridge Historical Society and is now an advisor.

MILLIE RAHN is a professional folklorist. She serves as coordinator of Club Passim's New England Folk Music Archive Project and has written and spoken about the 1960s folk revival in Cambridge. In 1995 she co-produced "Follow Me Down: A Folk Reunion," a documentary for WGBH about Club 47.

MARIAN CANNON SCHLESINGER grew up in Cambridge, the daughter of Dr. Walter Bradford Cannon, professor of physiology at Harvard Medical School, and Cornelia James Cannon, feminist and writer. A graduate of Radcliffe College, she is a landscape and portrait painter, the author of children's books, and has written for many magazines and newspapers.

ARNOLD SCHUTZBERG, the son of Russian immigrants, was born in 1927 in a three-decker at 320 Columbia Street, Cambridge. In 1935 the family moved to Fayette Street in mid-Cambridge. Schutzberg studied at the Longfellow School, the Hebrew School, and Cambridge High & Latin School. He later studied engineering at the Universities of Massachsetts and Michigan. Now retired, he pursues studies in political science and Jewish and Middle Eastern history.

ALAN SEABURG graduated from Tufts University and received a master's in library science from Simmons College. He has been librarian of the Crane Theological School at Tufts and curator of manuscripts at Andover-Harvard Theological Library, Harvard University. He is the author of *Cambridge on the Charles*.

O. ROBERT SIMHA served as the director of planning for the Massachusetts Institute of Technology from 1960 to 2000. He has worked on the Cambridge Planning Board, the Cambridge Citizens Advisory Committee, the Cambridge Economic Opportunity Committee, the Cambridge Community Center, and as president of Cambridge Community Services.

CHARLES M. SULLIVAN has been executive director of the Cambridge Historical Commission since 1974. He has overseen the expansion of the city's historic districts, secured the designation of landmarks and neighborhood conservation districts, and gained city-wide jurisdiction over the demolition of buildings more than fifty years old. He is the co-author of *Maintaining Your Old House in Cambridge, A Photographic History of Cambridge*, and the forthcoming *Building Old Cambridge*.

STEPHEN G. SURETTE recently retired from the Cambridge School Department, where he taught at Rindge Technical School and Cambridge Rindge & Latin School, serving as faculty advisor to the student newspaper for twenty-three years. He has compiled "Notable Cambridge Alumni" (2004), "Cambridge Football, 1886-2004," and other athletic records. In 1998 he received the Elijah Corlett Award for producing a 350th anniversary video history of the high school. In 2006, he began to publish an oral-history journal titled *Growing Up in North Cambridge*.

THE EDITOR

DAPHNE ABEEL is a book editor and journalist. An alumna of Radcliffe College with a master's degree from Columbia University, she has edited many works of fiction and nonfiction and published articles in a variety of periodicals, including *Harvard Magazine* and *The Boston Globe*. She is assistant editor of the *Armenian Mirror-Spectator*.

Index